SERIAL KILLERS

SERIAL KILLERS

by
RODNEY CASTLEDEN

A Futura Book

First published in Great Britain 2005 by Time Warner
Reprinted by Futura 2008

ISBN 978-0-7088-6116-5

Produced by Omnipress Limited, Eastbourne

Printed in the EU

Futura
An imprint of Little, Brown Book Group
100 Victoria Embankment
London EC4Y 0DY
www.littlebrown.co.uk

Photo credits: Corbis
Front cover images: *Aileen Wuornos,
Richard Ramirez* and *Ted Bundy*

*In memory of my father, Dennis Castleden,
a detective and police interviewer
who helped to bring two serial killers to justice.*

The views expressed in this publication are those
of the author. The information and the
interpretation of that information are presented in
good faith. Readers are advised that where
ethical issues are involved, and often highly
controversial ethical issues at that, they have a
personal responsibility for making their own
assessments and their own ethical judgements.

CONTENTS

Introduction 7

PART SEVEN: THE LADY-KILLERS

PART EIGHT: KILLING FOR THE STATE

PART NINE: KILLER DOCTORS

PART EIGHT: MADMEN & MADWOMEN

Introduction

A murder can be many things. An ordinary murder may be a reaction murder, an impulsive response to a quarrel or an insult, or it may be a calculated murder for gain, whether money, self-protection or power.

Serial murders are different from ordinary murders in several ways. A serial murderer has an in-built, long-term programme to kill, and very often the identity of the victim is of little or no consequence. A serial murderer goes on killing until stopped. A peculiarity of serial killing is that there is often a lull, a cooling off period that may go on for months or even years during which no killing happens, and then the killing starts again.

Serial murderers are difficult to catch because there is often no prior relationship between the victim and the killer. The victims may all have something in common, at least in the mind of the killer. They may, for instance, all be women of 25 with short red skirts and long brown hair and, as such, act as substitutes for the young woman who jilted the murderer many years earlier; the victims then become substitutes for the woman the murderer really wishes to destroy. He often sees his victims as completely worthless; this explains why he often selects his victims from certain sectors of society – migrant workers, vagrants, prostitutes, rent boys, runaways, missing children, single elderly women. It is not mere cowardice or sadism that drives a serial killer to choose powerless victims; their powerlessness and isolation make them easier targets and there will, in many such cases, be no anxious friends and relatives keen to see the killer brought to justice.

Serial killers are of many different types, but it is possible to sketch the commonest type. He is usually male, 25-35 years old, white, of average intelligence and chooses his victims from his own ethnic group. The age of his victims varies according to his particular interests and psychological history. He usually has no prior contact with his victims and has no personal hatred for them. There is great variability in terms of his social life. Some serial killers are complete outsiders, socially inept, unable to develop or maintain relationships – complete loners. These are people who often draw attention to themselves as likely suspects when there are unexplained killings in a neighbourhood.

But some serial killers appear to be completely normal. They may be married with children, and coping with a full-time job and a normal social life. For them, the killing involves a Jekyll-and-Hyde flip into an entirely different way of life. These are in some ways the hardest cases to deal with – hard for the police to solve, and very hard for the families and colleagues at work to come to terms with once the truth comes out. Ted Bundy is a prime example of a serial murderer who to all appearances was functioning well in society, and was therefore not suspected, even when his workmates noticed, with amusement, that he looked exactly like the photofit of the suspect.

A mass murderer is a very different type of killer. A mass murderer kills several people usually all in one place in a matter of a few hours at most, killing in a single sustained outburst, usually of rage or pent-up frustration, with no cooling off period. Serial killers may murder the same number of people in total, but over a period of weeks, months or years – this time with several cooling off periods when there is no killing and maybe no planning to kill either.

So, why do serial killers kill? There is the visionary type. This is the classic madman, the man who kills because the voices in his head tell him to kill. Frequently, serial killers on trial claim to be driven by voices, partly, I suspect, because this takes away from them the personal responsibility for what they have done, partly because if the plea is accepted they will be treated as insane and may therefore escape the worst penalties. Peter Sutcliffe is a good example of a visionary claimant.

A second type of serial killer is the missionary, the do-gooding killer who goes around eliminating what he sees as the scum of society. He is the puritanical prostitute-slayer, the homophobic gay-killer.

A third type is the thriller. Some people get a kick out of killing. These killers are sadists and their murders often become progressively more sadistic. The Jack the Ripper killings escalated in this way. A fourth type, often related to the thriller, is the lust killer, who gets sexual gratification from torturing his victims to death.

A fifth type is the tyrant. Heads of state have often been in the privileged position of legitimizing their killing. It is possible to see Hitler's determination to kill all the Jews in Europe as a manifestation of the missionary type of serial killer, but he was also a visionary. Whether Hitler was excited by all the killings he ordered is not clear – possibly not – but he certainly epitomizes the tyrant killer.

What makes people into serial killers? This is the great unanswerable question. It may be that the will to kill starts as an urge, then becomes a compulsion, and ends up as an addiction. Some experts say that serial killers enjoy being elusive and love the celebrity status they acquire. They have large egos, they want attention, they want to be known as notorious killers. With all of them, the motives are total, deeply embedded and personal. They feel no remorse and show total disdain for their victims. Often they display an inflated self-importance. The Unabomber demanded that the Washington Post and New York Times publish his manifesto. If he had kept himself in the shadows, he might have remained undetected; it was seeking publicity in this way that led to his capture. A similar ambivalence can be seen in Jack the Ripper's taunting letters to the police, which could easily have led to his arrest – though they did not.

Some profilers believe that serial killers don't learn from their mistakes. Others believe they do. Tod Burke, Professor of Criminology at Radford University, thinks they try to improve their technique. A greed factor sets in and they come to believe that the more they kill and get away with, the easier it will become. 'And that's when they get caught.'

Serial killing seems to thrive in urban societies. It has been estimated that 85% of all the serial killers in the world are

American. What we read into this I am not sure. It may be that the atomized society of modern urban living creates the conditions for serial killing; there are huge numbers of isolated people and therefore potential victims; extreme mobility also makes it easier for a killer to strike in several widely separated locations, making it impossible for the authorities to see any connections between the crimes; the division of policing into state authorities exacerbates this effect.

My father was one of the detectives who interviewed witnesses and suspects in two of the cases in this book – Haigh and Heath. He talked to me about his work over many years and left me with the overriding impression that cases like these are way beyond the comprehension of ordinary policemen, however conscientious. He was also profoundly disturbed as well as surprised at how easily people are taken in by psychopaths. He was particularly disturbed, shaken would not be too strong a word, by the ease with which one 'very nice young woman' he interviewed had been sweet-talked into spending a night with Neville Heath. She had been extremely lucky to survive, and both she and my father knew it. These are criminals who defy all our expectations of the way people around us are going to behave – and they are all the more alarming for that.

PART ONE

KILLER KINGS & QUEENS

William the Conqueror

stained from rivers of blood

England was conquered, in 1066, by a Norman Duke who had no hereditary right to the English crown; nor did he have an invitation or a welcome from the people of England. The invasion was an entirely unwarranted and gratuitous act of aggression on a country that had its own highly developed culture, its own customs and laws, and these were savagely overridden and suppressed by the invader. The invader, William 'the Conqueror', was no less than a thief on the grand scale, a thief who stole a nation.

William the Conqueror was born in Falaise in Normandy, the illegitimate son of Robert Duke of Normandy by a tanner's daughter called Arlette. Edward the Confessor died childless and William, a cousin of Edward's, claimed that the dead king had promised him the throne of England during a visit in 1051. He may have received such a promise, and the pope approved William's claim to the English throne, but it still does not amount to an entitlement. William assembled a fleet, crossed the Channel and defeated Harold Godwinson, the rightful English king, on 14 October 1066.

At the Battle of Hastings, the English King Harold made a courageous last stand with his house-carls as they gathered round the English standard. The Normans broke through their shield wall and butchered Harold and most of his house-carls. The last Saxon King of England was murdered. The following day, Harold's mother, Gytha, sent a request to William offering him the weight of the dead King's body in gold if he would hand it over for burial. William shabbily refused, insisting on giving the King an anonymous, unmarked grave on the beach he had tried to defend. Duke William added dishonourable behaviour to the crime of murder.

Duke William marched on Dover, where he stayed for a week before setting off for London by way of Canterbury, using the old Roman road. It was only in Southwark, on the southern edge of London, that William began to meet significant resistance. London did not give in so easily. Out of spite, William set fire to the area, turned away to the south and marched through Surrey, Hampshire and Berkshire, ravaging the countryside as he went. By the end of the year, William and his army had slashed and scythed a great curving swathe of destruction right round London. He then approached London again, this time from the north, via Berkhamsted. Demoralized by the reports coming in of the devastation all round London, the Londoners knew they had to give in. On Christmas Day 1066 William was crowned king of England – king by usurpation – in Westminster Abbey by Aldred, Archbishop of York. The

Abbey was almost completely deserted, emptied for security reasons. A disturbance outside the abbey was wrongly interpreted as an attempt to attack the new king and houses in the neighbourhood were gratuitously put to the torch.

On the strength of the one battle, William now claimed all of England, though the claim was not really supported by right or by military conquest. He had in truth only conquered those parts of England he had marched through. William saw that one way of avoiding further pitched battles was to allow the powerful lords of the north, such as Morcar, Earl of Northumbria, to hold their lands as a grant from him as their new lord. But most of the English landowners were robbed of their lands. William needed to reward the Norman knights and barons who had helped him win Hastings, and giving them lands in England was the only way he could do that. Some of the leading supporters were granted huge estates.

On 1067, King William I led his army on a tour of England. He organized the confiscation of land from English landowners and built wooden castles to keep the rebellious English under control. There seems to have been no major opposition to this intimidating behaviour, as William had by now acquired a reputation for being harsh and merciless, and he felt secure enough to leave Odo of Bayeux in charge of England while he returned to Normandy in the spring of 1067. While he was away, rebellions broke out in Kent, Herefordshire and the North, and in December

William had to come back to put down the rebellions. In a few months William had stamped them out, but in 1068 another insurrection broke out, this time in the West Country. This too he put down. Castles were shortly afterwards raised at Exeter and other key towns. A similar rebellion in Durham in 1069 was put down and a castle was built there too.

The English had not welcomed William as a saviour or rescuer, nor did they quickly come round to the idea that his presence in England was acceptable, desirable or necessary. There was resistance to Norman rule in one county after another. William was simply not wanted. The only way he could hold onto this kingdom was by force, and he did not flinch from using it. The spate of castle-building was a clear indication that the populace would be kept in order by military force.

Raids on the North led by King Sweyn of Denmark created further problems. In September 1069, Sweyn sailed a fleet into the Humber and up the Yorkshire Ouse – and burnt York down. William managed to beat the Danes into retreat, crushed a rebellion in Staffordshire, and then burnt houses and crops across the whole area between York and Durham. This devastation of the North was one of the most barbaric acts William carried out on a totally undeserving population. The chroniclers described the area as a desert after he had ravaged it. The ordinary people died of starvation. The Northern rebellion came to an end in 1070 when William took Chester.

William also dismantled the English Church, sacking

all but two of the English bishops and replacing them with Normans. Lanfranc became the new Archbishop of Canterbury. All this was with extraordinary speed by the end of 1070.

Then, in 1071, came one final revolt against the Norman invasion and usurpation. Under the leadership of the Saxon nobleman Hereward the Wake, the rebels occupied the Isle of Ely in the Fens. William led the Norman army in person against Hereward and his men. The rebels were savagely punished, with mutilation and life imprisonment. The English resistance was over.

After the series of rebellions, William thought it was safe to return to Normandy in 1073, but while he was away two English earls, Waltheof and Ralph, Earl of Norfolk, conspired against him. Geoffrey of Coutances dealt with the rising and afterwards ordered that every rebel should have his right foot cut off. William returned in 1076 and had Waltheof executed; Ralph had already escaped to Brittany.

William's rule was neither secure nor welcome in Normandy either. In 1077, William's eldest son Robert Curthose proposed that he should rule Normandy instead of his father. When Williamrefused, Robert rebelled and tried to seize Rouen;he failed and had to flee to Gerberoi. William laidsiege to his son, but his wife Matilda persuadedhim to end it and come to terms with his son.When William returned to England in 1082 hewas dissatisfied with the way Odo had been running England in his absence and, after a trial, threw him into prison for five years.

Then William launched his famous Domesday Survey of England. This was partly to assess people for tax, and partly to sort out exactly who owned some of the land. Today people look back on the Domesday Book as a valuable historical document, and are grateful to William the Conqueror for making it available to them, but at the time when it was compiled it was a culture shock, a phenomenon that was culturally alien to the way England was organized.

As he aged, William the Conqueror became very fat. In 1087, he was told that the French King Philip had described him as looking like a pregnant woman. William was incensed by this insult and consequently launched an attack on the French King's lands. On 15 August he captured the town of Mantes and set fire to it. While he was riding round the burning town, gloating over the destruction, his horse was startled by the flames and stumbled. William was thrown forward onto the pommel of his saddle. He sustained severe abdominal injuries, from which he died a lingering death in Rouen on 9 September. His doctors left him the moment he died; his sons had already left him; his servants stole his weapons, robes and other belongings and left the Conqueror's body half-naked on the floor.

The motive for the Norman invasion of England was very clear to the English. They wrote in 1087, 'King William and his chief men loved gold and silver and did not care how sinfully it was obtained provided it came to them. He [King William] did not care how wrongfully his men got possession of land or how many illegal acts they did.' As for the killing and the atrocities, William himself was directly involved and directly responsible. A Norman chronicler boasted that William dominated battles, always leading from in front. He must therefore take full responsibility for the scale of the killing. The Devastation of the North was a terrible and completely unjustified criminal act. Ordericus Vitalis, writing in 1142, said, 'In his anger, William ordered that all crops and herds and food of every kind should be brought together and burned to ashes, so that the whole region north of the Humber might be stripped of all means of survival.' This devastation was no random act of vandalism. It was a deliberate democide. There would be no further rebellions in the North for the simple reason that the North would be empty.

The Pope, Gregory VII, had reservations about William the Conqueror. In a letter to a friend he wrote, 'The King of England is not as religious as we would wish.' He was even so prepared to give him the benefit of the doubt as 'he neither destroys nor sells the churches of God'. William showed contempt for the lives and well-being of ordinary English people. He created large deer forests for his own amusement, but if any ordinary man dared to kill a deer he was to be blinded.

On his deathbed, William seems to have had belated qualms about his actions. Here, written right at the end, is his confession: 'I tremble, my friends, when I reflect on the grievous sins which burden my conscience, and now, about to be summoned before the awful tribunal of God, I know not what I ought to do. I was bred to arms from my childhood and am stained from the rivers of blood I have shed . . . It is out of my power to count all the injuries which I have caused during the sixty-four years of my troubled life.'

Vlad III

the Impaler

IT IS OFTEN assumed that Dracula was an entirely fictional character. To a great extent the high-camp anti-hero of Bram Stoker's novel has to be the product of the Gothic imagination. But elements of the character were real enough. If Dracula had any real-life existence outside Bram Stoker's Dracula, then it was in the form of a fifteenth century prince who lived in central Europe, Vlad Tepes or Vlad III – or Vlad the Impaler.

Vlad was born in the fortress of Sighisoara, in Transylvania, late in the year 1431. Vlad the Impaler's mother was rather improbably called Barbara. His father, Vlad II Dracul, was given the nickname 'Dracul' (Dragon), because he was a member of a crusading Catholic order of chivalry with that title. Vlad II had been admitted to the Order of the Dragon a year before the young Impaler was born. 'Dracul' was the nickname the Romanian boyars (noblemen) decided to call him. 'Draculea' means 'son of Dracul', and was often used by Vlad III to describe himself, which brings us very close indeed to the familiar name Dracula.

Vlad III supplied another element of Bram Stoker's story with his habit of drinking the blood of his victims, of whom there were many. Bram Stoker borrowed another element in the form of the Order of the Dragon's official uniform, a black cloak over a red robe.

His terrible reputation sprang from the horrible methods he used for killing his enemies. He sat down to dinner on one occasion, surrounded by a crowd of slowly dying victims. His dinner guests were nauseated by the screaming and the stench. One of them made the mistake of objecting and was himself impaled.

It was late in 1436 that Vlad became Prince of Wallachia, one of three Romanian provinces, the others being Moldavia and Transylvania. He took up residence at the palace in Targoviste, the capital. In 1442, Vlad III and his brother Radu were taken hostage by Sultan Murad II; he was held in Turkey until 1448, though Radu was kept until 1462. This period of Turkish captivity played a key role in the development of Vlad's black personality. He became profoundly pessimistic. The Turks set him free only when news broke that his father had been assassinated, at the orders of Vladislav II, who wanted the Wallachian throne for himself. He also then learned of the death of his older brother Mircea's death. Vlad was 17 and, supported by a force of Turkish cavalry, he made a move to seize the throne of Wallachia, but Vladislav defeated him only two months later. Then, in August 1456, Vlad was able to kill Vladislav and begin his longest reign (6 years). During this time he committed many cruel atrocities.

His first major atrocity was, inevitably, an act of revenge aimed at the boyars of Targoviste who had conspired to kill his father and his brother Mircea. On Easter Day 1459, he invited all the boyar families who were involved to a feast. He impaled the older ones and forced the rest to march fifty miles to the town of Poenari, where they were made to build a fortress overlooking the Arges River; many died during this ordeal. This building is what is today known as Castle Dracula.

This sick sadistic monster was, even so, regarded as a hero. He was a gifted general, and he succeeded in ending decades of feuding within his country. He also fended off the Turks who were constantly trying to encroach on his lands.

In 1462, Vlad launched a campaign against the Turks along the Danube, killing over 38,000 people. The Turks sent envoys to agree a peace settlement but, when the envoys refused to remove their turbans in his presence, Vlad had their turbans nailed onto their heads. This was risky, as the Sultan's army was three times larger than Vlad's, and the Sultan pushed his huge army forward. Vlad was forced to retreat to his capital. As he did so, he burned his own villages and poisoned the wells, so that there was nothing for the Turks to eat or drink. When the Sultan reached the capital, he was met by an appalling sight, the impaled bodies of 20,000 Turkish captives – the Forest of the Impaled. This tactic had the desired effect. The Sultan admitted defeat.

Vlad is perhaps best remembered for his favourite

method of execution, which was impaling his victims on stakes. This was an exceptionally slow and painful way to die, and Vlad usually insisted that the stakes should not be too sharp, so that it would take his victims longer to die. His preference for this type of execution led to his nickname, 'The Impaler', first recorded in 1550; even the Turks, who were frequently his victims, called him 'Kaziglu Bey', 'The Impaler Prince'. But he used other techniques too.

After the Forest of the Impaled, Vlad's support dwindled, and his brother Radu, with his own Turkish-supported army, pursued Vlad to Poenari Castle. According to legend, Vlad's wife committed suicide by throwing herself from the battlements. Vlad escaped the siege by using a secret passage. He made his way to Transylvania, where he met the new King of Hungary, Matthias Corvinus. Instead of offering help, Matthias arrested and imprisoned him at the Hungarian capital of Visegrad.

Vlad was allowed to return as Prince of Wallachia again in 1475, but this third reign was brief. He was assassinated in December 1476. His head was cut off and sent to the Sultan, who mounted it on a stake as proof that the Impaler was dead.

Dictators have often made free use of the death penalty as a means of getting rid of enemies, and as a deterrent to potential opponents. But what Vlad did went beyond this. He was a sadist who derived deep pleasure from watching other people's sufferings. We can only speculate that the extraordinary experiences of his boyhood must have played a great part in generating feelings of intense and violent rage towards others.

A beneficial effect of his brutal regime was that it was designed to enforce honesty and order, which to a great extent it did. Vlad placed a golden cup in the central square of Targoviste, for the use of thirsty travellers. It seems that it was never removed, that no attempt was made to steal it. Vlad was also concerned that everyone should be productive; vagrants and beggars were treated as thieves, because they were unproductive parasites. This sounds good, but Vlad took it to a surreal and cruel extreme. He invited all the poor and sick of Wallachia to a hall in Targoviste for a feast. Afterwards, he asked them if they would like never to be poor again. Naturally they said yes, so Vlad had the hall locked and set on fire. None of them survived. They were never poor again.

It is said that Vlad was buried at the Snagov monastery, which is situated on an island near Bucharest, but the tomb that is said to be his contains only the bones – of a horse. No-one knows where the Impaler's body is.

Suleiman the Magnificent

master of the massacre

SULEIMAN I (OR Soliman I) was the son of Selim I, and he became Sultan of the Ottoman Empire on his father's death in 1520.

Suleiman the Magnificent, who ruled from 1520 until his death in 1566, was the last great Sultan. In an age that produced many great and spectacular absolute monarchs in Europe and Asia, he was among the greatest and most spectacular. He was lucky to inherit a well-organized country, with full coffers and a well-disciplined army. He started his reign with huge advantages. To these he added his own personal qualities, among which was the invaluable ability to identify talented generals, admirals and viziers and exploit their abilities to the full. Suleiman was able to take the Ottoman Empire to the very peak of its power, but it goes almost without saying that this was achieved by unscrupulousness, bloodthirstiness and carnage on a huge scale. Some historians have fallen for the glitz of his military glory and praised Suleiman for his 'achievements'. He has even been praised for his justice, wisdom and courtesy. To later Turks he was 'The Lawgiver', because of his organization of the learned class; he set the mufti of Constantinople at the head of this body.

The large-scale killing started in the year 1526, when he invaded and annexed part of Hungary – some of Hungary was already in his domain – and organized a massacre of some 200,000 Hungarians. Two thousand of these were killed purely for his pleasure and delectation, as he watched the spectacle from a throne. He also took 100,000 slaves back with him to Constantinople.

Three years later, in 1529, when he laid siege to Vienna and that city refused to surrender, he ransacked the surrounding countryside for good-looking young women to stock the Turkish harems. Then he piled hundreds of Austrian peasants that he did not want onto a huge bonfire, close to the city so that the citizens of Vienna could see exactly what was happening. This display of military and political strength is not only evil but insane by any modern standards, but it was not exceptional – except in scale – in the sixteenth century. Cruelty, and cruelty towards the innocent and power-less, was a terrifyingly common way of demonstrating political strength at that time.

Suleiman the Magnificent died in September 1566 at the age of 72, while engaged in yet more mayhem, the siege of Szigetvar. He was buried in Constantinople in the precincts of the mosque that bears his name.

Henry VIII

Bluff King Hal?

HENRY VIII OF England was the younger son of Henry VII, the upstart king who won the Wars of the Roses by defeating Richard III at the Battle of Bosworth and, in effect, usurped the English throne. Henry VII consolidated his poor claim to the throne by marrying Elizabeth of York, whose claim was only a little stronger than his own. The young Prince Henry was brought up in a disciplined, scholarly way, developing interests in poetry, music and religious thought. As a young king, in 1521, he wrote a religious tract, which was in effect a reply to Martin Luther and a defence of the Roman Catholic Church, and for this work he was awarded the title Defender of the Faith by the Pope. No irony was intended, but subsequent events took both Henry and the English Church in exactly the direction indicated by Luther. Henry was much admired as the handsomest and most accomplished prince of his time.

Even so, right from the beginning there were hints, for those who were well-informed enough to read them, that Henry was going to be a ruthless, homicidal dynast. Henry was well aware of the weakness of his father's claim to the throne, and he knew others in the kingdom had superior claims. There was, in spite of the death of Richard III, still a rival Plantagenet line that could become a problem to him. Pretenders had appeared more than once during his father's reign. Potential claimants probably thought they were safe so long as they kept quiet and remained loyal, but it was not so. Henry VIII winkled them out one by one and had them killed. In 1521, for instance, he had the Duke of Buckingham executed on a trumped-up charge of treason; his only treason in fact was to be a descendant of Edward III and therefore a potential claimant to Henry's crown.

Although Henry VIII held the throne by inheritance from his father, Henry VII, Henry VII's claim to the throne was far weaker than that of the king he killed in order to take it – Richard III. Richard III had no living heir, but his elder brother, the disgraced and executed George Duke of Clarence, did. The son and daughter of the Duke of Clarence had a claim to the English throne that was stronger than Henry VII's or Henry VIII's. The dangerous son, Edward Earl of Warwick, was imprisoned in the Tower as a boy and died there unmarried and without issue. He was feeble-minded, but so had Henry VI been, and that had not prevented his accession. The almost equally dangerous daughter was Margaret Countess of Salisbury. Quite late in his reign, Henry VIII decided to do something about her ominous presence, so he brought a trumped-up charge of treason against her and she was sentenced to death.

The great Countess, who should by rights have been Queen of England, did not go to the block in 1541 with the traditional dignity and decorum. She knew exactly why she was being killed and she resisted her execution and her executioners, complaining and fighting to the last; she made them murder her – because murder is what it was. She had several sons – Henry, Geoffrey and Arthur – and Henry VIII saw to it that they died too.

Seven weeks after his accession, Henry married Katherine of Aragon, his brother's widow. This marriage, and subsequent marriages, proved to be a great problem to the king, who desperately needed a son and heir to consolidate his dynasty. It became clear that Katherine was not going to bear him a son. She had given birth several times, and all but one child had died in infancy; the only survivor was a girl, Mary Tudor. Henry saw a way out. Katherine had been his elder brother's wife first and marrying his brother's wife was against church law. The lack of sons was divine retribution for the invalidity of the marriage, which had been, in reality, no marriage at all in the eyes of God. Initially the Pope was inclined to agree to nullify the marriage and in 1528 sent Cardinal Campeggio to London to explore its validity. The visit was inconclusive, and the Pope referred the case to the Curia. This ruined Cardinal Thomas Wolsey – Henry's advisor and confidante – who now had no friends in England or abroad. In 1529, Henry stripped him of his goods and honours and dismissed him for failing. In

1530, Henry summoned him to London to stand trial for treason, but Wolsey died on the journey at Market Harborough. If Wolsey had survived the journey, Henry would certainly have had him killed.

The skilful Wolsey had failed, and the Pope refused to co-operate, yet Henry was still determined to have his marriage annulled – the more so since he was now infatuated with Anne Boleyn. Anne was bright and flirtatious and Henry was besotted with her breasts. Anne was not bowled over by the royal suitor, though. She had watched him seduce her sister Mary and then drop her when he lost interest in her. She was determined that would not happen to her.

In 1531 Henry VIII tried to bully the Pope into agreeing to the annulment by humiliating the entire English clergy; he accused them all of treason, but gave them the option of paying fines. He also extorted recognition as 'protector and supreme head of the clergy and church of England'. The English church, and by implication the English, were no longer bound by what the Pope agreed or did not agree. Henry accordingly went ahead and married Anne Boleyn, though he at least was circumspect enough to do so in private (1533). This wrenching doctrinal change was very hard for many to accept. Those who would not accept the royal supremacy were put to death. Bishop Fisher and Sir Thomas More, who had been his chancellor, were beheaded for refusing to support the new marriage. Many monks, Carthusians especially, were also put to death for refusing to acknowledge the royal supremacy.

Henry had Katherine of Aragon, the unwanted queen, moved to a cold damp house in the East Midlands. He hoped she would sicken and die there, to save him the trouble of divorcing her, but she stubbornly stayed alive. She outlived the trauma of the divorce, and did not die until 1536, the same year that Henry had her successor, Queen Anne Boleyn, executed for alleged treason. She was accused of infidelity, but the evidence was procured under torture and cannot be believed; the real reason seems to be that, like Katherine, Anne had failed to produce a son. Henry had also shifted his affections to Jane Seymour, a surprisingly straight-laced woman to whom Henry was betrothed the day after Anne Boleyn's execution. Jane, in spite of looking unpromisingly puritanical, supplied Henry with the necessary son, Edward VI in October 1537, but died immediately afterwards. Jane had died naturally, Katherine had died naturally, but her death was hastened by the bad living conditions provided by Henry; Anne died by the executioner's sword.

Thomas Cromwell was introduced to government service as a secretary for Cardinal Wolsey. Cromwell botched the arrangements for the next marriage. Henry expressed interest in the current troupe of princesses at the French court and proposed a beauty contest in Calais (still an English possession). The French ambassador, who obviously thought the idea preposterously tasteless, made the counter-suggestion that if the princesses were to be run round a ring like ponies why not mount them one by one to see which gave the best ride? The idea was dropped, though it might have worked better than Cromwell's botch-up. He supplied a Holbein portrait of Anne of Cleves that was far too flattering. Henry rashly agreed to marry Anne on the strength of the portrait, but found the reality unattractive. She was 'not as reported', he said; her breasts sagged, and she seemed generally in poor physical condition. Cromwell had made many enemies while in office, and those enemies were only too glad to exploit the king's indignation at having to marry an ugly woman. This was the opportunity they had been waiting for. The Duke of Norfolk accused Thomas Cromwell of high treason and Cromwell was executed without trial in 1540. It was another state murder committed by Henry VIII.

Henry next married Katherine Howard, who unwisely had affairs during her short marriage to the King, was found out and duly executed. In 1543, Henry married for the sixth time. Catherine Parr was lucky to survive Henry.

In Henry VIII, we have someone who was regarded by many of his contemporaries, the ordinary people of Tudor England, as an admirable king. He certainly looked the part. He was a fine big kingly man, who knew how to behave in public, and knew how to dress. We have inherited a view of Henry as a jolly, merry monarch with an eye for the ladies – Bluff King Hal. He was scandalous certainly, but in a roguish, raffish, forgivable sort of way. The occasional beheadings we shrug off as colourful lapses, and the monasteries – well, they were dens of corruption anyway and it was high time they went. The Hollywood and TV treatments of Henry have laundered his image several times over to give us the ultimate colourful costume drama king.

But Henry VIII committed a range of atrocities. He extorted a great deal from his people in the form of taxes. He was an asset-stripper of the worst kind. The elaborate infrastructure of the Church with its religious houses, hospitals, abbeys and priories had been built up and developed over a period of a thousand years. It had been a major force for good, in effect supplying social services for the poor and needy, offering many kinds of work, offering education for all, offering a route out of the poverty trap for aspiring young men and women, however low-born, and maintaining some sort of order even through major civil wars. Henry ripped all that apart for the sake of the wealth invested in it, and replaced it with – nothing. He turned a blind eye to what was happening in the country, where un-scrupulous 'improving' landowners turned people off the land by the thousand, disinheriting them and turning them into 'vagabonds' who could be disowned by any village they came to. With all this needless cruelty – evil by negligence – came the drift of country people into the towns hoping to find work. Henry knew these things were happening but did nothing at all to stop the landowners who were behind them.

And he was also a killer. He killed Katherine of Aragon by negligence, he killed Ann Boleyn for failing to produce a son, he killed Katherine Howard for infidelity, he would have killed Wolsey for failing to deliver the divorce had Wolsey not conveniently died first. He killed Fisher and More for refusing to agree to the divorce and the royal supremacy, and he killed off as many of the survivors of the Plantagenet line as he could lay his hands on.

Ivan the Terrible

IVAN THE TERRIBLE, the son of Vasily, Grand Duke of Moscow, was orphaned at an early age; his father died when he was three and his mother, then acting as Regent, was poisoned when he was eight. After that, Ivan claimed he had 'no human care from any quarter'. A power struggle followed his father's death, raging among the leading Muscovite families, and Ivan became a pawn in this struggle. One of his uncles was seized and murdered by a Moscow mob during a rising.

Ivan quickly learnt how to survive. He was 13 when he organized his own first political murder. He threw the body of a troublesome prince to his dogs. In 1547, Ivan became Tsar and at a specially convened beauty contest he selected a bride, a 15-year-old girl called Anastasia. She gave birth to six children, though four had died by the time she herself died in 1560. It is possible that the loss of the children followed by the loss of his wife, who was a stabilizing influence on him, caused him to topple over into bloodthirsty megalomania.

In his grief, he accused two of his closest advisers, Father Silvestr and Alexei Adashev, of plotting to kill his wife, and banished them both. Then he left Moscow and went into retreat. He was begged by the Muscovites to return, for fear of another power vacuum, and they must later have regretted doing so. Ivan agreed, but on condition that he would be free to govern with dictatorial powers, and he used them. He re-organized the country into huge administrative units; he would be absolute ruler in one, while the others were governed on his behalf by teams of bureaucrats.

This is when the terror began. He created a force of oprichniki, black-cloaked assassins riding black horses. In their saddles they each carried their emblems of office, a broom and a dog's head. The black riders descended like Furies on anyone who was suspected of opposing Ivan and slaughtered them. Ivan used them, among other things, to settle scores dating back to his childhood. Anyone he could remember thwarting him during his early years was marked for a visit by the black riders. He had over 4,000 aristocrats murdered in this way, including the entire Staritsky family; they were relatives of Ivan's, but because of this they were potential rivals too. When the leader of the Orthodox Church, Metropolitan Philip, condemned the oprichniki attacks and withheld his blessing from the Tsar, with ruthless inevitability the black riders came for him and executed him.

Throughout history, dictators have behaved in this way, getting underlings to commit their murders for them. Ivan was unusual in wanting to take part himself. He joined in orgies of rape, torture and killing.

The peak of Ivan the Terrible's terrible reign came

when he was informed that the city leaders of Novgorod, at that time the second city of Russia, were planning to rebel. Ivan's rage knew no bounds. He did not bother to check whether his informant was telling the truth, which he probably was not, but summoned the black riders and rode to Novgorod with them. First they laid waste to all the land within 50 miles of the city. Then Ivan ordered a wooden wall to be built round Novgorod to prevent anyone from escaping. For five weeks, he and his men slaughtered everyone inside the wall. Nor was the killing quick and merciful. Sometimes families were forced to watch while fathers, husbands or wives were tortured. Women were roasted alive on spits. Ivan joined in with relish. He mounted a horse, took a spear and rode about, running people through as if it was a sport.

Russian historians have been keen to keep alive the memory of a great king, and have put the death toll at Novgorod at 2,000, but historians in the West put it at 60,000. Ivan's sadistic savagery at Novgorod, and his similar treatment of Pskov on a similar pretext, had the effect of suppressing opposition. Many who knew they had become suspects killed themselves rather than risk the unimaginably horrible death that Ivan would inflict on them. When Ivan invaded the adjacent state of Livonia, one doomed garrison that was under siege blew itself up rather than risk falling into Ivan's hands.

In 1572, Ivan suddenly disbanded the black riders, and banned any future reference to them. Unpredictability and capriciousness are hallmarks of the dictator. Ivan was probably a manic depressive, with bouts of frenzied sadism alternating with periods of static religious depression. During these religious phases, he wore sackcloth and publicly confessed his sins. Perhaps it was genuine shame that brought the six-year reign of terror to an end. Perhaps there was no need to go on because all his enemies were dead; but that had not stopped him killing thousands of imaginary enemies. Perhaps there was a more political reason. Perhaps it was an attack from outside Russia that caused him to call off the weakening revenge attacks; the Turks were advancing from the south.

It is hard for a state to survive such destructive leadership. Ivan survived partly because he had the Orthodox Church's support. While Western Europe was going through the challenge of Protestantism, and the trauma of the Reformation was in full swing, Ivan was allowing no protest of any kind in Russia, and would maintain the status quo. Ivan took a predictably tough line on religious dissent, with the depressingly familiar burnings for heresy, and in this way he bought the support of the Church. In return, the Church acted as a propaganda machine for the Tsar. When peasant revolts were crushed with brutal cruelty, the atrocities were always blamed on the excessive zeal of underlings. It was never the Tsar who was behind them.

In 1581, Ivan murdered his son and heir, the young Ivan, with a spear during a quarrel. But his licentious sex life had left him riddled with disease; he was about to play a game of chess when he collapsed and died. But even Ivan's legacy was terrible. He had recently killed his heir and left instead his imbecile son Theodore on the throne. Russia was plunged again into decades of chaos, with invasions by both Poles and Swedes.

It is by no means clear whether Ivan was consciously evil, deciding to do bad things, or unconsciously evil because he was insane. Probably he was a manic depressive and the characteristics of both sides of his personality were exaggerated by the personal freedom that came with absolute power. As with Caligula, his existing personality traits became accentuated because there was nothing to hold him back.

Mary Tudor

MARY TUDOR WAS the daughter of King Henry VIII and Queen Katherine of Aragon. This should have been a great start in life, but it was not. Her father desperately wanted a son to continue the Tudor dynasty, and the fact that she was a girl was a great disappointment. The King seems to have been fond of her, even so, and saw that she was well educated, just as her half-sister, the yet unborn Elizabeth, would be. Mary's long unhappiness began when her father tired of waiting for her mother to produce a male heir and became infatuated with Anne Boleyn.

In the long struggle to have his first marriage annulled, Henry VIII pushed both Katherine and Mary to one side. When he finally married Anne Boleyn in 1533, Henry ordered that Mary should no longer use the title Princess, and that she should give precedence to the new Queen's daughter. The point Henry was trying to make was that the first marriage had been an illegal one and that therefore Mary was illegitimate; any children of the new Queen's would therefore take precedence over her. The old Queen was sent away to live in a cold, damp house at Kimbolton, while Mary was lodged with Anne Boleyn's sister at Hatfield. The severity of the King's treatment of Queen Katherine and her daughter aroused a great deal of sympathy in the country, especially when Katherine died, in 1536, without being allowed a visit from her daughter.

Mary's only ally through this difficult time was Charles V of Spain, her mother's nephew. The Spanish king's ambassador, Chapuys, tried to act on Mary's behalf when he thought her interests were threatened. At the same time, Chapuys had to advise Mary to behave a little more diplomatically; she was proud, hot-tempered and outspoken. Many believed that it was only the concern of the King of Spain that prevented Henry from permanently disposing of Mary, who was fast becoming a nuisance.

Suddenly things started to improve for Mary. Queen Anne was beheaded and Henry married Jane Seymour, who was far more compassionate towards Mary. The new Queen Jane advised Mary to show humility to-wards her father, agree to acknowledge the divorce and beg the King's forgiveness for her obduracy. Thanks to Chapuys' and the new Queen's persuasion, Mary signed the papers accepting her parents' divorce. After a few months, she was allowed back to Greenwich.

Jane Seymour gave birth to a son in 1537. This was the prince who would shortly become Edward VI, and Mary wisely recognized Edward's precedence over her. The fact that he was a boy was decisive, but by now

Henry had (for the time being) declared both Mary and Elizabeth bastards, so they were both out of the line of succession anyway.

Ten years later, Henry VIII died and was duly succeeded by Edward VI. He had tuberculosis and would not live long. Because of his illness and his youth, the real power lay in the hands of Edward Seymour, his uncle and the brother of the late queen. Seymour, a Protestant, became Lord Protector and together with Cranmer they attempted to establish a Protestant England. Once again Mary was in difficulties. She was a staunch, unswerving Catholic, and so found it increasingly difficult to remain at court, even though she was very fond of her brother, the King. She withdrew to the country and was allowed to say mass in private.

In 1533, Edward VI lay dying and Mary prepared to succeed, as Henry VIII had intended that she would. As her brother's death approached, she prepared to return to London, a rebellion was mounted by a group of Protestant nobles, who feared a return to Catholicism if Mary took the throne, not least because it would greatly reduce their own power and influence. The rebellion was led by the Duke of Northumberland, who supported the candidacy of Lady Jane Grey. She was Edward VI's cousin. She had no ambition to become queen, but this did not deter Northumberland, who married her to his son, Lord Guildford Dudley. Northumberland made the dying King sign a new will, bequeathing the crown to Lady Jane Grey and confirming, once again, that both Mary and Elizabeth were illegitimate.

Lady Jane Grey was queen for only nine days. A counter-rebellion to put Mary on the throne gathered momentum; most of the great barons wanted to be on the winning side. In July 1553 Mary was proclaimed Queen in London, to great rejoicing, and she entered the city in triumph. It was the high point of her reign.

Queen Mary was not magnanimous in victory. She set about getting rid of those who had acted against her. She was putting her popularity in danger, and her advisers proposed that she should marry in order to consolidate her position. After all, another Protestant candidate could quickly be found. Her old supporter Charles V of Spain offered her his son, Prince Philip, as a suitor. There were several problems looming. The prospective bridegroom was only 26, eleven years younger than Mary, and reported to be very virile. Mary disliked the idea of sex. She was naturally very reluctant, and feared marriage almost as much as her half-sister Elizabeth, and probably for a similar reason – the appalling example of their father's catastrophic marriages. She finally forced herself to accept the marriage, only to find that it was extremely unpopular with the English people. The Spaniards were, after all, 'the enemy'. There were riots. There were revolts, the most serious revolt being that of Sir Thomas Wyatt, a 23-year-old Catholic, who led an army of 15,000 to London before it was stamped out.

This experience hardened Mary's heart, and she now moved against all of those involved in the rebellions against her. Even Lady Jane Grey was executed;

although she was entirely innocent she would continue to be a focus for Protestant hopes.

Prince Philip of Spain arrived for the wedding in July 1554. Mary fell in love with him immediately, but he found her unattractive. He was courteous and attentive towards her in public, but privately she was a great disappointment to him, as her aversion to sex was all too apparent. Twice during their marriage Mary claimed that she was pregnant, but it turned out that she was swelling up because she had a diseased womb instead.

It was then that the persecution of Protestants began. She set up a tribunal in Southwark to question suspected heretics. The Bishop of London, Edmund Bonner, led a procession through London to celebrate the triumph of Rome. Bonner was quickly to gain an evil reputation as an inquisitor. He had suspected heretics to stay at his house, where he perfected the 'nice-and-nasty' style of interrogation. An invitation to stay at Bishop Bonner's house was no treat.

John Rogers, a married priest, was the first victim of the persecutions. He was burned at Smithfield in February 1555. The Bishop of Gloucester soon followed, a great surprise to everyone, as he had been loyal to Mary in spite of their difference in religion. Many Protestant bishops and theologians fled abroad. Those that remained went one by one to the stake. Hugh Latimer, Bishop of Worcester, who had helped establish the Protestant Church in England, was an obvious target. Ridley, the Bishop of London who had supported Lady Jane Grey, was another. The pair of them were taken to Oxford and burnt together in the town ditch (now Broad Street). Archbishop Cranmer was burnt shortly afterwards.

These were great men, who had taken an active part in public life. They had taken calculated risks and lost. Mary had them killed out of hand. But most of Mary's victims were ordinary people who had played no part in state politics and represented no kind of threat to her at all. Mary Tudor's persecution of these Protestant martyrs was callous and cruel – the clearest abuse of power. It was understandably generally assumed, because of the Inquisition in Spain, that her husband Prince Philip of Spain was egging her on, but in fact the opposite was the case. He urged her to stop it and practise more moderate policies. He had, meanwhile become disenchanted with Mary in every way. She had not yet reached 40, yet her face was heavily lined and she looked much older. She was carrying out pointlessly cruel persecutions of her subjects. Philip spent as much time overseas as possible, and whenever he left Mary wept.

Still the persecutions went on. People who saw the burnings came to regard those who were sadistically punished in this way as saints. Mary became very angry at the sympathy shown to the heretics, and demanded that anyone who voiced compassion for them should be punished too. In Norwich, a man who protested against the cruelty was given a flogging for it.

In 1558 Mary fell ill. It may have been dropsy. It may have been a malignant growth in her womb. She gave in to self-pity, weeping for Philip, weeping for the loss of Calais, England's last possession in France. Protestantism flourished everywhere, with secret prayer meetings and increasingly open demonstrations against the burnings – but still the burnings went on.

On 10 November she signed the death warrants for another five Protestants to be burnt in Canterbury, bringing the total number of Protestant 'martyrs' to 238. On 13 November, she mercilessly signed away the lives of two more men in London. On 17 November she died herself, just in time for the last two to be saved – and they were immediately set free. Mary's half-sister Elizabeth became queen. She generously laid on a lavish Catholic funeral for Mary, but the dead queen was to be remembered by the people of England, for ever after, as 'Bloody Mary'.

PART TWO

CANNIBAL
KILLERS

Sawney Bean

a Scottish bandit family

IN THE MIDDLE ages, all kinds of travel were dangerous. Travellers in those days sometimes went missing, as victims of falls, bandits, or simply losing their way at night and dying of the cold.

Towards the end of the fourteenth century it became evident that rather a lot of people were disappearing in Galloway in southwest Scotland. Galloway was always a bleak, windswept, empty landscape. Few people lived there and most of them lived on the low ground near the coast. By 1400 so many travellers were disappearing that the Galloway locals began to wonder if packs of wolves were on the loose in the hills. But there were no signs of attacks by wolves, no remnants of bloodstained clothes or other belongings.

James I of Scotland sent officers to Galloway to investigate. A few suspicious-looking vagrants and inn-keepers were rounded up and hanged, but the disappearances went on just as before.

Then, a man and his wife were riding home from a fair, both on the same horse, when they were set upon by a wild man who jumped out of some roadside bushes. The rider was armed and fired a pistol at the wild man. There was a shout, and more wild men appeared, surrounding the horse. The rider slashed at the attackers with a sword. His wife was pulled off the horse from behind and her throat was cut by one of the attackers; then the rider too was pulled down. Another moment and he too would have been killed.

As it happened, twenty people came into view at that moment; they too were returning home from the fair. They were stunned by what they saw. The poor woman's clothes had been ripped off her and she had been disembowelled. Her attackers were tearing at her flesh – and eating it. The horrified crowd shouted and the attackers ran off. The poor woman was dead, but her husband and the horse were still alive. They were the only creatures to have survived an attack from this pack of cannibals in 25 years. The woman's body had been dragged off the road for butchery. Any bloodstains there, among the heather, would not have been noticeable from the road. Within hours of the attack, no-one would have known anything had happened there at all.

The news was conveyed to the King in Edinburgh. In four days, he was in Galloway with four hundred men. They visited the scene of the ambush, where there were plenty of rocks and bushes to provide cover for the attackers; then they set off in the direction seen to be taken by the fleeing marauders. They soon arrived at the coast, where there were tall cliffs. They waited for the tide to fall so that they could ride along the beach to see if there were any hiding places. They came to some caves, but none of them was big enough to make a human dwelling. They were about to turn back when the dogs they had brought with them started barking at a crack in the cliff. It seemed hardly big enough to let a person in, but the dogs went in and started barking with excitement.

The King sent for torches while a few of his men went into the fissure. When the torches arrived, the King sent more of his men in. They followed the dark tunnel beyond the fissure until it opened into an evil-smelling cave. People could be made out, crouching in the corners, and everywhere there were piles of money and jewels. Human body parts dangled from the cave ceiling. The wild people were cornered and ready to fight, but they were quickly overpowered by the armed soldiers.

The cave-dwellers were the cannibals who had attacked the rider and his wife on the road, and scores of other unfortunate travellers before them. Almost unbelievably, they were eating human flesh raw. The soldiers buried the human remains from the cave in the beach sand and took the cannibals into custody at the Tolbooth in Edinburgh.

The head of this appalling cannibal family was Sawney Bean. He had been born in East Lothian, near Edinburgh. As a young man he had run off with a woman and they had ever since then lived in this cave where she had produced six daughters and eight sons; they in their turn had produced fourteen grand-daughters and eighteen grandsons, all sharing in the same debased and depraved lifestyle. It was difficult to know how to deal with such people. Were they really people at all? The authorities transferred the Bean tribe from the Tolbooth to Leith.

The Beans were given no trial. The chronicler of these events, John Nicholson, said that it was decided there was no point in bringing them to trial, 'It being thought needless to try creatures who were even professed enemies to mankind.' The Bean clan lived in a barbaric way. They died too in a barbaric way. The men's hands and feet were chopped off and they were left to bleed to death. The women were made to watch this grisly spectacle, which was not so different from the scenes they saw in their everyday lives, before being burnt to death on three fires. Nicholson said they died 'without the least sign of repentance, but continued cursing . . . to the very last gasp of life.'

In executing the Bean family without a trial, King James was in effect declaring that they were not in his view human beings but animals. It was an evil response to evil.

Peter Kürten

the Vampire of Düsseldorf

THE SADIST PETER Kürten started as a child sadist. When only nine years old he worked for the local dog-catcher near his home town of Cologne-Mulheim. He exceeded his duties, torturing the unfortunate animals he caught. Later he went on to torture pigs, sheep and goats. He was fascinated by the sight of blood and loved chopping the heads off geese and drinking the blood that came spurting out.

It was almost inevitable that, sooner or later, he would graduate to killing people. In fact Kürten was still a boy when he started killing his fellow human beings. Swimming in the Rhine one day with friends, he succeeded in drowning two of them.

As an adult, this profoundly dysfunctional person looked for new thrills, trying fraud, theft and arson. He also tried beating prostitutes. But murder was what he was destined for. It is rather strange, given the trail of death he had already laid, that the first premeditated murder he planned went wrong. He attacked a girl in a park and left her for dead, but she recovered and staggered away from the scene, too ashamed to report what had happened. The next attack was horrifically successful. He strangled and raped an eight-year-old girl he found asleep in a room over an inn at Cologne-Mulheim, then cut her throat. After this awful attack, Kürten locked the door, and went back to his home in Düsseldorf. He returned to the scene of the crime the next day and sat at a café opposite the inn. He felt elated and important when he heard people round him talking about the murder. This murder had an inevitable second victim – the man who was wrongly accused of the little girl's murder. He was the girl's uncle. He was arrested, tried and eventually acquitted, but the trauma and the 'no smoke without fire' suspicion that continued to hang over him wore him down; the poor man died prematurely two or three years later. This landmark in Peter Kürten's career of serial murder took place in 1913.

On the outbreak of the First World War in 1914, Kürten was called up. If he had stayed in the army, he would have had more than his fill of killing, but he deserted straight away and consequently spent most of the war in prison. When freed, he turned to fraud again and was sent back to prison. Then, in 1921, he was freed again and he made a decision to go straight. He married an ex-prostitute, started dressing smartly, and took a job in a factory. He was courteous and well-liked. But it did not last. In 1925 he started attacking prostitutes, then complete strangers in the street; he was still mesmerized by the sight of blood.

In 1929, Kürten attacked two sisters aged five and

fourteen as they walked home from a fair, strangled them and cut their throats. The next day he stabbed a housemaid with such ferocity that the knife-blade broke off in the young woman's back. She was lucky to survive; her screams attracted the attention of passers-by who came and saved her life, but unfortunately they did not arrive in time to catch Peter Kürten. With hindsight, it seems extraordinary that anyone could behave like Peter Kürten, committing one serious offence after another, and still remain at liberty. It is one of the quirks of a psychopath that he can assume 'normal' behaviour patterns at the drop of a hat, and show no detectable sign of disturbance, even after committing the most appalling murder.

By this stage, the city of Düsseldorf was in a panic. Police had records of over fifty attacks which they thought must have been committed by the same madman. He became known as The Vampire, but no-one knew who he was.

It seemed as though the attacks would go on and on, but in 1929 there was a breakthrough, when Kürten tried to set up another atrocity. A girl arrived at the main railway station in Düsseldorf on 14 May and was intercepted by a stranger who offered to direct her to a cheap hotel. He took her along a main street, but then proposed that they should walk through the park. At this point she became nervous, remembering the stories about the Düsseldorf monster. Just as the man was becoming frighteningly persistent, another man arrived to rescue her, introducing himself as Peter Kürten. The first man disappeared. Kürten, the rescuer, invited the girl to his house to recover and have a meal. She became uneasy when she saw how poorly furnished his attic rooms were. Then he walked her through the Grafenburg Woods, where he assaulted her. Suddenly, in the middle of his attack, Kürten changed his mind, released her and courteously escorted her back to the public highway. It was as if his 'normal' persona had reasserted itself in the middle of what would otherwise have been a murder. He asked her if she remembered where he lived. She had the presence of mind to say no, a white lie that saved her life.

As happens all too often in such cases, the girl did not report the incident to the police. Kürten might still have been in the clear, but for a strange coincidence. The girl wrote about the incident to a friend, but addressed the envelope incorrectly. A postal worker opened the envelope to find out the sender's address and his eyes fell on the account of the attack. He realised at once the significance of what he was reading and reported it to the police.

Policemen visited the girl and made her retrace her steps back to Kürten's house. She had not remembered the number, but picked out the likeliest. When she saw Kürten's room she was sure. At that moment Kürten came up the stairs, saw what was happening and ran off. The landlady gave the police his name. They spotted Peter Kürten, but he ran off through the city streets. As a last resort he turned to his wife. He told her everything. She was appalled, arranged another secret meeting with him and went straight to the police, who ambushed and arrested Kürten at the appointed meeting place.

Kürten was charged with nine murders and seven attempted murders. At his trial, Kürten was confined in a hastily improvised wooden cage, and startled the judge and jury with the clinical way in which he described his appalling crimes. His defence counsel was reduced to describing his client as 'the king of sexual delinquents, uniting nearly all perversions in one person, killing men, women, children and animals, killing anything he found.' The counsel's intention was to portray Kürten as a madman. It did not work. Kürten was sentenced to death. For a time it seemed the death sentence might not be carried out. There was lot of controversy about the use of the death penalty, which had not been carried out for three years, and Kürten appealed. On 30 June the Prussian Ministry of Justice turned down the appeal. He was guillotined at 6am on 2 July 1931 in the courtyard of the Klingelputz prison in Cologne. He went happily to his death, eating two breakfasts of Wienerschnitzel, fried potatoes and white wine and telling the prison doctor how he looked forward to 'the pleasure to end all pleasures, that after my head has been chopped off I will still be able to hear, at least for a moment, the sound of my own blood gushing from the stump of my neck.'

Fritz Haarman

the Vampire of Hanover

A CONTEMPORARY OF Peter Kürten, the Düsseldorf Vampire, was coming to the end of his criminal career in another German city. He was Fritz Haarman, known as the Vampire of Hanover.

Fritz Haarman was born in 1879 and spent the First World War safely in prison, serving a five-year sentence for theft. As the war ended, he came out of prison and returned to Hanover to try to make a living. He became a purveyor of meats, pies and second-hand clothes in a poor district of Hanover. His business was based on murder: the raw materials of his trade came from young men and boys.

Haarman went out at night, picking up homeless and jobless boys at the railway stations and offering them food and a bed for the night. When they reached Haarman's home they were fed and sexually abused. Some of them, though not all, were murdered, which they did not expect. Their bodies were butchered and their flesh cooked and put into Haarman's pies; their clothes too were sold.

It was the way Haarman killed his victims that gave rise to his nickname. He bit their throats.

Haarman was in regular contact with the police, who must have suspected at least the lesser of his crimes. He was a police informer, passing on information about suspicious newcomers to the town, the whereabouts of stolen goods and plans for criminal activities. The police were so used to working with Haarman that when a seventeen-year-old boy went missing and his parents raised the alarm, the police made only a cursory visit to Haarman's room, even though a witness had seen the boy with Haarman. Haarman later boasted at his trial that when the police visited his room the boy's head was there, wrapped in newspaper behind the oven.

Serial killers usually work alone. Haarman was one of the few who dared to trust someone else with their terrible secret – and take on a collaborator. In 1919, he acquired an accomplice, a twenty-year-old called Hans Gans. It became Hans's job to go out and select victims. Together, they stepped up the murder rate – and the production of meat.

It was becoming evident to the citizens that Hanover had become a very dangerous place. People were literally vanishing from the streets. The police found Haarman's information so useful that they turned a deaf ear to the stream of complaints about Haarman. People were reporting some very obvious clues to them: the one-way traffic of boys into Haarman's home, the buckets of blood being carried out, the bloodstained clothes he was selling – yet the police still took no action against him.

Then, beside the River Leine, two human skulls were discovered, one of them belonging to a boy. This finally pushed the police into action. More human remains were found along the river bank. Some boys found a sack packed with human organs. Hundreds of human bones were found on the river bed. Eventually, after numerous tip-offs, the police raided Haarman's blood-stained rooms.

Fritz Haarman and his assistant were put on trial in December 1924. When he was asked how many boys he had killed, Haarman said, 'It might be thirty, it might be forty.' He freely admitted killing them by biting through their throats. Gans was treated fairly lightly, given the horrific nature of the atrocities he was involved in, and there were no extenuating circumstances. He was given a life sentence, of which he served only twelve years. He was very lucky to have escaped the death penalty for his crimes. Haarman was found to be sane, in the sense that he was entirely responsible for his actions, and therefore sentenced to death by beheading. He said he looked forward to it.

Jeffrey Dahmer

the Milwaukee Cannibal

JEFFREY DAHMER IS another of those serial killers whose horrific deeds seem to be completely at variance with their mildness of manner.

Jeffrey Dahmer was a member of a white minority in a predominantly black neighbourhood, a run-down residential area of the city of Milwaukee. It was in the small hours of 27 May 1991 that three police answered a 911 call (the American equivalent of a British 999 call) from a couple of black teenage girls. They were deeply concerned about a young Asian boy who was running round stark naked in the street and rambling incoherently. The boy was so distressed he was unable to explain what had happened to him. Even so, the two eighteen-year-old girls, Nicole Childress and Sandra Smith, were convinced that he was genuinely frightened of the tall white man who had followed him out into the street and was trying to persuade him to go back with him into his apartment.

When the police arrived, their reaction was surprising. They paid more attention to what the white man was saying than the two black girls. The white man explained that the Asian was actually 19, was his lover and that they had simply had a lovers' tiff. Almost incredibly, the policemen escorted the Asian boy back into the white man's apartment, ignoring the protestations of the two girls, who were sure there must be some good reason for the Asian boy's fear of the white man.

When the truth of what was going on in Dahmer's flat emerged just six weeks later, the black community felt that the incident proved the inherent racism of the police.

The white man was Jeffrey Dahmer, a sadistic, depraved psychopath, and the Asian boy was Konerak Sinthasomphone who, thanks to the intervention of the police, had become the thirteenth of Dahmer's victims. Shortly after the policemen left, Dahmer strangled the 14-year-old Konerak, abused his body, then dismembered it. He kept some body parts to eat, and others as trophies. If the police had troubled to check Dahmer's record, they would have found that he was a convicted child molester on probation. As it was, the police were ready to believe his version of events, partly because he was white, partly, it may be suspected, because he was calm, rational and articulate. This was not just racial prejudice but cultural prejudice.

There is no suggestion that Dahmer was a racist. It is more likely that he was murdering Asians and blacks because they were more readily available, given the neighbourhood he was living in. The large black and Asian communities in Milwaukee, a city of 700,000 people, had suffered greatly from the social exclusion and alienation that was widespread in American cities. When in the hot summer of 1991 it emerged that a white man had murdered twelve black men, racial tensions rose dangerously – especially when it was clear that the police had failed to notice any connections between the disappearances of the many victims. Fortunately the impending race riot never happened. Even so it came as no great surprise when in 1994 Dahmer was battered to death in prison by Christopher Scarver, a 25-year-old black man suffering from Messianic delusions.

Disturbingly, Jeffrey Dahmer is by no means the only serial killer to have operated in a city without the city police having any idea of what was happening. The cases of Fred and Rose West, Harold Shipman, Dennis Nilsen and John Wayne Gacy are rather similar in that respect. All of these people managed to maintain an appearance of a normal lifestyle without the authorities even suspecting that anything was wrong.

Dahmer deliberately targeted young men on the fringes of society, transients who would not be missed. Many were living in a twilight world of drink and drugs. Many were loners and runaways who would not be missed by families; many were homosexual and therefore cut off from their families by homophobic prejudice; they had already left their families behind.

When Dahmer was arrested on 22 July 1991, the discoveries in his apartment horrified not only America but the world. The end of Dahmer's killing spree came in an incident rather like the Konerak incident. Two patrolmen were driving round Dahmer's area late one night when they spotted a black man stumbling about with a handcuff attached to his wrist. They pulled up beside the man, 32-year-old Tracy Edwards, and asked him what had happened. He told them a strange story about being invited back to the apartment of 'a weird dude' for drinks. He had become sleepy after a couple of drinks that might have been spiked. He had been handcuffed, then threatened with a knife while they watched a film on video. Tracy Edwards was still feeling light-headed, but he managed to punch his attacker and get himself out of the apartment.

The police officers were curious to find out more, and persuaded Edwards to take them to the apartment. Dahmer opened the door to them and gave them some sort of rational explanation. He had lost his temper because he had lost his job in a factory (which was true). He offered to get the key to the handcuffs from his bedroom. One of the officers followed him into the bedroom and saw scores of Polaroid photos of dismembered bodies, including photos of human skulls in a refrigerator. The officer was now very worried about what he had stumbled into. He walked through into the kitchen and noticed the same refrigerator as the one that appeared in the Polaroid shots. He opened the refrigerator door and, experienced and hardened though he was, he was horrified by what he saw. He instinctively shouted out to his colleague, 'There's a goddam head in here!'

Dahmer had been very calm and rational up to this

point. Now he started squealing and struggling as the two officers wrestled to get handcuffs on him.

Tracy Edwards' emotions can only be imagined, but he must have felt very uncomfortable about going back into the apartment in the first place. To hear that there was a severed head in the refrigerator must have been hard to take. He would have realised that Dahmer's wild threat to 'cut out your heart and eat it' had been no exaggeration at all. He had accepted an invitation home by a murderous cannibal.

Dahmer was taken to a police station for questioning, while officers carried out a thorough search of his flat – Apartment 213, Oxford Apartments, 924 North 25th Street. The results of that search were horrific. There was the fresh severed head in the refrigerator; there were three more human heads in the freezer, several pairs of hands and a penis in a stockpot in a cupboard, as well as a quantity of human flesh in the freezer. Several penises were preserved in formaldehyde and there was a bottle of chloroform, presumably used to overwhelm Dahmer's victims. There were also hundreds of grotesque photographs of the victims, both before and after death. The stench of death and decomposing human flesh permeated the apartment.

The residents of the other apartments in the block gathered in the hallway and outside the Dahmer apartment. People compared notes and realised, with hindsight, that there had been clues to what had been going on – they just hadn't realised their significance at the time. The reality was bewilderingly improbable.

The forensic experts looked at the human debris in the apartment, while Detective Patrick Kennedy gently interviewed Dahmer, and they came to the conclusion that the mild-mannered chocolate factory worker had killed sixteen people.

Later on it emerged that the killing had begun thirteen years before. A hitch-hiker called Stephen Hicks had been murdered near Akron in Ohio. That first murder had taken place when Dahmer was under a lot of stress. His parents were going through a particularly bitter divorce, though this does seem to have come at the close of what appeared to be a fairly happy and normal childhood. His father Lionel Dahmer remembered him becoming increasingly inward-looking and remote after the age of six, which suggests that something traumatic, but something we don't know about, happened to him at about the age of six. Lionel Dahmer tried to pull his son back, but fought a losing battle as Jeffrey sank further into his own private world. Lionel lost hope in his son when Jeffrey was convicted of child molesting in 1989. He said that the terrible reality dawned on him at that time that Jeffrey would 'never be more than a liar, an alcoholic, a thief, an exhibitionist, a molester of children.' The truth seems to be that Jeffrey had socio-pathic, perhaps psychopathic, tendencies from a very young age. As his father said, 'There was something missing in Jeff. We call it a conscience. That had either died or had never been alive in the first place.' That is almost a definition of what it is to be a psychopath.

The murder of Stephen Hicks had been an isolated event, and Dahmer had been able to keep whatever urges were simmering inside him under control for nine years. It was an unusually long cooling off period.

Dahmer had graduated from high school, dropped out of university, joined the army, been thrown out for drunkenness. Eventually he had wound up in the factory job in Milwaukee. While in Milwaukee he discovered the gay bars in the city and in one of them he picked up Steven Toumi, the 24-year-old who became his second victim. This second murder seems to have had the effect of unleashing the homicidal maniac within Dahmer.

The killing spree that followed escalated until by July 1991 he was killing one young man a week. His technique was to pick up young gay men in gay bars and offer money to pose for photos or just ask them back to his apartment to watch videos and have a drink. The drink was spiked, so the victim sank into a stupor. Then Dahmer stabbed or strangled them to death and dismembered them with a hacksaw.

He kept heads and genitals as trophies. Biceps were frozen for eating later. The rest of the body was dissolved using acids and disposed of down the drains.

Dahmer dabbled in the occult. He pondered on the existence of an evil force in the world – as well he might – and whether he might be influenced by it. He thought he might create a shrine to this evil force using his skulls and a statue of a griffin; he thought it would give him special powers. But the authorities in Milwaukee had other ideas.

At his brief trial, which opened on 13 July 1992, Dahmer pleaded guilty but insane. The jury found him guilty but sane. He was sentenced to 15 life terms, 957 years, in prison, and was to be murdered only two years later, still with 955 years to serve.

PART THREE
SADISTS

Gilles de Rais

a French Jekyll and Hyde

GILLES DE RAIS had a quite extraordinary double career, as a great land-owning French aristocrat and soldier, and as a black magician and serial child-killer. It is almost as if we are looking at the distinct and separate lives of two distinct and separate people.

Gilles was born on the border area between Brittany and Poitou, at Machecoul, in 1404. He was born into a noble French family, and became one of the leading figures of the French aristocracy. As a boy he showed intelligence and was a good pupil; he learned to speak fluent Latin.

At the age of 16, in 1420, he found himself at the court of the Dauphin, the then-uncrowned King of France. He was present at the Dauphin's court nine years later, when Joan of Arc arrived and proposed a plan for the Dauphin to retrieve his throne from England. From 1427 to 1431, Gilles de Rais served as a commander of some note in the Hundred Years War between France and England. His exploits in battle against the English made him almost as famous as Joan herself. After achieving a notable victory at the Battle of Patay, Gilles was rewarded with the post of Marshal of France.

He acquired five huge estates and ran a chapel that required the attendance of thirty canons. He had a proud, muscular bearing; he was cultured, sophisticated, rich, pious, and brave in battle; he was the epitome of the noblest medieval aristocracy. He fought with his personal retinue of two hundred knights alongside Joan of Arc and was so highly esteemed that in his post as Marshal of France he was able to crown Charles VII King of France. He reached a pinnacle of glory in France just as his contemporary, and apparent antithesis, Vlad the Impaler, was reaching a nadir of infamy. Yet Gilles de Rais was not what he seemed, not what he seemed to be at all.

There was another Gilles de Rais behind the public image that was a virtual mirror image of all that nobility. He had the darkest of shadow sides. He had become fascinated with alchemy and became convinced that to succeed in alchemy he would have to sell his soul to the Devil. A magician offered to introduce him to the Devil and, according to Gilles' story, persuaded him to sacrifice a child. It was by this route, he claimed, that he became a serial child-murderer. It is believed that he sadistically tortured and murdered somewhere between 150 and 800 children. He was so obsessed with the letting of blood that he would order his servants to stab his victims in the neck so that the blood would spurt over him.

Local children started to disappear, and their disappearance was noticed. The remains of many of these children were found in his castles of Machecoul and Champtogne. They were discovered in 1440, after Gilles quarrelled with someone to whom he had sold another of his properties.

Joan of Arc was famously charged and tried for heresy. Ten years later, Gilles de Rais was charged with heresy too, after attacking a priest. He was taken into custody on 13 September 1440 on a charge brought against him by the Bishop of Nantes. He denied this charge, but his accusers knew other things about Gilles – far worse things. He was then charged with a number of other offences including murder. His ecclesiastical accusers charged him with being a 'heretic, sorcerer, sodomite, invoker of evil spirits, diviner, killer of innocents, apostate from the faith, idolator.' It was an astonishing list of crimes, reading like a series of preposterous trumped-up charges. In fact the Church had good reason to want de Rais out of the way. He had become far too powerful in France and was a major threat to the power of the Church, and in particular to the Church's influence over the new King. Moreover, if de Rais was found guilty, the Church was in a good position to acquire some of his lands. The evidence against de Rais was acquired by force. His servants were tortured until they produced enough evidence to convict their master.

On the face of it, it would seem like any other medieval or Renaissance show trial, where the accused has committed no offence at all, and the perjured evidence has been wrung from witnesses by torture in order to achieve a conviction – and execution. But what is extraordinary about this case is that de Rais, who was evidently not tortured, freely admitted to his crimes. He made a full confession not only to the murder of the 140 children with which he was charged, but to the murder of at least 800. It is not at all clear why he made this confession, but then he was not a normal personality.

Most of Gilles' victims were young boys, whom he sodomized both before and after decapitating them. He killed some girls, but preferred boys. He enjoyed watching his servants butchering the children's bodies after the killings.

Gilles de Rais gave two reasons for committing these terrible crimes. One was the impact of a book. It was an illustrated copy of Lives of the Caesars by Suetonius, which included graphic descriptions of the mad sexual excesses of emperors such as Tiberius and Caligula, which included sadism – a word not yet invented, of course. The second reason he gave was the approach of an alchemist, Prelati, who promised to reveal the secret of turning base metal into gold by way of black magic rites and human sacrifices.

This was a time before the science of psychology had even been thought of, so de Rais did not have access to a mindset that would have allowed him to understand what he was doing; nor would he have had the vocabulary he needed to express it. We are probably seeing a medieval 'best-effort' at rationalization. Today his behaviour would be described using words such as paedophilia and sadism, though it has to be said that naming the impulses does not bring us much closer to understanding them. We have an illusion of analysis and understanding of sexual deviation which is really a self-deception. In the middle ages, concepts like sorcery, black masses and sacrifice came more readily to mind.

Inevitably, Gilles de Rais was found guilty of all these crimes. His reputation came crashing down in a spectacular fall from grace that must have delighted his envious rivals. In a public display of repentance he begged the forgiveness of the parents of the children he had killed. Like Joan of Arc, he was sentenced to burn, but he was shown some mercy because of the full confession he had made: he was garrotted before being burned. He was executed on 26 October, 1440.

Albert Fish

that old skunk

SERIAL KILLERS ARE deranged. Few killers in America's past have been remembered as more fiendishly deranged than the notorious Albert Fish, the man who ate children. Fish was the stuff of Victorian melodrama. In old age, with his silvery hair and white moustache, he looked like my grandfather – in fact, like everybody's grandfather. But at his back were his 'instruments of Hell', his meat cleaver, his butcher's knife and his saw.

Over a period of twenty years he sexually molested over 400 children and, according to one of the psychiatrists who examined him, lived a life of 'unparalleled perversity'. His career as a child molester and child murderer went on for an incredibly long time, and one of the most shocking aspects of his case is that he went undetected for so long. He is the oldest man ever to be electrocuted. But his execution came far too late to help his long list of victims.

Fish blamed his harsh childhood for his twisted personality. He was abandoned at an early age and put into an orphanage. It was there that he saw and experienced his first acts of sadism. When he grew up he worked mainly as a handyman and painter. He married and brought up six children. Although he appeared normal at this time, it is unlikely that he was; psychosis usually manifests itself early on. The first sign of serious psychological instability was when his wife left him for another handyman, John Straube, their slow-witted lodger. Fish came home from work one day to find his wife, Straube and all the furniture gone.

Mrs Fish, it might be thought, had acted wisely in running away from the maddest American ever, but she was herself not entirely sane. She returned to Fish one day, with Straube, asking Fish to take them in . Remarkably, Fish agreed to take his wife back, but drew the line at Straube, so she sent him away. A few days later, Fish discovered that Straube had not really been sent away; his wife had hidden him in the attic. Fish told her again that she could stay but Straube could not. This time she left and she was never seen again.

It was after this that Albert Fish started behaving strangely. He took his children to their summer home, Wisteria Cottage in Westchester County, New York. They were alarmed when he climbed a hill, shook his fist at the sky and shouted, 'I am Christ!' It became increasingly obvious that he enjoyed pain – his own or other people's. He love being smacked with a paddle, and ordered children, his own and other people's, to beat him on the backside until his buttocks bled. To ensure bleeding, he studded the paddle with one-inch nails. He also started inserting needles into his body, many of them in the genital area, and left them there for years, presumably to ensure continuous pain. He continually burnt himself with red-hot pokers and irons.

Another quirk was answering personal ads from widows looking for husbands, but answering them with letters full of obscenity, homing in on the idea of a life of beatings. Forty-six of these were retrieved and presented as evidence at his trial. It goes without saying that none of the forty-six widows accepted his offer.

Fish's children testified that on the night of a full moon he ate huge quantities of raw meat. Over a period of years, he collected published articles on the subject of cannibalism, showing the direction his fantasies were taking. Long before he started killing, Albert Fish was seen by psychiatrists. Each time they came to the conclusion that he was disturbed but sane and released him on an unsuspecting community.

It is not known when or where Fish carried out his first murder. He eventually admitted to six specific killings and referred vaguely to many more. It seemed he had committed so many that he could not remember the details of number, identity, location. He owned up to killing a man in Wilmington, Delaware. He admitted mutilating and torturing to death a mentally retarded boy in New York in 1910 and a negro boy in 1919. He admitted sexually molesting and killing a four-year-old boy called William Gaffney in 1929. He confessed that he had strangled a five-year-old boy called Francis McDonnell on Long Island in 1934. The most publicized of Albert Fish's murders was the killing of Grace Budd in 1928. Her abduction led to a search for the killer that dragged on for six years. Even then, it was only the slightest of clues sent to Grace's parents that led the police to Albert Fish.

Fish had insinuated himself into the Budd family in a way that aroused no suspicions. Grace's father earned a meagre living as a doorman, and he had a wife and four children to support. Their eighteen-year-old son, Edward, put a small ad in the paper to try to get a 'position in the country'. A well-dressed Albert Fish turned up at the Budds' home in Manhattan, introducing himself as Frank Howard, a farmer on Long Island willing to pay 15 dollars a week to a willing worker. After hearing a little about the farm, Edward Budd eagerly agreed to go. 'Mr Howard' agreed to return the next week and take not only Edward but his friend Willie to see the farm – there was enough work for them both, apparently.

For some reason Albert Fish could not make the appointment he made the following week, sent a telegram to apologize and visited instead a couple of days later.

The Budds were impressed by Howard's manners. He handed out treats and dollar bills to the children. On his second visit he said he would return to pick up the two young men later, but he had a special treat for Grace. He wanted to take her to a children's birthday party at the home of his married sister. He even gave the address. The Budds agreed and Grace left, holding

Fish's hand and still wearing the white dress she had worn to church that morning. The Budds waved goodbye to their daughter. They never saw her again.

That night, the Budds became concerned when Mr Howard did not return with Grace. They tried to persuade themselves that the party had overrun and that Grace was staying the night with Mr Howard's sister. The following morning, Albert Budd decided to go to the address 'Howard' had given them, only to find that it did not exist. In a panic, Budd went straight to the nearest police station. He was referred to the Missing Persons Bureau and the case was handled by the experienced detective, William King. The detectives were suspicious about the whole scenario, and they quickly established that there was no Frank Howard with a farm on Long Island. This meant that there was no way of knowing who Frank Howard really was, or where he lived, or where he might have taken Grace.

Fish had cunningly retrieved the telegram, saying that it was incorrectly addressed and he was going to complain to Western Union. King and his team spent 15 hours searching through the Western Union records for their copy of Fish's telegram. Eventually they found it. It had been sent from an office in East Harlem. The prospect of searching every home in that area of the city was rejected as impracticable. There was one other lead, the present of a tub of cheese and a carton of strawberries that 'Howard' had brought for Mrs Budd. The detectives managed to find the delicatessen in East

Harlem where 'Howard' had bought the cheese and the pedlar who had sold him the strawberries. The pedlar was able to describe Albert Fish in detail. Then that trail too petered out.

The disappearance of Grace Budd, and the particularly sinister circumstances surrounding her abduction, caught New York's imagination. The Budd family went to the media with their tragic story and Grace's photo was published on the front page of one newspaper after another. The weeks passed and one lead after another seemed to lead nowhere. But Will King was not a man to give up, and he went on following every call that reached his desk. At one stage, he thought he had his man. He had a file on a grey-haired con-man called Albert Corthell, who was on the run having tried to abduct another little girl – from an adoption agency. He certainly sounded like the same man. King tracked Corthell for months. When he finally found him, King was utterly defeated to discover that Corthell had been in prison in Seattle at the time of the Grace Budd abduction. Corthell was ruled out.

Meanwhile another suspect, Charles Pope, was arrested and charged with Grace's abduction. The case came to court, where Mrs Budd had to admit that she had identified the wrong man. Pope was released and it emerged that he had been framed out of malice by his ex-wife.

At the same time another silver-haired old gentleman was being interrogated in New York for sending obscene letters. These were letters Fish sent under the pretence of being a Hollywood producer, offering large sums of money in return for sado-masochistic favours. Fish was committed to a psychiatric ward for observation during the winter of 1930. The psychiatrists detected a range of sexual abnormalities, but thought him harmless and released him.

Meanwhile, the Grace Budd case seemed to defy solution. Then, in November 1934, six years after the abduction, Mrs Budd received an unsigned letter through the post. It claimed to be from a friend of 'Captain John Davis'. This seafarer had developed a taste for eating human flesh in the Far East. On his return to New York, he had killed two young boys, cooked their flesh and eaten it. The mad letter writer – and it does not take long to guess who it was – decided to try it for himself. He had visited the Budds' home and taken the girl away. Mrs Budd had to read on to find out the horrors that her daughter had been subjected to. The anonymous writer had taken Grace to an empty house in Westchester, allowing her to pick flowers in the garden while he took his clothes off. When he called her indoors and she saw the naked old man, she started screaming and tried to run away. He caught her, stripped and strangled her. Then he cut her body up and cooked and ate parts of it. The mad letter writer was keen to reassure the now-distraught Mrs Budd that he had not sexually molested Grace. 'She died a virgin.'

Mrs Budd passed the appalling document over to Will King, who had delayed his retirement in the hope that he could bring the Budd case to a conclusion. King compared the handwriting on the anonymous letter with that on 'Mr Howard's' original telegram blank. It was the same. King looked at the envelope under a microscope and found a tiny design on the flap. It consisted of the letters NYPCBA, which he discovered stood for New York Private Chauffeurs' Benevolent Association. The association let King look through its files to check the backgrounds of their 400 employees. Unfortunately he found no-one to match the profile of the mad cannibal. But Will King still didn't give up. He summoned all the employees together and asked for any information that might lead to the capture of the sadist. He offered immunity to anyone who might have stolen and sold on stationery.

After addressing all the employees together, King withdrew to a private office in the hope that one of them might come to tell him what he needed to know. Lee Sicowski knocked on the door to own up to taking association stationery home with him. he might have left some at a room he had since left. The detectives went to the rooming house and found nothing. Sicowski remembered that he had occupied a room at another address, at 200 East 52nd Street. Here the detectives finally struck lucky. The landlady, Mrs Schneider, said Sicowski's room had recently been occupied by a man answering 'Mr Howard's' description, but his name was Albert Fish. Then Will King checked the signature in the room register; the writing was the same as the handwriting in the appalling anonymous letter sent to Mrs Budd.

Will King was sure he had his man now. Fish had checked out of the rooming house, but returned every so often to collect a monthly cheque from one of his sons. King was obsessed with the Budd case, and moved into a room at the top of Mrs Schneider's house, where he had a view of the entrance and hallway. After three days waiting, King had to return briefly to the police station. While he was there, he had an urgent call from Mrs Schneider. Fish was back. King raced to East 52nd Street. Mrs Schneider met him at the door, to say that she had managed to keep him there half an hour by plying him with tea. King drew his revolver and went in.

Will King was surprised by what he found. Fish was a harmless-looking silver-haired old man with watery blue eyes, sipping a cup of tea. King identified himself and Fish made no secret of his own identity. Then King saw the other side of Albert Fish. Fish pulled a cut-throat razor from his pocket and lunged at him. Will King was ready for him, grabbed his wrist and forced him to drop the razor. He handcuffed Fish, then searched him and was horrified to find that he was armed to the teeth with knives and razors.

Later Albert Fish admitted that he had originally intended to abduct and kill Edward Budd, but when he met him and saw how stocky and strong he was he changed his mind, setting his sights on the smaller, more vulnerable Grace. He grinned as he described in detail how he had killed and dismembered Grace Budd at Wisteria Cottage. Detectives went to Wisteria Cottage and found the skeletal remains of Grace Budd, including her skull, buried beside a wall behind the cottage.

One of the few people who was not surprised at Albert Fish's arrest was his son, also called Albert. 'That old skunk! I always knew that he would get caught for something like this.' He told a journalist that he had come home one day to find his father naked and beating himself with a board studded with nails. He had thrown the old man out of his house not long afterwards. 'I've never wanted anything to do with him,' he said.

Albert Fish was examined by doctors and psychiatrists, and he relished their evident fascination. He told them in detail how he inflicted pain on himself: how he inserted needles into his body and left them there. X-rays confirmed that he did indeed have 29 rusting needles in his body. He seemed to be a walking compendium of every sexual perversion the psychiatrists had ever heard of. He admitted to carrying Grace Budd's ears and nose back home to New York; he had been intensely excited while carrying these trophies in a bag on his lap during the train journey.

One of the psychiatrists, Frederic Wertham, concluded that Fish was insane, that he was a sadist of unimaginable cruelty, and that he had probably raped over a hundred children. The evidence for his insanity was presented at his trial, but the jury nevertheless found Fish guilty of first-degree murder. He was sentenced to death by the electric chair. When told of the verdict, Fish said, 'Going to the electric chair will be the supreme thrill of my life.'

On 16 January 1936, Albert Fish was executed at Sing Sing Prison. He walked briskly to his death, eagerly helping the guards to attach the electrodes to his legs. The onlookers were horrified at his evident excitement at his own execution, which was the ultimate treat for a sado-masochist.

John Wayne Gacy

Pogo the Clown

JOHN WAYNE GACY was born in Chicago in 1942 His parents, Stanley and Marion, named their son after their favourite film star. They hoped their son would become as famous as John Wayne one day. Instead, he became one of the most infamous serial killers of all time, known as the Killer Clown.

When he was finally arrested and questioned by the Chicago police in 1978, Gacy freely admitted to murdering no less than 33 boys and young men. Gacy was a fat, over-sexed, unattractive and understandably lonely homosexual. He had difficulty in finding willing partners, so he had to take unwilling partners instead. He took boys, sexually molested and raped them, then strangled or stabbed them to death.

Gacy had ideas of being important in local politics. To make himself popular in his local Chicago township of Norwood Park, he tried to present himself as a benefactor to the children of the neighbourhood. He set about this with some panache, designing three clown outfits and creating a clown persona for himself. Now, instead of being the neighbourhood 'weirdo', which is how his immediate neighbours did see him in fact, he turned himself into a minor local celebrity. He became Pogo the Clown, performing in the streets and at children's parties. He was a great success. President Carter's wife posed with Pogo for a photograph and sent him a signed copy. To Gacy, this meant social and political acceptance.

But it was not enough. He was sexually unsatisfied. The only way he could have sex was by force. The Chicago police were puzzled by the disappearance of several local youths, but it was difficult to see any pattern to the disappearances, and a number of young people ran away each year anyway.

It was six years before the police realised what had been happening. When the truth came out – that Gacy had killed them all – the residents of Northwood Park were furious at the level of police incompetence this represented. They argued that if the police had been more efficient at least some of the boys might have been saved. The police did in fact have evidence against Gacy but failed to spot its significance. Gacy's name cropped up on police files four times between 1972 and 1978, as a suspect in the missing persons cases. He was very clearly a common factor and they should have spotted it. They should also have noticed, from their own records, that Gacy had been convicted twice for sexual assaults on young men.

Caught and interviewed at the Chicago Police Headquarters, Gacy obligingly drew the police a detailed plan of his property, noting the location of 28 bodies. After raping and killing the boys, he had buried most of them in the large garden of his ranch-style house, or in the space underneath his house. Five more bodies had been thrown into the Des Plaines River, which flowed not far from his home.

Gacy had had a strange upbringing, dominated totally by his mother and his twin older sisters Joanne and Karen. He carried within him a deep resentment towards women. Gacy's father had a violent temper and seems to have taken out some resentment about something or other on his son; perhaps he thought it was all right to beat boys, but not girls. On one occasion, Gacy was taken on a fishing trip by his father, whom he worshipped. The father, John Senior, failed to catch any fish. Characteristically, he blamed this failure on his son, lashing out at him verbally and physically. The father was an alcoholic with a fierce hatred of homosexuals; he would accuse his son of being gay, taunting him about his medical problems and accusing him of malingering. The boy suffered from black-outs from the age of eleven, the result of being hit on the head by a playground swing. In his teens he also suffered from a heart condition, which went on being a problem into adulthood.

John Junior had a lot of 'getting back' to do as an adult. In some ways John Wayne Gacy was a weak-willed man, but he was determined to succeed in business, and he did, building up a successful building firm.

Unemployment was rising in Chicago, and Gacy was able to exploit this by offering jobs to unskilled young men who stood little or no chance of getting any other work. The local boys he was picking up were mainly under the age of 20 and unemployed. The offer of work was a sure-fire way of winning them over and getting them to go home with him. Other youths he picked up at the Greyhound Bus Station in Chicago; they were frequently drifters who were heading west in the time-honoured American way, hoping to make their fortunes in California. Instead they found themselves travelling home with John Wayne Gacy.

Gacy told the police, 'I wanted to give these young people a chance', as if he had persuaded himself that he really had given them a chance. Gacy's teenage workforce were fairly well-paid and happy, apart from those who died. It seems that five of the dead youths were heterosexual teenagers who worked for his construction firm. The building contracts poured in and Gacy needed more unskilled labourers. At the end of a hard day's work, Gacy often drove down to the Bus Station to look for more prospective employees.

Gacy married in 1964. He managed a clothes shop for a while and married a co-worker called Marilyn Myer. Marilyn's father, Fred, persuaded them to move to Waterloo in Iowa, where Gacy was given the job of running his father-in-law's Kentucky Fried Chicken franchises in the town. For a time it seemed to work well. It was a reasonably happy marriage, and Marilyn gave birth to a son and a daughter. But Gacy was harbouring a secret love – for young men. In 1968 his aggressive homosexual tendencies led to the breakdown of his marriage. One of his employees at the KFC diner, a young man called Mark Miller, complained to the police that Gacy had tied him up and sexually assaulted him after luring him to his home. Gacy was sentenced to ten years in the state prison for sodomy. Marilyn divorced him and Gacy said he never wanted to see her or the children again.

Rather peculiarly, Gacy came out of prison on parole in 1970, after only eighteen months inside and seemed to be a completely reformed character. But it was a sham, and with hindsight we can see that the parole was a bad idea. If he had been kept in prison for his full sentence, the lives of many young men might have been saved. This was the view of the family of Gacy's final victim, Robert Piest, who filed a claim for $85 million against the Iowa Board of Parole, the Department of Correction and the Chicago Police Department.

At liberty once more, Gacy got himself a job as a chef in a Chicago restaurant, met Carol Hofgren. In 1972 they married and he bought the house in Summerdale Avenue. The second wife said that he had started taking home 'a lot of pictures of naked men' just before they separated in 1975. Both wives described him as 'mysterious', with unexplained nocturnal car trips a feature. There was a streak of violence too; he beat both of his wives.

Where was Gacy going at night? It eventually emerged that he was going to 'Bughouse Square', a low-life district of Chicago frequented by hosts of young gay men and rent boys. It was there that he picked up more young men, some of whom were murdered and buried at his home. The first of the murders happened as early as 1972, most of them in 1976, 1977 and 1978.

But all the time, Gacy was trying to build his imagined political career by winning friends with his Pogo the Clown act. His business success enabled him to make substantial financial contributions to the Democratic Party, which he supported. In the run-up to his arrest, Gacy had organized three consecutive annual political summer fetes, complete with music, hamburgers and beer. Each time 500 local politicians and tycoons attended, the proceeds going towards President Carter's re-election. His efforts were noticed at the White House.

In May 1978, a young man called Jeff Ringall was walking through the New Town district of Chicago when a thick-set man in a car called him over. The man offered him a ride. It was a very cold day, and Ringall agreed, disarmed by the man's open, friendly manner. The man offered him a joint, which he took. Without warning, the man jumped onto him and pressed a rag soaked in chloroform over his face. Jeff Ringall passed out.

Gacy could then drive off towards his home in the affluent suburbs, with his companion quietly sleeping beside him. Occasionally Jeff drifted back into consciousness, noticing road signs and landmarks. When Gacy noticed he was awake, he smothered him with the rag again. Once they reached Gacy's house, Gacy stripped, tied Jeff up and spent several hours molesting, torturing and raping him. It was evidently the same procedure he had used dozens of times before, to dozens of boys, and their rotting remains lay not far away, in the crawl-space under the single-storey house.

For some reason, Gacy decided not to kill Jeff Ringall. He just dumped him unconscious in Chicago's Lincoln Park. The following morning, Jeff woke up in the park, fully clothed, aching all over. Somehow he managed to stagger to hospital, where he spent the next six days recovering from his ordeal. He went to the police, but he had no idea who the man was or where the house was, so the police were unable to pursue this valuable evidence.

But Jeff Ringall was undeterred. He was determined that the fat stranger would not get away with what he had done to him. In a moment of lucidity during the drugged car ride, he remembered one particular highway exit. He sat in his car close to this highway exit, assuming rightly that his attacker would probably use this same route again, and waited for a car that he recognized. It was a long shot – a very long shot – but it worked. After some hours he saw the black Oldsmobile Delta that had picked him up. Jeff set off in pursuit, following the Oldsmobile all the way to a house in Summerdale Avenue, Des Plaines. He still had no idea who lived there, and it took him several weeks to find out that it was John Wayne Gacy.

Then he filed charges of sexual assault, which were being processed when another line of enquiry overtook him.

As is so often the case, it was chance that led to Gacy's arrest. One of Gacy's political acquaintances at this time had known the last of Gacy's victims and had pestered the police to mount a really intensive search for the missing 15-year-old boy, Robert Piest. The trail, as on earlier occasions, had led to Gacy's door. The boy had last been seen outside a pharmacy in Des Plaines – with John Wayne Gacy. The police checked his record and saw the highly significant conviction for sodomy in Iowa. The police raided his luxurious house in December 1978, arresting him and initially finding nothing at all except some documents and jewellery. The search team noticed a horrible smell, though they dismissed this at the time as probably due to a cracked sewer. Then they realised that the jewellery included a high school graduation ring belonging to a teenager who had gone missing a year earlier. The documents included a film processing receipt that a co-worker had given to Robert Piest just before he vanished. It was now clear that Gacy was closely involved in the disappearance of boys and young men. A second search was mounted; a small army of forensic scientists moved into the house, searching it for any clues.

The neighbours were horrified as they watched the police systematically digging up Gacy's landscaped garden and the crawl space under the house. By the third day, the remains of 28 different bodies had been dug up. At first, Gacy denied murdering anyone, then he admitted murdering a small number, then all of them. In the end he drew a detailed map of the property showing all the burial sites. Even the five bodies thrown into the Des Plaines River were recovered – by police frogmen.

Gacy's method of killing gradually emerged after forensic analysis of the remains and close questioning of Gacy. It seemed that Gacy had had an obsession with playing policemen as a boy; he loved the guns and the handcuffs. When he managed to lure a young man to his house, he would show him his handcuff trick. Once the handcuffs were on, the young man was at Gacy's mercy, and he would be subjected to a systematic sexual assault and rape. At some point in the rape, Gacy would say, 'The way to get out of those handcuffs is to have the key. That's the real trick.'

The handcuff trick was followed by the rope trick, which always ended in death for the victim. He put a loop of rope round the victim's neck, slipped a stick through the loop and slowly twist it like a tourniquet. The boy became unconscious within seconds; a few seconds more and he was dead.

The bodies were hidden in the crawl-space under the house. Gacy used powerful chemicals to speed up the process of decomposition, but the resulting stench was appalling. Yet still no-one suspected.

Gacy came to trial in 1979. Jeff Ringall was one of the witnesses. He had recovered physically from his ordeal at Gacy's house, but not mentally. He by this time understood all too well how close he had come to death and he found giving evidence against Gacy very difficult. He broke down, crying hysterically and vomiting at the memory of what Gacy did to him. William Kunkle, the Chicago District Attorney asked for the death penalty. Gacy, he argued, had systematically planned and executed his many murders. It was a time when many states in America had abolished the death penalty. The State of Illinois was currently debating whether to re-introduce the death penalty for certain types of murder. This certainly looked like one that would qualify.

Gacy claimed he was four different people. 'There are four Johns', he explained. There was a businessman personality, his politician personality, his voluntary worker personality. It was the fourth personality, Jack Hanley, as he called him, who was responsible for the killings. Gacy was attempting to build an insanity plea on the basis of a split personality. Gacy's defence lawyer, Sam Amirante, argued that Gacy was insane. But while a plea of temporary insanity might have been plausible for a single murder, it was not credible for a string of serial killings. The jury did not accept the multiple personality argument either, probably recognizing that we are all multiple personalities. They found Gacy guilty, after two hours of deliberation, of murdering 33 people.

On 13 March 1980, he was sentenced to death and sent to the Menard Correctional Centre. After 14 years on Death Row, the appeals ran out, he was transferred to the state penitentiary at Joliet, near Chicago. On 9 May 1994 John Gacy, now grossly overweight, feasted on a last supper of fried chicken, French fries, cola and strawberry shortcake. He chatted on the phone for a while with reporters, before being strapped down and given a lethal injection.

The case was notable for, among many other things, causing deep embarrassment to the Democratic Party and to President Jimmy Carter. Carter's weakness as a president had already been exposed during the US Embassy siege in Tehran; he was not helped by TV coverage of the ripping-apart of the home of one of his high-profile supporters in a search for murdered boys.

Fred and Rose West

the Cromwell Street killers

24 FEBRUARY 1994 was a very ordinary Thursday afternoon at the offices of the Gloucester Citizen. The reporters were trying to find ideas of news stories, when a scrap of information came in via the circulation department. A newspaper boy reported seeing policemen digging up the back garden of a house near the city centre. It was 25 Cromwell Street. A glance at the electoral register showed that the householders were Frederick and Rosemary West. Then someone in the office looked up the names in the cuttings library. Fred and Rose West had been cleared of sexually assaulting a girl after the key witness refused to give evidence. The police would only say that they were investigating the disappearance of the Wests' 16-year-old daughter, Heather, who had disappeared in May 1987, though her disappearance had not been reported by her parents, who claimed she had gone to work at a holiday camp in Devon. The Wests' surviving children kept a macabre joke going among themselves – that Heather was buried under the patio at 25 Cromwell Street.

In the summer of 1993, after allegations of sexual abuse had been made against the Wests, the six youngest children were taken into care.

The joke about Heather being under the patio reached DC Hazel Savage, whose dealings with Fred West dated back 30 years. She knew enough about the man to think it was worth following up. She finally persuaded her superior officers that they should issue a search warrant to enable them to dig up the Wests' garden. When the police came the door was answered by the Wests' 20-year-old son Stephen, who told them 'they were going to end up making fools of themselves'. Stephen and his mother tried hard to contact Fred West, who was working on a building 20 minutes' drive away. they got through to him at 1.50pm, when he said he was on his way home. He did not arrive home until four hours later. Those four hours were never satis-factorily accounted for. Several criminologists have speculated that he used the time to dispose of incrim-inating evidence, perhaps even visiting another burial ground somewhere in Gloucestershire where more of his victims were buried. This second cemetery has never been found.

On 24 February 1994, the day when the observant newspaper boy saw the police digging up the back garden, Detective Sergeant Terence Onions interviewed Mrs West about the disappearance of her daughter Heather. He did not get very far. All Rose West would say was that Heather had become difficult, at school and at home, that she was lesbian and had left home some time in 1987. DS Onions mentioned that the children had said Heather was buried under the patio, and Rose agreed that one of them had something about it. Did she think Heather was alive? 'Well, why not? Unless something horrible has happened to her. Come on – hundreds of thousands of kids go missing.' Mrs West was a hard case.

While the police dug away in their back garden, Fred and Rose West stayed up, discussing what they would do next. It is thought they made some sort of pact, and that Fred agreed to 'take all the blame'. When bones were found and he was taken in for questioning, Fred West admitted straight away to DC Savage that he had killed Heather, adding, 'The thing I'd like to stress is that Rose knew nothing at all'.

On 25 February, Rose West was interviewed again by DS Onions, who covered the same ground as before, but tried to get her to explain why she had taken no action about Heather's disappearance. Why had she not reported it to the police? Had she discussed the patio with her husband last night? She fell back on lies; her husband had seen Heather in Birmingham and Bristol. DS Onions strung Rose along for a while, asking how Heather had been when Fred had seen her, and so on. Finally, he delivered the *coup de grace*. 'Why do you think you've been arrested today? For the most grave of offences. There has been a major development this morning. Fred has confessed to murdering Heather.'

Rose said, 'What? So you know where she is?'

'He has told us where she is.'

'So she is dead, that right?'

'Fred has confessed to murdering Heather.'

'What?'

'And that automatically implicates you.'

Rose started crying, realising that the game was up.

Fred's story was that he had been arguing with Heather, who was headstrong, slapped her for insolence and then grabbed her throat to stop her laughing at him. He hadn't intended to harm her, but he didn't have the training to revive her. He dragged her to the bath and ran cold water over her, then he undressed her, lifted her out of the tub to dry her off. Then he tried to put her in the rubbish bin, but she wouldn't fit. He put her back in the bath ready to cut her up. First he strangled her because he didn't like the idea of her 'suddenly coming alive' while he was cutting her leg off. When he cut off her head, he found the sound, a horrible 'scrunching', very unpleasant. Once the head was off, he found cutting the legs off easier. West was trying to make out that the death was an accident and the concealment of the death an act of impulse. For that to be credible, Heather's death had to be the only one . . .

Fred West was the eldest of six children and his mother's favourite. He developed a distinct and rather feral look as he grew into adulthood, with a large greedy mouth. He did not perform well at school and left school at 15 almost illiterate. He was extremely aggressive with girls, taking any girl who took his fancy. Fred claimed that his father had sex with his daughters, treating his children as sex toys; it was what Fred himself would do later to his own children – the classic cycle of abuse. At 17, Fred West was injured in a motorcycle accident. He spent a week in a coma and had a metal plate fitted into his head. Some believed that this head injury made him prone to fits of rage when he completely lost control of himself.

It was after this accident that Fred met Rena. By the time she encountered Fred she had been in trouble with the police and was an accomplished thief. Their relationship was a stormy one. Fred had a job driving an ice cream van, which gave him unlimited access to young women, which he enjoyed, and this led to almost daily infidelities. Then in the early 1960s Fred was involved in an accident while driving his ice cream van. A boy was killed, and Fred expected to lose his job. It was then that Fred decided to move into Gloucester, where he got a job in a slaughterhouse. This seems to be where he developed a morbid interest in death, dismemberment and corpses. The way that he mutilated his victims was very peculiar; before he buried the body of little Charmaine under the floor at 25 Midland Road, he took off her fingers, toes and kneecaps. West cut off the fingers and toes of Anna McFall and Rena too. This morbid interest was developing at a time when his marriage to Rena had fallen apart; an unhealthy association between death, butchery, sex, danger and excitement was building up.

When Rena had wanted to take the two children back to Glasgow with her, Fred refused, so she went to Scotland on her own. She missed her daughters and in July 1966 she was back in Gloucester, where she found Fred living in a trailer with Anna McFall. Rena complained to Constable Haze Savage that her husband was a pervert and unfit to be in charge of children; that was truer than any of them could have realised at the time. At about that time eight sexual assaults were committed in the Gloucester area by a man answering Fred West's description. When Anna became pregnant by Fred in early 1967, she pressed him to divorce Rena and marry her. Fred's response was to murder her and bury her not far from the caravan site in July 1967. Fred allowed Rena to move into the trailer with him, and was happy for her to earn some money by prostitution.

In January 1968, a 15-year-old called Mary Bastholm was abducted while she was waiting at a bus stop in Gloucester. This is an unsolved crime, but there are reasons for suspecting Fred West. He was a customer at the café where Mary served. Mary had been seen with a girl who fitted the description of Anna McFall. One witness saw Mary in Fred's car. It seems probable that Mary was one of Fred West's uncounted victims. Then, in the November of 1968, Fred West met the love of his life, Rosemary Letts.

Interviewed about the bones the police diggers were finding in his garden, Fred West was hoping he would only have to own to the murder of his daughter Heather. Then professor Bernard Knight, the pathologist called in by the police to analyze the human remains, revealed that there was a third leg bone. There was more than one body buried at 25 Cromwell Street. Fred West decided to limit the damage by owning up to two more murders. He went back to the garden and pointed out where he had buried Shirley Robinson and Alison Chambers in the late 1970s. But he said nothing about the six other murder victims who were buried under the bathroom and cellar of his house. It seems he was less worried at the prospect of being labelled a serial killer than at the thought of the police tearing his house apart. Eventually, though, west was persuaded to admit that there were more bodies and he drew a sketch map to show where they were buried.

Like most serial killers, West was not very interested in his victims as people, and could not even remember their names. He described one as 'Scar Hand', because of a burn mark; another he described as 'Tulip' because he thought she might have been Dutch. He admitted to burying another victim, a girl of eight born to his first wife but fathered by another man, at another house in Gloucester. He also admitted to dumping two more bodies in fields near the village where he had been brought up, Much Marcle – his first wife, Rena, and his one-time girlfriend, Ann McFall.

Fred West's victims were an odd mixture. Some were family members who had got in his way somehow. The rest were hitch-hikers, lodgers, teenagers who had run away from home – classic serial murder victims, in fact.

One rather surprising victim was Lucy Partington, a 21-year-old student from a respectable family, and the cousin of novelist Martin Amis. She was waiting for a bus on the edge of Cheltenham one evening in December 1973. She would not normally have risked hitch-hiking, but was probably persuaded that it was safe to go with Fred West because his wife was in the vehicle with him. As she and other victims were to discover to their cost, Rose's presence was no guarantee of safety at all. She was kept prisoner at Cromwell Street for a week of torture and sexual abuse before she too was murdered and buried. Fred West cut himself so badly while dismembering Lucy on 3 January, 1974 that he had to go to hospital to have his wound stitched up.

Bondage had by now become a major part of the 'sex games' that Fred and Rose West played with their victims in the cellar. These were elaborated as they tortured the next victims, Therese Siegenthaler, Juanita Mott and Shirley Hubbard.

The police were convinced from the beginning that Rose West was deeply implicated in the murders, but she denied it and pretended to be shocked at her husband's confessions. At first she was not charged, though she remained under suspicion in a police safe house. The house was bugged, but Rose never said anything to incriminate herself. She was then, on 18 April 1994, charged with a sexual assault.

Rose West was born Rosemary Letts, in 1953 in Devon. Her father was a schizophrenic and her mother suffered from severe depression. The father was a domestic tyrant who enjoyed finding opportunities to beat his children with a belt or a piece of wood. The mother, Daisy, suffered from deepening depression which was treated with electric shock therapy. It was shortly after a number of these electric shock treatments that Daisy gave birth to Rose; the effect of electric shock therapy on the unborn baby is not known. She developed in a different way from her siblings, rocking in her cot, and later rocking her head for hours on end, producing a kind of self-hypnosis. She was not a very intelligent child and acquired the nickname 'Dozy Rosie'.

As a teenager she became sexually active, walking round the house naked , climbing into bed with her younger brother and fondling him sexually. She eventually picked up with Fred West. Her father disapproved of Fred West, but Bill Letts' judgement was worth little anyway. West was already in trouble with the police; he was sent to prison for various thefts and failure to pay fines for earlier offences. Rose went back to stay with her father, until he found out that she was pregnant. Then she left to take care of Charmaine and Anne-Marie. In view of what later happened to the two little girls, this was disastrous. In 1970, she gave birth to Heather. Rose now had three children to care for, a boyfriend in prison, serious money problems and none of the emotional or mental equipment she needed to deal with any it.

It was one day in 1971 that Charmaine went missing. Probably Rose simply lost her temper; Fred was in jail at the time and therefore could not have committed the murder. As Anne-Marie said, she was a woman entirely without self-control, turning into a kind of maniac. But the death of Rena's child presented Rose and Fred with a very specific problem. It was only a matter of time before Rena would come looking for Charmaine, and she would suspect that Rose had done away with her. In fact in August 1971 Rena did try to make contact with Fred's father in order to try to find out what had happened to Charmaine. Fred must have realised then that he had to kill Rena. Possibly he got her very drunk at 25 Midland Road, then dismembered her body.

Later the same year, Fred and Rose became friendly with one of their neighbours, Elizabeth Agius, who did some baby-sitting for them. When they returned home, Elizabeth asked them where they had been, probably expecting that they had been out for a meal or to the cinema, and was startled when they said they had been cruising around looking for young girls. Fred though that with Rose with him in the car a young woman might well risk a lift. Elizabeth Agius assumed they were joking. But they weren't.

In 1972, Fred and Rose were married and decided to move to a larger house. They chose 25 Cromwell Street, which had a cellar. Fred told Elizabeth Agius he would either make it into a place where Rose could entertain her clients – she was now earning money as a prostitute

– or he would soundproof it and use it as a torture chamber. Again, this remark will have sounded like a joke, but Fred West meant it. One of the first to be tortured in this dungeon was his own eight-year-old daughter, who was tied, gagged and raped. The poor little girl was in such a bad way afterwards that she was unable to go to school for several days.

In December 1972, Fred and Rose West picked up a 17-year-old girl called Caroline Owens and took her on as a nanny. Caroline quickly left this job when Rose made sexual advances. Three weeks after this, the Wests spotted Caroline in the street and offered her a lift, which she unwisely accepted. Rose began to interfere with her as soon as she was in the car; Fred drove them back to Cromwell Street where Caroline was stripped, tortured and raped. She promised not to tell anyone, but later went to the police. The Wests had let her live, and the result had been that they had later been prosecuted and fined for the offence. Evidently, they made a decision to kill their victims in future.

Fred and Rose befriended a young seamstress called Lynda Gough, eventually persuading her to move into Cromwell Street to take care of the children. Then she disappeared. Her mother traced her to the Wests' house, so she knocked at the door. Rose answered the door, wearing Lynda's slippers, and told Mrs Gough that Lynda had gone to Weston-super-Mare. In fact, she was dead, dismembered and buried in a pit in the garage.

The pattern was set. Young women went to stay at 25

Cromwell Street, whether as friends, nannies or lodgers, but few of them got out alive. The astonishing thing is that they were getting away with it. In 1973, they got away with torturing and raping Caroline Owens, and they got away with murdering Lynda Gough. It was also the year that Stephen West was born. Anne Marie was roped into the sex games against her will – how else could she have survived in that house? – and when she moved out to live with her boyfriend Fred turned his attentions to Heather and Mae. Heather put up a spirited resistance to his sexual advances and was given a beating for it. Meanwhile, the Wests probably continued their abductions and murders, but did not bury their victims at Cromwell Street, which was now 'full'; because the assumed 'second cemetery' has not been found it cannot be known how many more unfortunate young women met their death in this way.

In 1986, Heather told her girlfriend about her father's advances, about the beatings and about her mother's affairs. The girlfriend in turn told her parents, who unfortunately were friends of the Wests. Suddenly Heather's days were numbered. She was safe only so long as she could be trusted, and now she could not be trusted. In 1987, Fred and Rose murdered their daughter and told the remaining children that she had gone away. Fred got Stephen to help him dig a hole in the back garden. Then, he buried Heather in it.

But the Wests' luck was running out. People who had been assaulted by the Wests were talking, and some of this talk was getting back to DC Helen Savage – and she remembered the stories that Rena had told her, many years before, about Fred West's sexual perversions. So it was that the police arrived at 25 Cromwell Street on 6 August 1992, with a search warrant. They found some pornography and enough evidence to arrest the Wests for rape and sodomy of minors. The interviewing DC Savage did with Anne Marie convinced her that Heather had been murdered. She was unable to penetrate the 'joke' about Heather being under the patio, because the Wests' children were too frightened to say anything at all to the police, and rightly so because Fred West would not have hesitated to kill them too.

As he waited in prison in 1994, Fred West was kept going by the emotional bond with Rose, the bond of terrible shared secrets. He had it seems guaranteed to her that he would take all the blame. But he must have assumed she would in some way stand by him. As the case developed, Rose West distanced herself from Fred in order to save herself. She tried to present herself as the victim of a dominant murderous man. She did not convince the police working on the case, but she wounded Fred deeply. He co-operated with the police and helped them to find the bodies of Rena, Anna and Charmaine, but he decided not to co-operate when it came to the Mary Bastholm case. Her body was never found. When it came to their joint hearing, Fred attempted to console Rose, but she shrank from his touch. She told the police he made her sick. This rejection was devastating for Fred West.

Rose and Fred had been the ultimate partners in the ultimate crime. On 13 December, 1994, Fred West was charged with twelve murders. He wrote to Rose, but she brushed him off. Then as he waited in Winson Green Prison in Birmingham for his trial, Fred West took a momentous decision. Without Rose, there was no point in going on. It was not shame for the appalling murders, it was rejection by Rose that drove him to hang himself on New Year's Day 1995. He did it at noon, when the guards were having their lunch. It has been suggested that the Wests supplied the sacrificial victims for a coven, and that Fred West was silenced before he could reveal all, but that seems very unlikely in that Rose was allowed to go to trial – and she knew just as much as Fred.

Rose West's trial opened on 3 October 1995. Two murders were seen as happening before Rose West's arrival on the scene, so they must have been the work of Fred West alone. There were still ten murders with which should could be charged. The defence, led by Richard Ferguson, attempted to show that evidence of sexual assault, which Rose West was clearly taking part in, was not evidence of murder. The intention was to show that Rose did not know that Fred West was killing her play-mates after the sex sessions were over. It was a desperate defence, and not helped at all by putting Rose West on the stand. She came across as hard, defiant and cold-blooded – a completely unsympathetic figure. The prosecution showed her to be the 'perfect companion' for a serial killer. She kept her composure for most of the time, but the prosecution team, led by Brian Leveson, succeeded in showing the court what Rose West was like when she was angry. The jury were left in no doubt that she had treated the children very badly and was completely dishonest.

It became clear that the West family was seriously dysfunctional, with systematic sexual abuse of the children from an early age. Fred West's eldest daughter, Anne-Marie, accused her stepmother in court of embarking on a campaign of sexual abuse when she was only eight years old. Anne-Marie naturally found these terrible experiences difficult to talk about and the stress made her ill, causing an adjournment of the trial for several days.

The defence team's trump card was a recording of Fred West describing how he had murdered his victims while Rose was out of the house. This was intended to clinch the argument that Rose had had nothing whatever to do with the killings. But it was evident from inconsistencies that Fred was lying on certain key points, and that in turn implied that he was covering up Rose's now-undoubted involvement in the murders.

Some dramatic evidence was given by Janet Leach, who had witnessed Fred West's police interviews. Fred had told her privately that Rose had been involved in the murders, and also that Rose had murdered

Charmaine and Shirley Robinson without him. he also told Janet Leach what was now apparent to everyone, which was that he had made an agreement with Rose that he would accept complete responsibility for the murders. Janet Leach had become so stressed by carrying the burden of Fred West's confidential confession that she had a stroke. It was only after West's suicide that she had felt released from her promise of confidence and had told the police. She was evidently still distressed at having to breach a professional confidence – so much so that she collapsed after giving evidence in court and had to be taken to hospital.

Leveson described Rose West as the strategist behind the murders. In spite of the impression that both she and her husband had tried to create, it was she who was the dominant partner in these awful crimes. The jury took very little time to decide. They found Rose West guilty on all ten counts of murder – all the murders that led to burials at the house, in fact – and was given a life sentence. The Home Secretary has subsequently told her that she will never be released.

The house that she and her husband had loved, 25 Cromwell Street, was no longer a house that any sane person would want to live in. Clearly it would have to be demolished. The house was pulled down, and the site cleared; it has been turned into a broad, grass-lined footpath.

Fred West is dead and Rose is in prison, but the damage to the family continues. Fred West's brother

John hanged himself just ten months after Fred's suicide, while waiting for a jury to decide whether he was guilty of raping Anne-Marie. Anne-Marie herself is in a poor state; in November 1999 she was rescued after apparently jumping into the water from a bridge near Gloucester. In January 2000, Stephen West tried to hang himself after his girlfriend left him, but he survived when the rope broke.

The speculation that Fred and Rose West killed others, whose remains have never been discovered, continues to haunt many who were involved in the case. Family members say Fred admitted killing Mary Bastholm, a 15-year-old girl who disappeared in Gloucester in 1968. He said there were two more bodies in shallow graves in woodland, and that they would never be found. He said there were twenty other bodies scattered around. If he told the truth about these other murder victims, he took the secrets of their whereabouts to his own grave. Rose West meanwhile keeps her own counsel as she serves her life sentences for her ten murders at Durham Prison.

The thirteen likely victims of Fred West were as follows.

> 1967: Ann McFall, Fred's lover, found in Letterbox Field, Much Marcle.
> 1968: Mary Bastholm, 15 (probable?)
> 1970: Rena Costello, Fred's first wife, also found near Much Marcle.

1972:   Charmaine West, Rena's child,
found at 25 Midland Road,
Gloucester.

1973:   Linda Gough, 21, found (with all
the rest) at 25 Cromwell Street,
Gloucester.

1973:   Lucy Partington, 21.

1974:   Carol Cooper, 15.

1975:   Juanita Mott, 19.

1975:   Shirley Hubbard, 15.

1977:   Therese Siegenthaler, 21.

1978:   Shirley Robinson, 18.

1978:   Alison Chambers, about 18 (probable)

1987:   Heather West, 16.

PART FOUR

MURDER FOR PROFIT

Thomas Dun

dying piecemeal

THOMAS DUN WAS born in about 1100 into a very poor family in rural Bedfordshire, between Kempston and Elstow, an area that has now been developed into housing estates on the south-western edge of Bedford. Thomas Dun was a natural thief from childhood on; things just seemed to stick to his fingers.

He became a professional thief and highwayman, and owed his survival in this very risky occupation partly to his careful disguises. He would go out one day dressed as a merchant, another as a gentleman, another as a beggar. After committing each crime he would change the disguise so that he was impossible for witnesses to identify, sometimes even going to the lengths of covering his face with ointment, bandages and plasters. One crime would be committed in the guise of a blind harpist, another in the guise of a cripple with crutches.

Another reason for his continuing survival through over twenty years of highway robbery was his utter ruthlessness, cruelty and willingness to murder. On one occasion he saw a carter driving a wagon full of corn towards Bedford. He was seized with a kind of rage, fell on the unsuspecting carter, immediately stabbed him to death and buried him to conceal the evidence. Then he drove the wagon to Bedford himself, sold the wagon, the corn and the horses, and walked off with all the money.

At first Dun worked alone, but thought it would be safer to work with a gang. He set up his headquarters in some woods, and he was soon joined there by a gang of thieves who were every bit as unscrupulous as he was. The woods gave them protection. There were also caves and rocks that provided them with shelter. From this base, Thomas Dun's gang carried out many raids. The roads through the area became too dangerous for anyone to risk. The road that Dun made his main target was the stretch of Watling Street (which is today called the A5) between St Albans and Towcester. Along this road, Dun attacked all the travellers he met, murdering and robbing them without a second thought. It is said that Henry I founded Dunstable specifically to police the activities of the Dun gang.

Dun's gang consisted of a great variety of criminals, and he was quick to exploit their different talents. Some were expert pickpockets. Some were good at making keys. Some were clever at making 'deaf' files, which could be used to file through bars and padlocks silently.

One day Thomas Dun heard a rumour that the Sheriff of Bedford was searching for him with a band of men, and that the Sheriff's intention was to trap and attack him in the woods. Dun gathered his men together and took them into the deepest part of the wood. He then put on a canvas doublet and breeches, old boots and a steeple-crowned hat. In this disguise, Dun was able to approach close enough to the Sheriff's men to see how many of them there were and how well they were armed. He saw that they were no match for his gang, and returned to his woodland lair to reassure the gang.

Dun confidently led his gang into the attack when the Sheriff's men came near. It was a rout. Some of the Sheriff's men fled, eleven unlucky men were captured. Dun took the livery from the eleven and then hanged them from the woodland trees.

The Bedford Sheriff's uniforms were to prove a marvellous disguise for further robberies. Dun dressed some of his men in the livery and they boldly went to one of the local castles, pretending that they knew Dun and his gang were somewhere in the castle. They made a very thorough search, not for the criminals, who were easily found, but for money. Dun announced to the custodians of the castle that the gang had concealed themselves inside some chests. He ordered the keys to the chests to be handed over, opened them up and loaded himself and all his men with everything of value he could find inside the chests. Once Dun and his gang had gone, the lord of the castle discovered that his treasure had gone missing and naturally concluded that the Sheriff's men had robbed him. He complained to King and Parliament about the outrage and an order was sent out to examine the Sheriff's men. One of them was hanged, to see whether this produced an admission of guilt from the rest, but they all consistently and vehemently claimed that the raid had not been their doing. The enquiry revealed that eleven of their number had been taken by Dun and his gang earlier, and then it was realised that Dun had taken their uniforms.

Thomas Dun had by now acquired a terrible reputation throughout Bedfordshire and beyond. Peers, merchants and ordinary people alike feared him; he was no respecter of rank and he did not hesitate to kill his victims. He was so brutal that no-one dared to try to arrest him and bring him to justice. He carried on this extraordinary and very risky career in crime for more than twenty years before his infamy goaded people into action. One brave man in Dunstable arranged for a few of the Sheriff's men to go to his house to arrest Dun, who sometimes could be seen out walking by himself. Dun heard about this plan and paid a terrifying visit to the man's house one night, launching a string of terrible curses against the conspirator. But word got out in Dunstable that Dun was in town and the Sheriff's men arrived in force. Dun fled, and the Sheriff's men divided up into several groups to search the neighbouring area.

In the end, the Sheriff's men arrived at the house where Dun was hiding, posting themselves outside with a large crowd. Two men stood at the door ready to apprehend Dun when he came out. But Dun came out wielding a dagger and he used it to stab both of them to death. He mounted his horse and tried to force his way through the crowd on horseback, but they were having none of it. They attacked him with whatever they had – clubs, forks, spades, rakes – and managed to force him off his horse. But Dun was not finished yet. He managed to remount and get away into the fields. He was obliged to dismount to get away from the crowd chasing after him, and ran across the fields. It was not long before he was an incredible two miles away from them.

Just when he must have thought he was safe, having put this significant distance between himself and his pursuers, Thomas Dun found himself suddenly surrounded by three hundred men. Yet, undaunted as ever, he managed to get away from them too. He came to a river, undressed, took his sword between his teeth, and jumped in. The crowd followed to the river bank, some just to watch the historic moment of Dun's arrest, others to give chase. Some got boats ready. Dun swam this way and that to get away from his would-be captors. In the end his pursuers managed to hit him several times round the head with their oars. He was both tired and stunned now, and so much easier to catch, though the man's sheer energy and stamina were remarkable.

Once Dun was caught, he was taken to a surgeon to have his wounds dressed, then before a magistrate, who did not take very long to decide to commit him to

Bedford Gaol. Dun was taken there under a strong guard. Unusually, there was no trial. The terrible catalogue of crimes committed by Thomas Dun was so well known that there was no need to put him on trial. There was no question of his not being guilty.

About two weeks after his capture – and it is not clear why there was a delay – Thomas Dun was taken out into the market-place at Bedford. A scaffold had been erected for his execution and two executioners had been appointed. Right to the end, Dun showed neither fear nor humility – only unbridled aggression. In an act of extraordinary bravado, he threatened the two executioners. If they came anywhere near him they would regret the consequences. To convince the crowd that he was still a great force to reckon with, Dun grasped the two executioners and grappled with them. They tried to throw him down, but he kept leaping up again. The crowd saw him come up again nine times during this final struggle to go on living. He broke free and swaggered up and down the scaffold, continuously cursing the day he had been born and cursing those who had brought about his capture.

In the end, even the inexhaustible Dun ran out of energy and could no longer fight off the executioners. He gave in, and let them kill him. It was an unusually horrible execution, even by the barbaric standards of the middle ages. The executioners chopped off his hands, then cut off his forearms at the elbows, then his upper arms just below the shoulders. After this appalling sequence, they cut off his feet, then his lower legs at the knees, then his thighs five inches from the pelvis. Then, only then, did they cut off Thomas Dun's head. He died, as they said, piecemeal.

Patrick Flemming

the Irish highwayman

PATRICK FLEMMING WAS born in Athlone in Ireland. His parents were tenant farmers, growing potatoes and raising geese, hens and pigs. They all lived, parents, nine children and all the livestock together, in a house that was a single room. It was a poor and squalid household by any standard. Patrick Flemming was the eldest of the children, yet even he had virtually no education. What he lacked in knowledge he made up for in impudence.

When Patrick was thirteen he was lucky, and entirely undeserving, to be taken into the service of the Countess of Kildare as a foot-boy. She found that he was completely uneducated so she provided him with an education. Far from showing gratitude and taking advantage of this opportunity, Patrick was persistently idle and showed no inclination learn anything at all. The countess admonished him, and found that he was not only lazy but insolent. In the end, she dismissed him.

Young Patrick Flemming was given a second chance to make an honest living with the Earl of Antrim. In this household, he behaved even worse. The earl put up with Patrick's mischief-making for a time, in spite of the repeated complaints of the rest of his servants. The Earl of Antrim was a Roman Catholic and kept a chaplain and confessor in his house. All the servants were required to show this priest great respect. Patrick was often told off by this rather self-righteous and priggish priest for his disorderly behaviour, but then he found a marvellous way of getting his own back on the priest. Patrick happened to find the priest asleep in some private part of the house. The sleeping priest was in a very indecent pose. Patrick tiptoed away, gathered all the family together and took them to look at the indecency of the sleeping priest, who at that moment woke up. The servants were delighted and ridiculed the priest. When the earl heard about it, he assumed it was a malicious slander on Patrick's part, and dismissed him.

Before he went, Patrick helped himself to money and silver belonging to the earl to the value of about £200 and fled to Athenrea in Connaught. There he hid in a hut for about ten days until he thought the hunt for him would have died down, then he made his way to Dublin, where he made a living by house-breaking. Twice in Dublin he came close to being hanged for his many robberies. He became the talk of the city and he realised that it was not safe to stay there any longer.

After that, Patrick Flemming retreated into the green heart of rural Ireland, becoming a highwayman in the Bog of Allen. He attacked almost everyone who passed that way. He killed out of hand anyone who refused to hand over their money on demand. Within the space of just a few days he robbed 125 people on the mountain of Barnsmoor. Near it was a wood called Colorockedie, where he gathered round him a substantial gang of criminals. From time to time some of the gang members were caught and executed.

Some of Patrick Flemming's victims were very distinguished people. The Archbishop of Armagh and the Bishop of Rapho both had the honour of being held up by Flemming. The Lady Baltimore had the misfortune to be stopped by Flemming when she had her four-year-old son with her. Flemming took the boy and asked her to send a ransom within twenty-four hours or he would cut the young puppy's throat and make a pie of him. From the Bishop of Tuam he took a thousand pounds.

He was caught in Munster, and committed to prison in Cork, but the gaol was not secure enough to hold him. No sooner had he been locked up than his eyes were everywhere and his mind working on a plan for escape. He eventually succeeded in getting up a chimney and out of the building, avoiding for a time his almost inevitable hanging.

After this break-out, Flemming murdered five men, two women and a boy of fourteen. In addition to the murders, which were horrible enough, he committed a number of other atrocities on his victims. He held up Sir Donagh O'Brien, who possibly instinctively made some small resistance while Flemming was robbing him. Flemming's appalling response to this was to cut off Sir Donagh's nose, ears and lips.

The end came for Patrick Flemming when the landlord of a tavern he used to frequent near Mancoth decided to hand him over to justice. Flemming was becoming too dangerous even for his associates. The landlord courageously sent word to the sheriff of the county, notifying him of the times when Flemming was likely to be there. The sheriff arrived with a large force of men one evening. Flemming and his gang would have defended themselves, but the landlord had had the intelligence to wet all their firearms so that they would not fire. Flemming and fourteen others were captured in the ambush and taken off to Dublin.

Flemming was executed in Dublin on 24 April 1650, and his body hung in chains, as a warning to others, on the high road outside the city.

George Joseph Smith

the Brides in the Bath murderer

GEORGE JOSEPH SMITH was a man known by many names. He was Oliver George Love, he was Charles Olive James, he was John Lloyd, and he was Henry Williams. He was also found guilty of murdering three women, all in the same unusual way, by drowning them in the bath. Bessie Williams was found dead in a bath in 1912. Alice Burnham died in a bath in Blackpool in December 1913. Margaret Elizabeth Lofty was found dead in a bath in Highgate in December 1914.

When the case was under investigation, Detective Inspector Neil formed the opinion with the pathologist, the infamous Dr Bernard Spilsbury, that it would be impossible for anyone to drown accidentally in any of the baths in question.

Bessie Williams (maiden name Bessie Mundy) was found dead in her bath at 80 High Street, Herne Bay on 13 July 1912. One significant fact that made her death look arranged and deliberate, with malice aforethought, was that she had made a will in her husband's favour only five days earlier. That made her death look very suspicious indeed. Her husband, who was at that time calling himself Henry Williams, gained from Bessie's death to the tune of £2579, 13 shillings and seven pence.

Nevertheless, the doctor who examined Bessie's body immediately after her death believed that she had had an epileptic fit, and that this had caused her to drown. At the coroner's inquest he was asked if her had seen any signs of struggle on the woman's body. He said he had seen none. Had her death been due to anything other than drowning? He had no cause to suspect anything other than drowning. There was no request for a post mortem and a verdict of 'death by mis-adventure' was returned.

The reason why the doctor was in effect on Smith's side is simply explained by Smith's foresight. Shortly after the marriage, he persuaded Bessie that she had swooned or fainted. She had no memory of it, but that was because she had had an epileptic fit. With a great parade of concern, Smith then took Bessie to the doctor, who was both impressed with Smith as an immensely caring husband and predisposed to interpret what happened later in the light of Bessie's imagined history of epilepsy.

The very similar death of Alice Smith on 12 December 1913 was also the work of George Joseph Smith. Alice's father had not approved of her marriage to Smith. He had serious reservations about Smith, describing Smith during his daughter's engagement to him as being 'of very evil appearance'. His hunch that Smith was an evil man was absolutely right, but there was nothing he could prove, and nothing ultimately he could do to stop the wedding going ahead. On the evening when she died, Alice went for a bath at the apartments of Mr and Mrs Crossley, where she was staying with her new husband. She never returned from her bath.

Joseph Crossley noticed something odd when Alice's body was found some little while later. Her head was at the wrong end of the bath. Even so, the verdict of the inquest held on 13 December was that Alice had 'accidentally drowned through heart failure when in the bath'.

It emerged that there was a life insurance policy on Alice, and this meant £500 for George Joseph Smith as a result of her death.

In September 1914, under the guise of Charles Oliver James, Smith married another Alice – this time Alice Reavil. He married her illegally, robbed her and left her, gaining the princely sum of £76.

A similar life insurance policy to Alice Burnham's turned out to be the death warrant for Margaret Elizabeth Lloyd (born Margaret Lofty). John Lloyd – yes, George Joseph Smith again – rented rooms at a boarding house at 14 Bismark Road in Highgate, London, for himself and his new wife.

On the afternoon of 18 December 1914 Margaret Lloyd went to see her solicitor in Islington and made a will in her husband's favour. That evening, John Lloyd told the owner of the house that he would be going out to buy tomatoes for his wife's supper while she had a bath. When he returned form this errand he got no answer when he called out to his wife; when he went into the bathroom he found her dead in the bath. The inquest on 1 January 1915 returned a verdict of accidental death.

No connection was made between the three deaths. They took place in two different locations, Blackpool, Herne Bay and Highgate, and Smith used a different alias each time. Three unfortunate accidents happening to three entirely unconnected couples.

But Smith was careless. When the hearse drew up at Margaret's funeral, Smith crassly told the undertaker, Mr Beckett, 'I don't want any walking. Get it over as quick as you can.' After the funeral was over he said, 'Thank goodness that's all over.' And then someone did make a connection between two of the sudden deaths. Joseph Crossley noticed how similar the circumstances of Alice Smith's death were to those of Margaret Lloyd's. On 3 January 1915, Joseph Crossley sent the Metropolitan Police a newspaper cutting about Margaret Lloyd's death, and remarked in his letter that it was similar to the death of Alice Smith in Blackpool.

This was the starting point of the police investigation into the 'Brides in the Bath' murders. Gradually the story unravelled. George Joseph Smith had led a very sinister existence indeed. He had been born in Bethnal Green in January 1872. In 1898 he had married Caroline Thornhill. In 1908 he had married Edith

Peglar, under the name of Oliver George Love, though his first wife was still alive. He was a bigamist. He stole £30 and all her belongings from Edith Peglar. In 1910, when he married Bessie Mundy, Edith Peglar was still alive. He was a polygamist. From then on, murder and money took over. In October 1909, under the name George Rose, he married Sarah Freeman; from her he took £260 and all her belongings.

The only one of all of these women that George Joseph Smith was legally married to was Caroline Thornhill. She left him while he was serving a prison term in 1902, and emigrated to Canada, which was probably the wisest thing she ever did. The only one of all these women to whom Smith was loyal and faithful was Edith Peglar, whom he married in 1908. He did not take any money from her.

Detective Inspector Neil stopped Smith in the Uxbridge Road in London on 1 February 1915, and Smith appeared at the Bow Street Police Court a week later. To begin with he was charged with causing a false entry to be made in a marriage register – the police were onto the bigamy at this point – but as they enquired further the aliases started to emerge.

On 23 March 1915, Smith was charged with the murders of Bessie Williams, Alice Smith and Margaret Lloyd. At his trial he was found guilty and sentenced to death. He was hanged at Maidstone Gaol on 13 August 1915.

How were the murders committed, without leaving any injuries on the women's bodies, without leaving any sign of struggle? To begin with, Smith had the advantage of total surprise. His wives had no reason to suppose that they were in any danger from him at all. It seems likely that he grabbed their lower legs and pulled them out of the water. This would have pulled their heads straight under the water. Before they could do anything to save themselves with their hands, he may have pulled their legs up high, and twisted them so that they rotated and were face down in the water. No amount of flailing of arms would have saved them then. And, of course, because they had not been expecting the attack, they would not have taken a deep breath first. Unconsciousness and death probably came very quickly.

One of the baths was transferred to the courtroom, so that jurors could see how effective Smith's method was. A nurse lay in the bath and was ducked by having her legs pulled up. She showed signs of being in great difficulty immediately, and started to drown; she had to be artificially revived.

Praise was justly given to Detective Inspector Neil for the extremely competent and efficient way in which he handle the enquiry, but it is more than a little worrying to wonder how much would have emerged had Mr Crossley not noticed the parallels between the accidental drowning that happened in his own house and one reported but briefly in the newspaper – somewhere else. If he had not reported it, how many more innocent young women would have been ensnared by the callous Brides in the Bath murderer?

Al Capone

the Chicago gangster

ALPHONSE CAPONE WAS born in New York in 1899, one of nine children of Italian immigrants. From the start he was a street-fighter and a thug. He acquired the nickname 'Scarface' while working as a bouncer in a brothel in Brooklyn. He was involved in the killing of a policeman and when he heard he was wanted for questioning he knew it was time to get out of New York. He got in touch with Johnny Torrio, a Chicago gangster, who remembered Capone from his own street-fighting days in New York, and asked him to join his gang in Chicago.

It was in 1919 that Al Capone arrived in Chicago, where he found Torrio working for 'Diamond' Jim Colosimo, who was one of the older generation of Mafia tycoons. Colosimo acquired his nickname because he liked wearing jewellery. He ran most of the brothels in Chicago. Torrio was Colosimo's trusted Number Two, who had had to swear to guard his boss with his life. Colosimo regularly presided each evening at his restaurant, surrounded by his mobsters as well as politicians and entertainers. With the introduction of Prohibition, Torrio had tried to persuade Colosimo to expand the business into illegal alcohol, so that they could make even more cash, but Colosimo declined.

On 11 May 1920, Torrio asked Colosimo if he would be at the restaurant at a particular time to sign for a delivery. Colosimo was there, alone at the restaurant. Capone stepped out of a phone booth, shot Colosimo and took his wallet to try to make it look like a casual robbery. Capone was working to Torrio's orders, and he was soon back at Torrio's side joining in the weeping and grieving. Torrio and Capone took over Colosimo's empire, added bootleg alcohol according to Torrio's plan, and began to make huge amounts of money.

The Chicago underworld of the 1920s was divided between two rival gangs, the Torrio-Capone Mafia and the Irish gang of Charles Dion O'Bannion, 'Deanie' O'Bannion. O'Bannion was an unusual gangster. He was an angel-faced ex-choirboy who started off making a living as a singing waiter in a club frequented by gangsters; it was they who introduced him to the possibilities of earning more money. He developed into a gangster with a sense of humour and style, and with a certain contempt for the crudity of the Italian gangster way of doing things. He nevertheless made a strategic error in 1924, when he sold Torrio a half share in a brewery for half a million dollars, knowing that it was about to be raided. Torrio was booked. Torrio was furious, not least because up to that point he had very carefully avoided being caught by the police. He wanted revenge.

On 10 November 1924, three men arrived at O'Bannion's flower shop to buy a wreath. It was for him. The three men, Alberto Anselmi, John Scalise and Frank Yale, hired by Torrio and Capone, held O'Bannion down and shot him. The funeral of Deanie O'Bannion was spectacular. Murderers, bootleggers, gangsters and thieves mixed with local celebrities, to pay their respects to the man who was proud to supply them with the best alcohol in the city. Unfortunately it was only the first of many funerals. By killing O'Bannion, Johnny Torrio and Al Capone had begun a gang war that would run and run. During the next six years over a thousand people were to lose their lives.

Torrio was the first target for a revenge attack. Hymie Weiss and George 'Bugs' Moran lay in wait for Torrio as he left his home. They shot him and left him for dead, but he recovered. Then he was arrested over the brewery business and was jailed for nine months.

After that, Torrio seems to have lost his nerve. He was no doubt worried that he might be hit again by O'Bannion's men, or by Capone, who might by now begin to see Torrio as standing in his way. Torrio decided to retire, though he was only forty-three. He left Chicago for Florida, still with Weiss and Moran tailing him, and then went to live in Naples until things cooled off in Chicago. He decided in 1928 that it was safe to go back to America, but stayed in New York rather than risk returning to Chicago. In 1939 he was imprisoned for not paying his income tax. He lived on until 1967, when he died of a heart attack.

Torrio's departure from Chicago was good news for Al Capone. Capone was the legatee of the richest slice of the criminal underworld. Torrio had taken his share with him – over $50 million – but that left Capone a very productive business empire that yielded him a handsome income from gambling, extortion, boot-legging and prostitution. Capone ran his new empire in grand style from the Hawthorn Hotel in the Chicago district of Cicero. In 1926, Hymie Weiss and Bugs Moran returned to Chicago, having failed to kill Torrio, and decided they would do the next best thing which was to eliminate Al Capone instead. They drove past the Hawthorn Hotel, spraying it with submachine gun fire. It was more of a gesture than an assassination attempt. Naturally, they didn't hit Capone, but they did upset him. Capone had Weiss shot shortly afterwards. Moran was more elusive.

Capone had some business problems to attend to first. There was the question of the quality of the bootleg liquor he was selling. It was cheap, terrible and dangerous. Some customers were blinded, others died. Capone's main suppliers of whiskey and gin were the Genna family, a gang of four brothers. Capone quarrelled with the Gennas, not principally because of the low quality of the alcohol but because they were competing with him for power. One by one, he had them shot. Those that survived got the message and fled to other cities or even back to Italy.

Another of Capone's bootleg suppliers was Roger Touhy. Capone wanted him eliminated so that he could take over his business. First Capone kidnapped Touhy's partner Matt Kilb and demanded a $50,000 ransom. Touhy paid the ransom, but Capone shot Kilb anyway. Touhy bravely stood out against Capone's demands, so Capone had him framed for an abduction and got him a 199 year sentence. Touhy managed to escape and prove his innocence, but within days of gaining his freedom Capone had him shot in the street.

So far, all of these criminal activities were restricted to Chicago, but Capone's reach extended to New York when he needed it to. Frank Yale, one of the men who killed O'Bannion for him and Torrio, was suspected of cheating Capone on bootleg liquor deals. One day in 1927, Frank Yale was lured to an appointment in Brooklyn; when he reached the right address he was machine-gunned from a passing car.

But Al Capone's main enemy, his prime target, was still Bugs Moran, the O'Bannion heavy who had tried to kill Torrio. Capone commissioned a notorious hit-man, 'Machine Gun' Jack McGurn. Many of the mobsters had nicknames, but 'Machine Gun' Jack McGurn is unusual in that not one of his names is real; his real name was James Vicenzo de Mora. He was, in any case, a fearsome assassin. His calling card was a nickel coin pressed into the palm of the victim's hand. By 1929 the police had collected at least fifteen corpses bearing

Machine Gun McGurn's calling card. He had a fearsome reputation and his services didn't come cheap. He had been able to buy shares in several Chicago clubs.

It was on 14 February 1929 that Jack McGurn was ordered to get rid of Capone's great enemy Bugs Moran, who had made the mistake of abusing Capone recently, calling him 'Alphonse the Beast'. The Moran gang were expecting a delivery of liquor that day at a garage on 2122 North Clark Street. Seven gang members of the Moran gang were inside the garage. Three men dressed as policemen burst in with machine guns, ordering the gangsters to line up facing the wall. Then they mowed them down with their machine guns. The 'policemen' were two of Capone's hit-men, led by Machine Gun McGurn. But Bugs Moran himself was not there. He was not a victim of the notorious St Valentine's Day Massacre. Another adverse result of this incident was that the public, police and politicians all recognized that something serious had to be done to stop the escalating violence in Chicago. It was very bad news for McGurn, as it was well known that he had been involved in the killings, and Capone therefore wanted nothing more to do with him. McGurn thought he could hang up his gun and make a reasonable living out of his clubs. But one day McGurn was walking down a quiet street when he was approached by two gunmen who shot him at close range. The police found a nickel pressed in his palm and a cut-out paper Valentine heart beside him. It was 14 February 1936, the seventh anniversary of the St Valentine's Day Massacre.

The men who murdered Machine Gun McGurn were neither caught nor identified, but it is likely that one of them was Bugs Moran, taking revenge on McGurn for virtually wiping out his gang. Moran had more or less disappeared from view after the garage massacre in North Clark Street. He turned up in Ohio after the Second World War. He hadn't exactly gone straight: he was arrested for bank robbery. He died in prison in 1957, having survived almost all the other 1920s mobsters in Chicago, and outlived Capone by a decade. He must have been the only man marked out for death by Capone who survived.

The St Valentine's Day Massacre of 1929 had the effect of driving Moran out of Chicago, leaving Al Capone a clear run. He could now take over the whole criminal network of the city of Chicago. But his triumph was short-lived. The tax investigators succeeded where the police had never been able to make any progress at all; they caught Capone. On 24 October 1931, Al Capone was found guilty of tax evasion, fined $50,000, ordered to pay $30,000 costs, and sentenced to eleven years in prison. Capone did not take to life in prison at all.

When Al Capone was released from prison in 1939, he was suffering from syphilis and slipping into insanity. He buried himself away on his estate in Florida, avoided by his neighbours and regarded as a brutish anachronism by the new generation of Mafia leaders. Capone died, alone and deranged, in 1947.

John George Haigh

the Acid Bath murderer

JOHN GEORGE HAIGH was born at Stamford in Lincolnshire in July 1909. According to Haigh's mother, Haigh's father had lost his job as an electrician months before and had to borrow money from his fellow Plymouth Brethren to pay for the expenses of the birth. There is documentary evidence, though, to show that Mr Haigh Senior was more or less continuously employed, and could not have been out of work for more than a fortnight in December 1909. This highlights a major problem in exploring the Haigh case. Haigh himself told lots of lies – he was a con-man – but his eighty-year-old parents' version of events is not to be trusted either.

As a boy, Haigh was known as 'Chinky', because of his narrow eyes, to his contemporaries – one could scarcely call them friends, as he had none – and as 'Sonnie' to his parents. Even his final letters from the condemned cell were signed 'Sonnie'. One reason why he was separated from his contemporaries was that he was not allowed to play games. That was connected with his parents being Plymouth Brethren. They thought they were God's elect, too good to mix with ordinary folk. Poor Mrs Haigh. In old age, in the twilight period after her son had been hanged for murder, she had to recant. 'We used to despise the people in the village because we were God's elect. But we were not.'

The village she referred to was Outwood, where they moved to during John's childhood. Mr Haigh had got himself a job there as foreman electrician at the colliery. He was a tall, upright man with a waxed moustache. The chairs in the front parlour in Ledger Lane at Outwood were similarly straight-backed and well-waxed. There was also a harmonium, on which little Sonnie first showed his musical abilities, playing only the most dirge-like hymns – nothing uplifting. This interest in music he shared with George Joseph Smith, the Brides in the Bath murderer, who played Nearer My God To Thee after drowning at least one of his brides in an adjacent room. Charles Peace played the organ in a church in Peckham. Henri Landru sang in a choir.

Young Haigh was brought up in an uncompromisingly religious household, and a fundamentalist one at that. The literal truth of the Bible was a great focus. He was constantly reminded that misdeeds would bring down the wrath of the Almighty on his head. In addition, his mother smacked his hands with the bristle side of a brush. He said later that this drew blood, which he enjoyed licking. He also told doctors he had been locked in a room for two days with only bread and water. But there is a problem with Haigh's version of the past, because he was trying to establish – among many other things – that he was insane, in order to escape the gallows. So, some of the things he said about his past, his childhood especially, may not have been true.

Mr Haigh said, 'John was a good boy and right up to the time he left home he never misbehaved. He got on very well with the other boys and there was nothing wrong with him mentally.' That too may not be true. Indeed, whoever heard of a boy who never misbehaved? Every child misbehaves. It is also difficult to see how he 'got on very well with the other boys' when he was not allowed to mix with them outside the school or Wakefield Cathedral. There is in any case an anecdote told by a fellow chorister, who remembered 'Chinky' creeping from his place in the choir stalls on all fours to find the main electric light switch, in order to plunge the cathedral into total darkness while a dignitary was reading a Lesson on the theme 'And the Lord said Let there be Light'. This sounds much more like normal boyish behaviour than either Mr Haigh Senior's account or John George's. Another schoolboy remembers that he 'took some trouble when the opportunity presented itself of exposing himself to travelling schoolgirls'. There was another anecdote, told by a neighbour in Ledger Lane. The woman in question was scrubbing her doorstep, when young 'Sonnie' came along and stamped on her hand and ran off, laughing. This suggests that a nasty sadistic streak was there from early on.

The young Haigh enjoyed church, especially the High Church of Wakefield Cathedral. He loved the pomp, the near-Popery, the incense. He loitered in the Cathedral all day on a Sunday, gazing up at the gilded Christ crucified dominating the high altar. 'I gazed with fascination at the blood flowing from the wounds of the larger-than-life Redeemer.' It was intoxicating after the fire and brimstone Chapel in Leeds.

There is a letter, written by Haigh's father to a back-sliding colleague, and it shows the man to have been a religious maniac. He accuses the colleague of 'railing', by which he means vehemently disagreeing with other Brethren. The letter amounts to a kind of excommunication, and it concludes with a (faint) hope that the man's soul will be restored. This one letter shows how abnormal John George's childhood must have been. It also shows how the boy was driven to develop an inner life that he had to keep hidden, and driven to lie to the very odd couple that his parents were.

When older, Haigh had a string of attractive girl friends. He was very polite and gentlemanly with them, but the relationships always remained platonic. He took them to concerts, and sometimes to Madame Tussaud's where, one day, his own effigy would be on display in the Chamber of Horrors, wearing his favourite suit. He was described by one of the girl friends in later years as being over-smart, with glossy hair, wearing chamois gloves and driving a red sports car – surely always the hallmark of the bounder.

Haigh was a con-man and a thief. He would make his living by swindling other people. He came out of prison for the first time in December 1935. There was a pin-table machine craze. Among those making money out of them was a Mr McSwan who lived in Wimbledon. He and his son had made enough money out of pin-tables to buy property in Beckenham and Raynes Park. Mr McSwan decided he wanted a chauffeur and secretary, an odd combination at that time, but what we might now call a personal assistant. Just why John George Haigh was reading World's Fair, a journal of funfair folk, is one of many mysteries surrounding the man, but he was, and he saw Mr McSwan's job ad in it. He applied and got it. Haigh was soon appointed manager of a saloon in Tooting.

Within nine years, Mr McSwan, his wife and their son Donald had all vanished, and John George Haigh had killed all of them. The oddest thing is that no-one missed them. No-one reported them missing. During the Second World War, lots of people went missing.

But when Haigh stopped working for McSwan he and his family were all still alive. He went off to set himself up as a solicitor. He advertized that he was winding up an estate and had some shares to get rid of at below market prices. He asked people to send him a 25% deposit. Cheques flooded in. he cashed them, then moved on to another office and set up again under a different name. He made a slip-up on the letterhead for one of these outfits, misspelling the name 'Guildford'. Prospective investors started making enquiries, and this led to another spell in prison for John George Haigh – four years, starting in 24 November 1937.

By the time Haigh came out of prison, the Second World War was in full swing. He became a fire-watcher. In June 1941 he was sentenced to 21 months hard labour for stealing some bunks and kitchen equipment worth £17. Haigh never lost his big-shot view of himself, and was very ready to dismiss the other prisoners he encountered as 'cheap crooks', but here he was, serving a term inside for stealing a few bits and pieces worth £17.

In 1944, Haigh went to lodge at Northgate Road in Crawley, with the parents of Barbara Stephens. Barbara was still at school at this time, but they struck up a warm and real friendship. He took her to concerts. Barbara was to remain loyal to him even after all the murders had come out, even after he had been sentenced to death; she even wrote a touching letter to Haigh's parents as the execution approached.

Also in 1944, Haigh by chance met Donald McSwan in a pub in Kensington. McSwan admitted to feeling nervous about being called up for military service. Haigh advised him to run away, get lost. If he was not at home, he could not receive the call-up papers. McSwan said it wasn't so easy, with ration cards and so on. Haigh would set it up for him. They met again, several times, and there was a reunion with Donald's parents in Pimlico. What was Haigh doing these days? He was repairing pin-table machines in the basement at 79 Gloucester Road. Haigh said Donald should come round and see his workshop. On 9 September 1944, in the basement at 79 Gloucester Road, Haigh took a broken pin-table leg and battered Donald McSwann to death with it.

Haigh alleged that he cut Donald's neck, filled a mug with his blood and drank it. Then he realised he had to do something about the body and decided to dissolve it in acid. After that he went to see the McSwans to tell them that Donald had 'gone on the trot' to avoid the call-up. They were quite happy that Donald would not be called up. Haigh was not happy that it had taken him 72 hours to dissolve Donald's body. But at least there was a drain in the cellar, down which he could pour the remains of Donald McSwan.

Haigh was getting sums of money for Donald from the McSwans, and became impatient because they were so small. They in their turn became suspicious. Haigh would have to kill them too. He lured them to his cellar and battered them to death.

Then Donald McSwan had to be brought back to life to inherit. So Haigh posed as Donald, forging his signature on a Power of Attorney document. In this way Haigh acquired four freehold properties, one in Raynes Park, one in Wimbledon and two in Beckenham. On the strength of the cash he was now getting access to, Haigh was able to live it up a little. He moved into the Onslow Court Hotel, where he flattered and flirted with all the old ladies. This was where he met Mrs Durand Deacon.

At Notting Hill Gate, Dr Archie Henderson and his wife decided to sell their expensive house in Ladbroke Square, W11. They advertized. Haigh responded and insisted on giving them well over the asking price. Rose Henderson wrote to her brother, 'Of the scores of stupid people I've met, I've just been introduced to the greatest of them all. I offered him 22 Ladbroke Square, lock, stock and barrel for £7750 and he said "That's too cheap, but if you will accept ten thousand, it's a deal"'. Her brother wrote back, 'When you meet a man like that you should run for your life.' He was right. Haigh did not buy the house; as usual, he bottled out when it came to parting with the money. The Hendersons sold the house to someone else and bought something smaller – 16 Dawes Road in Fulham. Rather surprisingly, Haigh managed to remain friends with the Hendersons. They liked to hear him play the piano.

The Hendersons were fairly sophisticated people. It is surprising that they did not see through Haigh. They could not have known that he was a psychopath, but they could have spotted that he was a con-man, surely? One psychiatrist studying the Haigh case commented that his victims were as much in need of psychiatric treatment as himself. That is unfair. We all deal, on a daily basis, with a broad spectrum of humanity and, just to get through life, we have to assume the people around us are not going to stab us when we turn our backs on them for a moment. To defend ourselves against such low probability events would make our lives unmanageable. Haigh's victims gave him, as we nearly always give one another, the benefit of the doubt. For that they deserve our unreserved pity.

Haigh moved inexorably towards his next killing. He was £237 overdrawn and owed £400 to a money-lender. He afterwards claimed he saw in a dream a forest of crucifixes changing to trees dripping with blood; waking, he knew he wanted to drink blood again. The rich Archie Henderson was the obvious victim. He drove him from the Metropole Hotel in Brighton where he was staying to his premises in Leopold Road in Crawley and shot him in the head with his own revolver, which Haigh had stolen from Dawes Road. Haigh drove back to the Metropole in Brighton, told Rose her husband had suddenly been taken ill and offered to take her to him. Naturally she allowed Haigh to drive her to Crawley, where she walked into Haigh's slaughter house, was horrified to see the dead and bloody body of her husband, and was herself immediately shot dead by Haigh. He claimed that he drank blood from each of them. In his diary for 12 February 1948, Haigh drew a cross with a red crayon and the initials A.H. and R.H. There was a similar entry for 9 September 1944 – for Donald McSwan.

Interestingly, the '12 February' seems to have been either a mistake or a lie. The Hendersons were murdered on 15 February.

The next day, Haigh settled the Hendersons' bill at the Metropole Hotel, took their dog for a walk along the beach, then stole all the Hendersons' possessions. The relationship with the Hendersons had been a kind of asset-stripping exercise. He set about cashing in their assets. A week or two later he sold Mrs Durand-Deacon Mrs Henderson's handbag for £10. He sold Archie Henderson's car for £400. He forged deeds that gave him ownership of 16 Dawes Road. By the end of this asset stripping he was £7,700 better off.

In June 1948 Haigh's Lagonda was found at the foot of Beachy Head with the dead body of a woman nearby. Given Haigh's history, this looks like a very suspicious death, but he never admitted to this murder, which remains a complete mystery.

By New Year 1949, Haigh was in high spirits, writing yet more cheery 'Mum and Dad' letters, in which he showed off about meeting people in the film business, having dinner at the Savoy, wearing evening dress, describing attractive women he had met. Haigh's ultimate pin-up was Princess Margaret. In conversation and correspondence, he went on and on about her. But he also fancied Princess Elizabeth; 'They are both ideal princesses.'

Haigh's ninth victim was Mrs Olive Durand-Deacon. She was a Christian Scientist and a member of the Francis Bacon Society, a staunch believer that Francis Bacon had written Shakespeare's plays. She was the widow of a colonel, and lived on a pension of £1000 a year. She was 69 and weighed 14 stone. Haigh charmed her and then one day invited her to go with him to Crawley to see his workshop. Mrs Durand-Deacon was a woman of many interests, among them artificial fingernails, so Haigh pretended he was going into the business of manufacturing them.

Haigh shot her in the back of the neck while she was examining some paper he said he might use in making fingernails.

When Mrs Durand Deacon disappeared from the Onslow Court Hotel, the police had reports from all over England from people who thought they might have seen her. John George Haigh was the only person who knew what had happened to her, and he wrote excitedly to his parents from the hotel,

Dear Mum and Dad, Mrs D.D. has not returned and the Sunday newspapers are full of the most exciting stories imaginable. They are digging up chalk pits looking for her body and all sorts of things. Then a mystery call came through to the hotel last night. Somebody rang up to say that they had seen her (or been with her) last Sunday – 2 days after she had disappeared. The Pictorial speaks of the dapper young Mr Haigh and the Despatch of the handsome 35-year-old Mr Haigh. Which kindness rather surprised me

since I would give them no information and referred
them to the police station . . .

The letter gives a good idea of Haigh's heartless cruelty, shallow superficiality – and rather silly vanity. In fact he dismissed his victims in much the same way that his parents dismissed the 'offenders' and 'railers' who got the wrong side of the Brethren.

On 28 February 1949, Haigh had some more to say about Mrs Durand Deacon in a long statement he made at Chelsea Police Station. She was a confounded nuisance on account of her size and weight, and the difficulty he had in dissolving her body in a drum of sulphuric acid. 'I laid the barrel down lengthwise on the floor and with a minimum of effort pushed the head and shoulders into the barrel. I then tipped the barrel up by placing my feet on the forward edge and grasping the top of the barrel with my gloved hands. By throwing my weight backwards the barrel containing the body rocked to a vertical position fairly easily and I found I could raise a 15-stone body without difficulty. I then donned the rest of my equipment, for I had found it necessary to protect myself from the acid. I had a rubber mackintosh which I kept specially for this purpose, rubber gloves, a gas mask to protect myself from the acid fumes, a rubber apron and rubber boots. The question of getting the right amount of acid into the oil drum was only learnt by experience. Whether a person was thin or fat made a considerable difference.

Thin people were much more easily disposed of, for I found fat most difficult to dissolve. For this reason Mrs Durand-Deacon was a confounded nuisance – far more trouble than any of the others. She simply would not disappear and next day when I expected her body to be entirely dissolved I found a large piece of buttock floating on top of the sludge and grease that was the rest of her. I emptied off the grease and put in fresh acid, expecting that the next day to see the dissolution complete as in previous cases. She simply would not go and there were still some parts left, though quite unrecognizable for what they were, when I emptied the sludge onto a rubbish heap outside the shed and threw the drum carelessly among the other scrap iron and other drums that had been used on other occasions.'

After this ghoulish murder was over and the appalling clearing-up operation afterwards, Haigh 'went round to the Ancient Priors for a cup of tea'.

The police officer to whom Haigh was dictating this could not help but comment, 'You have made my stomach turn over. Do you really mean what you say?' Haigh was very matter-of-fact about the whole business. His method was a far better way of disposing of a body than a funeral.

After the statement was finished, Haigh was taken to Lewes Prison to await trial.

A month after this awful autobiography was dictated, Haigh was chirpily writing to his parents, who must by this stage have gone into shock,

Dear Mum and Dad, As you say this will be a big case: in fact I think the biggest case in British history, from so many angles. . . I have had two [Pharisees] to see me. The C/E Chaplain whose philosophical outlook is useless. No man who represents a church with such a diversity of contradictory opinions could hope to understand. The Wesleyan . . . was a more hopeful subject.

The newspaper Haigh mentioned was the Daily Mirror, who rashly ran the headline 'VAMPIRE – MAN HELD'. The police had leaked information to the press but made it clear that the matter was sub judice and therefore could not yet be published. The Lord Chief Justice, Lord Goddard, was very annoyed with the Mirror because their reporting could prejudice the forthcoming trial. The Mirror was fined £10,000.

The whole question of whether Haigh really did drink the blood of his victims had never been resolved. There are those who say that it would be physically impossible to drink more than a very small amount of blood. It is also more than likely that the blood-drinking claim was something Haigh latched onto as a way of escaping the noose. The theory that the police put the idea into his head seems to me extremely unlikely. The police thought Haigh was an un-scrupulous and dangerous man who needed to be got rid of; they had no interest in sparing his life. It is much more likely that Haigh wanted to portray himself as a vampire so that the jury would write him off as a madman and send him to Broadmoor instead of the gallows.

Detective Inspector Webb said that, when Haigh was on his own with him, Haigh asked him, 'Tell me frankly, what are the chances of anyone being released from Broadmoor?'

Webb's answer was scrupulous. 'I cannot discuss that sort of thing with you.'

Haigh then said, 'Well, if I told you the truth, you would not believe me; it sounds too fantastic for belief'.

Webb then formally cautioned him that anything he said would be taken down in writing and might be used in evidence.

Haigh said, 'I understand all that. I will tell you all about it. Mrs Durand-Deacon no longer exists. I have destroyed her with acid. Every trace of her has gone. How can you prove murder if there is no body?'

So another plank in his case was to be that in spite of his graphic confession, he could not be convicted of murder because there was no body. Haigh was supremely confident, which made the police even more determined to catch him out. He taunted them with the exact location of the human non-remains, his yard in Leopold Street in Crawley. The police called in Dr Keith Simpson, the pathologist. He visited Leopold Street and sifted through the soil in the yard. He found a set of dentures that turned out to have belonged to

Mrs Durand-Deacon; the handle of a red plastic handbag; a piece of elderly female pelvis. He also spotted the clincher in the case, several small brown pea-shaped stones; they were Mrs Durand-Deacon's gallstones.

The body had been found. I remember my father, who was one of the detectives involved in the case, proudly showing me the gallstones, as 'the evidence that hanged Haigh'. His admiration for Keith Simpson in spotting these small brown pellets among the yard gravel was unbounded. They worked together many times subsequently. Coincidentally, my father grew up in the same small village, Sevenoaks Weald, as one of the victims in the case; he went to school with Mrs McSwan, and her son Donald used to do clerical work for his uncle, Mr Paige, the wheelwright.

Haigh was careless and impatient in the way that he disposed of the human remains. With a little more care, he could have cleared the yard of any tell-tale evidence. That oversight was uncharacteristic, because he was in most ways a perfectionist. He is the only murderer in British history to have requested a rehearsal of his own execution. 'My weight is deceptive,' he said. 'I have a light springy tread and I would not like there to be any hitch.' The Governor at Wandsworth, Major Benke, assured him the executioner never miscalculated. Haigh persisted, but the governor was adamant; there was no rehearsal. It is hard to see what would have been achieved, other than some weird masochistic thrill for

Haigh himself, in that the crucial drop could not have been tested.

The trial routinely heard evidence from witnesses to show that Haigh had indeed taken Mrs Durand Deacon to Crawley and murdered her. It also heard from Dr Yellowlees, who gave evidence for the defence to support Haigh's insanity plea. The judge asked whether Haigh knew that what he was doing was punishable by law. Dr Yellowlees said, 'Yes, and he (Haigh) added that of course it did not apply to him.'

'What did not apply in his case?'

'What I have just said, that murder being punishable by law did not apply to him.'

'Does that suggest that he is not amenable to the law?' Mr Justice Humphreys asked.

'Yes, certainly.'

'Why was he not amenable to the law?'

'Because he says he is working under the guidance and in harmony with some vital principle that is above the law,' said Yellowlees.

'And because he said that, he thought that everyone else would believe it – is that what he told you?' The judge was scornful. The exchange went on like a game of table tennis. 'He thinks he ought not to be punished?'

'Yes.'

'But does he really think he will not be punished?'

'I asked him that and he said "I am awaiting the trial with complete equanimity; I am in the position of Jesus Christ before Pontius Pilate, and the only thing I have to say, if I was to say anything, would be, "He can have no power against me, unless it be given from above'".

'That may well be,' said the judge.

Mr Justice Humphreys showed the jury that he did not believe Haigh was insane, which was tantamount to directing them to convict on a death penalty. But later, when giving evidence himself to the Royal Commission on Capital Punishment, Humphreys made a revealing remark about another murder case. He said of the accused, 'I thought he was insane from the way he gave his evidence'.

He was then asked the inevitable question, 'You would not think it proper that he should hang?' Humphreys astounded the commission by saying that he thought it proper for the insane to be hanged.

In the Haigh trial, Yellowlees was cross-examined by Sir David Maxwell Fyfe. He had had five interviews with Haigh and thought Haigh was paranoid. He admitted that he had come to his conclusion that Haigh was insane as a result of what Haigh had said about himself and what others had said about him. Fyfe stopped him to say that that was second-hand evidence and therefore inadmissible. Yellowlees described Haigh's upbringing in a fanatical religious atmosphere, in social and mental isolation, as an explanation for his mental instability. Yellowlees also brought in the complete absence of sexual activity in Haigh's life – as further evidence of his insanity. It was 'a thing you find in a paranoic, who sublimates his sexual energies into this worship of himself and his mystic fantasy.'

The turning point in the trial came when the Attorney General, Sir Hartley Shawcross, stood up to cross-examine Yellowlees. He wanted confirmation that the doctor had seen the prisoner five times, as already mentioned. Yellowlees agreed, not seeing this as a trap. Then Shawcross delivered the coup de grace, giving the dates of the interviews – 1, 2 and 5 July – and there were two other occasions when he visited the prison but not the prisoner. Yellowlees was completely floored, and had to admit he had no notes with him of the dates when he saw Haigh. Suddenly the case for the insanity plea had fallen through. The psychiatrist was a flawed witness. Nothing he said could be trusted now.

The judge explained to the jury that in this case they had to follow the McNaughton Rules dating from 1843.

'Poor Daniel McNaughton had the delusion which is known among doctors as the delusion of persecution and which is very common. He thought that a number of people had conspired against him and that they used to send people into his room at night and worry him, and one of the people he thought had so conspired was the Prime Minister of the day, Sir Robert Peel, and he made up his mind to come to London with a pistol and get rid of Sir Robert Peel because, he said, "he is conspiring to make my life impossible". He came to London, he went to Downing Street, and there he shot the first person who came to the front door, he standing in the street. In point of fact, it was not Sir Robert Peel, it was Sir Robert Peel's secretary, a Mr Drummond, who was shot and killed. It makes no difference whatever in law that it happened not to be Sir Robert Peel but Mr Drummond who was killed; the man is prima facie guilty of murder.

'He was tried by Chief Justice Tindal, who directed the jury, and that direction was afterwards approved by all the judges. All of them agreed that Chief Justice Tindal was right according to the law of the land then, not according to the judges who made up the law at all but that it always had been – I will not say "always had been" – but had been for a long time – the law of the country.

'Chief Justice Tindal said – it is very relevant to the issue which you have to try – "The question is whether this man had the competent use of his understanding so that he knew he was doing a wicked and wrongful thing. If he was not sensible that it was a violation of the law of God or man, undoubtedly he was not responsible for the act or liable to any punishment whatever." That is what he told the jury.

'Had he [Haigh] competent understanding so as to enable him to appreciate that what he was doing was wrong?'

Thus far, the judge's summing up was masterly, but he then misrepresented Yellowlees' evidence, putting words into Yellowlees' mouth that had actually been put there earlier by the Attorney General. But he was right to remind the jury that committing lots of murders did not in itself prove insanity. The police view was that

Haigh was perfectly sane and the series of murders had been a callous business venture; all the stuff about drinking blood was to deceive the jury into thinking that he was insane.

When the jury was directed to retire to consider the verdict, the foreman did something very unusual – he almost asked to give the verdict there and then, but stopped himself mid-sentence, realising that it would look like unseemly haste. As it was, the jury was back in twenty minutes with its unanimous guilty verdict.

Haigh left the courtroom elated, full of praise for the judge. He wrote another gleeful, schoolboyish letter to his now totally crushed parents.

I have now had officially delivered to me the decision of the home secretary which I think you will have gathered from previous letters I was quite anticipating. There have been too many fours in this affair. This is my fourth conviction, it's my fortieth year, the shopping list mentioned as one of the exhibits was No. 4 on the list. I was on remand for four months. There were four remands.

He went on to complain that England was still executing her heretics. Perhaps he was mad after all.

Haigh wrote another of his chirpy 'Mum and Dad' letters the night before he was hanged. It ended with an incredible and semi-incoherent postscript;

The Chaplain has had a very beautiful note from Hugh R. Norton (Cathedral) who writes to have the privilege of consoling with: I have told the Chaplain that I am sure you will appreciate this. Sonnie.

Even at this late stage he was unable to strike the appropriate tone. But Haigh's parents were equally at sea in these uncharted waters. A friend had taken a selection of birthday cards for Mrs Haigh to choose one from – to send her son in the condemned cell for his fortieth birthday. Mr Haigh Senior took refuge in trying to explain his son's behaviour as a result of a minor accident in which he had banged his head; it had been on a Friday, and all of Sonnie's crimes had been committed on a Friday. The whole family had lost touch with reality. The photos of Haigh taken during his trial show him smiling triumphantly. He behaved like Douglas Fairbanks Junior at a film première.

When the day came for him to be hanged, 10 August 1949, he was marched at high speed from the condemned cell to the execution shed and hanged immediately. From condemned cell to hanging in eleven seconds – almost record time.

Whether he was sane or insane, they could not hang Haigh fast enough.

Zosimo Montesino

a Mexican contract killer

IT IS UNUSUAL to find killers speaking freely about their murders. A 22-year-old Mexican said, 'I started killing for pure pleasure when I was eight years old. Then I learned that you could good money for killing, so I set myself up in business.' His first victim had been a witch who bewitched his parents by giving them a strange brew to drink. He went on and on killing, until he reached a body count of 150.

Zosimo Montesino worked with a gang. His main assistants or lieutenants were two brothers called Alcocer. Together they prepared an ambush outside the town of Tepalcingo. They were hired by a farmer to kill a politician called Mendoza Omana. Menoza came along, accompanied by his wife and three-year-old son. The father and son were shot out of hand. The mother, by chance, survived. She sobbed as she lay beside the body of her son, begging passing peasants to help her. They dared not interfere.

Some weeks later the assassins were arrested in a shanty town on the edge of Mexico City. They were undaunted by their capture, freely admitting to the huge number of murders they had committed. Zosimo admitted to his 150 killings, done for prices varying from £3 to £150. But a week later he said that his confession had been induced by torture, that he had only killed half a dozen people, and mostly in self-defence.

Whether the higher or the lower figure is nearer the truth, the Mexican assassin showed scant respect for human life. It is also truly alarming that he might kill any one of us – and for such a small sum. Mexico has a very high murder rate, the highest in the world. More people die as a result of homicide than of disease. Mexico is in an unstable, transitional state, halfway along the spectrum of economic development. In some 'primitive' societies there is a high level of kindness and co-operation: these are high-synergy societies. In others people are mean-spirited and self-centred: these are low-synergy societies. Mexico is in the process of changing from a high-synergy to a low-synergy society as it develops economically. It may nevertheless return to a high-synergy once its economic development has peaked.

When questioned by the police, Zosimo said he did not know what all the fuss was about. He knew people who had killed more. He named a police captain: he was a real mass murderer. Zosimo and one of his associates had killed the police captain. It had taken thirteen bullets to kill him because he was so fat. Unfortunately, what Zosimo said was probably true. The police became so overwhelmed by the rising wave of crime that they formed a special execution squad. Known gangsters were taken for a ride, after which their bullet-riddled bodies were dumped in places where they would attract attention. Inevitably the squad got out of hand and had to be wound up – by the police themselves.

Another Mexican assassin was Martin Rivera Benitez, who was nicknamed 'Big Soul'. In a rather similar way to Zosimo, Martin Benitez told the police in 1972, 'I cannot count the number of people I have killed for money. I am so famous that I often had a long waiting list. In order to prove that the job had been done properly I would cut off the head and show it to the man who had hired me.' Benitez set up his own mortuary in the woods. Twelve headless bodies were found there, rather confirming his account, but the twelve probably represent only a fraction of the number of people he killed between 1969 and 1972. The police think he killed over fifty people.

Benitez could not see anything wrong in killing for money; after all, if he had not agreed to do it, someone else would have done it instead. The ethos of the Mexican assassins is not unlike the moral code of the London gangland killers.

PART FIVE

TEAM KILLERS

William Burke &
William Hare

the body-snatchers

IN THE WEST Port of Edinburgh in a period of just over a year from October 1827 to December 1828, there was a string of murders that horrified the whole of Britain. Murderers are usually loners, as much as anything because the crime is a secret too terrible to share. The West Port murders were murders in cold blood and they were carried out in a careful and business-like way. William Burke and William Hare were, in effect, partners in business. Their business was killing people and selling their bodies for medical research. As in any partnership, there was a dominant partner. In this partnership it was William Burke.

Burke was born in 1792 in County Tyrone, of Catholic parents. He left home at eighteen to become a servant in the household of a gentleman not far from his parents' home. Unfortunately his employer died within the year, and Burke had to find new work; he decided to join the Donegal Militia. After that Burke married a respectable young woman in Ballina, by whom he had seven children; all of them died except one boy, who was alive at the time of Burke's trial.

There was a falling-out, after which Burke left his young family and moved to Scotland. He worked as a labourer digging canals. Then he met a woman by the name of Helen McDougal at Maddiston in Stirlingshire, and they set up home together. Later he drifted into Edinburgh with his common-law wife, and they made a living of sorts peddling old clothes, human hair, second hand shoes.

In 1827 Burke and McDougal met William Hare. Hare was a hideous man to look at, and especially hideous when he smiled. He ran a sort of hostel for beggars in Tanners Close, West Port; it was called Logs Lodging, after his wife's previous husband. It was in this appalling den of vice and drunkenness, and general disorderly behaviour, that Burke and Hare were to carry out their series of murders.

They made their beginning in their new trade – in corpses – when in December 1827 one of the lodgers at Logs Lodging died. He was a tall, fat man who had met an early death through drink and general dissipation. Hare was annoyed, because the man had died owing him money for rent. Now he would never get it, unless... His funeral was organized in a decorous way – a coffin and mourners, and so on – but Burke and Hare had the ingenious idea of substituting a sack of tan bark for the body. The sack was buried with due reverence, according to custom, and after the funeral Burke and Hare set about selling the body. They contacted the medical school to arrange the sale. When night fell, the lodger's body was carried in a sack by William Burke as far as Bristo Port; there he needed a rest and William Hare carried the sack the rest of the way, to the dissecting rooms of Dr Knox in Surgeons Square.

They were paid seven pounds ten shillings for the body. The medics were ready to pay handsomely for bodies, because the medical schools were flooded with students and there were never enough bodies for dissection; they had to rely on executed criminals and a few donated bodies. Seven pounds ten shillings was also a lot of money to poor people with few prospects and Burke and Hare were understandably very excited. Hare was particularly pleased because the sum was about twice what the dead man owed him. This success was to be the start of a hideous roller-coaster of greed, cruelty and random killings.

If they could get hold of another body they could earn as much again. Inevitably it was not long before they started discussing ways of killing people. Their first victim was an old woman from Gilmerton, who was seen on the streets the worse for drink. Hare enticed her back to his lodging with the promise of a warm drink and a rest before the remainder of her long journey home. He and Burke gave her a lot more alcohol to drink and she fell asleep, then the two of them pinned her down, covered her mouth and held her nose until she stopped breathing. This was the method of killing they used again and again, as it left few visible signs. The old woman's body was taken to Surgeons Square, where they were paid ten pounds. Dr Knox was very pleased to do business with Burke and Hare and offered them a deal. He would pay them eight pounds for each 'subject' in the summer session and ten pounds in the winter.

The next victim was an English packman or pedlar who was unwise enough to lodge in Hare's house of horrors. After this, it is hard to give a continuous narrative of events as neither Burke nor Hare kept any record of their business, which in the circumstances was wise, and they lacked curiosity about the names of their victims. There was nothing personal in their murders at all, which in itself puts them in an unusual category. But in all there seem to have been about sixteen murders. There was the old woman from Gilmerton, the English pedlar, Joe the miller, Mary Haldane and her daughter, an old Irish woman and her grandson, a cinder gatherer, another old woman, Mary Patterson, a countrywoman, the girl McDougal, Mrs Osler the washerwoman, Daft Jamie, a girl Hare murdered on his own and, finally, a woman called either Campbell or Docherty.

The inmates at the lodgings seemed to be unnaturally healthy, so again and again Burke and Hare had to go out and accost people in the street, and persuade them to accompany them back to Hare's house. It seems extraordinary that so many were ready to go, especially since Hare was frightening just to look at. All of their victims were unknowing and entirely innocent, but there is something particularly touching and pathetic about the old Irish woman and her grandson. The pair were picked up off the street in the usual way by Burke, who invited them back to the 'inn' for drinks. Burke and Hare killed the old woman without any scruple or hesitation at all, but they wavered before killing the boy. He was very young, deaf and very vulnerable. Even Burke and Hare hesitated before killing someone as helpless as this. But kill him they did. It is said that they broke his back over Burke's knee. This may be true, but it seems a very clumsy way to try to kill someone, and would not necessarily result in death anyway. Given the effectiveness of their normal stifling method of killing, it seems likely that the poor little boy was killed in the same way as the others. This way of killing, which was perfected by Burke and Hare, brought a new word to the English language. To 'burke' is to annihilate something by silently smothering it.

Soon they began to quarrel. Burke discovered that Hare was killing and cashing in without involving Burke at all. Burke was very angry and moved out of Hare's house. They nevertheless still needed the money and so continued to work together; they were no longer friends, but still business partners. Even friends of Burke who came to see him were mercilessly killed and sold.

The biggest mistake they made was to kill a young boy who was not only well known in the neighbourhood but well loved. This was Daft Jamie. Hare found him wandering the streets looking for his mother, and took him back to his house. The boy fought for his life, but Burke and Hare managed to overpower him in the end. Jamie's mother looked everywhere for him and, as a last resort, visited the medical school. There, she found him. It emerged that Burke and Hare were the people who had brought the boy's body in for dissection; they denied it, but the staff at the medical school confirmed that it had indeed been them. There was public outrage and consternation; it was obvious that the boy had been killed and that Burke and Hare were to blame. The police soon moved in.

It was the last murder which proved to be their undoing. An Irish lodger called Gray and his wife were looking for a stocking and discovered the body hidden under a bed and covered with straw. Gray reported the find to the police, who promptly arrested Burke and his partner McDougal, and Hare and his wife. In the run-up to the trial, an offer was made to Hare that, if he would give enough evidence to ensure a conviction for Burke, he would be allowed to go free. He readily agreed to this deal.

The trial took place on Christmas Eve, 1828 at the High Court of Justiciary in Edinburgh. Burke was found guilty and condemned to death on Hare's evidence. Both his wife and Helen McDougal were given their freedom. The trial caused a sensation. Huge crowds converged on the Court and Parliament Square. The execution of William Burke, on 28 January 1829, pulled in even bigger crowds. It was estimated that there may have been as many as forty thousand people at the execution. Among the many boos and shouts of this huge mob, one voice could be heard crying out, 'You will see Daft Jamie soon!' The hanging took place at the top of Libertons Wynd, not far from Hare's appalling lodging house.

Those who were there that day never forgot the spectacle of William Burke's hanging. Many of the people in the crowd of spectators had assembled as early as two in the morning, in the cold and the rain, to be sure of getting a place with a good view. The whole event was more like a big public holiday, an occasion of rejoicing and celebration. It was not only the working classes who were there, either; many a fine lady in her Sunday-best could be seen at the windows of the buildings overlooking the spot. Long before the execution, the whole area was full of people. The Lawnmarket, High Street, County Buildings, the Bow – all were a solid mass of humanity. Unusually, there was not a spark of sympathy for the condemned man. When the workmen finally finished building the scaffold, after working on it all night long, a great roaring cheer went up that was heard for miles around.

When the clock of St Giles struck eight, the hour of the execution, the crowd fell silent. William Burke was led out with his confessor and Williams the executioner. His appearance was greeted with various shouts and remarks. After the execution was over, Burke's body was cut down and handed over to Professor Munro for dissection; in other words he was sent off to join his victims. When a public hanging was over, it was usual for people to disperse hurriedly and quietly, as if half-ashamed of having been there. Not so today. A feeling a of sweet revenge had swept across the crowd. There was a fear that the mob might try to get hold of Burke's body and degrade it in some way, so it was removed to the dissecting room.

The following day, many scientists and students crushed in to have a close look at Burke's body. Some of them made sketches of it. The body became the subject of a lecture on the brain, so Burke's head was sawn open to show what his brain looked like. The orderly anatomy lecture was soon interrupted by a crowd gathering outside, wanting to be let in. Stones were thrown and windows were broken. In the end the authorities had to intervene and allow members of the public to come in, huge numbers of them, fifty at a time, to view the corpse. This was a completely unprecedented exhibition of a corpse.

Some of the medical students succeeded in making off with trophies – parts of William Burke. They had pieces of his skin tanned. Someone bound a pocket-book in Burke's skin. It was dark, just like leather, and stamped in gold: 'Burkes Skin, 1829'.

The only murmur of discontent was the general feeling that Hare should not have been set free. There was an attempt to bring a second action against him, by

Mrs Wilson, the mother of Daft Jamie. After a long debate, it was thrown out and William Hare was declared a free man. But what sort of freedom was this – to walk out into the streets of Edinburgh and been torn to pieces by the mob? As in the more recent case of Maxine Carr, the authorities gave him the chance of escaping, creating a new identity and a new life. Now called Mr Black, Hare was taken one February night to the Old Post Office, Waterloo Bridge, and put on the mail-coach for Dumfries. From there he would continue into England, where no-one would recognize him. Once there, the sinister Mr Black would wander, like Cain, until time forgot him.

What became of William Hare is not known for certain, though there has been no shortage of speculation and surmise about his later life. He is said to have died penniless in London in 1859.

Mrs Hare, like her husband, was liberated, but barely escaped the wrath of a lynch-mob. She eventually reached Glasgow, where she boarded a ship, the Clyde steamship Fingal, that took her back to her native Ireland. Less is known of Helen McDougal. When she was released, she foolishly went back to her West Port haunts, where she was recognized and mobbed. She only escaped thanks to a ladder placed against a back window of the house. Some time later she turned up in the village of Redding. It is alleged that she eventually died in a house fire in New South Wales.

But what of the doctor who gave Burke and Hare

money and, in effect, bribed them to commit murder? Dr Knox must have known the bodies were murder victims, which made him an accessory after the fact, and yet he was never charged with any offence at all. He was even allowed to continue in his job at the medical school. But there was a cloud hanging over Robert Knox. The scandal would not die down. He went unpunished, but he was never forgiven by the community for what he had done. He applied for other posts but was rejected for all of them. He eventually went to work in a cancer research institute.

Ian Brady &
Myra Hindley

the Moors murderers

THERE ARE SOME murders which capture the imagination like no others, some that horrify like no others. There are some serial killers who inspire a particular revulsion like no others. It has little or nothing to do with the numbers of people they kill, but with the manner of the killing, the circumstances, the callous betrayal of trust. The recent Ian Huntley murders at Soham are a good example of a crime that inspired widespread revulsion. In the 1960s, it was the Moors murders. There were, to be honest, not many deaths, compared to many of the other serial killings investigated in this book – a mere five victims, which is a small number compared with the seventy that Tommy Sells is thought to have killed. But it is Ian Brady and Myra Hindley that we remember – not Tommy Sells.

These, in chronological order, are the known victims of Ian Brady and Myra Hindley;

Pauline Reade, 16 (murdered July 1963)
John Kilbride, 12 (murdered Nov 1963)

Keith Bennett, 12 (murdered June 1964)
Lesley Ann Downey, 10 (murdered Dec 1964)
Edward Evans, 17 (murdered Oct 1965)

One of the Moors murderers' victims was a ten-year-old girl, Lesley Ann Downey, who vanished on Boxing Day in 1964 after going to a funfair with her friends. The disappearance, and presumed death, of the little girl was hard enough for her mother to bear. But ten months later, when the full truth of what had happened to her little girl came to light, it was too much for her to endure. Mrs Ann West, Lesley's mother, found that her daughter had been abducted by a pair of total strangers, Ian Brady and Myra Hindley, and then, for no other reason than the pleasure of seeing her suffer, slowly tortured to death. The police found an audio tape of the girl screaming and pleading for her life. They wanted to be sure that the girl on the tape really was Lesley and – it is now hard to believe that they did this very cruel thing – they played the tape to Ann West.

Mrs West recognized that it was indeed her daughter on the tape. The screams stayed with her for the rest of her life, which was completely taken over with grief, anger and frustration over what happened both then and later. There were do-gooding liberals like Lord Longford who went on arguing that Myra Hindley was a changed woman, and should be let out of prison. Ann West was distraught at this recurring prospect. As far as she was concerned, a comfortable life in prison was far too soft a punishment for such a wicked act. She campaigned for years against the soft treatment the two killers were getting, and against the prospect of their release. For years, Ann West had to take valium to help her sleep and drive away the nightmares. She was overwhelmed by the stress and developed cancer in her breasts, ovaries, bowels and liver – and the cancer eventually killed her in 1999. Lesley was tortured to death by Myra Hindley and Ian Brady. So too was Ann, over a period of 35 years. Ann West was as much a victim of Hindley and Brady as any of those whose bodies were buried up on the Moors in the 1960s.

In Britain, a 'life sentence' usually does not mean that the convicted prisoner has to spend the rest of his or her life in prison. Usually it means spending only 12 years in prison; that is the average actual term served. Many people shared Ann West's view that 12 years was not long enough in relation to the horrific crimes committed. Quite apart from the question of whether 12 years was a severe enough punishment, many people felt that it was simply not safe to let such people out into the world where they might commit further horrific crimes.

This view was voiced with ever-greater vehemence as Hindley, in particular, began to lobby for parole. Brady seems not to have entertained the delusion that he could walk free; he has rather expressed the wish to be allowed to die. Public pressure about Hindley's case especially eventually produced a response from the

Home Office. In certain cases – and they were named – a life sentence really had to mean life. David Blunkett maintained that Hindley and Brady were members of a small group of offenders who could never be released. Rosemary West is another serial killer who can never be released. Above all else, the community at large has to be kept safe from such predatory monsters.

Brady and Hindley were hated for their crimes, and this hatred was exaggerated by their behaviour during their trial and subsequently in prison. The two personalities separately were very inadequate. Together, they were lethal. There was a terrifying physical and psychological reaction between them, which made them incredibly dangerous, in much the same way as Fred and Rose West. It is a reaction sometimes described as folie à deux – a joint madness that makes two people acting together commit crimes they would never contemplate had they been on their own. In fact it seems likely that in the case of Hindley and Brady neither partner would have been capable of murder if it had not been for the stimulus of the other. As Colin Wilson has said, 'Some strange chemical reaction seems to take place, like a mixture of nitric acid and glycerine that makes nitroglycerine.'

Ian Brady was Glaswegian by birth. He worked in Manchester as a stock clerk for a living. He was a quiet, brooding character who admired the Nazis, Nietzsche and the Marquis de Sade. It was a black day when the firm where he worked, Millwards Merchandisers in

Manchester, took on a new secretary in the form of Myra Hindley. Myra fancied Ian for a long time before he responded to her. He seems to have been one of life's loners, but he allowed himself to be 'adopted' by Myra.

When they became lovers, the dynamics of the relationship shifted, and Brady dominated her. She would listen captivated while he ranted about Nazis and Nietzsche. She changed the way she dressed to please him. She eventually agreed to join him in a murder spree too.

In later years, when she was trapped in prison, she tried to make out that she was a reformed character, a new woman, in fact not at all the woman who had done those terrible things – anything, really, to get parole. From early on she made out that it was Brady who made all the decisions, that she was a gullible, easily-led and easily-manipulated young woman. She had simply been unlucky, at the age of 19, to fall under the spell of such an evil man. But she was a very manipulative character and it has always been easy to see the ulterior motive behind these protestations. And there is the tape, the awful audio tape. The tone of her voice on that tape is harsh and cruel. Ian Brady himself claimed that Myra Hindley insisted on strangling Lesley Ann Downey herself and that Myra enjoyed toying in public places with the silk cord she had used to kill the little girl. Hindley was very far from being a passive and manipulated accomplice. She was at the very least an equal partner in evil.

The Brady-Hindley killings began in 1963. On 12 July that year Myra Hindley lured Pauline Reade into her car as the 16-year-old girl walked to a dance at a club in Manchester. Brady's version of events is different from Hindley's. According to Brady, Hindley persuaded Pauline to go with them up onto Saddleworth Moor to help her find an expensive glove she had lost up there. In return she would be given a stack of records. When they reached the moor they met Brady, who had ridden there on his motorbike. Then, depending on whose account you want to believe, Pauline was taken off to a remote spot well away from the road either by Brady alone or by both of them. Then she was raped, beaten and stabbed to death before being buried.

This ritual was repeated with variations at six month intervals. On later occasions they picked up a 12-year-old boy, John Kilbride, at a market in Ashton-under-Lyne, then another 12-year-old boy, Keith Bennett, as he walked to his grandmother's home in Longsight. Then they murdered Lesley. On each successive occasion, the process was drawn out longer, protracting the sadistic pleasure for themselves, protracting the fear and the suffering for their victims. They went to the lengths of making audio tapes of what they were doing. They also took pornographic photographs of Lesley, which were later found by the police in a luggage locker at Manchester Central Station.

The elaboration of the killing technique reached a point where Hindley and Brady wanted to involve a third participant. They invited a third person to join their killing club. This was, for them, a fatal mistake.

Brady saw Myra's brother-in-law, David Smith, as a potential partner in crime. Brady had been grooming him for some months and felt sure he could trust the 17-year-old with their terrible secret and get him to join in. Brady miscalculated badly. It was, all things considered, unlikely that he would find a third person to join him and Hindley in the enterprise. How many people would there be in the Greater Manchester area who would want to do the things they did? How many people with that particular strain of madness or wickedness? Would there have been any others at all?

But at the time, Brady was sure he had successfully brainwashed the boy. David Smith was writing in his diary such things as, 'Rape is not a crime, it is a state of mind. Murder is a hobby and a supreme pleasure.' He was an impressionable teenager, easily influenced by an older male whom he wanted to impress; he didn't really mean the things he wrote.

Suddenly the mere words became actions, and for David Smith that changed everything. On 6 October 1965, David Smith called at Brady and Hindley's house, 16 Wardle Brook Avenue in Hattersley. He went in and witnessed Ian Brady chopping Edward Evans, another 17-year-old, to death with an axe. It is very hard to imagine what that experience would have been like for the young Smith; presumably he was too stunned and frightened to react much at all. Edward

Evans was a total stranger, whom Brady had met and picked up earlier in the evening at a pub. David Smith was paralyzed with horror at what he saw happening. Fearing for his own life, he agreed to help Brady take the body upstairs to hide it in one of the bedrooms. Brady and Hindley laughed and joked as the three of them manhandled the bleeding corpse upstairs, making jocular remarks like, 'He's a dead weight'. Brady and Hindley were entertaining each other by remembering 'the look on his face', when Brady started raining axe blows on his shoulders. David Smith tried to join in as best he could, and did his best to convince them that he would keep quiet about what had happened. Above all he wanted to get out of that house alive.

Deeply shaken, David Smith went back home and told his wife, Myra's sister, everything that had happened. She persuaded him that the only thing he could do was to call the police. And that was how the killing was stopped. The following morning the police visited Brady's house. Brady and Hindley were arrested on suspicion, and the body of Edward Evans was found upstairs. Brady was charged with murder straight away. Hindley, even then, was expert at playing dumb, but four days later the police found a 'murder plan' in her car, implicating her very strongly in the murder or, as it now seemed, murders. She too was charged with murder.

Smith was able to tell the police that Hindley and Brady had boasted about killing other youngsters and burying them up on the moors. The police swung into action, organizing a huge search of Saddleworth Moor. During the following fortnight they found the bodies of Lesley Ann Downey and John Kilbride. The police had strong suspicions that Hindley and Brady had killed Pauline Reade and Keith Bennett, but they were unable to find their bodies and there was no specific evidence against them

In April 1966 Hindley and Brady went on trial at Chester Assizes, charged with three counts of murder. They both denied everything and tried, rather foolishly, to push the blame onto the 17-year-old David Smith. The jury saw through this wriggling and found Brady guilty of all three murders and Hindley guilty of two; in addition she was found guilty of harbouring Brady in relation to the John Kilbride murder. The sentence on both was 'life' and the dangerous possibility of release in 12 years was foreseen, so the judge recommended a minimum of 30 years in prison.

The strange and sordid love Ian Brady and Myra Hindley had for each other remained strong to begin with. They even asked for permission to marry, though this was refused. As the years passed, they drifted apart. Brady came to terms with his guilt, accepting it and not trying to excuse himself. Hindley continued to develop the theme that she had been innocent, gullible and easily-led. In order to take this line, of course, she needed to make Brady totally to blame for the murders. In 1970, she broke off all contact with him as part of her campaign of self-vindication. In 1977, she launched a campaign to get herself released; she was greatly encouraged in this by Lord Longford.

Hindley began to realise that while there were unsolved murders and unanswered questions about the graves of Pauline Reade and Keith Bennett she did not look totally repentant. In order to look something like a candidate for parole, she had to come clean about the other murders and give details of the whereabouts of the bodies. In 1986, she did this. In July 1987 police investigators went up onto Saddleworth Moor once more, and found the remains of Pauline Reade.

Hindley's supporters argued that this showed she had repented. He opponents argued that this showed how manipulative she was. She had known all along where the bodies were but had refused to co-operate; she was only co-operating now because she wanted parole – and release in 1996 at the latest. She had left all this twenty years too late. In any case the 30 years was not a maximum tariff: it was a minimum tariff. The Home Office felt it was appropriate to make it clear that Hindley would never be released, and this has been adhered to by successive Conservative and Labour Home Secretaries.

The situation eventually resolved itself. Myra Hindley's health deteriorated sharply, probably as a result of habitual heavy smoking. She died in November 2002 from a chest infection following a heart attack.

Brady is regarded as a monster, but Hindley is regarded as something worse. The fact that she was a woman made what she did even worse. It was Hindley who enticed the children into the car, Hindley who drove the car up onto the moors. Brady could not drive. Brady could not have committed the murders without Hindley's positive, active, practical participation.

Charles Manson

The Family

CHARLES MANSON WAS the self-style guru and leader of a 1960s religious cult that called itself The Family.

Charles Manson started life very differently; he was unplanned, illegitimate and unwanted. He was born on 12 November 1934 in Cincinnati, Ohio. His mother, Kathleen Maddox, was a drunken promiscuous 16-year-old who got herself into a great deal of trouble. In 1936, Kathleen filed a suit against Colonel Scott of Ashland in Kentucky for child support. She won her case but still never received any child support. Kathleen married William Manson, for a short time, and the boy was given his surname.

Kathleen Manson was the youngest of Nancy and Charles Maddox's three children. They were very fond of her, but indoctrinated her with their fanatical religious beliefs. The grandmother dominated the household and behaved like an Old Testament prophet, interpreting God's will with a flaming sword and demanding that all beneath her roof should abide by it. In 1933, at the age of fifteen, Kathleen could not stand any more and ran away from this suffocating home environment.

Charlie did not know his natural father at all and never had a father-substitute figure either. His mother was a broken reed, the kind of woman whose children are taken from and put into care. Kathleen disappeared for days or weeks at a time, leaving Charlie in the care of the grandmother or an aunt. Kathleen and her brother were imprisoned for armed robbery, and then Charlie was sent to live with an aunt and uncle in West Virginia. Once again, the aunt was religious and strict, and there was too stark a contrast with Kathleen's way of doing things. When Kathleen came out of prison she was unable to look after Charlie, and this made him more isolated than ever. He had in effect no parents and no friends either. He withdrew into a world of make-believe. He also started to steal.

When Charlie Manson was nine years old he was caught stealing and sent to a reform school. Three years later the same thing happened and he was sent to the Gibault School for Boys in Terre Haute in Indiana. This was in 1947. He ran away after about a year and tried to rejoin his mother, but she did not want him. He had to live, on his own, entirely by stealing and burglary. He was caught and sent to Father Flanagan's Boys Town. That did not last very long, as only a matter of days after arriving there he and another boy committed two armed robberies. There were more incidents of this kind, landing Charlie Manson in the Indiana School for Boys for three years.

In 1951, Charlie and two other boys escaped from the reform school and decided that they would try their fortunes in California. They would live entirely by burglary and theft; in particular they would steal cars. In Utah, he was caught and sent to the National Training School for Boys in Washington DC. He was subjected to various tests, which established that he was illiterate, which was not at all surprising, that his IQ was 109 and that his aptitudes in most areas were average.

Charlie was also examined by a psychiatrist, Dr Block, who was concerned by the 'marked degree of rejection, instability and psychic trauma'. He was a very insecure person, partly because of his small build, his illegitimacy, lack of parenting, lack of parental love; as a result he became very competitive, striving to improve (and prove) his status in relation to the other boys. For a while it looked as if things would improve, when his aunt agreed to take care of him again and the chances of getting parole were good. But then, just before the parole hearing, Charlie sodomized another boy while holding a razor to his throat.

Charlie was sent next to the Federal Reformatory at Petersburg in Virginia, where he was described as homosexual, dangerous and safe only under supervision. From September 1952, Charlie Manson's attitude change and he became more co-operative; educationally he started to make significant progress. By May 1954 he was released on parole. He was now 19.

For a time he lived with his aunt, then with his

mother, then in 1955 he married a waitress. She gave birth to a son, Charles Manson Jr. Charlie held down various low-paid jobs and supplemented his income by stealing cars. He was caught and sent to prison in San Pedro, California. After he been in prison three years, his wife divorced him. In 1958 Manson was out on parole. This time he took up pimping. He also took money from an unattractive but rich girl in Pasadena. Within the year he was in trouble with the law again, arrested for stealing a cheque and attempting to cash a stolen cheque. He was sentenced to ten years but then the judge relented and put him on probation. But he abused this kindness by re-offending.

It was only a matter of weeks later that he was arrested by the Los Angeles Police Department for stealing cars and credit cards. These charges had to be dropped for lack of evidence. It was a never-ending cycle of crime, punishment and re-offending.

Manson took to studying religious philosophies. As Kingsley Amis once said, it is a sure sign that someone has lost the plot when they start taking an interest in comparative religion. Religion? Maybe. Comparative religion? Definitely not. Manson dabbled in Scientology and Buddhism. He also had an obsession with the Beatles. He felt that if had the right opportunities he could be much bigger than the Beatles. While he was in prison, he befriended the gangster Alvin Karpis, then the sole survivor of the Ma Barker Gang, who taught Manson how to play the steel guitar.

When he was released, Charlie Manson was very frightened. 'I knew that I couldn't adjust to that world, not after all my life had been spent locked up and where my mind was free. I was content to stay in the penitentiary.' But he was released just the same. He did not adjust, but he did blend in with the hippy scene in San Francisco at that time. With his drop-out lifestyle and his guitar playing, he fitted into it quite well. The hippies taught him about drugs and how he could use them to influence other people.

Charlie Manson started to attract a group of followers, many of whom were girls with emotional problems and who were rebelling against society in general and their parents in particular. He broke down their inhibitions, questioned their ideas on the difference between good and evil. Most of Manson's followers were gullible, weak people who wanted someone to tell them what to think as well as what to do. Manson used LSD and amphetamines to change their personalities.

In the spring of 1968, Manson and his followers left San Francisco in an old bus. Eventually some of them moved in with Gary Hinman, a music teacher. Through Hinman, Manson was able to meet Dennis Wilson of the Beach Boys. Manson and his groupies started hanging round Wilson, but it was not long before Wilson became uncomfortable with Manson and asked him to leave. They then moved onto a ranch owned by an old man. Manson persuaded him to let them stay by offering him sex whenever he wanted it with one of his followers. Charlie Manson and The Family, as they began to call themselves, lived by a combination of stealing and scavenging; they found that supermarkets threw away quite a lot of food each day, so they helped themselves to it.

The bearded figure of Manson became a persuasive and charismatic leader. He discovered he could get his followers to do anything he liked. This was the challenge. He decided to test his followers by goading them into committing some atrocious murders. He imagined that these serial killings would spark a race war and that at the end of this war there would be only himself, The Family and some black slaves left. It was weird fantasy. He persuaded his followers to believe that he was Jesus Christ, growing his hair and beard in order to make his image fit the fantasy. Another, parallel, idea was that he was 'the fifth angel' – the other four being Paul McCartney, George Harrison, John Lennon and Ringo Starr.

Manson was still determined to make a career in music and used his contacts with Dennis Wilson. He had a plan to interest Doris Day's son, Terry Melcher, in financing a film using Manson's music. At the time, Melcher owned a house on Cielo Drive; it would eventually be leased to Roman Polanski and Sharon Tate. Melcher was invited to listen to some of Manson's music, which he did. He listened to Charlie singing his own musical compositions and playing the guitar; some of the girls sang too and played tambourines. Melcher listened carefully and even made a second visit, but decided that he had no interest in financing the project. What Terry Melcher did not realise was that Manson had staked everything, emotionally, on this one opening, this one contact with the music business. Charlie Manson was very angry that he had been rebuffed in this way, and blamed Melcher for disappointing him.

Side by side with the music, Charlie Manson worked on a set of religious beliefs to impress The Family. They involved a kind of Final Reckoning, the Last Things, an Armageddon that would involve a race war. The blacks would rise up and slaughter the whites. In 1968, the Beatles released their White Album, which included the track Helter Skelter. The lyrics suited Charlie's Armageddon scenario, so Charlie decided to call his Armageddon 'Helter Skelter'. Helter Skelter would begin in 1969, and that was when black people would start stealing from and killing white people. But Armageddon did not break loose in 1969, and Manson told his followers that the blacks would not know what they had to do unless the whites showed them. They, The Family, would need to initiate the killings.

Manson was never to be charged with murder. Instead he was imprisoned for ordering others to murder. Among the victims were Sharon Tate, a young movie star and former beauty queen who had the misfortune to be renting the house that Terry Melcher owned, Abigail Folger, heiress to a coffee fortune, and Jay Sebring, a hairdresser. Sharon Tate was eight months pregnant when she was murdered, so it was a particularly horrible and repulsive act. Several others too were killed by The Family acting under Manson's direct orders.

It was in the quiet and secluded valleys above Beverley Hills on 9 August 1969 that the Sharon Tate killings took place. Sharon Tate was missing her husband, the film director Roman Polanski, who was in Europe working on a film. She was a former beauty queen who had become a film actress. Her first big success had been in The Eye of the Devil with David Niven and Deborah Kerr. It had been while she was in London in 1966 for the filming of The Eye of the Devil that she had met Polanski, who cast her as the lead actress in his film The Fearless Vampire Killers and also in the role of Jennifer in Valley of the Dolls. It was only in 1969, the year in which she was to die, that they rented the house in Cielo Drive from Terry Melcher, Doris Day's son.

One the fateful August night, Sharon Tate was entertaining some friends in her home. They included the well-known hair stylist Jay Sebring, who was 36, Abigail Folger, a 25-year-old coffee heiress, and Abigail Folger's 32-year-old boyfriend Voytek Frykowski. It was a happy little gathering, with no apprehension, no prior warning that anything unpleasant was about to happen.

Winifred Chapman, Tate's housekeeper, noticed some unusual things when she arrived at the house at

8.00 in the morning. A fallen telephone wire was draped across the gate. There was an unfamiliar white Rambler parked in the driveway. The front door was open. Then she saw that there were splashed of blood everywhere. There was a body on the lawn. She screamed and ran through the house and down the driveway; on the way she noticed there was another body slumped in the car.

When the police arrived, they found two bodies on the lawn, not one. There was a young woman in a nightgown with multiple stab wounds and a man in his thirties whose face had been battered. His body was punctured with dozens of stab wounds. Later they were identified as Folger and Frykowski.

Unnerved, the police approached the house itself cautiously. They saw the word 'PIG' scrawled in blood on the front door, In the living room, they found the body of a heavily pregnant young woman lying on the floor, smeared with blood. There was a rope round her neck, which passed up over a rafter; attached to the other end was the body of a man, also drenched in blood. These two were later identified as Sharon Tate and Jay Sebring.

On the same night as Sharon Tate's ill-fated dinner party, two people arrived home from holiday in another district of Los Angeles. They were Leno and Rosemary LaBianca. Their home was 3301 Waverly Drive, in the Los Feliz district. The Family evidently finished their appalling massacre at Sharon Tate's house and then went straight to the LaBianca home, apparently choosing the house at random. The following day, Leno LaBianca was found dead with a pillow over his head, a cord round his neck and a carving fork sticking out of his stomach. The word 'WAR' had been cut into his flesh.

Los Angeles Police Department officers found Leno's wife in the master bedroom with a pillowcase over her head, a lamp cord tightly tied round her neck, and 41 stab wounds. As at the Tate house, there was writing in blood on the walls: 'DEATH TO PIGS', 'RISE', and on the refrigerator door 'HELTER SKELTER'.

The police were at a loss to understand what was happening. The murders were following a pattern, but had no obvious meaning or motive.

Then the case took a new turn when a woman awaiting trial for murder in an LA prison made a chilling confession. She was Susan Atkins. She was to be tried for an unrelated murder, but confessed freely to her cellmate her involvement in the Sharon Tate murders. Atkins seemed to be in a state of ecstasy, singing and dancing as she told how her lover Charles Manson was Jesus Christ and he was going to lead her to a hole in Death Valley where there was a secret civilization. Some people will believe anything, it seems. The cellmate must have been even more alarmed when Atkins described the Tate murders. Three girls and a man had done the killings, acting under Manson's instructions. She said they had chosen the Tate mansion because it was isolated and because they 'wanted to do a crime that would shock the world would have to stand up and take notice [of]'. Atkins confessions included the LaBianca killings too.

Atkins said there were several more celebrities on The Family's death list. She had planned to cut the words 'helter skelter' on the face of Elizabeth Taylor with a red-hot knife, and then gouge her eyes out. She planned to cut off Richard Burton's penis and send it in a bottle, along with Elizabeth Taylor's eyes, to Eddie Fisher. Frank Sinatra was to be skinned alive while being made to listen to his own records (the ultimate in torture). The Family was going to make purses out of Sinatra's skin and sell them in hippie shops. Tom Jones was to have his throat cut after being forced to have sex with Atkins.

It all sounded too mad to be true. Fortunately, the police had received some clues that The Manson Family might be involved from some other sources, including a member of a motorcycle gang called the Straight Satans, so they were readier to believe Atkins macabre confessions than they might have been. Even so, it was not until November 1969, three months after the murders, that they got round to interviewing Atkins' cellmate.

The case for the prosecution was not well founded. There was a shortage of evidence against Manson and The Family, but as the trial progressed it became obvious from the way Manson and his followers behaved that they were guilty. A small amount of forensic evidence pointed to The Family. A bloody fingerprint on the wall of Tate's house belonged to one of The Family.

Manson and Atkins stood trial together with two other cult members, Patricia Krenwinkel and Leslie Van Houten. Atkins showed no remorse during the trial, and happily repeated the story she had related in the cell for the benefit of the stunned jury.

Some apologists for Manson have said that Manson never killed anybody, but at least one criminologist believes he was at the murder scene, actively tying the victims up and ordering his followers to do the killing. Evidently, Manson's idea was to have the others commit the murders, so that he would not face a murder charge himself. The followers were indoctrinated to accept all the blame themselves and during the trial they told bizarre stories that were designed to incriminate them and divert attention away from Manson. Whenever any testimony emerged that might damage Manson, Manson himself created a diversion. On one occasion he lunged at the judge, yelling, 'Someone should cut your head off!' At this, Atkins, Krenwinkel and Van Houten started chanting loudly in Latin.

The trial of Charles Manson dragged on for an incredible 22 weeks. Then the judge called on the defence to present its case. The defence counsel replied disarmingly, 'Thank you, your Honour; the defendants rest'. There was no defence case. Then the three female defendants shouted that they wanted to testify that they planned and carried out the murder themselves, that Manson had nothing to do with it. At this, Van Houten's lawyer, Ronald Hughes, made a formal objection.

Because he was by implication wanting to spread blame from his client to Manson, he was to become the cult's next victim. A few days later, Mr Hughes disappeared, and his body was found wedged between boulders.

On 15 January 1971, the trial dragged to its close, seven months after it began. The jury left to consider a verdict. It took nine days to find all the defendants guilty of murder and conspiracy to murder. The recommendation was for the death penalty. At this, the female defendants, who had shaved their heads, threatened to have the jurors killed.

The trial of the fourth suspect in the tate and LaBianca killings was delayed. Charles 'Tex' Watson had left the state and there were extradition procedures to go through. He was tried and found guilty later in 1971. Later still, more Family members were brought to trial for some more cult murders, the killing of Gary Hinman and Donald Shea.

These are the innocent people The Family cruelly murdered;

Sharon Tate, 26
Abigail Folger, 25
Voyek Fykowski, 32
Jay Sebring, 36
Steve Parent, 18
Rosemary LaBianca, 38
Leno LaBianca, 44
Ronald Hughes, 36

George Spahn, 85
Gary Hinman, 34
Donald Shea, 36

In 1972, the California Supreme Court abolished the death penalty throughout the state, so all the death sentences were commuted to life sentences.

Manson exploited the immaturity and character flaws of his followers, providing them with the father figure he never had. He may in fact have got things so badly wrong simply because he had had no parenting himself. There was a lot of normal growing up that he missed. His idea of a patriarch was very wide of the mark by any adult standard, He even told some of his followers he was Jesus.

Members of the Manson Family appeared at his trial and when they did they behaved in a peculiar way, such as imitating his actions in the court room. At one moment during the trial, Manson cut a cross into his forehead. The girls did the same.

Immediately after the trial, which highlighted the sadistic cruelty that Sharon Tate and the other victims were subjected to, there was a rather surprising reaction. There were articles published that were favourable to Manson and The Family; it seemed that some observers had been hypnotized by Manson's charismatic 'act' and been turned into followers. There was a danger that Manson might even turn into some kind of cult hero. Fortunately that did not happen. Little now remains now of the Manson Family. But it is a sad fact that Charles Manson still gets a lot of mail, largely from young people desperate for a cause. Any cause will do, even a bad one.

Manson remains a fairly passive, well-behaved prisoner in Corcoran State Prison. It seems unlikely that he will ever be given parole. He may not be dangerous in person, but what he represents is extremely dangerous, that special someone that so many weak, morally and spiritually disaffected extremists, from Satanists to neo-Nazis, are on the look-out for – that special someone to lead them to Heaven or Hell.

Kenneth Bianchi &
Angelo Buono

'the Hillside Strangler'

ON 20 NOVEMBER 1977 some hikers found the naked body of Kristina Weckler on a hillside near Glendale in California. She had been sexually assaulted. On the same day, the bodies of two more women were found in the same hilly area. Over the course of the following four months, the police discovered ten more victims in the same Glendale area.

The Los Angeles Police Department, the Sheriff's Department and the Glendale Police assumed from the start that more than one person was involved in these killings. It was the media that created the singular nickname – 'the Hillside Strangler'.

After an intensive investigation, the police charged two cousins, Kenneth Bianchi and Angelo Buono, with all of these brutal murders. Bianchi had by this stage fled to Washington state, where he was quickly in very big trouble for committing similar crimes there. Specifically, he had raped and murdered two women he had lured to his home in Washington. His initial response when charged was to claim that he had committed the crimes in an altered unconscious state, and that he suffered from multiple personalities. Then he agreed to give evidence against his cousin.

Kenneth Bianchi left Rochester in 1975, when he was 26, and went to live in Los Angeles. At first he lived with his older cousin Angelo Buono. Several young women lived in the same apartment block. One of them was Kristina Weckler. She resisted his advances, though others were more receptive. He moved in with Kelli Boyd, a woman he had met at work. In May 1977 she told him she was expecting his child. Kenneth had set himself up as a psychologist, though he had no qualifications or credentials. Luckily, very few people went to him for counselling, and Kelli was angry about the scheme.

Kelli became increasingly dissatisfied with her relationship with Kenneth. Often she went off to stay with her brother, but kept returning. The baby, Sean, was born in February and for a while the relationship between Kenneth and Kelli was better.

The police released a photo of Bianchi to the media and got a call from David Wood, a lawyer. Wood had rescued one of two girls, Sabra Hannan and Becky Spears, from Bianchi and his cousin Angelo Buono, who had forced the two young women into prostitution by threatening them with violence.

Angelo Buono was an unprepossessing man, physically, intellectually and emotionally. He was coarse and vulgar and very successful with women. He had been married several times and had several children; he abused all of them physically and some of them sexually as well. He could occasionally treat women decently, mainly in order to have sex, but he had a deep-seated loathing of women and a desire to humiliate and wound them. Even as a 14-year-old boy he used to boast about raping and sodomizing girls.

But, for some reason, he was attractive to teenage girls – perhaps because of his overwhelming self-confidence.

In 1975, when cousin Kenneth (Kenny) turned up, he found an ageing Angelo, with dyed black hair, his neck hung with gold chains, a big gaudy ring on his finger and surrounded by a string of under-age girls. When Kenny was short of cash, Angelo came up with the idea of getting some of the girls to work for them as prostitutes. Two teenage runaways, Becky Spears and Sabra Hannan, fell under their control; they were forced into prostitution under threat of severe physical punishment. Becky met David Wood, a lawyer, who was horrified at the situation she found herself in, and arranged for her to escape. When Angelo realised what Wood had done, he threatened him. Wood reacted by sending one of his clients, a very big man, to persuade Angelo not to threaten Wood any more. That seemed to work; it was the sort of persuasion Buono understood.

Seeing that Becky had been able to escape, Sabra also ran away shortly afterwards. With the consequent drop in income, Kenny missed payments on his car, which was repossessed. Obviously they had to find more teenage girls. They impersonated policemen and tried to abduct a girl. Then they discovered she was Catherine Lorre, the daughter of the film actor Peter Lorre, and let her go. But eventually they found a suitable girl and installed her in Sabra's room.

They also bought from a prostitute called Deborah Noble a list of potential clients for prostitutes – a 'trick list'. Deborah and her friend Yolanda Washington delivered the trick list to Angelo in October 1977. Yolanda mentioned that she worked a certain stretch of Sunset Boulevard. Angelo and Kenny discovered that the trick list was fake or out of date; they couldn't get at Deborah, because they simply didn't know how to find her, but they knew where Yolanda worked because she had told them. So they punished her instead. She became one of their hillside victims.

Kenny was locked up in the Whatcom County Jail in Bellingham for long enough to think up a way out of the murder charges against him. He persuaded the lawyer appointed by the court to represent him, Dean Brett, that he was suffering from amnesia. Brett became convinced that Kenny might try to commit suicide and had a psychiatric social worker come in to counsel Kenny.

The District Attorney's Office offered Kenny a deal. If he pleaded guilty to the Washington murders and some of the Hillside Strangler murders, he would get life with the possibility of parole. He would also be allowed to serve his prison sentence in California, where the prisons were more humane than in Washington. In return for these favours, Kenny Bianchi would have to give evidence against Angelo Buono. The choice was not marvellous. It was a choice between death in Washington and life in California. Kenny agreed. It would not be possible to convict merely on the evidence of an accomplice, but if the accomplice's evidence was supported by other evidence a conviction was possible.

Kenny described how he and his cousin had pretended to be policemen, using fake badges to persuade girls to get into their car. The prostitutes went along with them surprisingly easily, they found, but it was much harder to get girls who were not prostitutes to get into the car. The investigator asked Kenny what sort of material they had used to blindfold Judy Miller. Kenny thought it was a piece of foam Angelo used in his upholstery business. The police had in fact found some fluff on the dead girl's eye-lashes; that could be the corroborating evidence he needed. It also emerged that the hillside area where the girls' bodies had been dumped had been chosen because Angelo knew the area well; one of his girlfriends had lived round there.

Kenny told the investigator about each murder in detail. He showed no regret, no concern for the suffering of the victims. He told of the long and awful death of Kristina Weckler. This particular killing was so awful that even Kenny did not want to talk about it. She was asphyxiated, very slowly, using domestic gas fed into a bag tied over her head. It had taken about an hour and a half for her to die.

Kenny had believed that by telling the police all the detail and laying much of the blame at Angelo's door he would somehow be let off, but his lawyer persuaded him that he had incriminated himself to such a degree that he had no choice now but to admit his guilt.

Kenny had supplied plenty of evidence of his cousin's involvement in the crimes. Angelo was arrested. The police shortly afterwards found his wallet, which clearly showed the outline of the fake police badge he had used to get his victims to go with him.

Rather oddly, the District Attorney's Office had dropped the five California murder charges against Bianchi, so that he no longer had the threat of the death penalty hanging over him. Now there was less incentive for Kenny to co-operate with the police. It began to look as if Angelo might not be brought to trial at all. Kenny himself was becoming unmanageable. The California police could not conceal the fact that they disliked him; Kenny found their disapproval hard to accept and started to make up stories to put himself in a better light; he even invented a third man who had been responsible for the killings. Then, he began to feel guilty about implicating Angelo and started to change his story. From the police point of view, Kenny was falling apart as a potential witness.

Kenny was in a difficult situation. If he simply gave evidence against his cousin in court and got him convicted, then he would come across as a straightforward police informer. For that he could be summarily executed by the criminal community. He would certainly become a target, even if he himself was in prison; a lot of scores are settled in prison. Kenny began to realise that the only way out was to start behaving like a very poor witness, and hope that the police would not want to call him as one.

Kenny was given two life sentences in the State of Washington, but was immediately transferred to California where he was sentenced to additional life terms. Bianchi is currently serving 35 years in California.

The jury agreed on 31 October 1983 that Angelo Buono was guilty of the murder of Lauren Wagner. On 3 November they found him not guilty of murdering Yolanda Washington. A few days later they found him guilty of killing Judy Miller. Then came the coup de grace. He was found guilty of murdering Dolores Cepeda, Sonja Johnson, Kimberly Martin, Kristina Weckler, Lissa Kastin, Jane King and Cindy Hudspeth. Under the law in California at that time, Angelo had now become a convicted 'multiple murderer' and therefore faced one of two futures – the death penalty or the rest of his life in prison, with no parole. The jury deliberated for an hour before deciding that Angelo Buono should have a life sentence.

The judge made it clear that he was unhappy about their decision. 'Angelo Buono and Kenneth Bianchi subjected various of their murder victims to the administration of lethal gas, electrocution, strangulation by rope, and lethal hypodermic injection. Yet the two defendants are destined to spend their lives in prison, housed, fed and clothed at taxpayer expense, better cared for than some of the destitute law-abiding members of our community.' But Angelo Buono did not live a long life in this comfort. He died in 2002 in Calipatria State Prison.

PART SIX
THE
EXECUTIONERS

Jack Ketch

the Punch & Judy hangman

JACK KETCH WAS possibly the best known and also the most incompetent English executioner. He was to become a black joke, almost a cartoon figure in the seventeenth century, and almost certainly the model for the Hangman in Punch and Judy.

One of Jack Ketch's predecessors, Derrick, was a celebrated figure who in about 1600 invented a huge gantry like a crane, which could hang as many as 23 people at once. This new type of gallows naturally became known as 'a derrick', and the word quickly passed into general usage as a nickname for any contrivance for moving heavy weights about; so by the middle of the seventeenth century the hangman's surname was applied, in jest, to any kind of hoist, such as a crane on a ship for lifting cargo on board. After Derrick, Gregory Brandon became the public hangman, then his son Richard Brandon inherited the post. It was Richard Brandon who executed Charles I. 'Squire' Dun followed.

Then came Jack Ketch, the notorious Jack Ketch. His real name was Richard Jacquet, but the surname became his whole name, and that became so well known that it was used as a nickname for his successors for nearly two hundred years. He was appointed public hangman in about 1663, in the reign of Charles II.

By 1672, Jack Ketch was a well-known public figure. It was in that year that a broadside was published entitled *The Plotters Ballad, being Jack Ketch's incomparable Receipt for the Cure of Traytorous Recusants and Wholesome Physick for a Popish Contagion*. These were certainly not Ketch's own words, but words put into his mouth by the anonymous author. It was quite common for 'Confessions' to be circulated at public executions; these too were 'fake'; although they purported to be by the condemned man or woman, they were not.

Ketch had a reputation for being a very incompetent executioner. He not only killed a lot of people: he caused them undue suffering. The high-profile execution of Lord William Russell on 21 July 1683 was carried out in a very clumsy way. A pamphlet has survived, which in this case may genuinely represent Ketch's words. In this pamphlet he makes his 'Apologie', claiming that the prisoner was to blame for not lying down properly. Lord William, he said, did not 'dispose himself as was most suitable'. Ketch also claimed he was interrupted while taking aim, which amounts to owning up to poor concentration.

There were many tracts aimed against Ketch. One was called *The Tyburn Ghost: or, Strange Downfal of the Gallows: a most true relation how the famous Triple Tree, near Paddington, was pluckt up by the roots and demolisht by certain evil Spirits, with Jack Ketch's Lamentation for the loss of his Shop, 1678.* The triple tree was a triangular gallows with three supporting posts. Each beam could carry eight people, so the whole structure could kill 24 at a time.

Jack Ketch became such a figure of folklore that for almost two hundred years 'Jack Ketch' was a nickname used for any hangman. A hundred years or so later, Ketch had become a character in Punch and Judy shows. As the executioner was nobody's friend, it delighted audiences to see Punch in the end succeeding in hanging the hangman. It was what the real Ketch justly deserved for the unnecessary suffering he inflicted. But the crowds loved to be shocked by this random cruelty: it was all part of the show. At Newgate in 1820, when the Cato Street conspirator Thistlewood and his companions were executed for treason, the sentence was to both hanging and beheading. The sentences were carried out and the executioner held up the heads one by one to show the crowd. He dropped the last one, and in the spirit of the occasion the crowd yelled, 'Oh, butter-fingers!'

Charles Sanson &
Madame Guillotine

CHARLES HENRI SANSON was born in 1739. He was the public executioner in Paris from 1788, the year before the French Revolution broke out, until 1795, when it was over. Sanson's great-grandfather, Charles Sanson, had received the office of executeur des hautes oeuvres de Paris in 1688, and this office became hereditary, passing from father to son. It was ironic that Sanson should be responsible for beheading Louis XVI, mainly for being an hereditary head of state, when he himself held office by hereditary right, but no doubt these small ironies were not noticeable during the melée of the French Revolution.

Executing was very much a family tradition, and Sanson's brothers followed the same grisly trade in other towns.

In the final days of 1789, Gorsas in the Courier de Paris accused Sanson of harbouring a Royalist press in his house. Sanson was brought to trial but acquitted, and Gorsas withdrew the accusation.

Sanson is closely associated with the hundreds of executions carried out in the Place de la Révolution, using the guillotine. The guillotine was at the time of the Terror not only a brand-new machine, but newly invented. Monsieur Guillotin's beheading machine was approved in principle in December 1789, partly on the grounds of humanity – it would behead quickly and reliably with one stroke – it would also treat all men equally. The same death for all. The guillotine was built, experiments were carried out successfully on several dead bodies, and it was first used for a 'live' execution by Sanson in the Place de Grève for the execution of the Highwayman Pelletier on 25 April 1792. Oddly enough, while the machine was in the experimental stage it was referred to as the Louisette. The King, who was so soon to die on the machine himself, was the one who suggested the sloping blade as more efficient. But from 28 April 1792, in other words once it was in use, it became known as la Guillotine after its main advocate and designer.

Many highly romanticized stories about C. H. Sanson were circulated, but they are probably fictitious. They seem to originate in the apocryphal Memoirs published in France in 1829, 1830 and 1863; these were almost certainly not based on any writings by C. H. Sanson. He seems to have been a meticulous and practical man. He for example drew his own plans and elevations for the construction of the guillotine that stood in the Place de la Révolution. Marie Tussaud managed to acquire the guillotine to put on display in he waxworks exhibition in London, and there it stood until the disastrous fire of the 1920s. Most of the guillotine was destroyed in the fire – most, that is, except the crucial blade, complete with its massive weight bolted onto it and the horizontal catch for releasing the blade. But Sanson's scale drawings survived and a facsimile has been built from these.

Probably the most momentous execution that Sanson had to carry out was the execution of Louis XVI on 21 January 1793. All the shops and places of business were closed to mark the solemnity of the day. The streets were lined with soldiers just in case there was an attempt to rescue the King. The King was taken in a carriage with his confessor, the Abbé Edgeworth, to the Place de la Révolution (now Place de la Concorde). The King mounted the scaffold and then broke away from his guards and began to address the crowd. An order was given to begin a drum roll; the sound of the drums drowned his voice. Sanson and his assistants took a firm hold of the King, strapped him to the plank, and tilted his body forward. The neck-piece was adjusted to hold his head in position and the knife released immediately. The confessor shouted, 'Son of St Louis, ascend to Heaven!' Sanson picked the head up from the basket and held it up for the crowd to see. The body was unstrapped from the plank, rolled into a basket and the remains were taken to the cemetery of the Madeleine. There young Marie Tussaud was waiting; she was forced by the authorities to make the death mask.

Following the execution of Louis XVI, Sanson had a

statement published in the Thermomètre politique, on 13 February 1793. He was concerned about some false statements that were put about with regard to the King's behaviour when confronted with death. He wanted people to know the truth of the situation.

In the autumn, it was the Queen of France's turn. Marie Antoinette was sentenced to death by the Revolutionary Tribunal at 4am on 16 October. Marie Antoinette was allowed to return to the Conciergerie prison for a few hours' sleep. She rose at 10am, put on a plain white dress. Sanson arrived to cut her hair short and to tied her hands behind her back. A much-hated figure – purely because she was foreign, it seems – she was made to ride to the guillotine in a tumbril, an ordinary cart, which swayed and jolted and exposed her to all the insults of the crowd. She travelled with her priest and her executioner, C. H. Sanson, for company. The cart stopped beneath the guillotine, red and forbidding against the sky. The Queen moved quickly up the steps to get the business over with and accidentally trod on Sanson's foot. She humbly begged his pardon. Sanson grasped her firmly and strapped her onto the plank. There was a brief pause while the neckboard was adjusted. There was a click as the lever released the blade, which rushed down onto her neck. The head and body were thrown onto a waiting handcart and wheeled to the Madeleine where, once again, Marie Tussaud was forced to make a death mask of a face that she was fond of. The face at least was serene in death. The head and body were then thrown, along with sixty other bodies, into a pit and covered with quicklime.

The victims of the Reign of Terror came to Sanson by the score. He can never have imagined when taking on the task in 1788 what he would be faced with. Hundreds of ordinary French people were to be beheaded, many because someone had denounced them and for no other reason. Then the organizers of the Revolution began condemning one another to death.

Jacques Rene Hébert, who had bitterly attacked Marie Antoinette, was sent to the guillotine for trying to bring the National Convention and the Paris Commune into conflict; Robespierre condemned him. Jean Paul Marat's assassin, Charlotte Corday, was executed by Sanson too.

Robespierre, the driving force behind the Terror, was himself executed by Sanson – on 28 July 1794. Jean Baptiste Carrier and Antoine Fouquier-Tinville, themselves responsible for sending hundreds to be beheaded by Sanson, were in their turn guillotined by him. Sanson was the legal executioner of all of these people; he nevertheless was the hands-on killer of an astonishing number of victims, a number that may run into thousands.

In 1795, possibly having had enough of killing, he 'abdicated' his office in favour of his son Henri, who had been his assistant for some time. Henri Sanson continued as executioner of Paris until his death in

1840; his son Clement Henri Sanson was the last of the Sanson dynasty to hold the office. There is no record whatever of the date or circumstances of the death of Charles Henri Sanson, the man who killed a King and a Queen.

William Calcraft

a callous hangman

IN THE TWENTIETH century, there was no shortage of executioners, or at any rate people who wanted to become executioners. The Governor of Wandsworth Prison in London in the 1940s commented to a Royal Commission on the Death Penalty that there were tremendous numbers of applicants for every job as hangman. The problem was picking the right man for the job and great care was needed to get the right man. 'A man who wants to be an executioner must be in a class by himself and I cannot answer for him. The executioners who have attended my prison have not shown any sign of brutality in the carrying out of executions or afterwards.'

The main problem in appointing an executioner was that, on the whole, any man who desperately wanted to do the job was almost certainly psychologically unbalanced and therefore unsuitable. It is likely that a man who wants to kill other people is going to be a sadist, and one of the requirements for an executioner is that the death needs to be swift, humane and efficient.

That at any rate is the modern view, the twentieth century view. Things were different in England in the nineteenth century.

William Calcraft, the principal British hangman in the middle of the nineteenth century, was not concerned to see his prisoners die quickly. He used the short drop, which left his victims suspended in mid-air, choking, sometimes slowly, sometimes quickly, to death. Dying by strangulation in this way might take two or twenty minutes, and this may be the origin of the old custom of leaving a criminal to hang for an hour – to make certain. But a humane death it most certainly was not.

Calcraft was the public executioner for an incredibly long time, from 1829 until 1872. When he started, he was hanging people in the ancient, medieval style. The gallows was often located in open country, outside a town, and at a crossroads. The victims were 'turned off' the back of a horse-drawn cart and left swinging in the wind. William Calcraft carried out just such an execution at Penenden Heath, a mile away from Maidstone Prison, in 1830. This was a classic crossroads gallows. On Christmas Eve 1830, Calcraft hanged three men together for committing arson. These were the last executions to be carried out at Penenden Heath. After that all the Maidstone hangings were carried out in, or in front of, Maidstone Prison. Calcraft carried out all 33 of the hangings at Maidstone Prison between 1831 and 1872, 28 in public and the remaining five , after 1868, in private.

William Calcraft it was who hanged the 14-year-old murderer John Amy Bird Bell in 1831 for cutting the throat of 13-year-old Richard Taylor. The tearful boy was led at 11 o'clock one morning, two days after his trial, to be hanged in front of a crowd of 5,000 people. Some may have felt justice was being done, but some also felt uneasy about it. In 1833, a boy of 9 was sentenced to death for burglary, but there was a huge amount of public agitation and he was reprieved.

William Calcraft travelled round the country, carrying out executions at all the major towns and cities and became a major public figure. He had his own carte de visite, which shows a broad solemn man with dark hair and a bushy white beard. He rests his right hand on a waist-high cenotaph with a wreath on its front. Prison governors might have been glad to have the public hangman's visiting card, but I doubt whether anyone else would.

The endless travelling from London out to one city after another must have been fairly arduous in the days of stage coaches. Calcraft's working life must have been made considerably easier by the coming of the railways in the 1860s.

William Calcraft presided over one of the biggest public executions ever to take place in Britain. The executions of Maria and Frederick Manning, on Tuesday 13 November 1849 at Horsemonger Lane Gaol, attracted the biggest crowd that is ever believed to have attended a public hanging. It is estimated that up to 50,000 people went to watch the Mannings die. Every possible space was filled with spectators and hundreds of policemen were needed to control the huge crowd.

The gallows, described at the time as 'a huge, gaunt and ominous looking structure', was erected as usual on the flat roof over the main gate at Horsemonger Lane Gaol (which now no longer exists). Maria Manning was William Calcraft's twentieth woman victim. At 8.15 am, the Mannings went into the prison chapel to take communion, then the prison governor arrived to hurry them along, no doubt alarmed at what the crowd might do if kept waiting. Calcraft came forward and Maria and Frederick Manning were taken to different parts of the chapel to be pinioned. Maria almost fainted while this was happening, so she was revived with brandy. She then produced a black silk handkerchief and asked to be blindfolded with it. This was allowed. She also had a black lace veil over her head, so that the public could not see her face at all.

A procession formed up at the back of the chapel. From there, with the prison bell ominously tolling, the Mannings were made to process to the gallows with Calcraft along a maze of narrow passages, incidentally walking over their own graves along the way, just as they had made their victim walk over his. Maria Manning managed to walk without faltering, led in her black silk blindfold by the prison doctor, Mr Harris. She was wearing a fine black satin gown, which deeply shocked the ladies of quality who watched the hanging. This lady's maid had certainly stepped well above her station.

Frederick Manning faltered and tottered on the long steep flight of stairs up to the roof where the gallows stood. Manning turned to look, awe-struck, at the colossal crowd gathered to watch him die and Calcraft drew a white hood over his head and fixed the noose round his neck. Then Calcraft moved to Maria Manning and pulled a similar white hood over her head and fitted her noose. He also tied a rope round her legs, to stop her dress billowing up when she dropped. After that, everybody left the roof except the husband and wife condemned to die side by side. Immediately, Calcraft pulled the bolt and the drop fell. Frederick hung almost motionless. Maria writhed for some seconds. Probably it took them five or as much as fifteen minutes to die; this was a short-drop hanging. Their bodies were left hanging for the customary hour before being taken down.

The huge crowd began to disperse at the moment of death. This often happened, and some have suggested that it was perhaps a feeling of shame at being present at a public hanging that made people hurry away afterwards.

Charles Dickens was one of the many spectators at the Mannings' hanging and wrote to The Times about it. 'I believe that the author has not seen a sight so inconceivably awful as the wickedness and levity of the crowd collected at that execution this morning... When the two miserable creatures who attracted all this ghastly sight about them were turned quivering into the air there was no more emotion, no more pity, no more thought that two immortal souls had gone to judgement, than if the name of Christ had never been heard in this world.' Dickens was among those campaigning to have public hangings stopped, and they were finally abolished in Britain in 1868.

Dickens' concern was for the effect the hangings were having on the spectators. They were a sadistic and voyeuristic form of entertainment, a kind of pornography of violence, and can only have fed feelings of morbidity or sadism. The victims often entered into their parts as entertainers. The Mannings appear to have dressed up for their execution, as many others had done before them. Maria's role as an entertainer continued well after her death. An artist from Madame Tussaud's was probably sent to the Old Bailey in anticipation, to draw her face to ensure a good likeness; William Calcraft seems to have sold the wax museum the dress she was wearing for her hanging, probably making a little extra money on the side. Shortly after the execution, the waxwork image of Maria Manning took its place in the Chamber of Horrors.

William Calcraft was also called down from London to despatch the Dorset murderess, Elizabeth Martha Brown. Her execution was set for 9am on Saturday 1856. Calcraft travelled down from London the previous day to make sure everything was set up properly. The Dorchester gallows was a tall and impressive structure, with the noose set very high to ensure that everyone could see. Elizabeth Brown had to climb endless steps to her death. She climbed the first flight of eleven steps, after which the hangman pinioned her arms in front of her before leading her up the next flight of nineteen steps, across a platform and then up another flight onto the trap. After he put the noose round her neck, Calcraft set off down the steps again to undo the bolts – there was no lever at this time. Someone pointed out to him that he had forgotten to pinion Elizabeth's legs. He went back to put a strap round her to stop her dress billowing up and showing her legs during the hanging. Then he went below and withdrew the bolts. Elizabeth fell about a foot. She struggled for a while. Death was certainly not immediate. Elizabeth Brown's execution led to a leading article in the local Dorset County Chronicle advocating the abolition of the death penalty.

William Calcraft was responsible for killing hundreds of people. Most of his victims died slowly and painfully – unnecessarily so. It may be that Calcraft believed that the suffering was an integral and essential part of the death sentence. It may alternatively be that he had grown up with the 'short drop' (because it had to be) off the back of a horse-drawn cart, the method that he had inherited from the eighteenth century, and never thought of anything more humane.

William Marwood

all Things Ready for the Execution

WILLIAM MARWOOD, THE great British executioner of the late nineteenth century, was born at Goulceby in Lincolnshire in 1818. He moved to Horncastle in 1855. There, living in a small cottage in what is now Church Lane, he ran a shoe-making and -mending business.

William Marwood was very much a self-made executioner. He was not following a long-standing family tradition; there was no particular connection that led him naturally into this career path. He just, it seems, fancied that he could do the job really well. He was a cobbler by trade, and lived in a small cottage in Horncastle in Lincolnshire. From there he touted for commissions, taking over from William Calcraft as England's public executioner in 1872.

A letter survives in which he touts for business in Dundee. His letter is addressed to The Governor, County Prison, Dundee, and dated 22 April 1873. It reads as follows;

Sir, Pleas I beg your Pardon in riting to you again to know if you are in the wants of a Man as Executioner at Dundee as I understand that thear is a Prisoner to be Executed on the 29th inst. Sir if my Service is wanted on the 29th I have all Things Ready for the Execution if thea are Wanted. Sir Pleas will you be so kind as to look after this Matter for me the Sentence of the Law shall be caried out in Due Form by me as Executioner. Please will you be so kind as to send me a Anser Back by the Return of Post I shall Esteem it a great Favour For the Time is getting near for the Execution. Sir Pleas I wait your replie. Sir I remain your Most Humble Servant, Wm Marwood.

Such a letter arriving on the desk today would be regarded as profoundly suspect. The letter writer clearly inhabits classic 'nutter' territory. Would any authority in its right mind employ this man to carry out executions? The simple fact of wanting the work so avidly would rule him out. But – the nineteenth century was obviously a very different place.

Luckily for Marwood, he was already acquiring a national reputation for being a very quick and efficient executioner. The reality of William Marwood was not quite as creepy as his letter suggests. He looked like Prince Albert, only more cheerful. He was also a more merciful executioner than his predecessor, William Calcraft. Marwood is alleged to have said that Calcraft hanged people, while he, Marwood, executed them. There was, even so, something very peculiar about a Horncastle cobbler reaching his early fifties before deciding on this weird career move. Why did he do it?

Possibly it was the money. Executioners were well paid for their work. It was when he was 54 that William Marwood persuaded the Governor of Lincoln Prison to let him conduct an execution. He duly hanged William Horry on 1 April 1874. Such was his efficiency on this occasion that he was shortly afterwards appointed hangman by the Sheriffs of London and Middlesex. They paid him a retainer of £20 a year plus £10 an execution.

It was William Marwood who developed the long drop technique. Until then, prisoners had been subjected to the short drop, which left them conscious and choking for several minutes. By leaving a long loop of rope hanging loose down the back, Marwood ensured that the body fell some distance before being checked suddenly by the taut rope. This broke the victim's neck, rendering him immediately unconscious, often killing instantly. It was a far more humane method of killing than Calcraft's. It also became a problem for the hangmen, prison governors, chaplains, warders and any other staff who had to be present, when public executions ceased in 1868 and the executions had to be witnessed, from very close quarters in what were often cramped execution sheds or cells. The long drop method was more humane for both the victims and those who had to witness the executions.

Marwood's hunch that killing people was a job that he could do really well turned out to be right.

When Horsemonger Lane Gaol closed in 1878 its execution shed duties were transferred to Wandsworth Prison and an execution shed was built in one of its yards. In all 135 prisoners were put to death at Wandsworth between 1878 and 1961. The seventeen executions in the nineteenth century were all for murder. Of the twentieth century executions all were for murder except ten for spying during the two World Wars and two for treason immediately after the Second World War – John Amery and William Joyce.

William Marwood carried out the first four executions at Wandsworth between 1878 and 1882. Bartholomew Binns hanged the next man and then James Berry hanged the next six between 1885 and 1891. The very first execution at Wandsworth was that of a 31-year-old man, Thomas Smithers. He was hanged on 8 October 1878 for the murder of his wife. This execution was followed by the high-profile execution of Kate Webster in July 1879, for the brutal and callous murder of her mistress; Kate Webster was the only woman to be executed at Wandsworth.

Marwood stopped Kate Webster on the chalk mark on the double trap door the execution shed, fitted the leather body belt round her waist and secured her wrists to it while his assistant strapped her ankles with a leather strap. She was supported on the trap in the usual way by two warders standing on planks. Marwood drew the white hood and the noose over her head, leaving the free rope hanging down her back. He quickly moved across to the lever and pulled it. Marwood's newly perfected 'long drop' meant that Kate Webster fell about eight feet out of sight into the pit, dying instantly of a broken neck.

The new execution method ensured that the whole business was over within two minutes. There were usually two newspaper reporters present, who were there to reassure the public that executions had been carried out 'expeditiously'.

Kate Webster was buried in an unmarked grave, Grave No 3, in one of the exercise yards. In all, 134 men and one woman were to be executed at Wandsworth.

Marwood himself hanged 176 people in all. Possibly his best known victim was Charles Peace, the Victorian burglar and murderer who had become a public menace. Marwood hanged Charles Peace at Armley Gaol in Leeds on 25 February 1879. He hanged Kate Webster at Wandsworth in July 1879. He hanged Percy Mapleton on 29 November 1881. Mapleton had murdered Isaac Gold on a train between London and Brighton, just for his watch and some coins. The Mapleton case gained a high profile because Mapleton escaped after his arrest and had to be re-arrested.

William Marwood it was who hanged the perpe-trators of the notorious political murders in Phoenix Park, Dublin. The murders – with surgical knives – of

Lord Frederick Cavendish, Chief Secretary for Ireland, and Thomas Burke, Permanent Undersecretary for Ireland, were committed by five members of the Invincibles gang. We would now call them terrorists. Whatever we call them, Joe Brady and four other men were hanged in Kilmainham Gaol in Dublin in 1883.

Marwood became a kind of folklore figure in popular culture. There was even a popular jingle about him:

If Pa killed Ma,
Who'd kill Pa?
Mar-wood.

William Marwood died in 1883.

James Berry
the recurring nightmare

JAMES BERRY WAS a Yorkshire police constable for ten years. During that time he made many friends and enemies. One acquaintance he made was William Marwood, an executioner who liked to give Berry blow by blow accounts of the methods he used to hang criminals. When Marwood died in 1883, Berry, who was then 32 years old, decided the police force did not suit him and left. Needing a new job, he decided he would be a hangman. He already knew a lot because of his conversations with Marwood, so Berry confidently applied for his dead friend's job. He was turned down.

Berry tried again, and his persistence was rewarded. He got his first fee – the huge sum of 21 guineas – for hanging two men at Calton Prison in Edinburgh. As part of the commission was a second-class return rail ticket from Berry's home town, Bradford, and cash to cover board and lodgings.

The night before Berry was due to hang the two men in Edinburgh, he had a nightmare about his new job – a classic insecurity dream, one might suppose. In the nightmare, James Berry found he could not hang his victim because the trapdoor would not open. The same dream recurred many times over the years. But the following morning, the double hanging went perfectly smoothly. The trapdoor opened and the two men died without any trouble.

On 15 November 1884, Miss Emma Whitehead Keyse, a former maid of honour and friend of Queen Victoria's, was found battered to death in her home at Babbacombe in Devon. Elizabeth Harris, Miss Keyse's cook, discovered her mistress's body in the dining room after waking up in a smoke-filled bedroom. She said that Miss Keyse's head had been beaten in and her clothes had been soused in lamp oil and evidently set on fire by the murderer. The police took a statement from the cook and then interviewed the other servant, the 19-year-old footman, John Lee, who was Elizabeth Harris's half-brother. Lee was a petty thief and had been taken on by Miss Keyse out of pity. The police saw Lee as the prime suspect, in spite of his histrionics when the police had first arrived; when he heard about Miss Keyse's death, Lee had broken down, sobbing, 'I have lost my best friend'.

But Lee had bloodstains on his clothing and an empty can that had contained lamp oil was found in his pantry. Eventually it emerged that Lee had a revenge motive. Just before her death, Miss Keyse had suspected Lee of theft and cut his weekly wages from four shillings to two. Lee had obviously killed her in anger.

There were rumours after the trial that there was another man involved, and another motive entirely. There were rumours that Elizabeth Harris had been caught by Miss Keyse having sex with a man. Miss Keyse had been outraged by this and taken a swipe at the naked couple. Out of panic, Elizabeth had lashed out at Miss Keyse with her fists and killed her. Elizabeth and her lover had then tried to cover up what had happened by taking the body into the dining room and giving it a beating to make it look as if there had been an intruder. Then Elizabeth realized the police would not be so easily fooled, so she sprinkled lamp oil on the body and set fire to it, to destroy the evidence. The attempt at cremation had failed, because John Lee had smelt the smoke and run in with a bucket of water to put the fire out.

The trial had nevertheless ended with Lee being found guilty and sentenced to death. On the eve of his execution, Lee was chatting to the prison governor and the chaplain. The governor told him there was no chance of a reprieve. Lee shrugged and said. 'Elizabeth Harris could say the word and clear me, if she would'. When the governor and chaplain left, he settled down to sleep. He had a strange dream. He was standing on the gallows with the noose round his neck, but the trapdoor would not open, even though the hangman was repeatedly pulling at the lever. It was a classic wish-fulfilment dream. Lee woke from his dream feeling there was nothing to worry about.

Just before 8am on 23 February 1885, James Berry led John Lee to the centre of the trapdoor, strapped his legs together, positioned the rope round his neck and pulled the hood down over his face. Berry threw the lever over, and the sound of the bolts drawing back under the gallows could be heard, but the trapdoor refused to open. John Lee's prophetic dream of the previous night – and James Berry's recurring nightmare – seemed to be coming true.

Berry was unnerved, took the hood and noose off Lee and tested the trap with a sandbag weighing the same as John Lee. This time the trap opened and the sandbag crashed through into the pit under the gallows. Lee was pushed back onto the trap, the noose and hood were replaced and once again Berry pulled the lever. But once again the trap would not open. Berry's face began to twitch. With shaking hands he took the hood and noose off Lee and took him off the trap. Berry had a discussion with an engineer and they called a carpenter. Obviously the trap door fitted the space a little too snugly, and the carpenter was asked to plane the edges of the trap door. The bolts were well greased. Berry ran a dummy run with a sandbag again and everything seemed to be all right.

John Lee was made to stand on the trapdoor for the third time. The lever was pulled. The chaplain was astonished when he saw Lee still standing on the trapdoor – and fainted. He was caught by a warder.

A decision was made to inform the Home Secretary

about the incident. Lee was asked if he would like breakfast. He agreed that he would. Berry was unable to eat anything. Nine hours later, a messenger arrived to say that the Home Secretary had reprieved John Lee. The death sentence was commuted to life imprisonment.

Lee was released in 1905 after serving twenty years. He married a childhood sweetheart who had waited patiently for him. They emigrated to America. John Lee died in 1933, still insisting that he had not murdered Miss Keyse. He also insisted that he was saved from hanging by divine intervention – because he was innocent.

PART SEVEN
THE
LADY-KILLERS

Jack the Ripper

the Whitechapel murderer

EARLY ONE AUGUST morning, a carter called George Cross was walking along Bucks Row in Whitechapel on his way to work. Bucks Row was a narrow cobbled street with a row of terraced houses on one side and the blank wall of a warehouse on the other. It was still dark, but Cross thought he saw a bundle of some kind on the pavement. Coming closer he saw that it was a woman lying on her back with her skirt pulled up. He assumed she was drunk and as another man came up he asked him to help him get her to her feet. The other man touched her cheek and felt that it was cold. He said she was dead and they had better get a policeman.

A few minutes later PC John Neil, following his beat, found the body for himself, beside a stable door. Neil had a lantern, and by its light he could see something Cross had been unable to see – that the woman's throat had been deeply cut, right through to the spine. When the body was stripped in the yard of the local mortuary, another wound appeared, a jagged knife slash a foot long down the woman's stomach. A Lambeth workhouse mark on her petticoat revealed that she was Mary Ann Nicholls, a prostitute. Shortly before her death she had lurched drunkenly back to her lodging house, admitted that she had not got the fourpence she needed to rent her bed for the night. She was turned away. 'I'll soon get the money', she called out good-humouredly, 'See what a jolly bonnet I've got'.

The police thought from witnesses who saw her shortly after this that she had approached a tall stranger with the line, 'Want a good time, mister?' She took him into the dark alley for sex and had her throat savagely cut. The police surgeon who examined her body said, 'I have never seen so horrible a case. She was ripped about in a manner that only a person skilled in the use of a knife could have achieved.' This idea that skill had been used was to return again and again, as people wondered whether the killer was perhaps a butcher or a surgeon.

The man she attracted with her jolly bonnet was the most notorious serial killer of all time. He was Jack the Ripper. This murder did not cause an immediate sensation in London, though. Murders of prostitutes happened all the time, even murders as violent as this one. Two other prostitutes, Emma Smith and Martha Turner, had both been sadistically murdered during the previous few months and, although these 'horrible murders' were duly reported in the press, they were treated as individual crimes. The thing that was sensational about the Jack the Ripper murders is that they were the work of one man, apparently a man on some sort of mission, a dangerous maniac who was systematically killing one woman after another.

The Jack the Ripper murders were really just one manifestation of a low-life nineteenth century East End of London. The awful slum conditions bred disease, poverty and violence. There were huge numbers of prostitutes, there was high child mortality, high incidence of sexual abuse of every kind – and lots of murders. Prostitutes were particularly vulnerable, then as now, and prostitute murders were two a penny. Jack the Ripper was responsible for only five of these murders – a drop in the ocean – and his reign of terror in the East End was a surprisingly short one, yet his name became notorious unlike any other murderer's before or since, a by-word for gratuitous, sadistic violence. The Ripper murders made a huge impact on late Victorian England.

One minor mystery is exactly when the Ripper murders began. It is generally agreed that the period over which they happened was fairly short – but how short? Some early victims have been suggested, such as Emma Smith. Emma was described as 'a drunken Whitechapel prostitute' which might make her look like a classic Ripper victim, but there the similarities end. She was staggering home drunk to her lodgings in Spitalfields on 3 April 1888 when she was attacked. Before she died of peritonitis, 24 hours later, she was able to tell the police that she had been attacked by four men, the youngest of them about 19 years old. She had been stabbed in the vagina with something like an iron spike and robbed. It has never been suggested that any of the authentic Ripper murders was carried out by a gang.

A second possible early victim was Martha Turner, another prostitute. She was seen drinking with a soldier late one night before being murdered – with thirty-nine stab wounds, nine in the throat, seventeen in the chest, thirteen in the stomach. It was a frenzied attack and looked as if it might have been done with two hands at once. Martha Turner was murdered on 6-7 August, 1888. Rather surprisingly, soldiers at the Tower of London took their bayonets with them when off duty. After the Turner murder that practice was stopped. All the soldiers at The Tower were lined up for an identity parade, but Martha Turner's friend, who had seen her with the soldier earlier in the evening of the murder, either could not or would not identify the murderer. Sir Melville Macnaghten, who was in charge of the CID after the last Ripper murder and had the job of wrapping the case up, discounted these two murders; he did not believe they were the work of the maniac who committed the Jack the Ripper murders.

The murders began on 31 August 1888, with the murder of Mary Ann Nichols, the poor woman who was found murdered in Bucks Row.

It was a horrible murder, but 'one-off' prostitute murders were relatively common, and the police assumed it was one of these. But a week later, at about 5.30 in the morning of Saturday 8 September 1888, another prostitute, Annie Chapman, was found dead in the backyard of a barber's shop in Hanbury Street close to Spitalfields Market. This was a place where prostitutes often took their customers. A neighbour had seen her talking to a dark-skinned man 'of foreign appearance', dressed in shabby, genteel clothes and wearing a deerstalker hat. Half an hour later, one of the lodgers, John Davis, came downstairs and out into the yard to go to the lavatory. There he saw Annie Chapman's body lying against a fence, he skirt pulled up to her waist and her legs bent at the knees. She had not only had her throat cut, her stomach had been cut open and she had been disembowelled, and her possessions as well as her entrails laid out beside her body. The thorough dissection of Annie Chapman suggested that the murderer had an interest, however warped, in anatomy. The killer had removed the uterus and the upper part of the vagina, presumably as a trophy.

The Annie Chapman killing woke London up to the fact that a sadistic monster was on the loose. The Star ran the headline, 'Latest Horrible Murder in Whitechapel'. Sir Melville Macnaghten, then Head of the CID, later recalled, 'No-one living in London that autumn will forget the terror. . . Even now I can recall the foggy evenings and hear again the raucous cries of the newspaper boys: "Another horrible murder, murder, mutilation, Whitechapel"'. A kind of hysteria swept across Britain, unparalleled since the Ratcliffe Highway murders of 1811 – which also remain unsolved.

Then, on 29 September 1888, came the first sensational letter from the Whitechapel murderer. It was sent to a Fleet Street news agency. 'Dear Boss,' it read, 'I keep on hearing that the police have caught me. But they won't fix me yet. I am down on certain types of women and I shan't quit ripping them until I do get buckled. Grand job, that last job was, I gave the lady no time to squeal. I love my work and want to start again. You will soon hear from me with my funny little game. I saved some of the proper stuff in a little ginger beer bottle after my last job to write with, but it went thick like glue and I can't use it. Red ink is fit enough I hope. Ha! Ha! Next time I shall clip the ears off and send them to the police, just for the jolly. Jack the Ripper.'

This was the first time the name had been used. If the letter was genuine, and there are many serious students of the Whitechapel murders who believe the letter was genuine, then the murderer himself chose his appalling nickname.

That same night, in the small hours of 30 September, he struck again. At about 1am a hawker by the name of Louis Diemschutz drove his cart into the backyard of a working men's club in Berner's Street. The pony shied, and Diemschutz saw a bundle at the pony's feet murdered. It was the body of Liz Stride, another prostitute. Jack the Ripper must still have been in the yard at that moment. By the time Diemschutz had fetched a lighted candle, the Ripper had fled. Diemschutz saw that Liz Stride had had her throat cut, almost certainly from behind, but was not mutilated in any other way, except that a start had been made on cutting off her ear.

The police, probably rightly, assumed that Jack had been disturbed during this murder and had run off before finishing the job. To compensate, he ran up Commercial Road and reached the Houndsditch area, just in time to meet a prostitute who had been let out of Bishopsgate police station only a few minutes earlier. She had been held for being drunk and disorderly. Her name was Catherine Eddowes. The Ripper was able to talk Catherine Eddowes into going with him into Mitre Square, a small square surrounded by warehouses, and another place ideal for prostitutes to take their clients. Here the Ripper killed again, for the second time in an hour. A policeman passed through the square every fifteen minutes. He passed at 1.30am and saw nothing out of the ordinary. At 1.45 he saw Catherine Eddowes lying on her back in the corner of the square, with her dress pushed up to her waist. Her face had been slashed, her throat had been cut and her abdomen had been cut open from the vagina up to her ribs. She had been disembowelled.

The murderer had evidently heard the policeman approaching and run off by way of a small passage running out of the square's north side. In this passage there was a public sink, and he had stopped there for a moment to wash his hands. In Goulston Street, about ten minutes away, he threw away a bloodstained piece of Eddowes' apron, which he may have taken to wipe his hands and his knife. The policeman who found the rag also found a message chalked on a wall nearby, blaming 'the Juwes'.

Another message from the Ripper arrived at the Central News Agency on the Monday morning, a postcard this time. 'I was not codding dear old boss when I gave you the tip. You'll hear about saucy Jack's work tomorrow. Double event this time. Number one squealed a bit. Couldn't finish straight off. Had not time to get ears for police.' The detail implied that the letter really had come from the killer.

Panic gripped Whitechapel. There was general public fury at the inability of the police to deal with the situation. Women began to equip themselves with whistles to raise the alarm and knives to defend themselves. The murderer was thought to be a doctor, so men carrying black bags were in danger of being attacked in the streets.

The Eddowes murder introduced a new dimension. Not only was it much bloodier than all the others – so far – but a trail of blood led to a wall where the message was inscribed in chalk: 'The Juwes are not the men who will be blamed for nothing'. Fearing reprisal attacks on Jewish men, the head of the Metropolitan Police Force, Sir Charles Warren, had the message scrubbed off. In doing so, he may have destroyed some vital evidence. It would be useful to know, for instance, whether the handwriting was the same as that in the 'Dear Boss' letter. The CID in fact pleaded with Warren for a delay until daybreak so that the inscription could be photo-graphed, but Warren refused.

Warren's fears about reprisals were well-founded. All sorts of rumours were going round the East End about the identity of the murderer. One suspect was Michael Ostrog, a Russian-born doctor; it was rumoured he had been sent from Russia to incriminate expatriate Russian Jews. Nevertheless, the spelling of 'Juwes' may suggest something else – the involvement of freemasonry. The disembowelling too may be connected with Free-masons' lore. The police were flooded with suspects nominated by the public, and the general atmosphere in the East End approached hysteria.

But October passed with no further murders and the public panic began to die down. Then came the melodrama of the final murder.

The Ripper's final victim was Mary Jeanette Kelly, a 25-year-old prostitute, who was murdered on 9 November in her rented room in Miller's Court off Dorset Street. The following morning at 10.45 her landlord, Henry Bowers, called to collect her rent. There was no reply. He looked in through the window and saw the horrific sight of Mary's dismembered body lying on the bed. The mutilations must have taken an hour to complete. The head was only hanging onto the rest of the body by a piece of skin. The nose had been removed. The embers of a fire burned in the grate, as if the murder had been committed by firelight. This time, no organs had been removed. 'I shall be haunted by this for the rest of my life,' Bowers told the police. The previous evening Mary had been desperately trying to earn her rent. She was seen approaching strangers for business. The last one she was seen approaching at about 2am was tall, dark, with a 'swarthy' complexion, and wore a deerstalker hat. He seemed well dressed and had a gold watch chain. Together they had walked into the narrow alleyway leading to her ground floor lodging. It is generally assumed that this swarthy gentleman was Jack the Ripper.

This murder caused the greatest sensation, and caused Sir Charles Warren to resign. Queen Victoria joined the chorus of well-intentioned helpers, suggesting methods for catching Jack.

After Mary Kelly's death there were no more Ripper murders, and that is in itself one of the great unsolved mysteries about them. Compulsive psychopathic killers tend to go on killing until they are stopped, yet the police had not apprehended anyone. There was no arrest, yet there were no more killings.

Theories abound, some sensible, some not. The first full-length book about the Ripper told an extraordinary story of a doctor visiting the bedside of a dying Englishman, a surgeon called Dr Stanley, under whom he had trained. Stanley told how his son Herbert had died of syphilis caught from a prostitute two years before. The prostitute's name was Mary Kelly. Dr Stanley swore to avenge his son's death and roamed the east End picking up prostitutes, questioning them about the whereabouts of Kelly, then killing them to ensure their silence. Finally he found Mary Kelly and killed her. After that he fled to Argentina.

This is a classic Ripper hypothesis, with its rational plotting, its surface plausibility, and its neat explanation for the ending of the reign of terror. But it is also typical in the way that it is riddled with flaws.

a) There was no Dr Stanley registered with the British Medical Association, no-one even resembling him in career.

b) If Stanley had existed and really had a vendetta against Mary Kelly, why did he not just stab or strangle the earlier victims? There was no need for all the mutilation if all he wanted to do was silence them.

c) Herbert is very unlikely indeed to have died only two years after contracting syphilis; it would be more likely to take ten or more.

d) Mary Kelly did not have syphilis.

Typically, the Dr Stanley hypothesis falls apart when it is looked at closely – like most of the other scenarios.

One possible explanation for the ending of the killings is that the Ripper was prevented from continuing by his own death, that he committed suicide. This has led to the identification of Montagu John Druitt as the Ripper. He was last seen alive on 3 December 1888, four weeks after the Kelly murder. His body was found floating in the Thames a few days later. Druitt was a failed barrister who had fallen on such hard times that he had to resort to teaching to make a living. In favour of Druitt as the murderer are the history of mental illness within the family and Druitt's acquisition of basic medical skills as a young man.

Druitt was born on 15 August 1857 at Wimborne in Dorset. His father William was a distinguished surgeon, a Justice of the Peace, a pillar of the community. Montagu Druitt was sent to Winchester in 1870 at the age of twelve. At school he was successful, except as an actor. Even the school magazine slated his performance as Sir Toby Belch. His great passion was for cricket. He went on to New College Oxford to read Classics, graduating in 1880. His decision to become a barrister seems to have been the beginning of a decline. He fell back on teaching at a private 'cramming shop' in Blackheath. He went on playing cricket. Interestingly, he is known to have been playing in matches the day before or the day after several of the murders – whatever that proves.

In 1888, Montagu Druitt was going to pieces, and finally killed himself in December. It may be that he even gave the police his address too. On 29 September 1888, the Ripper wrote from Liverpool, 'Beware, I shall be at work on the 1st and 2nd inst., in Minories at twelve midnight, and I give the authorities a good chance, but there is never a policeman near when I am at work.' After the Catherine Eddowes killing he sent another letter from Liverpool: 'What fools the police are. I even give them the name of the street where I am living.' Was Jack the Ripper really living in the Minories, a street near the Tower of London? Druitt had a relative called Lionel Druitt, who qualified as a doctor in Edinburgh in 1877, and he had lodgings near The Tower. It was at 140 Minories. Lionel seems to have moved in as a junior partner of Dr Gillard in Clapham Road in 1886, but it may be that the Minories rooms were passed on to his cousin Montagu, who was four years younger than him. It was quite common for upper and middle class young men to go 'slumming' in the East End. Charles Dickens and Wilkie Collins had done it when looking for material for their fiction; others did it when looking for sex. A room in a lodging house in the area would have been useful for the purpose. The connection between Montagu Druitt and the Minories is tenuous, but it is the address he mentions in his letter. It is also intriguing that Lionel Druitt left for New South Wales in Australia in 1886, yet he was able to produce, in 1890, a tantalizingly elusive document entitled The East End Murderer – I knew him. Since he was out of the country at the time of the murders, he can only have picked up the key information second-hand, perhaps from other family members. Unfortunately, though the title and author of this document are known, no copy has so far been traced. In spite of having a promising career in both medicine and cricket in England, Montagu's brother Edward suddenly decided in 1889 to emigrate to Australia. Maybe, after his brother's murder spree and suicide, England was no longer so attractive. In 1889, he doubtless met Lionel and told hem everything, supplying him with the material for the 1890 monograph.

Dr Neill Cream is a known murderer who may have the Ripper murders added to his CV. Cream's career as an arsonist, abortionist and murderer was brought to an end in 1892, when he was convicted of the murders of four London prostitutes. He had picked them up in the boroughs of Walworth and Lambeth and poisoned them with strychnine. It is said that on the scaffold he exclaimed at the last moment, 'I am Jack the – ' just as he dropped. Unfortunately, as well as the hangman, who swore that this happened, there were others present, including Sir Henry Smith, who later boasted that nobody knew more about Jack the Ripper than he did, and he did not mention this key information. Actually, even if Cream had claimed at that crucial moment that he was the Ripper, it could have been a ruse to gain a stay of execution. If he had owned up to being Jack the Ripper, surely those with him on the scaffold would have wanted to hear more?

In fact, regardless of what Neill Cream shouted, or whether he shouted at all, Cream could not have committed the Ripper murders. From November 1881 until July 1891 he was serving a life sentence for murder in Illinois.

Another convicted murderer often brought forward as a suspect for the Ripper murders is George Chapman. He was born in Poland in 1865 as Severin

Klososwski. He was hanged in 1903 for the murder by arsenic poisoning of Maud Marsh, Mary Spink and Bessie Taylor. He is linked to the Ripper cases by being, according to one source, in Whitechapel at the right time. He is said to have run a hairdresser's business at George Yard, which is where Martha Turner was murdered. Inspector Abberline, who led the Ripper enquiries, came to believe in his retirement that George Chapman was the Ripper. Abberline presumably suspected Chapman because he was living in the area (but so were a lot of other people) and he fitted the description of the man seen with Mary Kelly on the night of her murder. But the nature of the Ripper killings is totally different from that of the Chapman killings. One murderer used a knife; the other used poison. They could not have been more different.

Some writers have proposed that the Duke of Clarence was the murderer, on the grounds that the Duke was mentally unstable and keen on London low-life, and was confined after the Ripper murders. The Duke's sexual proclivities seem to have lain elsewhere, though, and it is difficult to see how he could have been involved in slaying female prostitutes. Many other people have been named as Ripper suspects, including the painter Walter Sickert, though none carry real conviction. The Jack the Ripper murders seem destined to remain the great unsolved murder mystery of modern times.

Who was he? At least we know what he looked like, because of one or two sightings of him immediately after the murders. The best description is the one given by a detective, Steve White, who saw a lone figure moving away from the scene of the Mitre Square murder. This is his memorable description of Jack the Ripper;

'I saw a man coming out of the alley [where the body was found two minutes later]. He was walking quickly but noiselessly, apparently wearing rubber shoes, which were rather rare in those days.

'He was about five feet ten inches in height, and was dressed rather shabbily, though it was obvious that the material of his clothes was good. Evidently a man who had seen better days, I thought. His face was long and thin, nostrils rather delicate and his hair was jet black. His complexion was inclined to be sallow and altogether the man was foreign in appearance. The most striking thing about him was the extraordinary brilliance of his eyes. The man was slightly bent at the shoulders, though he was obviously quite young – about thirty-three at the most – and gave one the idea of having been a student or professional man. His hands were snow white, and the fingers long and tapering. As the man passed me at the lamp, I had an uneasy feeling that there was something more than usually sinister about him, and I was strongly moved to find some pretext for detaining him; but it was not in keeping with British police methods that I should do so. . . I had a sort of intuition that the man was not quite right. The man stumbled a few feet away from

me, and I made that an excuse for engaging him in conversation. He turned sharply at the sound of my voice, and scowled at me in surly fashion, but he said "Good-night" and agreed with me that it was cold. His voice was a surprise to me. It was soft and musical, with a touch of melancholy in it, and it was the voice of a man of culture – a voice altogether out of keeping with the squalid surroundings of the East End.'

When Steve White's vivid description is compared with Montagu Druitt's photograph, there is no doubt that the two are strikingly similar. White got Druitt's socio-economic class right. He even got Druitt's age right. The rubber-soled plimsolls were consistent with Druitt's sporting activity. Immediately after the detective's encounter with Jack the Ripper, he was called urgently by one of the other officers to 'come along' and look at the body of a woman he had just found in the alley. Steve White went and looked, remembered the man he had just seen and ran after him as fast as he could.

But of course he didn't catch him.

Henri Landru

the impudent rascal

HENRI DESIRÉ LANDRU was born of fairly poor Parisian stock. His father worked as a fireman at the furnaces of the Vulcain Ironworks in Paris. Henri attended a Catholic school, leaving at sixteen to do his four years' military service, by the end of which he had reached the rank of sergeant.

Henri Landru had been considered a bright boy at school, and as a young man he realised that his easy line in conversation was useful in seducing young women. In 1891 he seduced his cousin. She became pregnant and gave birth to a daughter. Two years later, he married her. He was by now quartermaster of the regiment at St Quentin, but he left the military life behind when he got married and went into business, in a very small way, as a clerk. The young Landru was unlucky in his choice of employer, who absconded with the money Landru had given him as a bond.

This incident may have given Landru a motive to get back at society in some way, or just confirmation that the world is a jungle. From that point on, Henri Landru became one of the beasts of the jungle. In addition to being a furniture dealer and garage owner, Landru turned into a swindler. His victims were mainly middle-aged widows whom he met through his furniture business. Often they came to him with their possessions to sell, as a means of making some quick money. Landru preyed on their vulnerability, persuading them to let him invest their pensions, which he then stole. This trick worked for a time, but by 1900 he had been sentenced to two years in prison for fraud; he had tried to withdraw funds from the Comptoir d'Escompte using a false identity.

Over the next ten years, Landru was in and out of prison seven times. In 1908, undeterred by the law's opinion of his activities, he struck on a new scam. He put an advertisement in the newspaper, posing as a well-to-do widower looking for the companionship of a widow in a similar situation. It looked harmless and respectable enough. What he was looking for was more vulnerable widows, but this time he was going to get hold of all of their money in one go. Landru was becoming more ambitious. Mme Izore, a forty-year-old widow, was persuaded to hand over a 15,000 franc dowry with some fake deeds as surety. Mme Izore was left destitute. She went to court to get compensation and justice. Unfortunately the dowry had gone by the time the police caught up with Landru, so all she had was the satisfaction of seeing Landru going to prison for another three years.

Landru was released just before the outbreak of the First World War, probably on the understanding that he would re-enlist in the army. Landru's mother had died in 1910. His father had committed suicide, in despair over his son's lawless behaviour, which had left the family penniless and degraded. He drifted around the countryside, knowing that he had been convicted in absentia and sentenced to deportation, for life, to New Caledonia.

It is not clear what happened to Landru psychologically during the First World War, but something happened to escalate his criminal behaviour. Perhaps it was estrangement from his wife. Perhaps it was the death of both of his parents; he may have felt released from such slight moral controls as they had exerted over him. Perhaps it was the cumulative coarsening effect of too many years in prison. Perhaps it was the daily reports of terrible slaughter at the Front that made human life seem cheap.

The series of murders that followed do not fall into any 'normal' pattern of female serial killings. The motive does not seem to have been in any way sexual. Lust did not enter into it at all. Bloodlust does not seem to have been the motive either. In this case, killing was a means to an end. The murders are best understood in relation to the pattern of the earlier swindles. Landru started by buying furniture from vulnerable women, then went on to conning them of part of their pensions, then went on to conning a wealthier woman of her dowry. That was where he encountered a major problem; Mme Izore had afterwards brought a charge against him. If she had not been alive to bring the charge, there would have been no problem. So the logical next step was to take the money and kill the victims. The murders were therefore entirely cold-blooded.

He was not at all good-looking; he was rather small, with a bald head and a thick, reddish-brown beard, bushy eyebrows and sunken cheeks. He looked sinister or comical, and swept people along with his amusing patter. He was a good talker, even making jokes at his trial. It was not just women he charmed, but men. All the while he was robbing widows, he was defrauding discharged soldiers of their pensions too. What they all had in common was their position in society; they were all vulnerable people, and that tells us that Landru had no conscience.

He had a sense of right and wrong, but did not apply it to himself. He was able to justify swindling one soldier out of his pension on the grounds that he had a mistress, yet Landru himself had a mistress and was cheating on both the mistress and the wife. He expressed no remorse over the murders at his trial, only embarrassment that his estranged wife would now find out that he had been unfaithful to her. By that stage the unfortunate Remy must instead have been feeling very relieved that she had got away from Landru alive; the infidelity was a negligible detail.

Landru planned his killings with some care, making sure first that the victims were separated from their families. After he had killed them, he went to the trouble of assuring the families that they were alive and well. Landru sent postcards to Mme Guillin's friends to say that she was unable to write herself, which was true. He forged a letter from Mme Buisson to her dressmaker and another to the caretaker at her apartment in Paris. Landru posed as the solicitor of Mme Jaume, who had been in the process of divorcing her husband, and closed her bank accounts. The idea was to create the impression that the ladies were alive and well.

Two years after Mme Buisson had the misfortune to meet Landru, her son died. Obviously the family wanted to inform Mme Buisson, but could not contact her. Her sister remembered that she had said something about running away with a M Guillet, so she wrote to the mayor of Gambais to see if he could locate either of them for her. The mayor knew nothing of either party but resourcefully suggested that she should contact the family of Mme Collomb, who had also mysteriously disappeared in Gambais under rather similar circumstances. At that stage nobody knew where Mme Collomb had gone – except Henri Landru.

The mayor directed the Buisson family and the police to a villa. The tenant there was a M Dupont, but when the police called at the Villa Ermitage they did not find any of the people they were looking for. There was no Mme Buisson, no Mme Collomb, no M Dupont – and no Henri Landru either. The villa nevertheless belonged to Landru. Mlle Lacoste, who was the sister of Mme Buisson, went on combing the streets of Paris for her. She had a most remarkable piece of luck. She spotted the distinctive Henri Landru coming out of a shop and recognized him as someone she had seen accompanying her sister and who had been called 'Fremiet'. She lost him in the crowd but had the presence of mind to go into the shop to ask the man's name. She was told he was not M Fremiet but M Guillet, and that he lived in the Rue de Rochechouart. She called the police and Landru was arrested.

Landru was immediately suspected of murdering both Mme Collomb and Mme Buisson, but Landru was unhelpful and the police had no evidence on which to hold him. Where were the bodies? The police returned to Gambais, dug up the gardens, but found only the bones of two dogs. They searched another villa that Landru had occupied at Vernouillet, but found nothing there either. All the police did find was a notebook, in which Landru had usefully recorded all his financial dealings. Most of the contents looked un-promising, but there was one page that was a break-through in the investigation. It carried a cryptic list of names that told an alarming story: 'A. Cuchet, G. Cuchet, Bresil, Crozatier, Buisson, A. Collomb, Andrée Babelay, M. Louis Jaume, A. Pascal, M. Thr. Mercadier'. In the middle of the list were the names of the two missing women everybody was looking for, but who were these other people? Were they perhaps missing too? The police suspected at once that what they now had was a list of murder victims and that Landru was not just a killer but a serial killer.

Landru kept cool and maintained his silence; he was confident that with no bodies there could be no case against him. The police went on investigating the case remorselessly for two years, with Landru consistently and frustratingly refusing to admit to anything. But in spite of his obstinacy, the story began to emerge. Each of the missing women had answered Landru's marriage advertisements before disappearing. Landru had re-corded the purchase of tickets from Paris to Gambais – in each case return tickets for himself but one-way tickets for his victims. It was clear now that Landru had taken all the women to Gambais with the deliberate intention of killing them and disposing of their bodies there.

The police revisited the grounds of the Villa Ermitage and Vernouillet and dug them over again, but still with no result. Then the neighbours at Gambais mentioned the terrible evil-smelling fumes that had come from Landru's kitchen stove. The stove was examined and it gave the investigators the evidence they were looking for. Amongst the ashes they found the remains of fasteners characteristic of women's clothing. The Times added that they also found small human bones, though seems not to have been the case. The police could not tell how the eleven women had been killed, but it was now at least all too clear how their bodies had been disposed of.

Landru had cremated them. Landru could now be charged on eleven counts of murder and sent to trial.

Henri Landru's trial caused a sensation. In a depressing post-war world, the lurid details of Landru's shenanigans were a welcome distraction. The court case had all the ingredients of a high-camp melodrama; Landru's extraordinary villainous appearance, racy lifestyle and long criminal record made him a fascinating figure; his current mistress, Francoise Segret, was a 27-year-old he had picked up on a Paris bus; there was the sensational string of mysterious disappearances; there was the total mystery surrounding the deaths of the eleven women; finally, there was Landru's cavalier, rascally, impudent personality. There were queues to get places in the courtroom. On one occasion, there was such a scrum between some women fighting over seats that Landru called out to them that one of the ladies would be welcome to have his place.

Landru's trial opened in November 1921 and continued for a month. Landru was still convinced that he could not be convicted without the evidence of a body, so he carried on refusing to give away anything at all. His stock replies were that it was no-one else's business what he knew about the disappearance of the women, and that to say what happened would be to betray a woman's confidence. He also believed that because he had been judged sane enough to stand trial he would have to be found innocent, and said as much to the newspaper reporters, who enthusiastically covered his trial in great detail. Landru was bombarded with questions, day after day, but he stood firm. 'I have nothing to say.'

During the trial, Landru's health began to deteriorate, possibly because of the stress, and he became less circumspect in his answers. Although he never admitted killing any of the women, he said enough to show the court that he was deviously concealing a detailed knowledge of what had happened. This was a very serious error of judgement. He needed to create a favourable impression if he was withholding information, and he was creating a very unfavourable impression with his impudence and heavy sarcasm. Increasingly he came across as just the sort of devious, heartless, callous villain who would lure women out to his place in the country and kill them for their money. He increasingly came across as guilty.

It did not take the jury long to decide that he had indeed killed the eleven women, and he was duly sentenced to death. When Landru took his leave of his lawyers, he presented them with a picture. If they had looked behind the picture, they would have found Landru's written confession admitting to the murders, but they did not. Landru was guillotined in February 1922, and his confession remained hidden for another fifty years.

Reginald Christie

Ten Rillington Place

IN THE 1950S Ten Rillington Place became one of the most notorious addresses not only in London but the whole of England. One murder after another took place there and, after the truth came out, it became a pilgrimage focus for those of us with a morbid curiosity for such cases. The house itself became unlettable and unsaleable. Who would want to live in a house where such nightmares had taken place? The house was demolished, just as the Wests' house in Gloucester had to be demolished, and even the name of the street had to be changed – to Ruston Place.

In the 1940s and 50s, when the murders took place, Rillington Place was a cul-de-sac of run-down three-storey terrace houses. Ten Rillington Place was the last house on the left. Beyond it was a high brick wall, and beyond that was an industrial townscape including warehouses, a railway line and some smoking factory chimneys. Soot and grime coated the houses and paint flaked off the door and window frames. Number Ten was divided into three flats. Reg and Ethel Christie had moved into the ground floor flat in 1938. It consisted of a front room used as a sitting room and a back room used as a bedroom; alongside them was a stairwell and passage that led to the kitchen and the back door. This back door gave access to the garden, of which the Christies had exclusive use, and an outside lavatory and washhouse serving all three flats.

Possibly because they had the garden, possibly because their flat was next to the front door, the Christies felt themselves to be a cut above the other tenants. There was a second flat on the first floor, occupied by Mr Kitchener, and a third flat on the top floor.

Christie was a quiet, inconspicuous man in his forties, with ginger hair, pale blue eyes and horn-rimmed glasses. The only remarkable thing about his appearance was his huge domed forehead. His wife Ethel was plump, passive and sentimental. Their acquaintances thought she was afraid of her husband and had to do as she was told. They both thought themselves superior to their neighbours and, though they were friendly and pleasant, they maintained their privacy. To all appearances, they were a normal devoted couple, like thousands of others, taking care of their cat and their dog and taking pride in that great English virtue of keeping themselves to themselves.

For all that, Christie had no reason to think himself better than his neighbours. He was a post office clerical worker and, as it later emerged in the first murder trial, he had convictions for a range of minor offences. Yet the image he cultivated in Notting Hill was that of the professional man, the upright citizen.

As so often, Christie's aberrant behaviour was rooted in his childhood. Christie had been brought up in Yorkshire, a weaker child than his father would have liked, and therefore largely ignored by him except for beatings, of which there were plenty. Christie's father kept him at a distance, while his mother compensated by being over-protective. This smothering by his mother left him emasculated, a mother's boy. The effect was intensified by having four older sisters, who created a feminine atmosphere in the home but also dominated the little boy.

Christie discovered that he could gain attention in the family by exaggerating symptoms of illness – and attention was what he wanted. He also developed an obsessive horror of dirt. He did not make friends. He achieved quite well at school, took part in the church choir, played games and became a scoutmaster; he particularly enjoyed wearing the uniform, because it gave him an identity and a feeling of importance.

It was when he was eight that a decisive rite of passage took place. Christie lived in fear and awe of his father and grandfather. When he was eight his grandfather died; he was asked if he would like to see the body, which was laid out for the wake. He said he would. When he looked at the old man who in life had frightened him he felt a thrill of pleasure at the total absence of stress on meeting him like this. The experience haunted and fascinated him. It was something he would want to repeat. The little boy started to play in the graveyard and was absorbed by a broken tomb built over a vault housing the coffins of children; he used to peer through the cracks to see the coffins inside. The dead were safe. The dead could not criticize or jeer. The dead could not dominate him.

Given the family dynamics, it was not surprising that Christie was sexually inhibited. At the age of ten he was disturbed when he saw the legs of one of his older sisters. There was nothing unusual about this experience; people often learn about the anatomy of the opposite sex through siblings. But with Christie it was different. He resented this older sister who bossed him about, and now he found himself excited by her legs. His dawning masculinity was simultaneously aroused and stifled, and the result was a dangerous tension that would only be resolved through murder. As Ludovic Kennedy has said, 'There must have been many occasions when he thought of his grandfather and wished them all dead.'

The adolescent Christie experimented sexually with girls, but that experience seems to have been disastrous. He was sexually aroused enough to want to be successful, but the years of being dominated and stifled by his sisters made it difficult for him to perform the sexual act. He lost his erection. Girls in the neighbourhood ridiculed him, calling him 'Can't-Make-It-Christie' and 'Reggie-No-Dick'.

He left school and worked as a cinema projectionist. When the First World War broke out he became a signalman. In action he was knocked unconscious by a mustard gas shell and the shock made him lose his voice for three years. It was a hysterical reaction, produced by fear. From then, on through the rest of his life, he exaggerated his illnesses to avoid unpleasant situations. He became a hypochondriac. Christie left the army and took a clerical job.

In 1920 he married Ethel Waddington, but his sexual difficulties were far from over. Ethel seems to have been no help in this respect. Christie had begun the habit of visiting prostitutes. He had fewer difficulties with them, as the question of dominance or ridicule did not arise, but he still felt humiliated at having to visit them. After he married Ethel, he went on using them.

Christie became a postman. He stole some postal orders and was sent to prison for three months. He was still having trouble regaining his voice at this time. When he was 25, Christie was put on probation on charges of violence. Another difficulty now was that gossip about his visits to prostitutes got back to Ethel. He decided to leave her and move to London, leaving her in Sheffield, where she got a job as a typist. Within four years, he was in prison again, for nine months on two charges of theft. He moved in with a prostitute, but when he hit her over the head with a cricket bat he found himself back in prison for six months. He was suspected of violence against other women but, as is often the case with prostitutes, there was little evidence.

A pattern was emerging, of dishonesty, preoccupation with death, sexual difficulties with women that he was resolving through violence. Then he was arrested for stealing a car from a priest who was trying to help him. He wrote to Ethel from prison, asking her to come and live with him. After ten years of estrangement, she moved to London in 1933 to live with Reggie, little realising what she was agreeing to – but, then, how many of us realise that?

Shortly after this, he was hit by a car in the street and had to go into hospital. This started a long phase of hypochondria. He was at home off work, a great deal and made many visits to his doctor. The Second World War broke out and Christie signed up as a member of the War Reserve Police. Incredibly, no check was made of his criminal record, which these days would be standard practice; a check would have revealed a string of convictions for theft and violence that would certainly have debarred him from serving as a policeman. But Christie got his coveted uniform, in which he was photographed, as a Special Constable based at Harrow Road Police Station.

This was a happy time for Christie. He had a uniform, a role, an identity, and he had status as an upholder of the law. He became quite fanatical about his job and earned himself a facetious nickname, 'the Himmler of Rillington Place'. But he abused his position and his uniform to follow women. He also felt obliged to keep watch over his neighbours, boring a peep-hole in his own back door so that he could watch the comings and goings at his neighbours' back door. The abnormal, obsessive personality was becoming more and more evident as time passed; he went on with this for four years.

Ethel meanwhile must have wondered why she had agreed to return to Christie, and she took to visiting her relatives frequently. While she was away, Christie took the opportunity to have sex with other women. He found women who were responsive to him. He developed a relationship with a woman who worked at the police station while her husband was serving overseas. While Ethel was away, Christie went round to the other woman's house for sex. The husband returned unexpectedly and found evidence of his wife's infidelity. He even caught Christie in his house and gave him a beating before throwing him out; he then filed for divorce, citing Christie as co-respondent.

After this setback, Christie started inviting women back to Ten Rillington Place. In a pub he met an Austrian girl called Ruth Fuerst, a lively, energetic 21-year-old with brown eyes and brown hair. She worked in a munitions factory and lived in a bedsit close to Rillington Place. She seems to have earned some money by prostitution too, and that seems the likely starting point of the relationship: it is difficult to understand why else this good-looking young woman would have bothered with the seedy and unappealing Christie.

Ruth started visiting Ten Rillington Place when Ethel was away. One day when they were there, in bed, a telegram arrived to say that Ethel was on her way home with her brother. According to Christie, Ruth responded to this by impulsively asking him to run away with her. He refused. Then Christie had strangled her – while they were having sex. It is not clear whether he killed Ruth because he was afraid she would come round and make a scene when Ethel returned. It may have been a development of his association of sex with violence and death, and that he strangled her while he was having sex with her in order to intensify his pleasure. Christie later wrote, 'I remember, as I gazed down at the still form of my first victim, experiencing a strange, peaceful thrill'.

Christie wrapped Ruth Fuerst's body in her leopard-skin coat and hid it under the floorboards in the front room. When Ethel and her brother arrived the next day, they saw nothing out of the ordinary. Christie's brother-in-law left the day after that and Ethel went back to work. As soon as he was able, Christie took the body out of the house and put it in the washhouse. His plan was to bury it in the garden and he started to dig a grave. Ethel came back before he could finish, so he had to wait until she had gone to bed before finishing the job. He dragged Ruth Fuerst's body out of the washhouse and buried her in the pit. The following day, when he could see what he was doing better by daylight, he raked it over and tidied the garden up. Months later, he accidentally dug up Ruth's skull; he burnt it with some other garden rubbish. Ruth Fuerst was reported missing to the police, but no action was taken.

Christie had enjoyed his first sex killing. A year later he wanted to do it again. He had become a serial killer.

In the spring of 1948, when the Christies had been living there for ten years, some new people moved into the top flat at Ten Rillington Place. They were Timothy and Beryl Evans, who was expecting a baby. Timothy Evans was a 24-year-old van driver from South Wales. As a child he had been prone to temper tantrums. His father had run off and he did not get on with his mother who remarried a man called Probert; he moved in with his grandmother, who was unable to get him to go to school. He was a young man with a range of problems. He had had a disturbed childhood, he could scarcely read, he had an IQ of only 70, he was an inveterate liar. He was a 'Billy Liar' character, who invented fantasies about himself in order to increase his sense of importance.

Timothy met and married Beryl Thorley, who was another immature and unintelligent character; they were in a way well-suited to each other, though hopelessly ill-suited to deal with the problems that life would throw at them. They were, for instance, ill-equipped to deal with a monster like Reg Christie. The two of them had lived with Mrs Probert for a time, which was strained, but now that Beryl was expecting they had to get a place of their own. Evans's sister Eileen found Ten Rillington Place for them, and helped them to decorate and furnish the flat. Eileen was startled one day when Christie suddenly appeared beside her with a cup of tea. She said she didn't want it, but he made no move to leave. Finding his presence rather threatening, she said her brother was coming back soon and Christie vanished just as quickly as he had appeared. She was right to fear Christie. His offer of a cup of tea meant something far more sinister, as she later discovered.

When the baby Geraldine arrived, there were quarrels over money. They could not really afford to bring up a baby. Beryl also, perhaps predictably, turned out to be a hopeless housekeeper and cook. In August 1949, Beryl foolishly invited a friend of hers, a 17-year-old girl called Lucy Endecott, to stay with them. Lucy shared the bed with Beryl while Tim Evans slept on the floor in the kitchen. Lucy became interested in Tim and it was not long before there were three-cornered rows. Mrs Probert intervened and forced Lucy out. Timothy Evans responded to this by threatening to throw Beryl out of the window. Timothy followed Lucy back to another flat where she was staying, but she finished with him when she discovered that he was violent. This streak of violence makes what happened later more difficult to disentangle.

Meanwhile, Timothy Evans returned to Ten Rillington Place, where Beryl discovered to her horror that she was pregnant again. She was not very clever, but she knew they could not afford to have another baby.

Abortion was illegal in the UK at that time, but Beryl made it clear to her husband, who did not understand what all the fuss was about, and the Christies that it was an abortion that she wanted.

Christie had complained about the poor state of the building and workmen arrived on 31 October 1949 to rip out some of the walls and floors. They also worked on the washhouse. At the same time, old Mr Kitchener went into hospital and his flat was empty for five weeks.

Exactly what happened at Ten Rillington Place in November is still a matter of controversy. What did happen is that both Beryl and her baby were murdered. It is not known conclusively whether they were murdered by Christie or by Evans. Christie's version of events was given at Evans's trial. According to Christie, he and his wife were woken in the night by a loud bump overhead. The next day, Evans had told them that Beryl had gone to Bristol, though he told his mother that Beryl had gone to Brighton to see her father. The day after that, Evans told the Christies he had given up his job, though he had in fact been sacked. He had decided to sell all the furniture and join his wife. This he did, even though not all of the furniture was paid for, and he gave the dealer a false address in Bristol. He then sold Beryl's clothes to a rag merchant, which was odd, as he could have got more money by selling to a second hand clothes shop. Then he left by train for his aunt's home in South Wales.

Evans spent an uncomfortable week with his aunt

reciting strings of lies about what had happened. On 23 November he returned to Ten Rillington Place to discuss things with Christie, then went back to South Wales. No-one knew what to make of his erratic behaviour, but Christie's version of events incriminated Evans fatally once Beryl's body was discovered. Evans, with his history of temper tantrums, violence and lying, became the prime suspect but, as Ludovic Kennedy has carefully argued, Christie had set Evans up in such a way that Evans would be the prime suspect.

The alternative scenario is that Christie killed Beryl Evans. Beryl was not intelligent enough to know that Christie could not help her with something like an abortion. What she saw was a former police officer with a first-aid book and a determination to help her. Beryl told Timothy Evans on 1 November that Christie was prepared to give her an abortion, but Evans was not interested, even when Christie showed him the photograph of himself in uniform.

On 7 November, Beryl and Christie made arrangements for him to perform the abortion the following day. She told her husband, and he responded by shouting and slapping her. At midday on .8 November, while the workmen carried on working on the washhouse, Beryl lay down on a quilt in front of the gas fire and submitted to Christie's version of an abortion. It is likely that he used some rubber tubing and a makeshift mask to anaesthetize Beryl. She panicked, possibly when she saw the look in Christie's eyes, and Christie hit her, then strangled her. Then he had sex with her dead body.

Christie was taking terrible risks now. There were workmen in the house. There were also Beryl's friends. One of them, Joan Vincent, called just about the time he was killing Beryl. She was surprised to find the flat door closed. She tried opening it. It opened a short distance and then it was blocked. She sensed that someone was standing behind the door holding it shut. It was Christie, of course. In the end she went away, which was just as well, because Christie would certainly have killed her too.

When Evans came home from work, Christie met him at the foot of the stairs. 'It's bad news, Tim. It didn't work.' Evans went upstairs, distraught, and saw Beryl lying on the bed with a blanket over her. He pulled off the blanket and saw that she was bleeding from the nose, mouth and vagina. Christie explained that Beryl might have died from septic poisoning resulting from all the quack remedies she had tried. He also explained that he couldn't go to the police or they would both get into a lot of trouble – Christie for manslaughter and Evans for being an accomplice. Evans had a history of fights, and the police would naturally suspect him of killing Beryl. It did not take much for Christie to persuade Evans to keep quiet.

Christie offered to dispose of the body, but he could not carry it single-handed downstairs. Together they took Beryl down to Mr Kitchener's empty flat and left it in the kitchen. Christie said airily that he would put Beryl down the drain later. The next day, Christie offered to look after Geraldine. He knew a young couple who would take her. Evans was supposed to tell everyone that Beryl had taken the baby with her on holiday.

According to Ludovic Kennedy, Christie strangled the baby and put her body with that of her mother. On the same day, Joan Vincent inopportunely reappeared. Christie told her Beryl and the baby had gone away, but Joan noticed that the baby's pram and high chair were still there, so she was suspicious. Christie evidently noticed and told her not to come back.

The workmen, who knew nothing of the drama unfolding in the house, finished working on the washhouse, so Christie, alone this time, took the two bodies down and hid them under the sink in the washhouse. The following day he went to doctor complaining of terrible lower back pain, which Kennedy argues was very likely caused by hauling Beryl's body down the stairs and out to the washhouse.

When Evans returned on 23 November, he was expecting to see his daughter. Christie told him to leave or there would be trouble, fobbing him off with the prospect of seeing Geraldine in a few weeks.

Do we believe Christie or Kennedy? It could be argued that Christie had no motive for killing Geraldine – and indeed Christie refused to confess to that murder – whereas Evans might have killed both his wife and his daughter in a rage. On the other hand, as Kennedy has argued, it would be remarkable for two ruthless murderers, both stranglers, to be living by chance under the same roof. It is far more likely that there was one murderer than two murderers.

Mrs Probert was concerned that Tim and Beryl had disappeared. She quickly found that Beryl had not gone to Brighton. She went to Christie, who told her not to worry. Then she heard from her sister that Timothy was staying there and soon found that he had told a lot of lies. The aunt confronted him. Evans could not cope with this. He went straight to Merthyr Tydfil police station, where he told the duty officer, 'I have disposed of my wife. I put her down the drain'.

It was a curious pair of remarks. He had not confessed to murdering his wife, just to putting her down a drain. He was afraid to bring Christie into it, because he was afraid of him and of his imagined reputation as a policeman, so he claimed a stranger had given him something to help Beryl abort. He had given Beryl the bottle, warned her not to use it, but she had; he had arrived home from work to find her dead. He was too frightened to tell the police, so the next morning he had put his wife's body down the drain outside the front door. The Merthyr police phoned the Notting Hill police, who went to investigate. They realised at once that something was wrong with Evans's statement when it took three men to lift the manhole cover. Evans was 5 foot 5 inches tall and slightly built: he could not possibly have lifted the manhole cover by himself. And there was no body.

The Merthyr police told Evans what they had found, or rather had not found. He was astonished, and then offered to make a new statement. This time he would tell the truth. This time he told the version that incriminated Reg Christie. Unfortunately for Evans, he did not include everything in that second statement, but went on adding things, such as the detail that he helped Christie to carry the body downstairs. As far as the police were concerned, Evans was totally untrustworthy, and he stood little chance now of being taken seriously in court.

The Notting Hill police visited and searched Ten Rillington Place, but very superficially. They did not notice the human thigh bone, perhaps Ruth Fuerst's, propping up a fence. Christie's dog dug up a skull, but they did not notice that either. Christie threw the skull into the garden of an empty house nearby; when it was eventually found, there was speculation about the identity of the unfortunate air raid victim. What they did find they misinterpreted. In Evans's almost empty flat they found newspaper cuttings of a sensational recent murder case, the Setty case, which revolved round the unusual disposal of a corpse. The police saw this as incriminating Evans. It did not occur to them that as Evans was barely literate this was much more likely to be a plant put there by Christie to cast suspicion on Timothy Evans.

Christie was interviewed at length but, because of his Special Constable background and general plausibility, especially by contrast with Evans, everything he said was accepted. Christie was able to tell the police about the violent rows the Evanses had had. The police searched Ten Rillington Place more thoroughly, and this time they found the body of Beryl Evans and baby Geraldine, which had been hidden in the washhouse for about three weeks. Both had been strangled. Beryl had been beaten round the face. For some reason the police asked Christie (now apparently very much one of them) about the clothing found with the bodies. Christie said he did not know about the tie that had been used to strangle the baby, but he thought he might have seen Evans wearing it. It was another clever plant. In fact the tie had probably belonged to the absent Mr Kitchener. I wonder if he ever missed it.

Timothy Evans was taken back to London, told that the bodies of his wife and daughter had been found. Tears came to his eyes as he realised that Geraldine too had been murdered. Now in shock, Evans admitted that he was responsible for their deaths; in a sense, in exposing them to Evans, he was responsible. The police got him to sign a statement saying that he had strangled his wife during a quarrel over the debts she was running up, and he later strangled the baby too. Dates were included but, as Kennedy has pointed out, they could not be right, as the bodies could not have been put in the washhouse while the workmen were still in there.

Nor could the bodies have been hidden with planks of ripped-up flooring on 8 November, since the floorboards were not taken up until 11 November. Evans was then interviewed at even greater length and signed yet another statement, probably, as Kennedy has argued persuasively, strongly guided by the police. Each successive statement made it more certain that he would hang.

Later, far too late, Evans would tell his mother, 'I didn't do it, Mam. Christie done it.' The problem is that he was coached by the police, just as earlier he had been coached by Christie.

The only things that make me wonder if, after all, Evans was guilty were the remarks he made about the Setty case. He mentioned that he and Hume, the man who killed Setty, had been together at Brixton and that he had often talked about that case. So it is, after all, just possible that he did keep cuttings about the Setty case, and got people to read them to him. The way Beryl's body was parcelled up was reminiscent of the way Hume parcelled up Setty.

Timothy Evans went on trial for the murder of his baby on 11 January 1950. The case for the prosecution was presented by Christmas Humphreys. The defence lawyers seem to have felt the case was hopeless from the start and they failed to question Joan Vincent, who would have shown Christie in a new light, or the carpenters. They never fully investigated Christie's criminal past, which would have thrown doubt on his credibility as a witness and revealed him as a potential suspect. In fact there were many loose ends that might have been pursued to help Evans. One oddity was Ethel Christie's written statement that she used the washhouse every day to get water, but had never noticed anything unusual. That would mean that she went into the tiny room, not much more than one metre square, twenty or more times when Beryl's decaying body was right under the sink – and never smelt anything peculiar. That statement would have been accessible to the defence lawyers, who failed to notice a lie, probably coached by her husband. They also failed to notice that once she got to court she claimed she never used the washhouse – a significant discrepancy. If it had emerged that the Christies were lying, the trial might have taken a different direction.

The carpenters too would have been useful in court. The police evidently pressed them to say the flooring had been taken up a few days earlier, so that it would have been available for Timothy Evans to hide Beryl before he went to South Wales. In fact Mr Anderson recognized the planks as those he had taken up on 11 November, but was, like so many before and since, browbeaten into changing his story to suit the case against the accused.

The post mortem evidence from Dr Teare the pathologist suggested that someone had tried to have sex with Beryl after her death. He saw this as a sign of sexual mania. The defence lawyer, Malcolm Morris, decided not to use this as it might put Timothy Evans in an even worse light. But what should have occurred to him is that Evans had had no problem in having sex with his wife while she was alive – she had become pregnant twice, after all – and would certainly not have needed to kill her for sex. The sexual motive indeed points away from the husband and towards the greedy, envious stranger. If Malcolm Morris and his colleagues had had any real understanding of sex murders they would have known that this evidence pointed not to their client, the accused, but to the prosecution's star witness. Evans kept telling Morris that 'Christie done it', but even Morris could not bring himself to believe it.

The trial was dominated by the contrast between Evans and Christie as witnesses. Evans came across as guilt-ridden and dazed, a man in pieces. Christie was pleasant, thoughtful, made sure the jury knew about his service in two world wars and the physical ailments he still suffered from. His quietness was probably produced by mortal fear; at any moment the trial could turn against him. Morris did manage to get Christie's criminal record into the open, but Christie was able to impress the court by having gone straight for 17 years.

Evans tried to tell the court that 'Christie done it'. He was asked why Christie would have killed his wife and daughter and poor Evans couldn't think of anything better than, 'Well, he was home all day'. If he was innocent, how had he been able in his statements to describe the murders so well? He said, probably truthfully, that the police had given him enough information to do so. Then the police themselves denied it, and were believed.

The coup de grace was the unexpected brevity of the prosecution's closing speech. The counsel mentioned that Christie was far too ill to have done what Evans claimed he had done, that Christie had no motive, and that Evans was obviously guilty. That was it. It was all over in ten minutes. Morris, the defence lawyer, had assumed that he would have the evening to get his notes together and prepare a convincing speech, but now he found he had to go ahead at no notice. He tried to argue that the jury did not need to decide that Christie had done it, only that there was significant doubt as to whether Evans did it. The following morning, the judge gave a loaded summing up which was heavily prejudicial to Evans.

After a forty minute deliberation the jury decided Timothy Evans was guilty. Outside the courtroom Evans's mother caught sight of Christie and shouted at him, 'Murderer, murderer!' Ethel told her he was a good man, and probably believed it. Timothy Evans was hanged two months later, after a failed appeal, on 9 March 1950.

Christie was a free man. He had by this stage killed four people: Ruth Fuerst, Muriel Eady, Beryl and Geraldine Evans. It could be argued that he brought about the state murder of Timothy Evans too, making five. But Christie's career as a serial killer was far from over. Back at Rillington Place, Mr Kitchener had moved out, oblivious to all that had gone on in' the flats above and below him, and probably not even missing his tie. Some Jamaicans moved into the top flat and Ethel Christie thought it was time to move out. She thought Jamaicans were low class and frightening and she did not like the idea of sharing a toilet with them.

Christie had sunk into a deep depression following the trauma of the trial. He had lost his job at the post office after the disclosures about his convictions. A psychiatrist advised analysis in hospital, but he said he could not leave his wife alone. He gradually improved with weekly support from his GP, and got himself a new job with British Road Services. Then he gave that up, saying he had a better job lined up, though there was nothing.

Ethel was not pleased that he was at home all the time, under her feet in that small flat. Christie hoped she would go on visits to relatives as she had before, but she did not. She was under his feet, and he had things in mind that he wanted to do at home with Ethel out of the way. That was the answer, of course: Ethel out of the way. She made the mistake of taunting him about his impotence, and this touched a very raw nerve. On 11 December 1950, Ethel Christie visited a friend to watch television. On 12 December she went to the laundry. Then no-one ever saw her again. Christie told neighbours his wife had gone to Sheffield. They were surprised she had not said goodbye or mentioned that she was going. Unfortunately for him, Christmas was fast approaching and he had to sign Christmas cards from both of them, arousing suspicion. He started sprinkling the house and garden with a strong disinfectant.

In January, Christie seems to have decided to expose himself to capture by preparing to leave Ten Rillington Place. He sold the furniture, his wife's wedding ring and her watch. He had an old mattress to sleep on, three chairs and a kitchen table. For the next two months he lived in this extraordinary frugal way. He was un-ravelling. He had not entirely given up, though, as one of the three chairs he kept was his killing chair.

One day he spotted a woman looking for a place to rent and he invited her to look at his. He evidently had plans for Mrs Reilly, as he was clearly disappointed when she turned up at Ten Rillington Place with her husband. They decided to take the flat and gave him three months rent. Christie moved out with a suitcase on 20 March, leaving them his cat and a very evil-smelling flat. The Reillys were only there for a day when the landlord called to tell them Christie had no right to sub-let. They had lost their rent money, but the flat smelt so appalling that they were glad to get out.

Christie lived the life of a vagrant. Really, he was waiting for the terrible secrets of Ten Rillington Place to be uncovered. Then it could only be a matter of days before he was arrested. The landlord meanwhile had an empty flat, and he may have felt the property would be more secure with the ground floor occupied, so he

The people of Kasan bow their heads as Ivan The Terrible marches through on horseback. Considered mad by some, admired by others, Ivan The Terrible was one of the most ruthless tyrants in history.

Suleiman the Magnificent ruled from 1520–66. He took the Ottoman Empire to the very peak of its power, but it goes without saying that this was achieved by unscrupulousness, bloodthirstiness and carnage on a huge scale.

Dapper John George Haigh arrives at the court building to stand trial for the slaying of wealthy widow Mrs Olive Durand-Deacon. British police authorities claim Haigh dissolved her body in an acid bath, and also claim that Haigh confessed to five other murders, boasting that although his first murders were 'messy affairs' his 'technique improved' as he went along. Grisly details abound, including a boast to police that he had sucked the blood of victims through a straw.

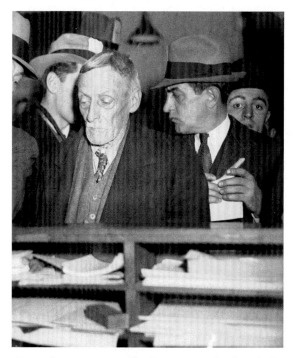

Few killers in America's past have been remembered as more fiendishly deranged than the notorious Albert Fish, the man who ate children. Here, Fish appears in court, captured by detective William King after a six year search.

Seven deputies escort Charles Manson, leader of The Manson Family, from the courtroom after he and three followers were found guilty of seven murders in the Tate-LaBianca slayings.

Henri Landru was accused of murdering 11 people, 10 of them were former sweethearts. He expressed no remorse over the murders at his trial, only embarrassment that his estranged wife would now find out that he had been unfaithful to her.

A police officer carries a bundle of bones, wrapped in newspaper, to a waiting police van outside 10 Rillington Place, London. The bones are those of the fifth person to be killed by the serial murderer John Reginald Christie, former resident of the property.

Ted Bundy leans on the Leon County jail wall as an indictment charging him with the murders of two FSU coeds at the Chi Omega house is read by Leon County Sheriff Ken Katarsis.

Suspect Richard Ramirez, the 'Night Stalker', flashes his left palm showing a pentagram, a symbol of satanic worship, at his former attorney Joseph Gallegos. Ramirez pleaded innocent at the hearing to 68 felony counts, including 13 murder charges. He was found guilty.

Arguably the most powerful and murderous dictator of all time, Joseph Stalin ruled Russia with a regime of terror, causing the death and suffering of tens of millions of his own people.

Ho Chi-Minh, leader of the Communist Vietnminh forces. His leading characteristics were his refusal to negotiate and his preference for armed struggle.

Dr John Adams waves in celebration after having the doctor's plaque outside his Eastbourne home restored, and his name returned to the Medical Register following a period of suspension. Over a period of 35 years in general practice in Eastbourne, Dr Adams had suspiciously been named as a beneficiary in 132 of his patients' wills.

Serial killer and prostitute Aileen Wuornos taking an oath during a murder trial in 1992. Wuornos was convicted of killing six men and was executed in 2002.

David Berkowitz, a 24-year-old postal worker, is taken from the Gold Street station house to Brooklyn Criminal Courts Building. Berkowitz was arrested outside his Yonkers home as a suspect in the 'Son of Sam' murder case.

allowed the upstairs tenant, Beresford Brown, to use the kitchen.

The kitchen was in a very squalid state. Mr Brown noticed the terrible smell and decided to clean it up. He also decided to put up a shelf for a radio. He tapped the walls to find a suitable wall to fix brackets to, and found one wall that sounded hollow, it was evidently a papered-over cupboard door. Mr Brown pulled away some of the wallpaper along one edge and shone a torch through the crack. He was horrified by what he saw inside the cupboard. He recoiled from the door, from the kitchen, and went for the police. He had seen the back of a naked woman.

The police opened the cupboard and saw the corpse of a woman, doubled up as if bowing to them, showing her bare back. The body was removed and put into the front room for examination. Her wrists were tied in front of her and she had been strangled. Then they noticed that there were two odd-shaped bundles in the cupboard that had been hidden behind the woman's body. They were two more bodies, stacked upside down. They too were taken out of the cupboard. The three women were prostitutes, all in their twenties, brought home by Christie to his almost empty flat: Hectorina McLennan, Kathleen Maloney and Rita Nelson. Then the police noticed that some of the floorboards were loose in the front room. They took them up, found a pile of loose rubble. Underneath it they found the body of Ethel Christie.

A police guard was left for the night. The investigators would return the next day to search the entire house. They were fully aware that this was the house where a double-murder had taken place over a year earlier, and that a man had been hanged for it. What were they discovering now? The police searched the garden, thoroughly this time, and found the human thigh bone propping up the fence. Bits of human bone were found in the flowerbeds. The remains when reconstructed turned out to belong to two women, one about 21, the other about 33. The younger was Ruth Fuerst, who had arrived in England from Austria in 1939 and disappeared in 1943. The other was likely to be Muriel Eady, who had worked in a factory with Christie.

The common factor was Reg Christie. However the police and the legal profession might wriggle, it seemed to many people that it was likely that a gross miscarriage of justice had occurred. Many remembered the pathetic cry of Tim Evans – 'Christie done it' – and realised that the wrong man had been hanged. Christie's photograph was published in the newspapers. He saw the photograph and tried to disguise himself by giving away his raincoat. He ran out of the Reillys' rent money fairly quickly and took to sleeping rough on park benches and in cinemas. He was wandering along the Embankment at Putney when a policeman thought he recognized him. He asked him to take off his hat. When he did, he revealed the huge domed forehead. The policeman arrested him at once.

In his statement, Christie tried to limit the damage to himself by saying that some of the women had struggled, that he had 'blacked out' and then woken up to find that he had strangled them. In other words he hadn't killed them on purpose. This was all very unconvincing, as it was evident from the gear the police found that he had devised a system for killing. He placed his victims in a special chair. He also had an inhalant device, which enabled him to administer gas to his victims, and of course he had his strangling rope to hand as well. There was corroboration for this from Mrs Forrest, who had met Christie and made an appointment to go to Christie's house to be treated for her migraines. He had mentioned to her that it would involve gas. For some reason she failed to turn up. Christie went looking for her, made it clear he was cross with her and insisted that she went to his house at once. She agreed, but then lost the address.

Christie admitted to killing Beryl Evans, but made out that it was a mercy killing. She had tried to kill herself with gas and Christie had rescued her; then she had begged him to help her commit suicide. None of that is likely to be true.

Christie went on trial on 22 June 1953, pleading not guilty by reason of insanity. The plea was rejected because although Christie had an hysterical personality and was a sexual pervert he still appreciated the criminality and immorality of his actions. He was asked why during his lengthy confession he had not mentioned

Beryl Evans. He said he had forgotten that one. Since he had given evidence at Timothy Evans's trial only four years before, it could not have gone clean out of his mind. This showed a calculating, devious mind. It was a short trial, given the complexity and high significance of the events. After four days, Reg Christie was found guilty and sentenced to death. He was hanged at Pentonville Prison on 15 July 1953.

The Evans-Christie case left an unpleasant question hanging in the air. Had the British legal system failed to identify Christie as the killer responsible for all the murders at Ten Rillington Place? Had Evans been wrongly hanged? The Recorder of Portsmouth, John Scott Henderson, was assigned to look into the case. His report, published the day Christie was hanged, concluded that Evans had indeed strangled his own wife and child. That conclusion has been challenged again and again since 1953, among others by the psychiatrist hired by Christie's defence lawyers, F. Tennyson Jesse, who wrote The Trials of Evans and Christie, and Ludovic Kennedy, who wrote Ten Rillington Place.

Kennedy believes that little reliance can be put on a confession by a mentally-deficient man under intensive police interrogation; the confession is likely to be false if forced. He also argues that there was evidence that other women were offered medical services by Christie to lure them into compromising positions, fitting the pattern into which Beryl Evans's death fits. The clincher is the absurdity of the underlying Henderson thesis –

that there were two lady-killers, both stranglers, coincidentally operating in the same way in the same house at the same time.

An inquiry carried out in 1965 yielded the very odd opinion from a pathologist that Evans strangled Beryl but not Geraldine. Christie did that. But that is a very odd conclusion to come to, when Geraldine, being a baby, was the one victim who would not have been seen by Christie, give his psychological make-up and interests, as a worthwhile victim. Christie would have had no motive whatever to kill Geraldine – except to cover up the murder of Beryl, and then only if he had murdered Beryl himself. Even so, the thrust of the report was to exonerate Timothy Evans of the murder with which he was charged, and Evans was in 1966 granted a posthumous pardon.

If Evans had been given a prison sentence, the later revelations about Christie would almost certainly have led to Evans's release. The Timothy Evans case was a landmark in British legal history in generating a groundswell of opinion that would lead to the abolition of the death penalty.

Peter Manuel

a Glasgow sex attacker

IN SPITE OF his Mediterranean-sounding name, Peter Manuel was a Scot, though a Scot by a rather unusual route. He was born in 1927 to Scottish parents who had emigrated to the USA. He moved with his parents back to Scotland in 1932. Peter Manuel had a troubled, dysfunctional personality and his youth was spent in and out of approved schools and borstals for a string of minor offences including theft and burglary. He was always a loner, unable to form proper relationships with other people, and ended up still living with his parents in Birkenshaw when he was an adult. He felt more secure in the dark, and took to prowling the streets at night.

He became a sex offender and picked up several convictions for sexual assault and rape. His need for sexual gratification culminated in a series of killings in 1957—58. It is thought that they all took place in the Glagow area where he lived He was eventually charged with eight murders, though it is believed that he killed as many as fifteen people in all, using a Webley revolver, a Beretta pistol and an iron bar; some victims were strangled.

He was arrested on 14 January 1958 and tried at Glasgow Crown Court in May that year. He decided to conduct his own defence, and acquitted himself well, though he did not succeed in getting himself acquitted. He was found guilty of seven of the eight murders with which he was charged and sentenced to death.

Peter Manuel was hanged at Barlinnie Prison on 11 July 1958. Before he was executed he confessed to all of the murders, plus a few others that he had not been accused of. It is not certain how many murders he committed altogether, partly because there was so much variation in the way he killed, but it is believed that he killed fifteen people, possibly more. It was believed by local people, for instance, that Manuel was responsible for killing Anne Stelle in Aberfoyle Street. A woman living in Alexandra Parade reported to the police that she had seen a man running along the Parade from the direction of Aberfoyle Street at about the time of Anne Stelle's murder, but the police did not get back to her. It was one of the murders that was not laid at Peter Manuel's door. Manuel's known victims were Anne Knielands, aged 17, Marion Watt, aged 45, Vivienne Watt, aged 17, Margaret Brown, aged 41, Isabelle Cooke, aged 17, Peter Smart, aged 45, and Michael Smart, aged 11.

Ted Bundy

'My name is Ted'

TED BUNDY WAS born on 24 November 1946 in a home for unmarried mothers in Burlington, Vermont. He started life as Theodore Robert Cowell. To cover up his illegitimacy, his mother, Eleanor Cowell, told the boy he was her brother, leading him to believe that his grandparents were his parents. It has been suggested that the grandfather may also have been the father, and that the trauma of discovering that he was the product of incest may have tipped the boy towards psychopathic behaviour; but none of that is certain. Nothing is known about Ted Bundy that can satisfactorily explain the series of brutal killings that began in 1973.

In 1950 Eleanor Cowell moved to the West Coast, where she settled in Tacoma, Washington. There she changed the boy's name from Cowell to Nelson. It is not clear why she did this. Then a year later she married John Bundy, and the boy took his step-father's surname. There seem to have been no abnormal childhood problems except for these changes of identity and the rather unsettling fact that Ted referred to Eleanor alternately as his sister and his mother. Changing his name twice in quick succession suggests a level of confusion. In his teens, Ted Bundy started stealing on a regular basis and, on his own account, he was socially backward.

Bundy attended the University of Puget Sound for two semesters, then transferred to the University of Washington, where he met and fell in love with Stephanie Brooks. Stephanie was a good-looking young woman with long dark hair parted in the middle. She was strikingly similar in appearance to the young women Bundy would later murder; probably Bundy was consciously or unconsciously killing Stephanie, over and over again. Back in 1966, the relationship with Stephanie was developing smoothly, but by 1968-9 difficulties were emerging and Stephanie broke it off. Bundy was devastated.

It was at this time that he revisited Burlington, the place where he was born, and looked up the records to check whether Eleanor was his sister or his mother. She was his mother. A man called Lloyd Marshall was listed as his father. No-one had ever mentioned him at all. It is not known what effect these significant revelations had on Bundy, but he returned to Washington to try, unsuccessfully, to restart the affair with Stephanie.

Bundy started relationships with two more young women at this time, with Liz Kendall and Ann Rule. To all outward appearances, Bundy was perfectly calm and normal. In 1973 he entered law school. Then came the crisis. He abruptly dropped out of law school – and the killing started.

A 15-year-old girl called Kathy Devine was given a fatal lift in a green pick-up on 25 November 1973. Her body was found a couple of weeks later; her throat had been cut. In January 1974 Bundy brutally attacked 18-year-old Jonu Lenz in the basement bedroom of a house she shared with some other girls in Seattle. She was sexually assaulted and savagely beaten over the head; she was very lucky to survive this attack. The third victim, on 1 February, was Lynda Ann Healy. She was abducted, again from a basement bedroom. The fourth was Donna Manson, who was abducted from Evergreen College; Donna's body was never found. The list of abductions and murders went on, seemingly endlessly: Susan Rancourt, Kathy Parks, Brenda Ball, Georgia Hawkins, Brenda Baker, Janice Ott, Denise Naslund.

A prolific and savage serial killer was on the loose.

The police had little to go on, except the report of a green pick-up and the description of a man with a plaster cast on his arm who was seen by several people approaching women and heard introducing himself as 'Ted'. The composite sketch was published in the press. The likeness was good enough for Ted Bundy's workmates to tease him about being the serial killer. Ted Bundy got well enough with the people he worked with to be able to carry off this chaffing easily enough. He still showed every outward sign of being socially integrated.

One of his victims was discovered near Lake Sammamish, but by then Bundy had moved on to the University of Utah, where he started killing more young women: Nancy Wilcox, Melissa Smith and Laurie Aimee. Then one of the abductions went wrong for Bundy. He approached a young woman named Carol DeRonch on 8 November 1974 at a shopping centre in Murray. He pretended to be a policeman and told her that her car had been broken into. He got her into his car, pulled out a gun and snapped a handcuff onto one of her wrists. Before he could secure the other cuff, Carol realised what was going on and had the presence of mind to get away and flag down a passing motorist who took her straight to the police. Unfortunately there were no fingerprints left on the handcuffs that were clear enough to be used for identification. Bundy was still free to go on killing, and another long list of victims followed: Debbie Kent, Caryn Campbell, Julie Cunningham, Denise Oliverson, Melanie Cooley, Lynette Culver, Susan Curtis, Shelley Robertson, Nancy Baird and Debbie Smith.

By now the authorities in Washington knew they had a massively prolific serial killer on their hands, and the Utah authorities knew that they did too, but because of Bundy's travelling it was difficult to be sure whether the killings were linked. One murderer? Or two, three or four? The scale of the mystery escalated when an investigator found the crushed skulls of several of the missing girls, one of them transported 260 miles from the scene of the abduction. Frequent crossings of state boundaries would make it easier for Bundy to stay at large.

The task force in Washington made gradual progress,

compiling a list of suspects. Using a computer, the list was reduced to twenty-five. They were interviewed one by one. Bundy was on the list. As it happened, Bundy was to be interviewed next, when a Highway Patrol officer, Bob Haywood, noticed an unfamiliar light-coloured Volkswagen in his neighbourhood. When he turned his car lights on the vehicle, it sped away, and Haywood gave chase. Eventually Haywood caught up with the VW and made it pull over to the roadside. He asked for identification. It was Ted Bundy. Haywood noticed that the vehicle had been customized in an unusual way. The passenger seat had been removed. Haywood decided to search the vehicle. He found a bag containing a stocking mask, an ice-pick and some handcuffs. Haywood arrested him for evading a police officer and then released him.

Soon after that, the investigators began to make a link between Bundy and the DeRonch attack. They searched his apartment but found nothing significant. Bundy's photograph was circulated, but unfortunately Carol DeRonch could not positively identify Bundy. A witness at one of the other abductions did recognize him, though. Bundy's girlfriend was interviewed and she told police about his odd collection of possessions, such as a false moustache, crutches and plaster of Paris. It was one of Bundy's favourite tricks to pretend to be disabled by an arm or leg injury, and use this disability to persuade a girl to load something into his car for him. Once the girl was halfway into the car, the plaster cast and crutches would be thrown aside and the girl bundled into the vehicle. It became increasingly obvious that Bundy was the serial abductor and killer.

Almost incredibly, Bundy was granted bail and he moved in with Liz Kendall until his trial. He was convicted of aggravated kidnapping and sentenced to up to fifteen years in prison. The main purpose of this conviction was to hold Bundy until he could be tried for one or more of the murders. The first murder charge would be for the death of Caryn Campbell, one of whose hairs had been found in Bundy's VW. The preliminary hearing was nearly a fiasco when one of the witnesses, asked to identify Bundy, pointed to someone else. The case was still supposed to go to a full trial, though. During a visit to the courthouse on 7 June 1977, Bundy leapt to freedom from a second storey window. He spent several days in the woods near Aspen, but was then caught while driving yet another stolen vehicle through the streets of Aspen.

Once again he was in captivity. Once again he escaped. On 30 December 1977, he broke out of his cell in Colorado Springs by dismantling an old light fixture in the ceiling. He took a bus to Denver, and then a plane to Chicago. By the time the Colorado Springs authorities knew he had gone he was hundreds of miles away. Once in Chicago, Bundy stole another car, drove to Atlanta in Georgia and took a bus to Tallahassee in Florida, where he assumed two new identities – Chris Hagen and Ken Misner.

Travelling long distances and repeatedly crossing state boundaries, Bundy was cleverly exploiting the disunity of the United States. He just might have got away with his appalling list of past crimes, but for the fact that he just couldn't stop committing new ones. He launched into a new series of killings, while he lived off the proceeds of shoplifting, purse-snatching and stolen credit cards. On one night, 14 January 1978, Bundy attacked five girls: Lisa Levy, Margaret Bowman, Karen Chandler, Kathy Kleiner and Cheryl Thomas. They were all housemates at the Chi Omega sorority in Tallahassee. Four of them were sexually assaulted and strangled, bitten and beaten to death; Cheryl survived, but in a terrible state; she suffered permanent hearing loss. Bundy was a psychopath who would only be stopped by capture or death. The unparalleled savagery of the Chi Omega killings showed that Bundy was falling apart psychologically.

Bundy tried to abduct a fourteen-year-old girl in Jacksonville on 8 February 1978, using a stolen van. Luckily the girl's brother turned up just in time and frightened Bundy off. The next day would prove to be the last in Bundy's career as a serial killer. On 9 February he abducted a twelve-year-old girl, Kimberly Leach, from her school campus in Lake City, Florida. It was the first period of the day. She had left one school building to go to another to collect her purse. She got her purse, but was intercepted by Bundy before she made it back to her classroom. She was last seen by a passer-by, who saw Kimberly being led towards a white van by an angry-looking man. The witness did not interfere, assuming that the pair were father and daughter. Poor Kimberley's body was found a month later 30 miles away underneath an old pig shed.

After this final murder, Bundy dumped the stolen van in a high-crime area, presumably guessing that it would be stolen; it was in fact never found, so he was probably right. Bundy stole another vehicle, was stopped by the police, but managed to escape while the officer was checking the registration number. He returned to his Tallahassee apartment, wiped it clean of fingerprints, stole yet another car, and left Tallahassee. Yet again Bundy was stopped by police, when an officer recognized the stolen number plates. He tried to make a run for it, pretended to be shot when fired at, then leapt up ready to fight off the policeman, but was eventually overpowered.

This time it was all over for Ted Bundy. He attempted to pass himself off as Ken Misner, but by now his photograph was to be seen everywhere – he was on the FBI's Ten Most Wanted list – and he was identified as Ted Bundy. He was taken to Tallahassee and charged with the Chi Omega killings on 27 July 1978. In court, Bundy was confident, controlling and aggressive, unsuccessfully demanding that the judge and defence lawyers should be replaced. The Chi Omega trial was held in Miami, and he was found guilty on 23 July. There was overwhelming forensic evidence tying him to the atrocity; the bite marks on one of the victims matched his teeth. There were character witnesses at the trial, including Bundy's mother; Bundy wept as she gave her evidence of his good character. On 31 July, he was sentenced to death. Then he was tried and convicted for the Leach murder. During this trial, Bundy exploited an odd law that allowed marriage in a courthouse, and he married his current girlfriend, Carol Boone, while she took the witness stand.

Bundy was condemned to death twice over, but he still did not give up. He exploited the lengthy appeal procedures in place in America to prolong his life. The final death warrant was issued on 17 January 1989. He tried through his lawyers to get an extra three years to enable him to have time to confess properly to all the killings. They even tried to press the families of missing girls to plead for a stay of execution on this basis, but none of them supported it. They knew it was a ruse to extend his life. Bundy gave a lot of interviews during his last few days, confessing to some murders but not others. He was unwilling to own up to the killing of the younger girls, perhaps because in a corner of his warped mind even he recognized that that was wrong, perhaps because he knew they were too young to have been Stephanie.

Refusing a last meal, Ted Bundy was electrocuted early in the morning on 24 January 1989.

Neville Heath

the sadistic charmer

IN THE STRANGE half-world of post-war England, there were a great many men who had played their part in the war effort, but who were now in serious financial and emotional difficulties. Demobilization was in effect large-scale redundancy. All over the country there were 'war heroes' who needed help and support of every kind. People were inclined to give them that support. But there were also a lot of cads about who were not war heroes or heroes of any kind, and who were ready to trade on the sympathy of others. Neville Heath was one of these cads. Neville George Clevely Heath was a clean-cut, good-looking man of 29, with big blue eyes, wavy fair hair and a fresh complexion. He was charming. He had perfect manners. It was easy to imagine that he was the top-drawer war hero he wanted people to believe in.

There was a hidden dark side, though – and a very dark side it was. He already had a criminal record. He had served time in civilian prisons for a string of petty crimes – theft, fraud and false pretences – and he had been court-martialled from no less than three armed services for criminal activities. He had been court-martialled by the British RAF in 1937 for being absent without leave, escaping while under arrest and theft of a car. He had been court-martialled by the British Army in 1941 for going absent without leave and issuing dishonoured cheques. He had been court-martialled by the South African Air Force in 1945 for wearing unauthorized decorations and undisciplined conduct. In April 1946 he was fined £10 by magistrates in Wimbledon for wearing decorations he was not entitled to. It may be that someone with Heath's personality defects can only be kept out of major trouble in wartime. Certainly by the time he was washed up in post-war London he was short of challenges and short of excitement, and this may be what led him to try out far more dangerous new thrills.

Heath nevertheless successfully play-acted a series of suave army colonels and daring air force captains in order to attract the ladies round the clubs and res-taurants in London. The adoption of the alias 'Brooke' was a deliberate and cynical reference back to the similarly good-looking poet of the same name. He was never short of a pretty woman at the end of an evening.

The problem was that he did not just want sex, he wanted sex and violence. He was a vicious sadist. It was relatively easy to find women who liked a little bit of smacking or whipping, or being tied up, but he wanted something much stronger than that. In March 1946, the month before he was fined for wearing false medals, there was an incident at a London hotel that showed where Heath was heading. The house detective at a hotel in the Strand broke into one of the rooms after guests reported hearing a woman screaming. He found Heath savagely whipping a naked girl whose hands and feet were bound. The girl did not want to make a formal complaint to the police, because she did not want the publicity that would involve. The hotel management did not want that sort of publicity either. So Heath was allowed to get away with this sadistic attack.

But in May, he did it again, and this time the woman died. His first murder victim was a masochist, a woman who was on the look-out for men who would satisfy her craving for bondage and flagellation. Margery Gardner was 32, and known as 'Ocelot Margie' to the doormen at the clubs where she turned up in her trade-mark ocelot fur coat. She had been married but was now separated from her husband. She went with Neville Heath to the Pembridge Court Hotel in Notting Hill Gate with Heath, expecting a whipping. She got it too, but the noise once again drew the attention of other guests. Once again the hotel detective intervened and the thrashing was stopped.

Unfortunately Ocelot Margie was ready to try again and she agreed to another date with Heath at the same hotel, expecting more violent sex. She got much more than had reckoned on. At 2pm the next day, the chambermaid went into Room 4 on the first floor and was horrified when she drew back the curtains and saw what lay on one of the beds. The two single beds were in disarray and covered in blood. On one of them was the dead body of Ocelot Margie.

The pathologist's report on her damaged body told a terrible story. She was murdered by suffocation. Her ankles were tied tightly together with a handkerchief. Her face was bruised as if someone had used great force to keep her mouth shut, and covered with criss-cross knife slashes. Her body was covered with blood seeping from diamond-patterned whip marks. Her nipples had been bitten off. The interior of her vagina had been badly torn by some sort of blunt instrument that had been inserted and savagely rotated. Oddly, her face had been washed clean, though congealed blood still filled her nostrils and eyelashes. There was no evidence that any normal sexual intercourse had taken place.

The sheer savagery of the murder put London into a panic. A depraved monster was on the loose. Scotland Yard had a marvellous lead to go on, of course – the hotel register. The gentleman booked into the room in question was none other than Neville Heath.

Evidently Heath had taken great pleasure in this first killing – it is always assumed that the Margery Gardner murder was his first – and wanted to repeat the experience.

A couple of days later, Heath was in Worthing, having dinner with the girl he had shared Room 4 at the Pembridge Hotel immediately before Margery

Gardner. She was Yvonne Symonds, a 19-year-old who had met Heath at a club in Chelsea a week earlier and consented to spend the following night with him after he proposed marriage. She was back at her parents' home in Worthing now. Heath booked himself into the Ocean Hotel and took Yvonne out to a club at Angmering for dinner.

Over dinner, Heath told her a version of what had happened at the Pembridge Hotel. He had met Margery Gardner on the evening of 20 June. She had asked to borrow the room he had booked (for himself and Yvonne, originally) so that she could entertain another man, as they had nowhere else to go. Heath himself had slept somewhere else and had been taken to the room by an Inspector Barratt the day after the murder and shown the body. 'It was a very gruesome sight', he told Yvonne. The killer, he reflected, must have been some sort of sexual maniac. Well, he would know.

Yvonne may have accepted Heath's version of events, but both she and her parents were perplexed the following day when they read in the Sunday papers that the police were looking for Neville George Clevely Heath. According to what he had told Yvonne, they had already seen him. Inspector Barratt had shown him Margery's body. Still not realising the awful truth, Yvonne decided to ask Heath to explain the situation, and phoned him at the Ocean Hotel. He told her he was going back up to London to clear up what was obviously some sort of misunderstanding.

He settled down to write a letter to Inspector Barratt at Scotland Yard, signing it with his real name, saying he felt he should report what he knew of the case. He decided the story he told Yvonne was good enough for the police. He had given Margery his room key, because she wanted to sleep with the other man for financial reasons. She had hinted that that if Heath arrived back at 2am she would spend the rest of the night with him. He had gone back at the appointed hour and found Margery 'in the condition of which you are aware'. He had panicked and run away because of his invidious position.

Heath gilded the lily by giving the police a description of the other man. He was slim, dark-haired (unlike Heath), and he was called – Jack. Presumably at some level in his mind Neville Heath was aware that he was behaving like that notorious other Jack, Jack the Ripper. Heath thought he would be extra helpful by sending Barratt an artefact. 'I have the instrument with which Mrs Gardner was beaten and am forwarding this to you today. You will find my fingerprints on it, but you should also find others as well.' Obviously Heath was not thinking very clearly when he offered the whip. If he had been horrified and revolted by the gruesome sight of Margery Gardner lying dead in his hotel room, his natural instinct would have been to touch nothing and get out as fast as possible – not collect souvenirs.

The letter did much to incriminate Heath. The whip never arrived at Scotland Yard, but Barratt was not surprised by that. He was now extremely suspicious of

Neville Heath but, for some unaccountable reason, did not issue a photograph of him. This put any number of young women in extreme danger during the next fortnight.

Heath did leave Worthing as he told Yvonne, but not to return to London. Instead he went west.

On 23 June 1946 Neville Heath booked into another hotel, this time the Tollard Royal Hotel in Bournemouth, this time under the name Group Captain Rupert Brooke (which was surely far too good to be true), and stayed there for two weeks, going to shows, drinking copiously, chatting up girls who were there on holiday. He chatted to a young woman who was staying at another hotel nearby, the Norfolk. She was 21-year-old Doreen Marshall from Pinner and she was in Bournemouth convalescing after a bout of influenza. Doreen Marshall agreed to a dinner date on 3 July. That night at midnight she disappeared.

Two days later, the manager of the Norfolk Hotel reported that Doreen Marshall was missing. She had last been seen going off to have dinner at the Tollard Royal. The manager of the Tollard Royal asked 'Captain Brooke' if he knew what had happened to his dinner guest and recommended Brooke to get on to the police. Heath did as he was told, to avoid suspicion falling on him, and identified Doreen from photographs he was shown. He met Doreen's father and sister, who were in by now in some distress. But one of the policemen thought Captain Brooke bore a close resemblance to a man wanted by Scotland Yard. Heath was asked directly if he was the man wanted for questioning about a murder at Notting Hill Gate in London. He denied it, but the policeman delayed him at the station long enough for several other officers to get a good look at him.

As the evening drew in, Captain Brooke complained of feeling cold, so as a kindness one of the officers went to the Tollard Royal Hotel to collect Brooke's jacket. The officer naturally had a look in the jacket pockets and found what they were looking for. There was a single artificial pearl and a left-luggage ticket issued at Bournemouth West railway station on 23 June. It was for a suitcase full of damning evidence; clothes labelled 'Heath', a bloodstained neckerchief, a scarf with women's hair stuck to it, a vicious leather riding crop with a criss-cross weave. The end of the crop had been worn away and there was blood on the exposed wire.

It was five days since Doreen's disappearance and she had still not been found, but Heath was taken to London without delay and charged with the murder of Margery Gardner. It was 8 July. That same evening, as Heath arrived in London, Doreen was found.

A woman walking her dog in a deep wooded valley called Branksome Chine, about a mile west of the Tollard Royal Hotel, noticed swarms of flies buzzing round a patch of undergrowth beside the footpath. She remembered the report of the missing girl and called the police. On investigation, the police found an appalling sight. Doreen's body was found hidden inside a clump of rhododendrons. She was naked except for one yellow shoe. She had been savagely mutilated with a knife. Her clothing, a yellow jacket, an inside-out black dress and her underwear, had been draped casually over her body after the murder. Doreen's empty handbag was found tossed away nearby, rifled by Heath for anything of value, along with her ripped stockings and broken pearl necklace.

As with Margery Gardner, the nipples had been partially bitten off. There was a jagged slashing wound that zig-zagged up from her vagina right up to her chest, reminiscent of one of the hallmarks of a Jack the Ripper killing. Another weapon, probably a branch ripped from the rhododendron bush, had been used to violate her vagina and rectum. Some of the stab wounds were an inch deep. Her throat was slit twice causing great loss of blood, and this was the likely cause of death. Doreen's hands were badly cut; these were probably defence wounds, acquired while the poor young woman was fighting for her life. Her hands were tied together. One of her ribs was broken and sticking into her lung, as if her killer had knelt on her to hold her down. It was an unusually brutal and savage killing.

Neville Heath told the police that he had left Doreen near the pier and watched her walk back towards her hotel through some public gardens. He went back to his hotel at about half past midnight. He knew the night porter would be waiting for him, and decided to play a practical joke on him. He climbed up to his room using a builder's ladder that had been left outside. He described this jape as 'a small deception'. The police dismissed this and everything else Heath said as large-scale deception.

Amongst Heath's belongings, the police found plenty of evidence connecting him with both Margery Gardner and Doreen Marshall, including handker-chieves, scarves that had belonged to them and weapons stained with their blood. Heath was charged with both murders, but tried for only one of them. Heath's defence lawyer decided not to put him on the stand. He was such a boaster that he would have sunk the case the lawyer was trying to build. A plea of insanity was entered – a desperate measure on the part of his defence counsel. The psychiatrist who was called to support this plea was a distinguished figure in his day, Dr William Henry de Bargue Hubert, who had been psychotherapist at Wormwood Scrubs Prison. He made out a very weak case for Heath's insanity, a case that was totally demolished by the prosecution's cross-examination.

Dr Hubert claimed Heath knew what he was doing when he tied up and whipped Margery Gardner, but did not know it was wrong. The prosecution counsel asked, 'Did he then think it was right?'

'Yes', Dr Hubert replied.

'Are you saying, with your responsibility, that a person in that frame of mind is free from criminal responsibility if what he does causes grievous bodily harm or death?'

Hubert replied, 'Yes I am, because sexual perverts often show no regret or remorse.'

Hawke, the aptly named prosecuting counsel, asked, 'Would it be your view that a person who finds it convenient at the moment to forge a cheque in order to free himself from financial responsibility is entitled to say that he thought it was right, and therefore he is free from the responsibility of what he does?'

'He may think so, yes.'

'With great respect, I did not ask you what he thought. I asked whether you thought he was entitled to claim exemption from responsibility on the grounds of insanity.'

Hubert was falling apart now. 'Yes, I do.'

Hawke continued, as if in disbelief, 'You are saying that a person who does a thing he wants to do, because it suits him at the moment to do it, is entitled, if that thing is a crime, to claim that he is insane and therefore free from responsibility?'

Hubert was now irrevocably caught in his own trap. 'If the crime and the circumstances are so abnormal to the ordinary people, I do.'

Even Heath could see that Hubert was damaging his prospects. He dropped urgent notes to his own counsel to drop the insanity plea. In 1946, the dividing line between being hanged and being confined to a mental hospital was the dividing line between being diagnosed psychopathic and being diagnosed psychotic. At that time, psychopaths were considered capable of controlling their urges to commit crimes, while psychotics were not. If Hubert was to do his job for Heath successfully, he had to prove Heath was psychotic, not psychopathic. Heath was in great peril, as two prison doctors had diagnosed him as abnormal, a sadistic sexual pervert, and a psychopath. Therefore, given the legal technicalities of the time, Neville Heath was not insane.

Not only had Hubert lost the case for Heath, he had emerged from the trial a totally discredited figure, his own reputation in ruins. He committed suicide the following year.

The jury took an hour to decide that Neville Heath was guilty of murdering Margery Gardner. He was sentenced to death and sent off to Pentonville, where sentence would be carried out. He did not bother to appeal, and expressed no remorse for the sufferings of his victims, no sympathy for their families.

In a typically grand gesture, Heath asked that his diaries, containing details of his sexual conquests, should be destroyed in order to protect the reputations of the women involved. The sadism was probably a constant and permanent part of Neville Heath's make-up, but it is not at all clear why he started murdering when he did. It is known that he had been a petty criminal for some time. It is known that he had had a few drinks before each of the two murders, but the consumption of alcohol is not usually enough to trigger violent sadistic killings like these. The Heath case is something of a puzzle. Maybe the diaries should have been preserved after all.

Neville Heath wrote two final letters to his mother before he was hanged on 26 October 1946, one regretting that he had been an unworthy son, which was certainly true, and the other regretting the approaching dawn, when he would hang, and asking her not to grieve for him. The cad's last request was for a whiskey. Then he thought for a moment, realising perhaps that someone else was paying for this round, and said, 'Make it a double.'

Albert De Salvo

the Boston Strangler

ALBERT DE SALVO is generally believed to have been the notorious Boston Strangler. The reign of terror of the Boston Strangler was as brief as that of his notorious London counterpart, Jack the Ripper. It is often forgotten that the Jack the Ripper murders all took place within a period of only four months. All the Boston Strangler murders similarly happened within a short period, in the Strangler's case an eighteenth-month period between June 1962 and January 1964. Between those two dates, thirteen women of various ages, but all single and living quiet, self-contained lives on their own, were murdered in the city of Boston, Massachusetts. The youngest victim was nineteen years old, the oldest was eighty-five. All of them were murdered in their own apartments, first sexually assaulted and then strangled with items of their own clothing. A peculiarity of all the cases was that there was no sign of forced entry into the apartment, implying that either the murderer was known to the victim or he was extremely plausible and persuasive, able to talk his way in. Somehow and for some reason that we still don't know, in each case the women invited the murderer into their homes.

A complication in this case is that the attacks were not necessarily all the work of the same person. The police working on the murder cases at the time were not convinced that a single serial killer was to blame. There is always the possibility, when details of a crime are well-publicized, that attention seekers will copy the crime. Nevertheless, the people of Boston believed that the murders were all committed by one man, and this real or imaginary man became known as the Boston Strangler.

De Salvo might have got away with the string of thirteen murders, but in the end he gave himself away. It is often the way with psychopaths that they have a psychological need to be caught or stopped; often after a run of 'successful' killings, they will unconsciously give themselves away, and make it easier for the police to apprehend them. Sometimes they advance deeper into insanity. Sometimes they become aware that they are increasingly out of control. Sometimes they simply get careless.

Police investigators made their breakthrough in identifying Albert De Salvo as the Boston Strangler in the autumn of 1964. On 27 October, De Salvo got into a young woman's apartment posing as a detective. He tied the victim to her bed, sexually assaulted her and then suddenly changed his mind, apologizing to her and leaving. The woman was lucky to have survived this visit, particularly because she was later able to give the police a detailed description of her visitor. This led to the identification of the attacker as Albert De Salvo. Even at this point, the police were not thinking of this attacker as the Boston Strangler, but when he was charged with rape and interviewed, De Salvo confessed in detail to all the crimes of the Boston Strangler.

The case against Albert De Salvo might therefore seem to be open and shut. But there was no physical or witness evidence, no evidence of any kind, to support his confession, and it is relatively common for people with personality disorders to confess to crimes they have not committed. There is in addition something profoundly disturbing, disorientating, even disintegrating, about being questioned by professional interrogators, and history is littered with the corpses of unfortunate people who have agreed under pressure of questioning to all manner of crimes they have not committed, confessed to almost anything.

There were discrepancies between De Salvo's account of the killings and the pathologists' reports on the victims' bodies. Both investigators and psychiatrists were ready to discount his implausible and apparently rehearsed or coached confession.

Showing remarkable self-restraint, the law enforcement officers decided that De Salvo was not to be charged with the serial stranglings at all, but for some earlier crimes, robbery and sexual assault. He was found guilty of these and sentenced to life imprisonment in

1967. There was a general assumption that the Boston Strangler had been captured and de-activated, and that he was now safely behind bars, but some criminologists remained (and still remain) convinced that there was more to the series of killings than had been satisfactorily explained. The case is not closed.

De Salvo himself was unable to throw further light on the matter, as he was murdered in prison six years later, in 1973. One reason for believing De Salvo was not responsible for the crimes was that people who knew him personally were convinced that he was not capable of committing such crimes. On the other hand, we know from the lives of many other psychopathic serial killers that this is a common pattern. A great many quiet, kind, well-mannered people have turned out to be serial criminals of one kind or another.

There is some forensic evidence in favour of De Salvo's innocence. The eleventh of the Strangler's victims, nineteen-year-old Mary Sullivan, who died on 4 January 1964, may not have been killed by De Salvo. She was found dead by her room-mates, strangled with a stocking. Her nephew Casey Sherman later explored the crime scenes, the initial police investigations, the prime suspects, and also De Salvo's confession tapes, which have never been made public. Casey Sherman believes that the Boston Strangler Task Force was driven by political motives, and that the defence attorney manipulated De Salvo's confession. Casey Sherman also gathered forensic evidence, including DNA evidence, that suggests that Mary was not killed by De Salvo but by somebody else. Sherman's campaign led to his forming an alliance with De Salvo's family; together they attempted to get the law enforcement officers in Massachusetts to declare De Salvo innocent and re-open the Mary Sullivan murder enquiry. Sherman believes he knows who the real killer of Mary Sullivan was.

A disquieting aspect of Sherman's line of enquiry is that, if De Salvo did not kill Mary Sullivan, then quite possibly he did not kill any of the other victims either.

In 1971, Albert De Salvo was awarded an extraordinary commendation by the Texas House of Representatives, who in their citation said that he was 'officially recognized by the state of Massachusetts for his noted activities and unconventional techniques involving population control and applied psychology.' The commendation was made at the instigation of Texas legislator Tim Moore, with the idea of highlighting the lack of legislative scrutiny in Massachusetts.

Behind and beyond all these complex political and criminological wrangles rests a truth that is uncomfortable to live with. Albert De Salvo may have been the Boston Strangler. If so, he was sent to prison, even if for another crime, and because he was stabbed to death while in custody he was unable to re-offend. Society was saved from further attacks. But if De Salvo was not the Boston Strangler, then somebody else was – and that somebody else was never caught.

Peter Sutcliffe

the Yorkshire Ripper

DURING THE LATE 1970s and early 1980s, women in the north of England lived in fear of a serial killer known as Wearside Jack and the Yorkshire Ripper. As with the notorious Whitechapel murders, there was a very high level of public criticism of the way the police handled the case. There was also tremendous relief when the Ripper's reign of terror came to an end, with the arrest of a prostitute, Olivia Reivers, and her client. She may not have realised it at the time, but the arrest saved Olivia's life. She had been about to become the Ripper's fourteenth victim.

The Yorkshire Ripper murders started in October 1975, with the killing of a 28-year-old prostitute named Wilma McCann from the Chapeltown district of Leeds. She had gone out for an evening's work, kissing her four young children goodnight. She had spent the evening drinking in various pubs and clubs, and ended up touting for business after midnight. The Ripper picked her up in a lime green Capri and took her the Prince Philip playing fields. She got out of the car, started to remove her trousers and snapped at him, 'Come on, get it over with'.

The Ripper muttered, 'Don't worry, I will', as he reached for his hidden hammer. Then he started battering Wilma McCann over the head. As she lay on the grass, he stabbed her in the neck, chest and abdomen, 'to make sure she was dead', he later explained. Her body was found on the Leeds playing field the next morning. It had some distinctive wounds – hammer blows to the head and some stab-wounds inflicted with a screwdriver. Three more murders, all of prostitutes in the Leeds-Bradford area, followed a similar pattern.

Peter Sutcliffe later told police that he had driven home to his wife, Sonia, a schoolteacher. 'I carried on as normal, living with my wife. After that first time I developed and played up a hatred for prostitutes in order to justify within myself a reason why I had attacked and killed Wilma McCann.'

The pattern changed in June 1977 when a 16-year-old girl, not a prostitute this time, fell victim to a Ripper attack. This 'innocent' victim was a girl of sixteen, a shop assistant called Jayne MacDonald. After a night out in Leeds city centre she had walked home along Chapeltown Road. At 2am she stopped and chatted to two prostitutes. She may have stopped just to ask them the time, but the conversation was enough to persuade Sutcliffe, who was following her, that she too must be a prostitute. He followed her and attacked her with a hammer and a kitchen knife. Then he dumped her body in a school playground.

The murder of Jayne MacDonald shocked the whole country, not least because it showed that no young woman was safe from the attentions of the Ripper. West Yorkshire Chief Constable Ronald Gregory appointed his most senior detective, George Oldfield, to investigate the Ripper murders.

Alarmed by the escalation of police attention, the Ripper turned to Manchester for his next attack. Jean Jordan, a young woman of 20, was murdered in October 1977. Her body was mutilated. Sutcliffe had even tried to cut off her head. Before killing her, Sutcliffe had paid her £5, which she put in her handbag. After killing her, he threw the handbag into some shrubs nearly 60m away from the body. The police did not find the handbag during their initial search. Sutcliffe went back to the crime scene because he feared that the five pound note was traceable back to him. It was brand-new. Sutcliffe could not find the bag, but the police did, and they traced the note to the payrolls of several Yorkshire firms. One of them was a road haulier firm, T. and W. H. Clark – and one of their employees was Peter Sutcliffe.

Sutcliffe was interviewed, but provided what seemed like a sound alibi: he and his wife had been giving a house-warming party. It was only later that it emerged that Sutcliffe had driven to Manchester after the party. Sutcliffe was elated by his escape from arrest, and became bolder in his attacks. Three prostitutes were killed in the space of four months in early 1978, in Bradford, Huddersfield and Manchester. They were Yvonne Pearson, Helen Rytka and Vera Millward.

George Oldfield was out of his depth. He was given lots of officers and huge resources, but the volume of data coming in was too great to handle. The evidence was not being entered onto computers, either, which was a major mistake. Computer analysis would have revealed that the name Peter Sutcliffe was coming up again and again. There were repeated glints from the needle in the haystack, but George Oldfield could not see them.

In the years 1978—1980, few woman would venture out alone at night in Manchester, Sheffield or Bradford. If they wanted to go out, it had to be in company. Peter Sutcliffe warned his sister of the dangers of going out at night alone, and often gave her a lift to ensure her safety. In some northern cities, groups of vigilantes walked the street, occasionally attacking men who resembled the photofit images circulated by the police.

A Halifax Building Society employee called Josephine Whitaker was murdered in Halifax in April 1979. Then Oldfield made a tragic mistake. He decided that a series of letters posted in Sunderland and claiming to be from the Ripper must be genuine. In June, the letter writer went a step further by sending Oldfield an audio cassette. Oldfield was convinced this was the Ripper, and sent his officers on a wild goose chase looking for a

'Wearside Jack' with a Geordie accent. Arguably, this wrong turning in the enquiry cost the lives of several more young women.

In July 1979, Peter Sutcliffe was interviewed by the police investigating the Ripper murders – for the fifth time. DC Andrew Laptew and DC Graham Greenwood were suspicious of Sutcliffe, but their report was marked 'to file', simply because his voice and handwriting did not fit Oldfield's idea of Wearside Jack.

In September 1979, the Yorkshire Ripper – and it was Peter Sutcliffe – struck again. He killed a young woman called Barbara Leach in Bradford. A month earlier, George Oldfield had had a heart attack, and it was clear it was time for him to retire. After the Ripper had killed two more victims, Marguerite Walls and Jacqueline Hill, Oldfield was forced to retire. In November 1980, Oldfield was replaced on the case by Detective Chief Superintendent James Hobson, who clearly did not believe in the Wearside letters and tape, but who loyally did not publicly refute the Wearside connection either.

It was almost by chance that the Ripper was caught in January 1981, and when he was caught the police had to admit that the Wearside connection had been a complete red herring. There have been rumours that the tape and letters were the work of a malicious police officer with a grudge against George Oldfield, but an investigation was unable to prove anything.

The Ripper was discovered by Sheffield police in his brown Rover with a 24-year-old prostitute named Olivia (or Ava) Reivers. The car had false number plates and carried the Ripper's sinister armoury: a garotte, a hammer and a sharpened screwdriver. Olivia Reivers had been plying her trade in the red light district of Sheffield when a client pulled up in a brown Rover. They agreed a price, she got into the car and the man drove her to a quiet spot in Melbourne Avenue. Ten minutes later, a police car turned into the drive where they had parked. Sergeant Robert Ring and Constable Robert Hydes went up to the Rover. The driver gave his name as Peter Williams and told the policemen that the girl was his girlfriend. When asked her name, he admitted he didn't know. 'I haven't known her that long.'

The police were suspicious, and decided to check the Rover's registration number with the police national computer. They found that the number plates belonged to a Skoda, not the brown Rover. Reivers and her client, 'Williams', were arrested and taken to Sheffield police station, though the police first allowed him to go and relieve himself behind a storage tank.

When the suspect was taken into custody for questioning, it emerged that he was Peter William Sutcliffe, a married man living in a respectable middle-class district of Bingley. He had had a variety of jobs, including digging graves in Bingley cemetery. It also emerged, worryingly, that the police had interviewed him no less than nine times before and not realised that he was their man. But Sutcliffe went to sleep in his police cell, confident that he would only be charged with stealing the number plates from a Dewsbury scrapyard.

Sergeant Ring was nevertheless not happy about the man. He decided, playing a hunch, to go back to Melbourne Avenue and have another look at the scene of the arrest. He remembered Sutcliffe's request to relieve himself behind the tank. He went to have a look. There he found a ball-pein hammer and a knife. Sutcliffe had gone behind the tank to get rid of the weapons he had been about to use on Olivia Reivers. It was 11pm on 3 January 1981 – and the hunt for the Yorkshire Ripper was over.

Then Sutcliffe was confronted by Detective Inspector John Boyle of the Ripper Squad. 'I think you are in serious trouble.'

Sutcliffe said, 'I think you have been leading up to it.'

'Leading to what?' asked Boyle.

'The Yorkshire Ripper.'

'What about the Yorkshire Ripper,' asked Boyle.

Then Sutcliffe blurted out, 'Well, it's me. I'm glad it's all over. I would have killed that girl in Sheffield if I hadn't been caught. But I want to tell my wife myself. It is her I'm thinking about – and my family. I am not bothered about myself.' Sutcliffe went on over the next 15 hours to give a detailed account of his life as the Ripper.

Sutcliffe was described by a friend as a quiet, un-aggressive man. One of a family of six, he had left school at fifteen and gone through a series of different jobs including labouring and two spells as a gravedigger. A workmate recalled that his behaviour even then was irregular. He usually opened the coffins and robbed the corpses of rings or other jewellery. Even more macabre, he would sometimes play with the corpse like a ventriloquist's dummy. He was eventually sacked from this job for poor time-keeping. Sutcliffe had married a schoolteacher called Sonia Szurma in 1974 and started murdering women just a year later. Sonia had a history of mental instability, and it is possible that Sutcliffe was in reality releasing the aggression and frustration he felt towards his wife. Although outwardly demure, Sonia was giving him a difficult time at home, frequently shouting at him. In response, the slightly built Sutcliffe did no more than ask her to keep her voice down. There was a great deal of tension in the relationship, and it found its outlet in the series of terrible killings.

Whether Sutcliffe was also a missionary serial killer is less certain. He certainly hated prostitutes. This hatred may have stemmed from an incident when he was ripped off by a prostitute in the Manningham Lane red light district of Bradford. He started attacking women in the summer of 1975. He attacked two in Keighley and one in Halifax. Characteristically, these early victims survived, reported their experience to the police and the police did not make any connection between the attacks. In this way, the series of attacks paralleled the Jack the Ripper attacks, in that it is not clear exactly who the earliest victims were.

The Yorkshire Ripper attracted a great deal of press interest, not merely because of the series of horrible murders, but because of the suspicion that mishandling of the case by the police had delayed the arrest and therefore allowed Sutcliffe to kill more women. The manhunt, costing £4 million, had been seriously misled and substantially delayed by three letters and a tape that had apparently come from the Ripper in 1978. The police accepted the tape as authentic. The voice on the tape had a Geordie accent, which meant that police for a time ruled out non-Geordies from their enquiries; meanwhile the murders continued. The tape turned out to be a hoax. The result was a depressingly long list of victims;

30 Oct 1975: Wilma McCann, 28
20 Jan 1976: Emily Jackson, 42
5 Feb 1977: Irene Richardson, 28
23 April 1977: Patricia Atkinson, 32
26 Jun 1977: Jayne MacDonald, 16
1 Oct 1977: Jean Jordan, 20
21 Jan 1978: Yvonne Pearson, 21
31 Jan 1978: Helen Rytka, 18
16 May 1978: Vera Milward, 40
4 April 1979: Josephine Whitaker, 19
2 Sep 1979: Barbara Leach, 20
20 Aug 1980: Marguerite Walls, 47
17 Nov 1980: Jacqueline Hill, 20

Another cause for interest in the case was the application of the 1957 Homicide Act. Under this Act, Sutcliffe asked for a reduced charge of manslaughter on grounds of diminished responsibility. He was in effect pleading insanity. The Attorney General and the judge were uneasy about shrugging off a whole series of murder charges, and it was with murder that Sutcliffe was charged. The Attorney General said what the jury had to decide was whether Sutcliffe as 'a clever, callous murderer, deliberately set out to create a cock and bull story to avoid a conviction for murder.' He added that there was a marked difference between the stories Sutcliffe had told the police and those he told the doctors. It is still uncertain whether Peter Sutcliffe was technically insane or not. Sutcliffe's defence went in the direction of establishing his unfitness to be tried for murder, and he claimed that he heard 'voices' telling him to kill prostitutes. He had a divine mission from God to kill prostitutes. He was examined by psychiatrists in prison, and they reported that he was a paranoid schizophrenic, but it is possible that Sutcliffe was fooling them. There are good reasons for supposing that he was faking insanity. For instance, in prison he was overheard telling his wife Sonia that he expected to get thirty years for what he had done but if he could convince people he was mad he might only get ten years in a 'loony bin'. He did not mention the heavenly voices in the initial interviews at all. In court, he was careful to give no clue as to the state of his mental health. More damning still was the fact that not all the victims were prostitutes. Jayne Macdonald, Josephine Whitaker, Barbara Leach, Jacqueline Hill and Margo Walls were numbered among Sutcliffe's victims, and none of them were prostitutes.

It turned out that Sutcliffe normally went out murdering on a Friday or a Saturday night, the two nights when Sonia worked as an auxiliary nurse. For the Crown, Mr Ognall asked one of the consultant psychiatrists, "Why did God only direct him on Friday and Saturday Nights?' Mr Milne, the psychiatrist, answered, 'Paranoid schizophrenics are extraordinarily cunning, extremely involved in premeditation and determined not to be found.' Mr Ognall replied, 'That isn't the hallmark of a schizophrenic. It is the hallmark of the normal criminal.'

Much of the case hinged on Sutcliffe's motive for killing. It was fairly clear that there was a sexual motive; he had actually had sex or attempted to have sex with several of the victims while he was murdering them. But Sutcliffe was intelligent enough to know that he had to deny, if possible disprove, a sexual motive if his insanity plea was going to work. The voices, the divine mission, had to be the reason for the attacks, not sexual gratification.

In May 1981, only five months after his arrest, it took the jury at the Old Bailey just six hours to find Peter Sutcliffe guilty, by a majority of 10 to 2, of thirteen charges of murder and seven charges of attempted murder. He was given life imprisonment with the recommendation that he should serve not less than thirty years. The judge added that the psychiatrists were of the opinion that he should never be released. Sutcliffe was sent to Parkhurst Prison on the Isle of Wight, but later transferred to Broadmoor Secure Hospital in Berkshire after another inmate at Parkhurst slashed his face with a broken coffee jar. Sutcliffe has been attacked several times. In 1997 he was attacked by a fellow patient at Broadmoor, who stabbed him in both eyes with a pen. Sutcliffe has lost the sight in his left eye.

Sutcliffe spends his time at Broadmoor, diagnosed with paranoid schizophrenia, his state of mind having deteriorated markedly since going into prison. It is a chilling thought that this man will, according to the judgement passed on him, possibly be at liberty again in 2011. Whether mad or faking, there can be no doubt that Peter Sutcliffe is an extremely dangerous man.

Richard Ramirez

the Night Stalker

THE CRIMES RICHARD Ramirez committed on the streets of California over a one-year period in the mid-1980s were beyond the imagination of the Los Angeles journalists who reported on the case. They called him 'The Night Stalker', which gives a good idea of the fear his crimes spread through the city and its suburbs, especially through the long hot summer of 1985. His capture after a car chase through the streets of Los Angeles became one of the most memorable in the city's history; it was only eclipsed a decade later by the car chase that culminated in the arrest of O. J. Simpson. His trial was equally a matter of public interest, not just because of the nineteen death sentences that it was leading up to, but because of Ramirez' erratic and callous behaviour, which seemed to make him a kind of demon king.

Richard Ramirez was born in February 1960. He was the youngest of seven children of a Mexican-American railway worker living in El Paso. Texas Ricky, as the young Richard liked to be called, was a lonely, sad child who played truant from school and spent hours in the town's amusement arcades, sniffing glue or smoking marijuana. It was an unpromising beginning.

While he was still a boy he started shoplifting, picking pockets and burgling people's houses to raise cash for drugs. His school reports were very poor. In 1977, he was sent to a special home for juvenile delinquents; this was a landmark year, the year when his criminal record began. A few years later he was put on probation for possession of marijuana.

Ramirez tired of El Paso and moved first to San Francisco, then to Los Angeles. There he developed new interests in guns, knives and satanism. He also got himself addicted to cocaine. He was by now sleeping rough and wearing filthy clothes; his teeth were bad because he never brushed them; his skin was poor because of his diet of junk food, cakes and cola. He was a very unprepossessing figure. He had no job, yet he always had money. He was a car thief and burgled houses and warehouses for electrical appliances that he could sell on to pay for his cocaine and junk food. In due course, the Los Angeles Police Department caught up with Ramirez and served a prison term for car theft.

It was shortly after his release from prison in 1984 that the criminal career of Richard Ramirez took a new turn, towards serial killing.

On 28 July 1984, a warm, humid and oppressive evening in Eagle Rock, a suburb of Los Angeles, Jennie Vincow, a woman of 79, left her window open to let some air circulate into her stuffy ground-floor apartment. Ramirez slipped in through the open window, attacked the old lady as she slept, sexually assaulted her and stabbed her. Ramirez ransacked the apartment and left bloody fingerprints all over the place. Mrs Vincow's son was living in the apartment above, but heard nothing. He came down and found his mother's body the next morning. Her throat had been so viciously cut that she was nearly decapitated.

The police were mystified by the crime. It looked like killing – and sadistic killing – for fun. The odd thing is that there was no further attack for eight months, a long cooling off period. But the monster attacked again, and once again it was an attack on an apartment block in Los Angeles, the Rosemead suburb. It was 17 March 1985 and at 11.30 at night Maria Hernandez pulled her car into her garage, unaware that the killer was watching her from behind a pillar. As she got out of her car, the killer emerged from the shadows and raised a gun. She pleaded with him not to shoot, but he fired. She stumbled at the impact and fell. The stalker stepped over her to get in through the side door of her apartment. He thought she was dead. In fact the bullet had bounced off the car keys in her hand and she only received a hand wound.

Maria's roommate was not so lucky. When Maria finally managed to get indoors, she found her roommate had been shot dead by the stalker. Dayle Okazaki, a 34-year-old Hawaiian, lay in a pool of blood, her skull smashed by a shot fired at very close range. Once again, the police were puzzled by the attack. At least this time one of the victims had survived and this living witness could give some kind of description. The stalker was tall, gaunt, dark, possibly Hispanic. There was another clue too, a baseball cap bearing the logo of the heavy metal band AC/DC.

On the same night, the stalker struck again in Monterey Park, shooting dead a slightly built 30-year-old Taiwanese woman called Tsai Lian Yu. She was driving a yellow Chevrolet down North Alhambra Avenue in Monterey Park, not far from Rosemead. The stalker forced his way into her car, shot her, then disappeared into the night. At this stage, it was not clear whether the attacks were linked, or the work of several different attackers.

On 27 March 1985, just ten days later, Vincent Zazzara (aged 64) and his wife Maxine (aged 44) were found dead in their home in the prosperous middle-class suburbs in the San Gabriel valley. This was another brutal attack. Vincent Zazzara had been shot in the head while he was dozing on the sofa, and died at once. Maxine Zazzara was subjected to a frenzied attack. Mrs Zazzara's eyes had been gouged out, her face mutilated out of recognition and her upper torso had been stabbed again and again.

Investigators discovered footprints made by a tennis shoe in a flowerbed, so it was possible to reconstruct the means of entry and general modus operandi. The police were beginning to realise that the Vincow, Okazaki, Yu and Zazzara cases were linked; they were the work of one man. The police pleased for witnesses to come forward, but there was virtually nothing to go on.

On 14 May the stalker slipped through a window into the residence of an elderly couple, Harold and Jean Wu. The first Mrs Wu knew of the intruder was a loud bang that woke her up. She saw the figure of the intruder standing over her with a smoking gun in his hand. Beside her, her husband was groaning. He had been shot in the head. Then the intruder started to punch, slap and kick her, demanding cash. He tied her hands behind her, then threw her across the bed on top of her dying husband, as he went rummaging round the house looking for money. Jean Wu could hear Harold gasping for breath, furniture being rifled and the stalker's curses as he found nothing of any value. He came back to the bedroom, angry, and savagely raped Mrs Wu. She survived this terrifying attack, and was able to tell the police that the attacker was tall, gaunt, dark and Hispanic.

Two weeks after this attack, Ramirez attacked Ruth Wilson, a 42-year-old Burbank woman. Ruth was woken up in bed by the blinding beam of a torch. She could see the barrel of a gun. The intruder asked, 'Where's your money?' before she could answer he had pulled her out of bed by the sleeve of her nightdress and led her to her son's bedroom. He used the frightened boy as a hostage, insisting that she produce something of value. So she told him where an expensive piece of jewellery was hidden. He seemed satisfied as he handled the diamond necklace, and Ruth Wilson began to think he would leave without harming either her or her son. She was wrong. The attacker took the precaution of locking the boy in a closet, pushed Ruth back into her bedroom and sexually assaulted and raped her. Ramirez left Ruth Wilson, telling her, 'I don't know why I'm letting you live. I've killed people before. You don't believe me, but I have.' This chivalry was expensive, though. Ruth Wilson was able to give the police a good description of her attacker. He was tall, thin, dark-haired, Hispanic and had bad teeth and bad breath. The Los Angeles Police Department published a photofit of Ruth Wilson's attacker, and it was shown widely on TV. He was clearly of Hispanic descent, 25—30 years old, with long unkempt black hair hanging in greasy strands over a high forehead and straggled down a skeletally thin pock-marked face. He had prominent cheekbones, sunken cheeks, thick lips and a square jaw. On each occasion he had worn all-black. It was a good description.

Yet still the violence continued. On 1 June 1985, in the Los Angeles suburb of Monrovia, another old woman was beaten to death. Ramirez battered 83-year-old Malvia Keller to death with a hammer. Her sister, an 80-year-old named Blanche Wolfe, survived. When their gardener found them the next morning he could see that both old women had been beaten across the head with a hammer. Blanche Wolfe was bleeding, but still alive. Malvia Keller was dead. She had been tied hand and foot and then been crushed by a heavy table which the killer had upended onto her chest. The police found a Satanic symbol drawn in lipstick on Malvia Keller's thigh. Another had been drawn roughly on the bedroom wall where Blanche Wolfe lay unconscious.

These signs of devil worship were no surprise to the police. The County Sheriff, Sherman Block, was a very experienced officer and had seen many different sorts of homicide. This was now looking like a particular type of serial killer who was feeding on his crime, growing stronger as he committed more killings, a typical 'vampire' killer. The killings did indeed become more brutal and degenerate. During the next few weeks, panic spread through Los Angeles. It seemed no apartment was secure, no security system proof against the Night Stalker. Throughout his *modus operandi* remained the same; a break-in, a brutal and sadistic attack, an attempt at theft, a rape

Later the same month a 29-year-old called Patty Higgins had her throat cut in Arcadia. Five days after that yet another old woman, Mary Canon, was brutally murdered at her home, not far from Patty Higgins' address. Another attack in Arcadia three days later left a 16-year-old girl badly injured, but she survived.

The connections among the attacks now became clearer. The violence was accelerating and the attacks were happening after shorter intervals.

On 7 July, Joyce Nelson was found dead at her home

in Monterey Park. Another woman, a nurse, was robbed and raped by Ramirez on the same night, but she survived the attack. The attacks came faster and faster on each other's heels, and the police were under enormous pressure to catch the Night Stalker. A special Night Stalker task force was set up in early August, with 200 dedicated detectives led by Detective Sergeant Frank Salerno. Posters showing a composite sketch of the Night Stalker were produced, so that Ramirez' image was to be seen everywhere. The increased level of publicity made the LA population more prepared, more on its guard. People bought guard dogs and burglar alarms. Some even made cardboard cut-outs to place in lighted windows to make the killer believe that someone at least was still up and awake at night.

The increased pressure forced Ramirez to move along the coast to find a new hunting ground. He attacked an elderly Chinese couple, Mr and Mrs Pan in Lake Merced near San Francisco. The 66-year-old Mr Pan was shot dead. Mrs Pan was sexually assaulted and then left paralyzed by a gunshot wound. Ramirez daubed satanic slogans and symbols on the walls with lipstick before leaving. The satanic element alerted the San Francisco police, who realised that the Los Angeles Night Stalker was on their patch.

A week later, Ramirez attacked again. This time he struck at Mission Viejo, halfway between San Diego and San Francisco. The 29-year-old William Carns somehow survived being shot three times; his 27-year-old girlfriend Renata Gunther was sexually assaulted but left alive. This was to be Richard Ramirez's last attack. The net was closing on him. A multitude of small clues from the earlier attack were pointing, as yet vaguely, towards him. The vital clue came from a teenager at Mission Viejo, James Romero, who had had the presence of mind to write down the registration number of a Toyota station wagon; he had become suspicious when it was driven past the house three times. Some hours later, after being attacked, Renata Gunther saw her attacker driving away in the same car.

The police put out an APB (all points bulletin) on the Toyota, which was eventually found abandoned. A new technique was tried to reveal the Stalker's fingerprints inside the car. A saucer of superglue was left inside the Toyota, which was then locked with the windows firmly shut. The idea was that the fumes from the superglue would react with moisture to make any latent prints visible; these could then be enhanced by a laser beam. It worked. A single fingerprint was found and checked at the new California state computer in Sacramento. It produced an instant match. The print belonged to the 25-year-old Richard Ramirez, and his prints had been logged back in 1983 at the time of his conviction for car theft. Then the police photos of Ramirez were brought out of the police records; the tall, scruffy Hispanic was obviously the right man. The police photo was published in the Los Angeles papers.

When Richard Ramirez stepped off a Greyhound bus

in Los Angeles on 31 August, he glanced at a newspaper rack in a liquor store and saw his own photograph under a headline, 'Police Identify Stalker Suspect'. He knew then that he was finished. He ran for two miles. Police cars converged on the area as reports came in that the Night Stalker had been sighted. Ramirez tried to hi-jack a car, but its owner – a woman – managed to fight him off; some bystanders rushed to her aid. He jumped over fences and across the back yards of East Los Angeles. It was a tough area, one where many fugitives would stand a good chance of being hidden and protected by the local population. But not this fugitive. No-one had any sympathy for the Night Stalker. A carpenter who saw him coming over his fence hit him with his barbecue tongs.

Eventually Ramirez found a car he could hi-jack, but its owner, 56-year-old Faustino Pinon gripped him in a headlock as he tried to turn the ignition key. Ramirez broke free and ran to another car, which was about to be driven off by Angelina de la Torres. He threatened her and she started shouting, 'El Matador! El Matador!' (The Killer, the Killer), and slammed the car door onto him. Soon a crowd of her neighbours armed with steel bars and various tool was on the spot, surrounding Ramirez. He tried to run, but they cornered him after a twenty-second dash and beat him to the ground, pinning him there until the police arrived. When the police did reach Ramirez, he had had all the fight knocked out of him by the vigilante group. The man who had terrorized, raped, maimed and killed without mercy was now cowering like a frightened puppy.

As the deputy arrested him, he sobbed, 'Shoot me now, man. I don't deserve to live.'

At first Ramirez admitted he was the Night Stalker, humming the tune of AC/DC's song Night Prowler, and saying, 'You think I'm crazy, but you don't know Satan'. At that stage it seemed as though a conviction would be straightforward, but when the case eventually came to trial – there were several delays caused by Ramirez sacking teams of lawyers – he claimed he was innocent, that he was the victim of a case of mistaken identity. His lawyer claimed that because pictures of Ramirez had been used repeatedly on TV, it would no longer be possible to get reliable evidence of identification – that the identification evidence had in effect been contaminated. An expert witness on identification told the court that people often have trouble identifying people of different racial type, and their judgement is often faulty when they are held at gun- or knife-point.

Julian Ramirez also helpfully gave evidence that Richard had been at home in El Paso on the night of Mabel Bell's murder.

There were many delays. One juror was murdered and had to be replaced. Another juror feel asleep during the trial and therefore had to be replaced. But, in the end, Richard Ramirez was found guilty of thirteen murders and thirty other serious offences. The lawyers representing Ramirez tried to claim that Ramirez was not responsible as he was possessed by the Devil. The jury would have none of it and he was given 19 death sentences for his appalling crimes.

Ramirez said to the judge, 'You don't understand me. You are not capable of it. I am beyond your experience. I am beyond good and evil.' Almost incredibly, Ramirez had plenty of fans. He received fan mail from many young women on Death Row at San Quentin Jail. In October 1996, in a simple ceremony at San Quentin, he married Doreen Lioy, a highly intelligent freelance magazine editor. She said in an interview, 'The facts of his case ultimately will confirm that Richard is a wrongly convicted man, and I believe fervently that his innocence will be proven to the world.'

Richard Ramirez remains on Death Row at the time of writing. The state of California has not executed a prisoner since 1967. Ramirez himself is probably indifferent to his fate. When he was being led away after receiving 19 sentences of death, he was heard to say, 'No big deal. Death always comes with the territory. I'll see you in Disneyland.'

The Zodiac Killer of San Francisco

THE NIGHT STALKER was a nickname made up by journalists to highlight and dramatize – if it needed dramatizing – a running newspaper story about a Californian serial killer. With The Zodiac Killer it was different: he made up his own nickname, just as Jack the Ripper did. He was like Jack the Ripper in some other significant ways too; he taunted the police with letters and clues, and in spite of offering this help he was never caught and never even identified.

The Zodiac Killer stalked the San Francisco area for over ten years, starting one cold moonlit night over the Christmas of 1968. A couple of teenagers had drawn their car up in an open space next to a pump house in the Vallejo Hills above San Francisco. It was a favoured spot for lovers. David Faraday and Bettilou Jensen hardly noticed the cold and they were so involved in each other that they scarcely noticed another car pulling up three metres away. Suddenly a bullet smashed into the rear window, smothering them with broken glass, and a second banged into the car bodywork. Bettilou jumped out of the car and tried to run away. David put his hand on the door handle, preparing to get out, when the gunman reached in through the door window and shot him in the head. Then the gunman ran after Bettilou. She had only got ten metres when he fired five shots at her. She fell, dead, and the gunman got back in his car and drove away.

Just a few moments later a third car came along. The woman driving it saw Bettilou's body lying on the ground and, instead of stopping, she stepped on the accelerator with the idea of getting help quickly from the next town. She saw a police patrol car coming the other way and flashed her headlights to make it stop; she told the patrolmen about the body. Together, they went back to the pump-house. They found Bettilou dead, and David still alive but unconscious. They got him to hospital, but he died shortly after arrival.

There was very little for the police to go on. David had not been robbed. Bettilou had not been sexually assaulted. The police looked at the possibility that the murderer was a jilted lover, but investigation showed that there were none. The teenagers had been ordinary students whose lives concealed no secrets. It became an unsolved double murder.

On 4 July 1969 the same killer struck again, at another 'lovers' lane' spot, this time at Blue Rock Park, but only 3km from the place where David and Battilou were murdered. Michael Mageau was sitting in his car with his girlfriend, a 22-year-old waitress called Darlene Ferrin. They were not entirely alone, because other courting couples had also driven there, for the same reason. They did not notice when a white car pulled up beside them for a few minutes. It drove off, then came back and stopped on the far side of the road. A spotlight was suddenly shone onto them and Mike saw a figure approaching. He assumed it was a policeman and reached for his driving licence. The figure opened fire on them. He shot Darlene first, then Mike. The gunman walked back to his car, fired some more shots at them from there, and then drove off at high speed.

It was only a few minutes later that a man phoned the Vallejo County police station to report a murder on Columbus Parkway. He said, 'You will find the kids in a brown car. They are shot with a 9mm Luger. I also killed those kids last year. Goodbye.' When the police arrived, Darlene was dead. Mike was still alive, but the bullet had damaged his tongue and he could not speak. There was one more possible lead, though.

Four months earlier, Darlene's babysitter had been aware of a white car parked outside Darlene's flat, and she had felt uncomfortable about it. She mentioned it to Darlene, who said, 'He's checking up on me again. He doesn't want anyone to know what I saw him do. I saw him murder someone.' The babysitter had seen the driver of the white car and could describe him. She told the police he was middle-aged with brown wavy hair and a round face. As Mike recovered, he regained the use of his voice and was able to confirm that the gunman had brown hair and a round face.

About two months after the shooting of Darlene and Mike, handwritten messages arrived at the offices of three local newspapers. They were written in capital letters, either because the writer was mad – for some reason mad people often write in capital letters – or because he wanted to disguise his handwriting. All three began in the same way: 'DEAR EDITOR, THIS IS THE MURDERER OF THE 2 TEENAGERS LAST CHRISTMAS AT LAKE HERMAN & THE GIRL ON THE 4TH OF JULY'. He went on to give exact details of the gun and ammunition he had used, to make it clear to the police that he really was the murderer. He also sent an extra sheet of paper covered with a strange code, demanding that the editors publish it on their front pages. If they didn't, he threatened, he would go on killing lone people in the night. The letters were signed with a cross in a circle – a gunsight.

The three newspapers went along with the mad gunman's request. Cryptographers worked to decode the secret message. Eventually a teacher named Dale Harden cracked it. He looked for a group of symbols that could stand for the word 'kill'. He found it and after many hours of work he deciphered the whole message: 'I like killing people because it is so much more fun than killing wild game in the forest because man is the most dangerous of all to kill.' He boasted that he had killed five people in the San Francisco area and when he was reborn in paradise his victims would be his slaves.

The publication of the strange message produced a massive public response. People volunteered all sorts of information, but none of it led anywhere. Then the killer volunteered another clue, a nickname for himself that he must have known would ensure that he got into the headlines; 'DEAR EDITOR, THIS IS ZODIAC SPEAKING'. The police were being fed clues, but no positive leads. And the killing continued.

On 28 September 1969 Bryan Hartnell and his girlfriend Cecelia Shepard – he was 20, she was 22 – were having a picnic on the shore of Lake Berryessa, 20km north of Vallejo. It was about 4.30pm and they had finished eating, and were lying on a rug, kissing, when they saw a stocky man with brown hair walking towards them across the clearing. He disappeared for a moment into a wood, then came out wearing a mask and carrying a gun. As he came closer, Bryan saw that the mask had a symbol painted on it – a circle with a cross inside it.

The gunman was not particularly threatening in manner and had a soft voice. 'I want your money and your car keys.' Bryan explained that he only had under a dollar, but the man was welcome to that. The gunman started to chat, explaining that he was an escaped convict and that he would have to tie them up. After tying them up, he said, 'I am going to have to stab you people'. Bryan asked him to stab him first, because he couldn't bear to see his girlfriend stabbed. The gunman agreed, knelt calmly down beside Bryan and stabbed him several times in the back with a hunting knife. Bryan felt dizzy and sick, but was still conscious when the madman turned to Cecelia. After the first stab, he went berserk, stabbing again and again while she frantically thrashed about to try to avoid the blows.

Finally the girl lay still. The Zodiac Killer regained his composure, walked over to their car, pulled a felt pen from his pocket, drew something on the car door, and walked calmly away.

A fisherman heard their screams and ran over to find that Bryan and Cecelia were still alive. The police arrived almost immediately, having had an anonymous tip-off; 'I want to report a double murder'. The caller had given them the exact location. When the police arrived, Cecelia was unconscious. She died two days later without regaining consciousness. Bryan made a full recovery and was able to describe the killer. The symbol he had drawn on the car door was a gunsight, so it was obviously the Zodiac Killer again. The police found the telephone where the tip-off call had been made, and were able to get three high-quality prints from it. Unfortunately the owner of these fingerprints did not have a criminal record. Still the police were unable to identify this dangerous killer.

Two weeks later, on 11 October 1969, a fourteen-year-old girl was looking out of the window at her home in San Francisco. She saw a stocky man sitting in the passenger seat of a parked taxi, going through the pockets of the driver, who appeared to be dead. She called her brothers to come and watch. Together, they watched the man get out of the taxi, leaving the driver slumped across the seat, and wiping the door handle with a piece of cloth before walking off. They called the police, but the details were not taken down correctly, perhaps because the children were over-excited, and the police thought they were looking for an NMA, a negro male adult, when the killer was white. A patrolman stopped a stocky white man near the crime scene to ask if he had seen anything unusual; he had not, so the policeman let him go. He did not, after all, answer the description of the wanted man. The taxi driver was found to be dead from a gunshot wound in the head. He was a 29-year-old called Paul Stine.

A local San Francisco paper received a letter from Zodiac. 'THIS IS THE ZODIAC SPEAKING. IAM THE MURDERER OF THE TAXI DRIVER OVER BY WASHINGTON ST AND MALE ST LAST NIGHT, TO PROVE IT HERE IS A BLOOD STAINED PIECE OF HIS SHIRT'. The piece of cloth did indeed match the shirt of the taxi driver. The bullet was a .22 fired from the same gun that had killed Bettilou Jensen and David Faraday. Just like Jack the Ripper, he taunted the police with their incompetence. 'THE S.F. POLICE COULD HAVE CAUGHT ME LAST NIGHT. SCHOOL CHILDREN MAKE NICE TARGETS. I THINK I SHALL WIPE OUT A SCHOOL BUS SOME MORNING. JUST SHOOT OUT THE TIRES AND THEN PICK OFF ALL THE KIDDIES AS

THEY COME BOUNCING OUT.' The letter was signed with the now-familiar gunsight symbol.

The descriptions from the children who had seen the murder of the taxi driver and from the various earlier victims all matched. A composite image of the Zodiac Killer could now be drawn up and issued to the public. The killer was a white male, 35—45, with short brown hair, possibly with a red tint; he was 5 feet 8 inches tall, heavily built, wearing glasses.

In the middle of the night on 21—22 October 1969, someone claiming to be the Zodiac Killer called the police, wanting them to arrange his 'appearance' on a talk show. He wanted to talk, on air, to F Lee Bailey or Mel Belli, who were the leading criminal lawyers in the USA at the time. Mel Belli agreed to appear on Jim Dunbar's early morning talk show. At 7.20am the man phoned in, saying that he was Zodiac, though he preferred to be called Sam. Then he blurted out, 'I'm sick. I have headaches.' The call was traced back to Napa State Hospital. The caller was a psychiatric patient, and so probably not the real Zodiac Killer.

The following Christmas, Mel Belli received a card: 'DEAR MELVIN, THIS IS THE ZODIAC SPEAKING. I WISH YOU A HAPPY CHRISTMAS. THE ONE THING I ASK OF YOU IS THIS, PLEASE HELP ME. I AM AFRAID I WILL LOSE CONTROL AND TAKE MY NINTH AND POSSIBLY TENTH VICTIM.' It was very much a call for help. The killer knew that ahead must lie capture and trial, and that he would be needing help from a first-rate criminal lawyer. But he was also admitting that he was running out of control and needed to be stopped. It was classic psychopathic serial killer territory. He had reached a point where he wanted to be caught; in fact the whole business of writing letters and giving the police clues was to do, at some level, with wanting or needing to be caught. A handwriting expert said that Zodiac's mental state was deteriorating.

On 17 March 1970, Kathleen Johns was driving in the Vallejo area, with her baby in the back of the car, when a white Chevrolet drew up beside her. The driver indicated she had something wrong with her rear wheel, and she pulled over. Kathleen said he was a neatly dressed, clean-shaven man. He said her wheel was wobbling and offered to tighten the wheel nuts for her. She agreed to let him do this, but when she drove off, the wheel came off altogether; he must have loosened them rather than tightened them. Then the neat man offered to give her a lift to a service station, but when they reached it he drove straight past. 'You know I am going to kill you', he said. When he slowed down on a bend, Kathleen had the presence of mind to open the car door and jump out, with her baby in her arms. She ran and hid in an irrigation ditch.

The neat man stopped the Chevrolet and started searching for her with a torch. He was approaching the ditch where she was crouching when, luckily for her, a lorry came along and caught him in its headlights. This distracted him and he gave up looking for her. He drove off. She made her way to a police station to report the incident and while in the police station she saw the Zodiac Killer poster on the wall; she identified him as the man who had abducted and threatened her. The police drove her back to her car, and found that the Zodiac Killer had gone back to it and set it on fire.

The police were still a long way from identifying the Zodiac Killer. Detective Sergeant Lundblatt had an idea that he was Andy Walker, who had known Darlene Ferrin. Darlene's sister had also identified him as the man who had waited outside Darlene's flat in the white car. Andy Walker also bore a strong resemblance to the man who stabbed Cecelia Shepard to death. Walker was known to suffer from bad headaches and to get on badly with female colleagues. He had also been in army where he had studied codes.

But there was a problem. Not everything matched. Andy Walker's fingerprints did not match the one left in Paul Stine's taxi. His handwriting did not match the writing in Zodiac's notes. The police then discovered that Andy Walker was ambidextrous, and his handwriting varied according to which hand he used. It was also possible, the police believed, that the murder of Paul Stine had been planned so that the Zodiac Killer used the severed finger of an unknown victim to plant 'fake' fingerprints in the taxi in order to fool the police.

The police decided they needed to match Walker's palm print with the one they found on the telephone after the Paul Stine murder. An under cover policeman managed to get Andy Walker to carry a goldfish bowl for him, but the palm prints he left on the bowl were not clear enough to be of any use. Walker quickly realised he was being targeted by the police, and got a court order to stop the police pestering him.

More Zodiac letters arrived, again containing all sorts of clues, though none of them crucial. It seemed he was a Gilbert and Sullivan fan, as he was taunting the police with a parody of a G & S song, listing those he wanted to kill with the chorus, 'Titwillo, titwillo, titwillo'. There were no killings during the entire run of The Mikado at the Presentation Theatre in San Francisco. He also seemed to be preoccupied with water and flooding, leading the police to believe that he might live in a flood-prone low-lying area.

The Zodiac Killer's demands became more absurd with time. He was obviously a fantasist and a megalomaniac. He demanded that everyone in San Francisco must wear lapel badges carrying his symbol. They did not, of course and, when he realised it was not going to happen, he threatened to kill Paul Avery, the crime writer on the San Francisco Chronicle. Journalists started semi-facetiously wearing badges saying 'I am not Paul Avery'. Avery unsportingly wore one too and took to carrying a gun.

New leads were few, though one correspondent suggested that the Zodiac Killer was possibly responsible for an earlier murder, the killing of Cheri Jo Bates in November 1966. That murder, like the later ones, had been followed up with crank letters.

On 7 April 1972, a law secretary called Isobel Watson was getting off a bus when a white Chevrolet swerved across the road and nearly hit her. The car stopped, the driver apologized and offered to give her a lift. She wisely declined and he jumped out and stabbed her in the back. She screamed and her neighbours ran out to help. The Chevrolet driver drove off. Isobel was able to describe her attacker. He was 5 feet 9 inches tall, white, in his early forties, wearing black-rimmed glasses. He was almost certainly the Zodiac Killer.

Time passed and the case was no nearer resolution. The inquiry was wound down. Eventually there was only Inspector David Toschi left on the case. The Zodiac Killer's correspondence stopped for almost four years. It was possible he had committed suicide, but Toschi believed the killer got his kicks from the publicity rather than from the killings themselves. If he had killed himself, it was likely that he would have drawn attention to the fact by leaving a note or writing a letter to the press. On 25 April 1978 Toschi got confirmation that Zodiac was indeed still alive; he sent a letter to the San Francisco Chronicle.

There were references in the letters to films, so it seemed likely that the killer was a film buff. One of the local cinemas had the constellations painted on its ceiling, and that may have been the origin of the Zodiac Killer's name for himself. It was also possible that the 'gunsight' logo was not intended to be a gunsight at all but the symbol that appears on the cinema screen as a projectionist's guide. The police hoped to use the killer's obvious love of publicity to trap him. A film was made about the Zodiac Killer, and when it was shown in San Francisco a suggestion box was set up in the foyer, where people could leave any information or ideas they had about the identity of the killer. It was a big box, and it had a detective hidden inside it. He read each letter with the aid of a torch as it was dropped in and the idea was that he would raise the alarm if there was anything that looked as if it might be from the Zodiac Killer himself.

The Oakland police thought they had the killer at one point. The suspect had seen the film three times and had been observed acting strangely during the showings. But he turned out to be a Vietnam war veteran who was sexually excited by the scenes of violence – and his writing did not match.

Police in San Francisco thought the Zodiac Killer was either dead or serving time for a crime committed in another state. But one criminologist at least thought the killing went on at a different location. There were several murders of young women, often hitch-hikers or students, in the Santa Barbara area in the early 1970s. They had been killed in different ways, and none of them had been sexually molested.

One possible suspect was a former boyfriend of Darlene Ferrin, who had lived at Riverside at the time when Cheri Jo Bates was murdered. He lived with his mother, whom he hated, and cut up small mammals as a hobby. During the puzzling 1975–1978 period, when the Zodiac Killer had been completely inactive, this suspect had been in a psychiatric hospital after being charged with child molesting. In spite of these promising-sounding leads, it has nevertheless proved impossible so far to identify the Zodiac Killer with any certainty.

The Green River Killer

another unsolved series

THE PUBLIC CV of the serial killer, the string of sadistic murders with all their peculiar circumstances that make up the hallmarks of the particular psychopath, is often at variance with his everyday persona. The serial killer is often a quiet, ordinary-looking, ordinary-behaving person holding down an ordinary job. The mismatch is of course why he remains unidentified, uncaught for so long. As we saw, the Zodiac Killer was a neat, tidy man wearing glasses, a mild-mannered man with a soft voice. Nobody would suspect him of doing the terrible things he did – and that was why in the end he was never caught.

The Green River Killer was another serial killer of this type, a killer who killed at least 42 women.

In July 1982, two boys were cycling along beside the Green River, near the Seattle-Tacoma Airport in the state of Washington. They had their fishing gear with them and were intent on their afternoon's fishing, when one of them saw what he thought was a log floating in the shallow water close to Peck Bridge. He was curious about it and waded in to roll it towards the bank to get a better look. It was the body of a 16-year-old girl, Wendy Coffield, and she was, as far as we know, the first victim of the Green River Killer.

To begin with, the police thought they were dealing with a fairly straightforward sex killing. Lieutenant Jackson Berd thought it was the usual case of a man who had had too much to drink and lost his judgement, picked up a girl for sex, encountered some resistance to his advances and tried to use force; the girl started screaming; the man tried to silence her, instinctively putting his hands to her mouth and throat; the girl died by suffocation or strangulation and then her body was dumped. It was a crime that happened all too often, a nasty crime, but far removed from the cold-blooded serial killing.

Wendy Coffield was a runaway, a child prostitute who had been missing for three months when her body was found. She fitted the sex killing pattern.

Five weeks later, the picture changed very significantly. In one day, the bodies of three more young women were found at separate locations along the same river. During the years that followed, more bodies appeared, all of women between the ages of 15 and 36, all over King County, the area round the Green River. Two bodies were found across the state border, in Oregon.

A huge police investigation was mounted to try to identify and catch the Green River Killer. The cost of such operations is huge, and this one alone cost over £14 million. A Green River Task Force was set up, waiting 24 hours a day for some new information to turn up. A major problem faced by the King County police was the attitude of local people. Although they were petrified that they might be attacked by the killer, they developed an unhealthily complacent attitude towards him because so many of the victims were involved in prostitution. If the killer was targeting that particular minority, the moral majority had nothing to worry about. The Yorkshire Ripper murders showed how false that kind of thinking can be. You do not have to be a prostitute to become the victim of a committed prostitute-slayer; you only have to be mistaken for a prostitute by someone who, by definition, is not thinking straight. Complacency can be very dangerous.

The mother of one of the Green River Killer's young victims made another interesting observation. She complained that people were missing the point by demanding tougher action against prostitution. 'Our kids are being penalized again,' she complained. 'It sounds silly, but how can you be penalized any more after you've been murdered? We admit that our kids had problems but Tracy didn't deserve to die because she wasn't living what was perceived to be a perfect life. The issue was and is this maniac out there, not the lives that some of his victims were leading.'

The Green River Killer is believed to be of the same psychological type as the Zodiac Killer and Jack the Ripper – a psychopathic sex killer who will not stop until he is stopped. Lieutenant Nolan, who was second-in-command of the Green River Task Force, has a strong feeling about the type of man he is looking for. 'The man we are looking for is a shade of grey. He is very innocuous, fits right into the community. That is what makes him so very dangerous.'

To safeguard their investigation, the Task Force has revealed little of what of what they know about their suspect, though they have released a photofit picture. They were prepared to admit to the following details, though; the killer is middle-aged, an outdoor type who knows the mountains, ravines and streams like the back of his hand. He is physically strong, strong enough to be able to carry the body of a full-grown woman for some distance. There were a few witness sightings, when people caught sight of the victims with strange men not long before they were found dead. From these fragments of descriptions, the police thought they knew some significant details about the killer. They believed, for example, that he drove a pale blue pick-up speckled with primer paint to cover rust spots.

The forensic evidence from the bodies of his victims gave more specific information about him. The Green River Killer was a sexual psychopath. As such, he must have been a deeply troubled and tormented personality, his sexual personality twisted by some terrible childhood secret which has left him with a simmering anger. The Task Force did not reveal details of the way he killed his victims, though one of their collaborators, a psychologist, has implied that strangulation was the favoured method and that it was favoured so that the killer could watch his victims suffer.

The Green River Killer used the open country within 45 miles of Seattle as a dumping ground for his victims. The bodies have been spotted by a wide variety of countryside visitors: hunters, joggers, walkers, mushroom pickers,boy scouts, fishermen.

There were 10,000 calls to the Task Force centre offering information and ideas, including several false confessions from mad attention-seekers. Lieutenant Nolan was disappointed not to have caught the killer, and he said that he and his team had got used to the disappointment. By 1985, they were even having to call in clinical psychologists to help them deal with the stress their sense of failure was inducing. Nolan said, 'I would love to capture him, to get him to sit down and tell me just why he did this, what drove him. I don't have any idea what this guy's going to tell me, what his secret is.'

What did develop within the Task Force was a kind of sneaking admiration for the Green River Killer's intelligence. Members of the force recognize that the killer chose his victims very cunningly, leaving the police little in the way of witnesses or clues. The killer is good at concealing the bodies, which in turn creates a range of problems for the police. The longer the time that elapses between the murder and the discovery of the body, the harder it is to determine the time of death, and in some cases even the cause of death.

In the late 1990s the killings stopped. Why? Is it that the Green River Killer is dead or in prison for some other crime? Is it that he has moved to another state and therefore the sequence has been interrupted? Or is it just that he is having a long cooling-of period and the killings will erupt once more? It is very unlikely, given the psychological profile, that the Green River Killer would simply voluntarily stop killing because he had had enough. Someone who has killed that number of people – 42 at least – is unlikely to find that he has had enough of killing.

Tommy Lynn Sells

an angry young man

IT WAS IN the small hours of 31 December 1999 that two friends, 10-year-old Krystal Surles and 13-year-old Kaylene Harris, were attacked by a homicidal maniac who had somehow got into their house in Del Rio in Texas. The intruder had a 12 inch long boning knife and used it to cut their throats. Kaylene died almost at once. Somehow, in spite of having her windpipe severed, Krystal survived. She managed to stagger to a neighbour's house for help. With medical treatment, she made a full recovery from this terrible attack and was able to help police in identifying the maniac.

It was just two days later that the police picked up Tommy Lynn Sells, a 35-year-old drifter. From Krystal's description, a sketch artist had prepared an impression of what the man who had killed Kaylene looked like. The police recognized Sells as the man in the picture. The police questioned Sells closely and he admitted to committing dozens of murders during the previous twenty years.

Tommy Lynn Sells was a school dropout, and after

leaving school took various jobs as a truck driver and fairground worker. He committed his first murder in Hollywood, in a street fight. Sells told the police that he had killed people all over the country, from California across to West Virginia. Some of the policemen who interviewed Sells were overwhelmed by the magnitude of Sells' crimes. It was hard for them to believe that he had done all the things he claimed to have done. What was most remarkable of all was not that he had killed so many people, but that he had got away with the killings.

Sells said that he killed people when they annoyed him. His anger was responsible for making him kill. 'I lose it. I lose control of my thoughts, I lose control of my emotions. When you're not in control, bad things happen.' He told the police that he had never left a living witness to his crimes until Krystal Surles. He also told them that he had only been caught because he left someone alive.

Sells claimed that he had a difficult childhood. His family had criminal tendencies. His mother abandoned him before he was two years old. He was sexually abused by a man living in the same neighbourhood. He took to the life of a drifter when he was only 13. He naturally drifted into crime, and had served stretches in prison in several states in America, for a variety of crimes, including car theft and assault.

Sells' trial for the first-degree murder of Kaylene Harris opened on 12 September 2000. He was in effect on trial for his own life. The key witness at his trial was the sole living witness, Krystal, who was now 11 years old. He was doomed, and he knew it. When asked about the significance of a tattoo on his wrist, the number thirteen and a half, he explained it; 'Twelve jurors, one judge and a half-assed chance'.

Sells had shocked the police investigators with his stories of how he had criss-crossed America killing men, women and children in many different states. One of the murders he confessed to was a 13-year-old case in Illinois. In 1987, Elaine Dardeen, who was seven months pregnant at the time, was bludgeoned to death along with her 3-year-old son Peter. The shock of the attack caused Elaine to give birth. The new-born baby, who is believed to have been alive at the time of the birth, was also clubbed to death. Elaine's husband, Keith Dardeen, was found in a field nearby; he had been shot in the head. The detective who had originally investigated the case, John Kemp, admitted to being deeply shocked by these murders. 'How you can kill a 3-year-old and also kill a new-born infant – that just goes beyond explanation.'

Sells admitted to killing scores of murders. So far the police investigators have linked Sells to 13 murders, including the killings of 13-year-old Haley McHone in Lexington, Kentucky and 9-year-old Mary Perez of San Antonio, Texas.

They cannot be sure of the exact number. The Texas Rangers who investigated the Kaylene Harris case took

Sells to various locations, so that he could show them where he had buried a body or got rid of a murder weapon.

The Kaylene Harris murder trial was straightforward and the verdict almost a foregone conclusion. After two hours of deliberation, the jury returned a guilty verdict with a recommendation for the death penalty. Krystal, whose evidence was so important in getting a conviction, afterwards said that the one good thing that came out of her terrible ordeal was 'that he got caught and that no-one else will get hurt from him'.

Sells was moved to death row, but Texas has an automatic appeal procedure in capital cases, so it may be a long time before a date is set for execution. One drawback in the current situation is that Texas law prohibits death row prisoners from leaving prison on any pretext at all. This means that it is now impossible for Sells to accompany investigators to the many murder scenes where unsolved murders took place. The investigators are sure that Tommy Sells committed 13 murders, but he may have committed as many as 70.

There is very little in the way of a visible pattern to Tommy Sells' killing. He killed men, women and children, even entire families, but it looks as if he had a preference for killing women and girls. The other murders may have been motivated by a need to remove witnesses. On his own account, he killed out of anger. But what force generated such anger? Was it pent-up frustration arising from having been a failure at school, or a failure at work? Or was it frustration at not having a clear enough personal identity? Was he one of those serial killers who need to kill in order to validate their sense of self-worth, who have to surround themselves with death in order to feel truly alive?

Cary Stayner

the Yosemite murders

CARY STAYNER HAD the strangest childhood imaginable. On the face of it he was a member of a normal enough family. There was a father, Delbert Stayner, who was a maintenance man who worked a hard six-day week at a cannery. There was a mother, Kay Stayner, who was a Roman Catholic raising her children as Mormon. Here was where some of the abnormality started. Kay had been educated at a Roman Catholic boarding school. While there she was physically and emotionally abused and later found that as a mother she could not hug and kiss; she looked after her children to the extent of keeping them clothed and fed, but provided them with no emotional warmth. Then there were the children, five of them: three sisters and a brother called Steven. Cary was the oldest.

Already, by the age of three, Cary Stayner was showing signs of psychological disturbance. He started pulling his hair out. The condition, an obsessive-compulsive disorder, was diagnosed as trichotillomania. He was given medication. Then, at the age of seven, he had his first violent fantasy about women; he wanted to capture women and kill them.

But there was something else wrong with the Stayner family, something unique. Cary shared a bedroom with his younger brother, Steven, through their childhood, but there was a seven year long gap – the time when Steven was abducted.

Kenneth Parnell decided that Steven was the boy he was going to kidnap after he was told by the postman that Steven was spanked by his father. That gave Parnell the idea that young Steven would obey him; the beatings would be likely to make him compliant, take orders, and it would also make the boy believe that his parents did not really want him any more.

The disappearance of Steven in 1972 was a great shock to the family. Delbert in particular was deeply affected. He would go through Steven's drawers, touching his belongings, and weep openly in Cary's presence. Steven had scratched his name into the paintwork on the garage door; when Cary painted over the name, Delbert beat him for it. It is difficult to gauge the effect all this had on Cary, not least because Cary never talked about his brother, but it may be that the loss of his brother, the preoccupation of his father with Steven and the continuing coldness of his mother made him feel undervalued.

After the kidnapping, the initial shock wore off and Delbert tried hard to get his family back to normal. In fact a family friend said that he managed to continue with as little disruption as possible. He bought a big caravan and took them all to the Grand Canyon or Death Valley; he made a point of laying on big family holidays. They were always together. Delbert and Kay never quarrelled and the house was always well maintained. The strictness, to the point of harshness, was maintained. Some of it was understandable, such as the insistence that the children could never go anywhere without proper permission, simply because of what had happened to Steven. Delbert and Kay were always concerned about their children, always wanted to know where they were, who they were going out with; they would not let them go off with anyone until they had met them.

One young friend of the children was invited to stay with them for a summer holiday. Delbert enlarged a closet to create space for a bed for her. But after only four days Kay told the girl it was time to clean the bedroom. She realised then that things were not normal in the Stayner home and decided it was time to leave for her own.

The Stayners had come to terms with the abduction and probable murder of Steven. No body had been found, but after seven years there was no hope of finding him alive or dead. Yet, somehow, Steven Stayner managed to get away from Kenneth Parnell and find his way home. He had been virtually brainwashed by Parnell, to the point where he did not really know who he was. One of the things he said to the police when they interviewed him was 'I know my first name is Steven'.

The police assumed he had been abducted by a paedophile and that he has been sexually abused. To begin with, Steven denied that he had been molested by Parnell. But then the police found sexually explicit photos of him and he admitted it. The sexual abuse was something Delbert and Kay would not discuss with him and the boy was never given any counselling after his ordeal. Steven recognized his mother and father when he returned, but not his brother and sisters.

A neighbour commented that Cary must have been affected profoundly by Steven's return. Suddenly the missing brother – the missing, presumed dead brother – was back in the room they had shared seven years before. Steven was very much in the spotlight and receiving all the care. Cary himself commented that he never really got on with his brother after he came back. 'All of a sudden Steve was getting all these gifts, getting all this clothing, getting all this attention. I guess I was jealous. I'm sure I was. I got put on the back burner, you might say.' He was right, and the extent that he was pushed into the background by his parents was extreme. One evening, Kay had finished setting the table for a meal, when Steven commented to her that she had forgotten one place setting. 'Who?' she asked. Steven pointed at his brother. 'Oh yes. Cary,' she said. The exchange is revealing, in that place settings are not personalized, and both Kay and Steven assumed that if there was one person who would be, or might be, left out then that one person would have to be Cary.

The family dynamics were destined to fuel Cary's development into a startling assertion of ego. Cary wanted his share of the attention that his brother was getting. One common trait of serial killers is an overriding to be noticed, to be a celebrity, to be talked about by everybody. That need is often rooted in a fundamental insecurity; in Cary Stayner's case it is very clear where that insecurity came from. His apparently normal family was in reality very abnormal.

Cary was also becoming interested in girls. A cousin noticed Cary drawing pictures of naked girls on a notepad. A girl who went to stay at the Stayners' house when Cary was 16 remembered him stealing into her room as she slept and reaching into her bed to touch her breasts. She told him to go away, which he did, but then reappeared in the doorway, naked. She told him to go away a second time. This time he went. But Cary seemed to be unable to make or sustain a relationship.

Instead, he took refuge in fantasies about killing people. He also tried to draw attention to himself by claiming that he had seen Bigfoot. In 1979, his classmates voted him the most creative student in his class. It looked as if he might go on to become a graphic artist or a cartoonist. But fundamentally he was known as the boy whose brother was kidnapped.

Steven – really, against all the odds – seemed set fair to become a relatively normal adult. He got married in 1985 and had two children before he was killed in a motorbike accident in 1989.

Cary, meanwhile, was a psychological time-bomb. He told a work-mate that he felt like driving a truck into the office and killing his boss and everyone else in there, then setting fire to the place. The friend suggested he might have a chemical imbalance. Cary agreed and said that it had been diagnosed, but nothing had been done about it. He was taken to a psychiatric centre where he was, belatedly, given some counselling. He mentioned to a work-mate that he had been diagnosed as compulsive-obsessive, but that it was nothing that could not be cured by smoking a joint.

Cary was sharing a house with Jerry Stayner. Then, in 1990, the police found Jerry Stayner shot dead in the house. Cary had an alibi which the police were unable to crack, so the murder remains unsolved. The shadow of suspicion nevertheless falls on Cary. He was plotting a campaign of violence for many months. One wild fantasy was to kill his girl friend, rape her two daughters and then burn down their house.

Then the real murder spree began.

In February 1999, Cary Stayner walked past the room of three tourists in the Yosemite National Park. There were two girls watching television while a middle-aged woman was reading. The middle-aged woman was Carole Sund, who was 42. The girls were her daughter, Juli, who was 15, and their Argentinian friend Silvina Pelosso, who was an exchange student. The room was isolated, so no-one would hear their screams.

He persuaded Carole Sund to let him check the

plumbing in the bathroom. Then he pulled out a gun and killed Carole. He drove Juli to a reservoir, where he cut her throat. The bodies of Carole and Silvina were found in the forest, in the boot of their rented car, over a month later. Cary Stayner had set fire to the car. The fire as the finishing touch seemed to be a recurring feature of the violent fantasies he had been having for twenty years. Now the fantasies were being turned into horrible realities.

Cary Stayner was arrested six months later. Before he confessed to the murders of Carole, Juli and Silvina, Stayner owned up to killing a fourth woman, also in the Yosemite National Park. This victim was a 37 year old naturalist called Joie Ruth Armstrong. He said he had beheaded her. Cary Stayner was given a life sentence for that murder. Oddly, when the audio tape was played for the jurors to hear, Stayner clamped his fists to his head and put his fingers in his ears.

He told his FBI interrogators, 'I didn't realize how hard it is to strangle a person. It's not easy. I had no feeling.' He also said he had no feeling as he tightened the rope round the neck of one victim he felt had been easy prey.

Delbert and Kay Stayner were sent reeling by this new horror. Delbert cried for three days. A spokeswoman for them said, 'It's killing them. We've always been a real close family. Most of Cary's friends are his relatives. There was nothing out of the ordinary that would make us imagine, ever, that he could be responsible for such a thing.' This is no more than saying that the Stayners wanted to be a normal family, but it's clear that they were very far from being normal. Delbert Stayner insists that 'Cary was a good kid, one who kept to himself, got good grades, and had friends. We didn't know anything about him having problems or hearing voices.' Delbert and Kay go to see Cary every week, but they don't discuss anything to do with the serial killings. 'We don't ask questions or ask him why this or why that . . . He's just not the villain like people have wrote him up to be. We go to see him every week, me and Kay. It's getting a little easier to see him. We still cry, but you only have so many tears. I wish some day somebody would pinch me and this would all be over. I love my son.'

Even if the Stayners try to maintain the fiction of an integrated and caring family, the world outside that family is less forgiving. That world outside goes on staring unflinchingly at the horrible things Cary Stayner did, callously, unfeelingly and cold-bloodedly to Carole Sund, Juli Sund, Silvina Pelosso and Joie Armstrong. In that outside world, the real world that Cary Stayner never adjusted to, cold Justice waits with her unsheathed sword.

The jury rejected Cary Stayner's plea of insanity. On 12 December 2002, the 41 year old Cary Stayner was sentenced to death by lethal injection for murdering Carole Sund, Juli Sund and Silvina Pelosso. The retired judge who was assigned to the case, Judge Thomas Hastings, was emotional. Members of the victims' families wept. Jurors wept. Judge Hastings said the evidence against Stayner was overwhelming. Cary Stayner is to die for his terrible crimes, but the path through death row to execution can take a long time. Death row is overcrowded, the legal procedures that have to be gone through are intricate and time-consuming. It may be decades before Cary Stayner is executed. Meanwhile, Delbert and Kay Stayner will go on with their weekly visits – still not talking about the most important things that have happened to their family.

PART EIGHT
KILLING FOR THE STATE

Jean-Baptiste Carrier

the Butcher of Nantes

JEAN-BAPTISTE CARRIER was another of the high-profile serial killers produced by the French Revolutions. Robespierre and Marat were national figures, leading the way in Paris. Carrier was a similar figure but active in the provinces. He earned himself a kind of immortality by killing huge numbers of people, in the name of the Revolution, in Nantes.

The same standards of bloodlust and cruelty that prevailed in Paris prevailed in the other towns and cities too. The main guillotine, the one that stood for most of the French Revolution in the Place de la Révolution, which is now the Place de la Concorde, dealt with huge numbers of victims. The place became a place of terrible misery for the victims and their families but also a place of grisly popular entertainment. Huge crowds turned out to watch, laying bets on the order in which each batch would lose their heads. The English writer William Hazlitt described the scene.

The shrieks of death were blended with the yell of the assassin and the laughter of the buffoons. Whole families were led to the scaffold for no other crime than their relationship; sisters for shedding tears over the death of their brothers; wives for lamenting the fate of their husbands; innocent peasant girls for dancing with Prussian soldiers; and a woman giving suck for merely saying as a group were being conducted to slaughter, "Here is much blood shed for a trifling cause".

The Paris guillotine was so busy that people living in the Rue Saint-Honoré close to the Place de la Revolution, complained that the smell of blood running in the street was a health hazard and reduced the value of their houses. Ironically, the Rue Saint-Honoré was where Robespierre himself lived.

Sometimes, the purges outside Paris were even more vicious than those in the capital. Hazlitt said, 'The whole country seemed one vast conflagration of revolt and vengeance'. In Lyons, 300 people convicted by the Committee of Public Safety and sentenced to death were barbarically mown down with a cannon.

Jean Baptiste Carrier, who was a lawyer like Robespierre, was responsible for the carnage at Nantes. Carrier was born at Yolet in the Auvergne in 1756. He became an influential member of the Cordeliers club and he was also a prominent Jacobin. In March 1793 he took part in the formation of the Revolutionary Tribunal. After a mission to Normandy in July, he went to Brittany in August. While there he received instructions to secure Nantes against counter-revolutionary forces in the Vendée, the neighbouring district.

Carrier arrived in Nantes in October, set up a revolutionary tribunal, but also set up a vigilante group, a gang of desperadoes he named the Compagnie Marat, the Marat Company. He in effect created a kind of terrorist hit squad. He gave them the job of destroying as fast as possible the crowds of prisoners in the gaols. He soon dispensed even with the formality of trials. The Marat Company went into the prisons and simply cut, shot or cudgelled to death any inmates theyencountered.

Like Paris, Nantes had its guillotine, but Carrier found it too slow. Nantes stands on the Loire estuary, and Carrier had the idea that he could use water as a faster means of killing the nation's enemies. He loaded his victims into barges with trapdoors for bottoms, had them towed out into the middle of the river, then scuttled them, so that everyone on board was drowned at once. Various refinements were introduced. Some couples were stripped naked and strapped together, face to face, for this final ordeal. Carrier stationed men with hatchets along the river banks to make sure that no-one escaped.

Carrier had over two thousand people killed in the Loire in this way. But Nantes was a port. Sailing ships came and went. When they weighed anchor, the sailors were dismayed to find human corpses hooked onto their anchors. The water in the estuary became so polluted, stinking with decaying corpses, that fishing in it had to be banned.

Although Carrier did use the guillotine he found it unsatisfactory for killing children. It is not clear why he found it necessary to execute children, but in the hysteria of the Revolution whole families were wiped out. The beheading machine was designed to deal with adult heads. The small heads of children were often sliced in half by the falling blade, which was awful for everyone who had to watch. Not surprisingly, even one of the hardened executioners collapsed and died after the traumatic experience of having to behead four little sisters.

Carrier's solution was not the obvious one – to stop killing children – but to have the children taken to a field outside Nantes. There they were either shot or bludgeoned to death. He had 500 children killed in this way.

Given the speed of Carrier's killing it is hard to believe that any of his victims lingered in prison, but the prisons were filled to overflowing and filthy. Disease swept through them, killing 3,000 people before Carrier and his company of murderers could lay hands on them.

The appalling scale of Carrier's killings in Nantes became a matter of national comment, and after a few months he was recalled. In February 1794 he was summoned to Paris by the Committee of Public Safety. Carrier audaciously took part in the attack on Robespierre which led to Robespierre's execution, but was himself brought to trial before the Revolutionary Tribunal a few months later, in November, and guillotined on 16 December 1794.

Maximilien Robespierre

the Sea-Green Incorruptible

MAXIMILIEN MARIE ISIDOR de Robespierre was born on 6 May, 1758 in the French town of Arras. He was the eldest child of François de Robespierre, a lawyer, and Jacqueline Marguerite Carraut, the daughter of a brewer. Robespierre's childhood was unhappy, especially after the death of his mother in 1767, and he was left, along with three orphaned siblings in the care of relatives when his father abandoned them. The father left Arras immediately after his wife's death, wandering disconsolately round Europe until he too died, in Munich, two years later.

The young Robespierre was sent to the college of Arras and the college of Louis-le-Grand in Paris. It was in Paris that he met and befriended Camille Desmoulins. As a boy and as a man Maximilien was nervous and hesitant when speaking, disliked crowds, and might have been thought timid and lacking in self-confidence, but his reserve concealed a steely certainty and an underlying arrogance.

In spite of the hesitancy of his ordinary speech, and his solitary nature, he turned out to have the gift of oratory and he became the greatest public speaker of his time.

In 1780, Robespierre became a Bachelor of Law, receiving his licence the following year and opening a law practice in his home town of Arras. As a young man he had a reputation for honesty and compassion. He was not a good lawyer, and lost many of his cases, though he began to think of ways in which society might be reformed through the law. He wanted to see the death penalty abolished and, when he became a criminal judge in the diocese of Arras in 1782, refused to give a death sentence when the law required it. He resigned his post rather than pronounce the death sentence, which is astonishing, given the number of people he enthusiastically sent to the guillotine just ten years later. It is as if he underwent a complete change of personality during the Revolution.

In the 1780s, Robespierre turned to literature and society. He came to be admired as one of the best writers and most popular dandies of Arras. He was a member of a musical and literary society known as 'The Rosati'. It was the beauty of his speaking voice when he recited at meetings that won him great applause rather than the quality of his verses, which were not very good.

In 1788 Robespierre took part in the discussion on the way in which the Estates General should be elected. He argued lucidly that if the old mode of election was used, the next Estates General would not represent the people of France.

In this way the following year he found himself elected, at the age of only 30, to the Estates General, to represent Artois. He gravitated to the extreme left wing and soon commanded attention because everything he said was aflame with fanatical fervour. His charisma ensured that his influence grew daily. Initially he had no intention of overthrowing the monarchy or setting up a revolutionary government. Mirabeau referred to the left wing contemptuously as 'the thirty voices', because they were so few, but they were fanatically determined. Mirabeau's death brought Robespierre into higher profile. The radical Jacobin Club to which Robespierre belonged was soon advocating exile or death for the aristocracy.

In 1791 Robespierre proposed the motion that no member of the present Assembly should be eligible for the next, and revealed for the first time in public the streak of jealous suspicion that would come to the fore during the Terror to come. Robespierre's first great triumph as a demagogue came on 30 September, when the Constituent Assembly was dissolved and the people of Paris crowned Pétion and Robespierre as 'the two incorruptible patriots'.

In August 1792, Robespierre presented to the Legislative Assembly a petition for a Revolutionary Tribunal and a new Convention, where some bitter attacks launched against him by the Girondins threw him into a closer alliance with Georges Danton. Interestingly, and somewhat inconsistently, during that summer Robespierre took no part at all in the movement to end the Bourbon dynasty. At this stage, almost incredibly, it seems that Robespierre was still shocked at the idea of shedding blood. Robespierre opposed the Girondins' idea of a special appeal to the people of France on the King's death. By December 1792 his position had changed to the extent that it looks as if his personality had changed. He said, 'This is no trial; Louis is not a prisoner at the bar; you are not judges; you are – you cannot be – statesmen, and the representatives of the nation. You have not to pass sentence for or against a single man, but you have to take a resolution on a question of the public safety, and to decide a question of national foresight. It is with regret that I pronounce the fatal truth: Louis ought to perish rather than a hundred thousand virtuous citizens. Louis must die, that the country may live.'

The execution of the King without appeal to the people on 21 January, 1793 represented a personal triumph for Robespierre and inaugurated the final life-and-death struggle between the Girondins and the Jacobins.

Robespierre's personality changed, or rather different traits emerged, after he gained power. There was now a strong streak of paranoia. He became extremely intolerant. He treated people who disagreed with him and criticized his ideas as 'enemies of the nation', and suspected conspiracy everywhere. In his position as leader of the Committee of Public Safety, he was easily able to send those enemies of the nation to the guillotine. People became terrified of him. Robespierre now developed a great appetite for power and acquired a reputation for self-righteousness and cruelty. He used his great skill as an orator to win the death sentence for both the King and the Queen.

It was largely due to Robespierre's efforts that Louis XVI went to the guillotine in January 1793 and Marie Antoinette followed ten months later. The first Committee of Public Safety was decreed in April 1793. It assumed the governance of France and now Robespierre, elected in July, formally became one of the rulers of France along with the rest of the Twelve. In his capacity as ruler, Robespierre supervised a three-year Reign of Terror. During this terrible episode, Robespierre and his associates committed the wholesale murder of entire families of aristocrats, and sent thousands of ordinary people to their death without proper trials.

The one-time president of the Revolutionary Parliament, Pierre Vergniand, had warned France, 'it is be feared that the Revolution, like Saturn, will end up by devouring its own children'. Now his prophecy came true. Vergniand was one of the 20 high-profile moderates brought to trial and condemned to death. One of them managed to stab himself to death in the courtroom when he was sentenced. Such was the fanaticism gripping the Revolutionary Tribunal that his dead body was taken to be publicly beheaded the next day.

Over three thousand other Parisians followed, many of them executed for entirely non-political reasons, some for absurdly trivial reasons. One man was executed for shouting 'Vive le Roi!' after being sentenced to 12 years in prison for another offence. A general was executed for dining with aristocrats. Madame du Barry was executed for allegedly mourning the death of Louis XVI while she was in London. One unfortunate man was executed 'for not giving his testimony properly'.

Robespierre could not of course have sustained this programme of cruelty without the eager support and connivance of others. One of his associates was Louis de Saint-Just. He said, 'We must rule by iron those who cannot be ruled by justice. You must punish not merely traitors, but the indifferent as well.' Robespierre was more extreme than any of them, and it was not long before he was ordering the trial – and therefore execution – of his own supporters. One was Camille Desmouslins. Robespierre was Desmouslins' friend and the godfather of Desmoulins' son, but it made no difference. Desmouslins had rashly said, 'Love of country cannot exist where there is neither pity nor love for one's countrymen, but only a soul dried up and withered by self-adulation.' He did not mention Robespierre by name, but everyone knew this was remark was aimed at Robespierre. It sounds like a modest enough criticism, but in Robespierre's eyes it was treason, and Camille Desmouslins had to die for it.

Desmouslins' wife pleaded with Robespierre for her husband's life, so she was a traitor to the Revolution; she had to be executed too. Robespierre callously orphaned his own godson.

Robespierre's highest-profile associate was Danton. Robespierre was austere, cold, celibate, whereas Danton enjoyed all the pleasures of life. He loved food and women. Robespierre decided that such a notorious womanizer was not fit to champion the Revolution. Danton decided not to fight his accuser, on the grounds that 'far too much blood has been shed already. I had the Revolutionary Tribunal set up. I pray to God and men to forgive me for it.' So Danton went to the guillotine.

Robespierre was capricious and inconsistent. His paranoia led him to suspect everyone about him. He had sent his friends Danton and Desmoulins to the guillotine. He then placed new men in all positions of influence in the Commune of Paris and assumed complete control of the Revolutionary Tribunal. Jacques-René Hébert, an atheist, closed the Catholic churches and started the pagan-style worship of a Goddess of Reason. Robespierre condemned this Cult of Reason and sent him and his friends to the guillotine in March 1794, and then in May recommended the Convention to acknowledge the existence of God. On 8 June he introduced his own alternative faith, the Reign of Virtue, at the inaugural Festival of the Supreme Being. It says a lot about Robespierre's vanity and megalomania that he thought he could make up a whole new religion and force France to adopt it. He gave an extraordinary speech 'On the Festival of the Supreme Being', the text of which has survived. It is full of ringing generalities and eloquence.

'The day forever fortunate has arrived, which the French people have consecrated to the Supreme Being. Never has the world which He created offered to Him a spectacle so worthy of his notice. He has seen reigning on the earth tyranny, crime and imposture. He sees at this moment a whole nation, grappling with all the oppression of the human race, suspend the course of its heroic labours to elevate its thoughts and vows toward the great Being who has given it the mission it has undertaken and the strength to accomplish it.

'Is it not He whose immortal hand, engraving on the heart of man the code of justice and equality, has written there the death sentence of tyrants? Is it not He who, from the beginning of time, decreed for all the ages and for all the peoples liberty, good faith and justice?

'He did not create kings to devour the human race. He did not create priests to harness us, like vile animals, to the chariots of kings and to give to the world examples of baseness, pride, perfidy, avarice, debauchery and falsehood. He created the universe to proclaim His power. He created men to help each

other, to love each other mutually and to attain happiness by way of virtue.'

After reading a page or so of this a kind of ethical weightlessness takes over, and then one can begin to sense what it must have been like to be there, listening to Citizen Robespierre persuasively rhapsodizing as the death sentence becomes more and more certain for some unlucky victim.

'O hapless People, would you triumph over all your enemies? Practise justice, and render the Divinity the only worship worthy of Him. O People, let us deliver ourselves today, under His auspices, to the just transports of a pure festivity. Tomorrow we shall return to the combat with vice and tyrants. We shall give to the world the example of republican virtues. And that will be to honour Him still.

'The monster which the genius of kings vomited over France has gone back into nothingness.'

And so on.

Robespierre's friend St Just demanded the creation of a dictatorship in the person of Robespierre. On 8 July, the dictator delivered another long and neurotic tirade, this time complaining that his enemies were out to get him. Many felt threatened and menaced by his tone.

Robespierre's grasp of France was mercifully short-lived and imperfect, so at least his Reign of Terror was quite brief. He succeeded in the course of a few months in executing many of his enemies, but the groups opposed to him quickly recognized that they must act against him or they too in their turn would be executed. The only way to save themselves was to bring Robespierre down.

In 1794, the Committee of Public Safety impeached Robespierre. Most of his co-members of the Jacobin Club betrayed him during this trial. St Just was a rare exception. When Robespierre hesitated in his own defence, someone shouted, 'It's the blood of Danton that chokes him!' He had sent one too many of his comrades to the guillotine. He was rescued from prison and taken to the hôtel de ville, but Barras followed him there with the national guards to re-arrest him. They found Robespierre signing an appeal to one of the sections of Paris to take up arms for him. A young gendarme fired his pistol at him and hit him in the jaw. After a night of agony, Robespierre was taken before the tribunal where he was identified as an outlaw and taken away to be executed. On 28 July, 1794, Robespierre was taken to the Place de la Concorde along with nineteen of his comrades and executed with the same guillotine, on the same spot, as Louis XVI.

The Reign of Terror came to an end with Robespierre's death. At the time, Robespierre was blamed for instigating many of the horrors, and probably rightly. Robespierre did not single-handedly invent the Terror, but he served it and sustained it with his oratory. He persuaded his hearers of his honesty and virtue and made it seem that everything that happened was laudable and necessary, rather than monstrously evil. Robespierre liked to lay 'all the crimes and misfortunes of the world' at the door of the poor, dead, feckless King Louis, but the Reign of Terror was a child of Robespierre's imagination, not the King's. He spoke of 'all mortals bound by a boundless chain of love and happiness' and willed 'the tyrants who have dared to break it' to perish. Robespierre was himself the tyrant and deserved to be consumed by the machinery of the Terror.

In himself, Robespierre was a respectable, hard-working, well-dressed, well-mannered, honest, truthful, charitable man. But for the Revolution, he would probably have made a comfortable and happy life for himself as a provincial judge and a writer – a traditional pillar of eighteenth century bourgeois society. But reading Rousseau when young gave him disturbing, subversive, revolutionary ideas. Even those might not have led to trouble, but for his election to the Estates General, where he met a score of other fanatical young Rousseau addicts – and there among them the Revolution was kindled. It was a personal tragedy that the honest and incorruptible idealist who detested the idea of sentencing someone to death should have ended up successfully arguing for the death of his King and his Queen and thousands of other innocent people besides.

Heinrich Himmler

administrator of death

LIKE ADOLF HITLER, Heinrich Himmler may not have killed anybody with his own hands. It is doubtful whether either of them had the temperament for that. Himmler was an official, an administrator, a bureaucrat: he made other people do his killing for him. Himmler was born in Munich in October 1900, the son of a Roman Catholic schoolmaster. Himmler served as a cadet in the Eleventh Bavarian Regiment at the end of the First World War, afterwards studying agriculture at the Munich Technical High School. He always regretted that he had been too young, though only by a year or two, to have taken an active part in the Great War; he idolized the war heroes he saw coming back from the front. Perhaps what came later was to some extent a way of compensating for that perceived earlier lack of heroic action, that inadequacy.

Himmler started his adulthood modestly enough, working as a fertilizer salesman, but then joined in the Munich Beer Hall Putsch in 1923 as standard-bearer beside Ernst Roehm. After marrying in 1927, Himmler went into poultry farming for a time, but proved hopelessly unable to make it work as a business. In 1929, he made another sideways step into the twilight world of Nazism when he became head of Hitler's personal bodyguard, the SS (Schutzstaffel), at that time a small group of 280 men; under Himmler's leadership, it would expand enormously and become a major force within the Nazi state.

In 1930, Himmler was elected to the Reichstag, and concentrated on extending SS membership, which soared to 52,000 by 1933. He also organized a security survive, the SD, under the leadership of Heydrich, and the two men together tightened the Nazi grip on Bavaria. In 1934, Himmler also became head of the Prussian Police and Gestapo. A major turning-point in Himmler's career was the master-minding of the purge of June 1934, which destroyed the SA (the Sturmabteilung) and ensured the emergence of the SS as a powerful organization, safeguarding Nazi principles – especially racist principles. By June 1937, Himmler had succeeded in making himself the chief of the political and criminal police throughout the Third Reich, becoming head of the Gestapo as well as Reichsführer of the SS.

Himmler was an able organizer and administrator, efficient, hard-working but also power-crazed, as can be seen from the way he collected official posts and titles the way small boys used to collect postage stamps.

Hitler was a monster, and it was Himmler who enabled him to be a monster. Himmler was largely responsible for organizing and perfecting methods of state terrorism against the regime's enemies, real and imagined. It was Himmler who in 1933 set up the first concentration camp at Dachau. With Hitler's encouragement, he greatly extended the categories of people who qualified for imprisonment in the camps, which quickly became death camps.

Himmler had some very peculiar obsessions. He thought he was the reincarnation of Henry the Fowler. He was interested in mysticism, mesmerism, the occult, herbal remedies – and there was the major and fanatical obsession with the narrow racialism of Nazism. The mission of the German people was 'the struggle for the extermination of any sub-humans, all over the world, who are in league against Germany, which is the nucleus of the Nordic race.'

Himmler's death camps were the negative side of that racism. The dream of a race of blue-eyed, blond heroes bred by selective breeding (eugenics) was the positive side of it. He wanted to rear a new synthetic, racially pure aristocracy that would lead a vast colonization of the East. He organized a state-registered human stud farm known as Lebensborn, where young, perfectly formed 'Nordic' girls would breed with SS men and their offspring would be cared for.

Himmler looked harmless and inoffensive, like a teacher or a bank clerk, but he was seething with mad and dangerous visions. He appeared to have no emotions, no nerves at all, but he suffered from a variety of severe psychosomatic disorders, including violent headaches, intestinal spasms and occasional unpredictable squeamishness. On a visit to the Russian front, he watched a hundred Jews, both men and women, being executed by shooting for his benefit. He felt nauseous and almost fainted. After this, he ordered a more humane method of execution; this involved using poison gas in specially built gas chambers disguised as shower rooms. Here was a curious glimpse of something approaching 'normal' sensitivity and humanity. But he still wanted the killings to go on, and on other occasions he showed no qualms about the sufferings of others at all.

Himmler made a speech to SS Group Leaders in 1943. He said, 'What happens to the Russians, what happens to the Czechs, is a matter of utter indifference to me. Whether [these] other peoples live in comfort or perish of hunger interests me only in so far as we need them as slaves for our civilization. Whether or not 10,000 Russian women collapse from exhaustion while digging a tank trench interests me only in so far as the tank ditch is completed for Germany. We shall never be rough or heartless where it is not necessary; that is clear. We Germans, who are the only people in the world who have a decent attitude to animals, will also adopt a decent attitude to these human animals.'

Towards the end of the Second World War, as it became increasingly obvious that Germany was going to be defeated, Himmler made plans to save himself.

He sought to win asylum for himself and 200 other leading Nazis in the final days of the war, after the D-Day landings, by offering deals to the Allies behind Hitler's back. This is the same man who had exacted revenge on all those involved in the Stauffenberg plot by having them executed by hanging with piano wire, yet he himself was now betraying the Führer. Himmler offered money and the freedom of 3,500 Jews held in concentration camps. According to documents recently released by British intelligence documents, the concentration camp victims – and quite a small number of them, really, considering the astonishing deal he was trying to pull off – were to be sent to Switzerland in two trains.

After Hitler's suicide, Himmler was so far detached from the reality of the situation that he deluded himself into believing he could succeed as the new German leader. But Grand Admiral Doenitz was the Führer now, according to Hitler's will, and Doenitz dismissed Himmler from all of his posts as he was considered 'politically questionable'. Doenitz must have known that Himmler was guilty of a string of monstrous crimes against humanity, not just war crimes but crimes dating right back to the early Thirties; Himmler would have to be called to account for those.

Ditched by Doenitz, Himmler knew the game was up. He did what he could to escape from Germany. In the confusion and chaos that followed Hitler's suicide and the invasion of Russian, American and British troops, there was a chance he could escape. He took off his glasses, changed his name to Heinrich Hitzinger, and tried to lose himself in the great milling crowds of soldiers, refugees and displaced people trying to find their way home all over a Germany that was confused in defeat. Himmler almost escaped from Germany but gave himself away in the oddest way at the last moment as he joined a queue of people trudging across a bridge at Meinstedt. Perhaps his obsession for bureaucratic correctness got the better of him but, whatever the reason, he offered to show his papers to the British soldiers who, up that point, had not been paying much attention to the endless column of people. He was instantly suspected because of his odd behaviour in drawing unnecessary attention to himself. He seemed to be trying to tell them something. The soldiers did not recognize him straight away, but his behaviour was certainly suspicious enough to make them arrest him. It was only later that he was recognized.

In prison he admitted he was Himmler and asked to be taken to Montgomery. When this request was refused and British intelligence officers arrived to question him, he bit on a cyanide capsule concealed in his teeth and died instantly. His body was taken to the Lüneburg Heath and buried in an unmarked grave in the woods. Only the five soldiers who buried him knew the location of the grave of the second most feared man in the Third Reich.

Joseph Stalin

the greatest serial killer of them all?

IT IS EASY to forget that Stalin was not a real person at all. Behind the pseudonym, the famous alias, and the equally famous smiling moustached face seen on a thousand posters, was a real man called Josip or Joseph Dzhugashvili. He was born at Gori in Georgia on 21 December, 1879. His parents were illiterate peasants: in fact, they were serfs at the time of Stalin's birth. He was severely beaten by his father, who was an alcoholic, and this bad treatment in childhood may explain his harshness and the vengeful feelings he had towards anyone who might wield authority over him. The young Joseph was forced to work with his violent father as a cobbler until he was eleven, when his father was killed in a fight. His mother enrolled him in a religious seminary with a view to his becoming a priest.

While Joseph Dzhugashvili was at the seminary he came into contact with socialists and this led on naturally enough to his involvement with the socialist movement. In 1899 he failed to turn up for school examinations and as a result of this he was expelled. For ten years after that, he worked as a political activist in Georgia. From 1902 onwards he was repeatedly arrested and sent to Siberia. Among other things, he had robbed banks in Georgia to raise funds for the Bolshevik cause.

He admired Lenin's idea of a strong centralist party of professional revolutionaries, and he would be one of them. His practical experience in Georgia made him useful to the Bolsheviks, and he gained a place on the Bolshevik Central Committee in 1912. Some historians think that at this time Stalin was not a genuine revolutionary at all but a Tsarist spy infiltrating the Bolshevik movement. Certainly Stalin was capable of playing a double game like that; he was certainly not interested in personal or group loyalty. It was in 1913 that he adopted the name Stalin.

His revolutionary nickname was Koba, the name of a Georgian, Robin Hood-like folk hero. Stalin used a dozen other secret names to ensure his own anonymity before the Russian Revolution. The nickname 'Stalin', combining 'stal' (steel) with Lenin, was one of his noms de guerre from revolutionary days, and that was the one that stuck.

In the Russian Revolution of 1917, Stalin was at first opposed to the idea of overthrowing Kerensky's provisional government, and he was only won over to Lenin's position after Lenin returned from exile in April 1917. He played only a minor role in the Bolshevik seizure of power in November. His stand-off at this crucial moment is very peculiar, and would fit in with the idea of a lack of genuine commitment; it would also fit in with the proposition that Stalin was an observing agent rather than a real revolutionary. If so, it would account for the thoroughness of his later purges; he would want anyone who had known what he was really up to during the First World War – and survived – eliminated so that they could have no power over him. It is probably best to think of Stalin as a personal and political opportunist, not an idealist; like many others, he was able to exploit a chaotic political situation for personal advancement.

Stalin spent the first years after the Revolution in a sequence of senior posts in the government and party. He became General Secretary of the Communist Party in 1922, and built up the post into the most powerful position in the state. Lenin was not happy with Stalin, and was probably one of the last people in Russia for over thirty years to be able to criticize Stalin and not risk death as a result. Lenin did not want to see Stalin in a post of high responsibility at all, let alone as his successor. He urged his colleagues to find someone who was 'more tolerant, more loyal, more polite, more considerate, less capricious. Comrade Stalin had concentrated boundless authority in his hands and I am not sure whether he will always be capable of using that authority with caution.'

Lenin's remarks urging caution turned out to be prophetic, and they came too late. Stalin was already too powerful.

When Lenin died in January 1924, the party hierarchy tried to act on Lenin's advice by limiting Stalin's power. They sought to do this by appointing Zinoviev and Kamenev to share the leadership with him a triumvirate consisting of Stalin, Kamenev and Zinoviev ran the party, putting themselves ideologically between Bukharin (on the right) and Trotsky (on the left). Stalin advanced a policy of building 'Socialism in One Country', in stark opposition to Trotsky's policy of 'Permanent Revolution', which would involve working towards triggering revolution in other countries. Stalin and Bukharin joined forces against Trotsky, Kamenev and Zinoviev. By 1928, Stalin had emerged as supreme leader and the following year Trotsky was exiled. After that, Stalin exercised dictatorial power until his death in 1953. Nikolai Bukhanin had been one of Lenin's closest associates and could have expected to play a leading role in the post-Lenin era, but Stalin ousted him. Bukhanin confided to a friend, 'Stalin is a Genghis Khan who will kill us all'. Bukhanin's remark turned out to be all too accurate. Stalin was a born killer.

Russia was at the time of the Revolution the poorest and economically the most backward country in Europe. To modernize its economy, Stalin introduced a system of centrally-organized Five-Year Plans. These involved ambitious programmes of rapid industrialization and collectivization of agriculture. The industrialization programme involved creating a massive iron and steel manufacturing industry. All over Russia huge new collieries and iron and steel works were built. The cost in human life was enormous. An American observer estimated that Stalin's steel programme alone cost more lives than the Battle of the Marne in the Second World War.

The first two Five-Year Plans were nevertheless successful in achieving rapid industrialization. In fact if economic statistics alone are used, the whole sequence of pre-Second World War plans looks to have been successful; in 1935, industrial production in Russia was four times higher than it had been in 1913. This growth was financed by restraining consumption by ordinary Soviet citizens and the ruthless extraction of wealth from the peasants. It was odd. Stalin came from the peasant class, yet these were the people he treated worst.

The agricultural collectivization scheme was a disaster. In theory the large new mechanized farms would produce more food more efficiently than the small-scale and inefficient peasant farms. But collectivization meant destroying a way of life that had gone on for centuries, taking control over the land and food production away from the peasants, and their consequent loss of motivation. Under Lenin, the peasants (kulaks) had been allowed to sell their surplus food to ease shortages. Stalin was not going to let them dothat any more. The whole class kulaks was abolished; the peasants lost the small amount of land they had and were ordered to join huge new state farms.

The process also meant a drastic fall in living

standards for many peasants. Many of them violently resisted the collective movement. Between 1929 and 1933 Stalin introduced shock brigades to go in and force peasants to join the collectives. Many peasants slaughtered their livestock rather than give in, leading to a major drop if food production. Stalin blamed this on the kulaks, rich peasants who were 'capitalist parasites' and therefore enemies of the people. Kulaks who resisted collectivization were to be shot, transported to Gulag labour camps or deported to remote areas.

These measures were the background to thousands of infringements of human rights, thousands of deaths and untold misery throughout the Soviet Union. The disruption caused by collectivization led to major famines and up to five million death in 1932–33, especially in the Ukraine and lower Volga valley. Ironically, at this time Stalin was exporting millions of tonnes of grain. The loss of human life in Stalin's Russia was on an unimaginable scale. There was a census in 1937, which revealed how few people there were in Russia; population experts reckoned in 1939 that 20 million people had been lost. The demographic statistics, which revealed the scale of human suffering, had to be suppressed.

On the good side, Stalin invested heavily in the provision of basic medical services, increasing the number of doctors and launching campaigns against diseases such as typhus, cholera and malaria. Infant mortality rates steadily dropped. Education was another major growth area.

Like many another dictator, Stalin feared opposition. The fear was justified. He robbed, disinherited and killed many and there were many who would have like to get revenge. On a day-to-day basis, he disliked attending functions where he had to cross rooms full of people; these were places where he might be assassinated, and he feared assassination. He organized a Great Purge designed to get rid of all actual and suspected political and ideological opponents. Some were imprisoned in the labour camps, some were executed after show trials, some were assassinated. Trotsky and Kirov, the Leningrad party chief, were both assassinated. Stalin is said to have personally signed 40,000 death warrants, but many more than this died. During this reign of terror, there were mass arrests, torture and executions without trial. Anyone suspected by the secret police of opposing the regime was rounded up and killed. The word 'troika' acquired a horrible new meaning – a quick trial by a committee of three – it was a euphemism for summary execution. The scale of the atrocities ordered by Stalin is hard to imagine. There were three major purges, in 1935–38, 1942 and 1945–50. During those purges about a million people were shot and millions more were deported to labour camps.

The big show trials in Moscow were intended as examples for local courts to follow across the rest of the Soviet Union. The big show trials included the Trial of the Sixteen in 1936, the Trial of the Seventeen in 1937, the Trial of the Red Army Generals in 1937 (halving the

Red Army leadership) and the Trial of the Twenty-One, which included Stalin's old colleague Bukharin, in 1938. Stalin was never to be known for personal loyalty. Bukharin, Zinoviev and Kamenev were all removed. He ordered the assassination of Trotsky in 1940, eliminating the last of his opponents from the old Party leadership. Only two men now survived out of Lenin's Politburo, Stalin and Molotov, and Molotov must have felt very lucky to be alive, though not very safe.

Stalin had an endless capacity for evil. It is possible to see, behind the purges, a deep insecurity in the man. He could not bear to have people near him who might know more than he did, or who might contradict him. Anyone with experience, rank or ideas was ruthlessly eliminated. He was not absolutely sure of President Kalinin's loyalty, so he had his wife imprisoned as a hostage; she was kept in a prison camp for seven years, just to ensure her husband's good behaviour. In addition to the judicial murders, and an estimated half million people were summarily shot, he uprooted and deported hundreds of thousands of people. During the Second World War, he organized deportations an a massive scale. Over 1.5 million people were sent to Siberia and central Asia. The reasons given were separatist movements, resistance to Soviet rule, and collaboration with the Germans. Underneath this whole programme there seems to have been an unspoken desire for ethnic cleansing. Various ethnic minorities were removed from the Black Sea region: Tatars,

Kalmyks, Chechens, Ingush, Karachai, Greeks and Armenians. The conditions under which these deportations took place were appalling. It is estimated that 60% of the 200,000 people deported from the Baltic states died. Half of the Crimean Tatars died of hunger within a year of being deported.

In 1956, three years after Stalin died, Khrushchev condemned Stalin's deportations as contrary to Lenin's principles. He said the Ukrainians escaped deportation by Stalin only because there were too many of them. Not only were the deportations a savage and totally unjustified act, they left a legacy of hatred which lives on. The memory of the deportations still plays a major role in shaping and driving the separatist movements in various parts of the former Soviet Union long after Stalin's death. The Baltic States were among the first to demand independence from a collapsing Soviet Union; Chechnya still hopes for separation.

Overall, the famines, deportations, prisons, labour camps, torture and political purges accounted for around 20 million deaths, maybe more. Stalin himself was responsible for these, in many cases directly responsible by issuing direct orders, in other cases indirectly responsible by creating situations in which he knew people would die. Some people had emigrated, some people had starved, some had died in industrial accidents, some had been killed in purges. Stalin acquired a reputation for ruthless brutality. It is said that Stalin had to have a medical team in constant attendance at his reception desk, because people who were summoned to an interview were literally in fear of their lives and often had to be sedated either before or after seeing him. It is also said that he had a button under his desk. If Stalin was not getting the answers he wanted, or he had found out enough to be sure of the interviewee's guilt, he just pressed the button and two or three men came and dragged the interviewee away to be shot. The harshness and cruelty of the man are hard to understand, yet the simplest explanation may be the right one – that he was getting his own back for the unjustified violence he himself experienced in childhood.

Even his own wife was horrified by what she saw Stalin doing. In November 1932, Nadezhda Alliluevna shot herself with a revolver. She had started as a secretary in Lenin's office, helping Stalin by passing on secrets that she thought might help Stalin's career. But during the next ten years, the years when Stalin was in power, she became alienated by his increasing brutality, at home as well as 'professionally', as head of state. He had become foul-mouthed, hard-drinking, given to violent rages and capricious acts of cruelty. On one occasion he stuck five tubes of paper onto his secretary's fingers, then lit them like candles. He watched, grinning, as the man's fingers were burnt; he knew the poor man would not dare to remove the burning paper. Pure sadism.

Stalin was cruel, but he also lived in fear. A Finn who knew Stalin well, said, 'The more ruthless and cold-blooded he became, the more he lived in an almost insane fear of his life'. Even when he was safely inside the Kremlin, which is a fortress, Stalin took the precaution of wearing a bullet-proof vest. He had tunnels dug so that he could reach other government buildings from the Kremlin without going outside. The Moscow underground railway was secretly extended to reach his villa at Kuntsevo. When he was forced to go out into the street and travel anywhere by car, Stalin used an armour-plated vehicle with bullet-proof windows three inches thick. Beria's secret service squads checked every route he travelled and lined the roads as he passed along them.

Stalin's food always came from special farms run by the NKVD to ensure that it was not tampered with. The food was always analyzed and tasted before he ate it. His tea was always taken from a freshly opened packet. When Stalin's tea lady was spotted taking tea from a packet that had already been opened, she was thrown into prison for negligence.

Stalin's daughter Svetlana said, much later, after Stalin's death, that her mother's death was a final personal disaster. Nadezhda was one of the last remaining checks on Stalin's psychopathic behaviour. Svetlana said Nadezhda's death 'deprived his soul of the last vestiges of human warmth'.

Not long after his wife's death, Stalin tightened up the process leading to execution. In December 1934, a young Communist shot dead Party Secretary Kirov in

St Petersburg, which had been renamed Leningrad. As a result of this assassination, Stalin ordered the speeding-up of the processing of cases involving terrorist acts. Courts were instructed to carry out death sentences immediately, since the government would no longer consider appeals. Khrushchev was later to comment that this led to 'mass acts of abuse against socialist legality'.

In August 1939 Stalin signed the Molotov-Ribbentrop Pact, a non-aggression pact with the Nazis. It was a sleazy and cynical deal. The Russian NKVD swapped notes with the German Gestapo on their respective dissidents. Jewish prisoners in Soviet gulags were swapped for concentration camp prisoners that Stalin wanted to lay hands on. Stalin was given a free hand in some areas to extend his reign of terror. The Red Army was allowed to march into the Balkan States to 'protect their neutrality'. Poland was callously divided in two, the western half to be German, the eastern half Russian. Stalin sent troops in from the east, capturing over a quarter of a million Polish officers and men. 14,000 of them were massacred. Of those, 4,000 were massacred in the Katyn Forest near Smolensk. Their remains were found in 1943. Most of the bodies had their hands tied behind their backs and bullet wounds in the nape of the neck. A few had smashed skulls. What happened to the missing 10,000 Polish soldiers has never been established for certain. It is thought that they were loaded onto barges that were

towed out into the White Sea and sunk by the Russian NKVD.

Stalin evidently felt safe in behaving in this way inside Europe because he trusted Hitler, but Hitler was, in his way, even more of a monster than Stalin. By 1940, Hitler was planning to betray Stalin – with Operation Barbarossa.

Stalin got a well-deserved nasty surprise in June 1941, when Hitler broke the Molotov-Ribbentrop Pact, which divided Eastern Europe into agreed German and Russian spheres of influence. Hitler surprised Stalin by invading the Soviet Union, with the intention of reaching, and helping himself to, the Baku oilfields on the shores of the Caspian Sea.

Hitler's troops crossed the Russian border at dawn on 22 June 1941. Stalin had not expected this invasion and was not prepared for it, either militarily or psychologically. In fact, he was too stunned to react appropriately to the invasion for eleven whole days. During these eleven days, the Red Army, weakened by Stalin's massive leadership purges, was beaten back in total disarray. The Germans advanced quickly, capturing or killing hundreds of thousands of Soviet soldiers. Stalin had very unwisely executed many of his most experienced Red Army generals. Now he needed them. Stalin addressed the Soviet Union for only the second time in his thirty year reign. On this memorable occasion he told the Russian people two very big lies – that the Germans had lost 4.5 million troops and that

Soviet victory was near. Neither of these facts was true. Russian losses were staggeringly high and Russia was losing the war. Stalin had executed his generals. Now he started executing his soldiers. Order 227 (27 July, 1942) dictated that any soldier who retreated or left his position without orders would be summarily shot. He also ordered a scorched earth policy. Infrastructure and food supplies were to be destroyed before German troops could make use of them; this inevitably meant that even greater suffering was inflicted on the civilian population. In the end about 25 million Soviet citizens died in the war between Germany and Russia.

The towns and villages invaded by the German troops welcomed them, assuming that the German regime must be better than Stalin's. None of them dreamed that Hitler would be as bad a master as Stalin. Oddly, Hitler refused to capitalize on this goodwill. Almost a million Russian troops wanted to join the German army to fight against Stalin under the rebel General Vlasov, but Hitler turned down their offer. It might well have decided the outcome of the war.

Beria's NKVD, acting under Stalin's instructions, took savage revenge on anyone they suspected of collaborating with the Nazis. Whole peoples from outlying areas were transported to camps in Siberia or central Asia where they were left to starve to death – the Crimean Tatars, the Kalmyks, the Karachi-Balkars, the Chechens. Even Russian soldiers who returned from captivity or victory in the west were thoroughly interrogated to find out whether they were truly loyal to Communist Russia. Those soldiers who innocently admitted to being impressed by what they saw in the West were either shot or imprisoned. Stalin was (still) very insecure. He could not bear the idea that Russian soldiers might spread stories to the masses that ordinary people in the West had a better standard of living than ordinary Soviet citizens. Svetlana said her father was 'as bitter as he could be against the whole world. He saw enemies everywhere. It had reached the point of being pathological, of persecution mania'.

Even Soviet war heroes were not immune. The writer Alexander Solzhenitsyn was twice decorated for bravery as an artillery officer, but then imprisoned in a labour camp for eight years for 'insulting Stalin'.

This episode was a traumatic experience for Stalin, and shaped his post-war strategy in Europe. Communist-led governments were installed in the East European countries occupied by Soviet troops, forming a Communist Bloc. This was to be a buffer zone, protecting Russia from Germany. It was strengthened in 1955 in the Warsaw Pact. So, the freezing of eastern Europe into a Communist zone was the joint posthumous legacy of two evil dictators, Hitler and Stalin.

The knock-on effects were to be global. Many in the West believed that the Soviet Union's encroachment in Eastern Europe was a sign that the Soviet Union intended to spread Communism round the world. But that was Trotsky's aim – it was never Stalin's. Stalin only ever wanted control over the Soviet Union. The misunderstanding nevertheless led to a Cold War, a long period of distrust and tension.

In the post-war period, Stalin promoted himself as the great war-time leader who had defeated the Germans. He also cultivated the image of the wise and genial elder statesman, and the thousands of gigantic posters showed him as affable, kindly 'Uncle Joe'. Many in the West fell for this image; it was not until after his death that the full horror of the purges and the labour camps became known. One of the points agreed at the Yalta Conference was that the Western leaders would return to Stalin his prisoners of war but refugees from Soviet rule. Some of these were not recent refugees connected to the Second World War at all. Some were White Russians who had fled after the Russian Civil War ended in 1921. In fact over three million of these genuine refugees were living in the West in 1945. By 1948 nearly all of them had been repatriated by force. Britain alone sent 30,000 back. It could be argued that Churchill too was guilty of a monstrous crime; it was after all a kind of mass murder. But it is very hard to tell to what extent Churchill knew what Stalin was going to do with these people, though they knew perfectly well what fate lay ahead. At Scarisbrook Camp on Merseyside, one man hanged himself rather than fall into Stalin's hands. Another man cut his throat as he was being loaded onto a ship in the docks in Liverpool. Yet another beat his own brains out with a stone.

When these unfortunate people got back to the Soviet Union, they were marched straight from the boats and trains into makeshift execution yards. Soviet Air Force planes flew low overhead to drown the sound of the shooting. Others were loaded onto closed trains and sent to the gulags, where they died more slowly.

In the aftermath of Stalin's death, his successors, Malenkov, Bulganin and Khrushchev, launched a programme of de-Stalinization in an attempt to put the record straight about Stalin's period in office. A distance had to be created between much of what Stalin had done and those who had survived. The infamous NKVD had to go, though it was replaced by the KGB. Beria himself would be shot within a matter of months of his master's death. Stalingrad would, within a few years, become known as Volgograd. Meanwhile, behind the genial smiling posters, the repression and the executions continued. In 1953, Stalin was apparently preparing a new purge – this time of Jews – but he died before he could put this scheme into action.

The West understandably treated Stalin with circumspection. One young post-war British MP, Alice Bacon, found herself lucky enough to be included in a routine diplomatic mission to Moscow, where she expected to meet British Embassy officials and maybe some Russian bureaucrats. There was a drinks party at the British Embassy in Moscow. Suddenly, without warning, the doors burst open and in walked Stalin with a group of heavies. Alice Bacon instinctively cringed for safety behind someone else as she saw Stalin advance across the room in her direction. But there was no escape. He walked straight up to her, smiling the big 'Uncle Joe' smile of the gigantic posters and asked her who she was. She told him she was a British Member of Parliament. 'Which constituency?' he asked. 'Liverpool East,' she said. 'Ah,' said Stalin, 'there are two constituencies in Liverpool: Liverpool East and Liverpool West. There is a labour dispute going on there at the moment.' He was interested, friendly, charming. It was as if he was going back to his roots, checking on the fomenting of unrest in Georgia – but his detailed knowledge of what was going on in Britain was more than a little unnerving. How did he know there was a labour dispute in Liverpool West? Was he reading British newspapers or did he have other sources? Alice Bacon didn't ask.

On 1 March 1953, the 73-year-old Stalin had a long dinner with Beria, Malenkov, Bulganin and Khrushchev: too long a dinner – he collapsed at the end of it. He had been raging because some members of the Politburo had opposed his scheme to transport thousands of Soviet Jews to the East and dump them in the wilderness near the Chinese border. The rage apparently brought on a stroke, though the cause of death is still uncertain; Molotov later claimed that Beria boasted to him that he had poisoned Stalin. Either way, because of the centralization of power in the person of Stalin himself, none of the others felt they could take any action. That at any rate is the story they later told, but it may instead be that they deliberately did nothing for several hours in order to ensure that he died. They were safer with Stalin dead. Everybody was safer with Stalin dead. He died four days later on 5 March aged 73. At the time of his death he had killed over 20 million Soviet citizens and still held an incredible 14 million people imprisoned in the gulags. Scarcely a single family in the Soviet Union had been left untouched by Stalin's murderous hand.

Stalin's body was embalmed and displayed, for a time, alongside Lenin's; Lenin, it should be remembered, had disliked Stalin intensely and warned his successors to get rid of him. If only they had taken his advice, Eurasia would have been spared the worst democide the world has ever seen.

Ho Chi Minh

'Uncle Ho'

HO CHI MINH was born in Vietnam in 1890. His father, Nguyen Sinh Huy, was employed by the French colonial authorities as a teacher. He was a highly intelligent and able man, but he was dismissed from his teaching post because as a matter of political principle he refused to learn the French language, the language of the colonial power. To try to make a living, Nguyen Sinh Huy was reduced to travelling round offering help in the form of letter writing and medical services to the peasants. Nguyen was a committed nationalist and he brought up his children to resist French rule – and they did. Ho Chi Minh would contribute greatly to the ejection of the French from Indo-China and go on to achieve something even more remarkable, the ejection of the Americans from Indo-China too. In many respects, then, Ho would turn into a patriotic hero. But it was his refusal to compromise, his refusal to wait, that would cause so much unnecessary loss of life. If he had not involved himself in the affairs of South Vietnam, the Americans would have stayed out, so he was to a great extent responsible for the huge loss of life in the Vietnam War.

But all that lay ahead. Ho Chi Minh's sister got herself a job with the French Army, using her position to steal weapons which she hoped could one day be used to drive the French out of Vietnam. Eventually she was caught and sentenced to life imprisonment.

Nguyen sent the young Ho to a French school, which he thought was the best way to prepare the boy in the struggle against the colonial occupation. Ho himself became a teacher for short time before becoming a sailor. This enabled him to travel. He saw several other countries that were suffering from exploitation by the French, and this reinforced his view that the French presence in Indo-China must be ended. In 1917, Ho settled in Paris, where he read Marx and other left-wing writers; he became a convert to Communism. In December 1920 the French Communist Party was founded, and Ho was one of its founder members. Like many others in his group, Ho had been inspired by the recent Russian Revolution, and in 1924 he visited Moscow. From there he wrote to a friend that it was the duty of all Communists to go back to their own countries, 'Make contact with the masses to awaken, organize, unite and train them and lead them to fight for freedom and independence'.

Ho also knew that if he returned to Vietnam straight away he would be arrested by the French authorities, so he went instead to China, settling close to the

Vietnamese border. While he was there, he organized other nationalists in exile into a Vietnam Revolutionary League. A recurring theme in his political and military strategy is co-ordination

The Japanese invaded Indo-China in 1940. Paris was occupied by German troops, so the demoralized French troops in the East did not have the heart to resist the Japanese; instead they surrendered. Ho Chi Minh saw this as an opportunity to liberate Vietnam, and formed a new organization called the Vietnminh, which would run a guerilla war against the Japanese. The Vietnminh campaign was supplied with arms by the Soviet Union. After the bombing of Pearl Harbour by the Japanese, the Vietnminh got supplies from the USA as well. The events of the Second World War unfolding round them taught the Vietnminh a lot about military tactics, and they were able to apply this knowledge in the following years.

When the Japanese surrendered at the end of the Second World War, the Vietnminh were in a strong position to take control of Vietnam. In September 1945, Ho Chi Minh declared the foundation of the Democratic Republic of Vietnam. What Ho did not know was that Roosevelt, Stalin and Churchill had already decided at Potsdam what was going to happen in Vietnam. They had decided that Vietnam would be divided in two, the north under Chinese control, the south under British control. It turned out to be even more complicated than that, as the French, excluded from the Yalta Conference, decided unilaterally that they wanted their colony back.

In January 1946 the British agreed to withdraw their troops from the south. Later that year the Chinese agreed to leave the north – on condition that France relinquished its claims to territory in the region. But the French did not agree. Fighting soon broke out between French troops and the Vietnminh. At first the Vietnminh, under General Vo Nguyen Giap, found it hard to match the highly-trained French troops. Their situation improved after 1949, when Mao Zedong and his Communist forces created a safe haven in China where they could train and care for their wounded.

The Vietnminh controlled large areas in North Vietnam by 1953. Meanwhile, the French were maintaining a firm hold in the south, where they had installed the former Emperor of Vietnam, Bo Dai, as head of state. The war dragged on, so the French tried to strike a deal with the Vietnminh, offering to set up a national government with a view to granting Vietnam eventual independence. Ho Chi Minh did not trust the French, though, and went on fighting. This refusal to negotiate, to prefer armed struggle, was his leading characteristic.

Ho Chi Minh was a butcher, in spite of his mild and genial appearance,.

In France, there was general loss of confidence in the war in Indo-China. By 1952, as many as 90,000 French soldiers had been killed. France was trying to rebuild its war-damaged economy and the foreign war was costing too much in cash as well as lives. There were also many in France who, in a post-war world, no longer believed in colonialism. In Europe generally, there was no stomach for colonial adventures any more.

In Vietnam, the French commander General Navarre saw that time was running out. He needed a quick victory. He was sure that if he could engage the Vietnminh in a large-scale battle the French were bound to win it. So General Navarre misguidedly – tragically, as events turned out – set up a defensive position at Dien Bien Phu, to block the path of the Vietnminh troops attempting to return to their camps in Laos. Navarre thought this would force General Giap to mount a mass attack on the French at Dien Bien Phu. General Giap took up Navarre's challenge, but in an unexpected way. Instead of mounting a huge frontal attack on Dien Bien Phu, he took his time, surrounded it and ordered his men to dig an encircling trench. He laid siege to the great fortress. Then trenches and tunnels were dug radially inwards towards the French, who now realised they were under siege. More Vietnamese troops were brought in. By the time the battle started, General Giap had 70,000 soldiers surrounding Dien Bien Phu, five times the number of French troops bottled up inside.

Navarre realised now that his situation was desperate. He could see that he and his men were fatally trapped and appealed for help. Some US advisers considered the possibility of using nuclear weapons against the Vietnminh. Others thought conventional air raids would be enough to overcome the forces of General Giap. Eisenhower, the US President, in any case refused to intervene without the participation of the other Western Allies. Churchill declined to get Britain involved while the peace negotiations were taking place in Geneva; he perhaps felt that it was through their own folly that the French were in this mess – and they should be left to get themselves out of it. It was on 13 March, 1954 that General Giap launched his attack, a relentless and terrifying attack that went on for 56 days. The French were pushed into a smaller and smaller area of Dien Bien Phu. The French artillery commander, Colonel Piroth, blamed himself for the tactics that were obviously failing, told his fellow officers that he was 'completely dishonoured' and committed suicide by blowing himself up with a grenade.

On 7 May the French surrendered; 7,000 French troops had died at Dien Bien Phu, and the remaining 11,000 were taken prisoner. The next day the French announced they were withdrawing from Vietnam. An international conference agreed a division of Vietnam; North Vietnam would be ruled by Ho Chi Minh and South Vietnam would be ruled by Ngo Dinh Diem, who was strongly anti-Communist. The French would withdraw from the South and the North, the Vietnminh would withdraw from the south, and the Vietnamese could choose for themselves whether they were going to live in the Communist North or the non-Communist South.

Ho Chi Minh accepted this as a temporary solution, and was sure that in the promised General Election the Vietnamese would elect a Communist government for the whole of Vietnam. Eisenhower shared Ho Chi Minh's view; he later said, 'Had elections been held at the time of the fighting, possibly 80% of the population would have voted for the Communist Ho Chi Minh'. But further problems lay ahead. In 1954 the French argued that Ngo Dinh Diem, the proposed new ruler of South Vietnam, was 'not only incapable but mad'. They had a point. It turned out that Diem had no intention of holding elections that might result in a united Vietnam, and cancelled them.

The only solution seemed to be violence against the Diem regime. In 1959, it is estimated that as many as 1,200 of Diem's government officials were murdered by guerillas. At first Ho Chi Minh was against the idea of joining in the violence in South Vietnam and offered non-military support to South Vietnamese opposition forces. He sent a trusted adviser, Le Duan, to South Vietnam to report on the situation. Le Duan returned with the advice that North Vietnam had to encourage armed resistance to Diem; it was the only way to unite the country.

Basing his decision on Le Duan's advice, Ho Chi Minh sent guerilla units and encourage the various different armed bands to join together to make a more effective resistance organization. This was agreed and in December 1960 they formed the National Front for the Liberation of South Vietnam (NLF). The Americans were later to call them the Vietcong, and they were made up of many different political and ethnic groups. They were led by Hua Tho, who was a lawyer from Saigon and, as it happened, not a Communist. The tactics of the NLF were very similar to those used by Mao Zedong in China, the tactics of guerilla warfare. Working in small cells with little knowledge of one another, little damage was done to the overall strategy if an individual was captured and tortured; he would know only about his own cell. Ho Chi Minh's speciality was an eye for effective organizational structure. The NLF were under strict instructions to do no damage to the fields and houses of the peasants, but rather to do everything they could to help them. What they actually did, of course, was to implicate the villagers in the campaign of military and political subversion, just by passing through and getting supplies from them, and drew terrible reprisals on them first from the Diem regime and later from the American troops, who notoriously engaged in village massacres.

Just three months after being shot into the Presidency by the Kennedy assassination, Lyndon B. Johnson launched Operation Rolling Thunder. This was a brutal bombing campaign aimed at destroying the North Vietnamese economy and stopping the North Vietnamese from interfering any further in South

Vietnam. The plan was for an eight-week campaign; it lasted for three years. In that time, the Americans dropped a million tons of bombs on Vietnam.

Ho Chi Minh himself lived right through all of this, dying in 1969.

He was the visual stereotype of the oriental ascetic, with his emaciated figure, goatee beard, enigmatic smile, mild manner and threadbare bush jacket. He cultivated the image of a humble, benign 'Uncle Ho', perhaps with 'Uncle Joe' Stalin consciously in mind. But behind this mild image was a seasoned, uncompromising and ruthless revolutionary. He was also totally single-minded. He wanted the French out of his country, he wanted a Communist regime, and he wanted unity. He fought three wars: one to get rid of the French, one to get rid of Diem, one to get rid of the Americans. He was not only single-minded, he was ready to lose a lot in order to win. In 1946, when war with the French was looming, he warned the French, 'You can kill ten of my men for every one I kill of yours, yet even at those odds I will win.' The French ignored his stark warning, and suffered severely as a result. In a very similar way, the Americans were the victims of cultural chauvinism. They were convinced, then as before and subsequently, of their own technical superiority and certain that they could win the Vietnam War fairly quickly. They were wrong too. Just like the French, they eventually had to withdraw in total humiliation. Ho Chi Minh and his supporters were too ruthless for even for the Americans to deal with.

Ho Chi Minh was responsible for much of the bloodshed by his refusal to compromise. He could have improved the lot of the North Vietnamese people by holding back from interference in the South, however unsatisfactory it might have seemed to him that unification was being postponed. North Vietnam was a poor country, in need of careful development, and it was not enriched in any way by Ho Chi Minh's doctrinaire policy regarding his neighbour. The orders he gave to the NLF for their behaviour towards the peasants were of an idealistic nature that is reminiscent of eighteenth century France. French revolutionary idealists such as Robespierre spoke in high-flown language (often drawn from Rousseau) about love, nature, peace and patriotism, while all around them, precisely because of their actions, the streets ran with blood. It was the same with Ho Chi Minh. In pursuit of the ideals of anti-colonialism, Communism and nationalism, enormous numbers of innocent Vietnamese people had to die. The sacrifices he made to achieve his goals were too great. General Giap spoke in 1990 about the Vietnamese struggle for independence. Asked how long he could have resisted the American onslaught, he said, 'Twenty years – maybe a hundred years – as long as it took to win, regardless of cost.' But the cost was terrible. Three million Vietnamese people in the North and South died.

Jean-Bedel Bokassa

the Cannibal Emperor

BORN AT BOBANGUI in the Central African Republic on 22 February 1921, Jean-Bedel Bokassa became one of the most infamous tyrants ever to have ruled in Africa.

Bokassa started off as a career soldier, enlisting in the Free French Army in 1939, and ending the Second World War as a Sergeant Major with the Légion d'Honneur and the Croix de Guerre to his name. By 1961 he had risen, rather slowly, to the rank of Captain. He left the French Army for the army of the Central African Republic. Here he advanced more quickly, possible because he was the cousin of the President, David Dacko, and the nephew of the previous President, Barthelemy Boganda. Bokassa was duly promoted to Colonel and then Commander-in-Chief of the armed forces.

On 1 January, 1966, Bokassa successfully overthrew his cousin, David Dacko, in a quick and efficient coup; he assumed power for himself as President of the Republic and leader of the country's one and only party, the Movement for the Social Evolution of Black Africa (MESAN). By 4 January Bokassa was abolishing the 1959 constitution and ruling by decree. He had become a dictator.

In April 1969 there was an attempt to topple him, which gave Bokassa a marvellous excuse to strengthen his personal power. It was just what he wanted. In 1972, he made himself President for Life. He survived another attempted coup in December 1974 and an attempt on his life in February 1976.

After meeting Colonel Gadaffi of Libya, President for Life Bokassa decided he would convert to Islam. This involved changing his name to Salah Eddine Ahmed Bokassa.

In September 1976, Bokassa dissolved his government and put in its place a Council of the Central African Revolution. Megalomania was now taking over in a big way. On 4 December 1976, Bokassa told the MESAN congress that the country was no longer a republic but a monarchy, called the Central African Empire. He issued an imperial constitution, converted back from Islam to Catholicism, and had himself crowned Emperor Bokassa I on 4 December 1977.

In the run-up to his coronation, Bokassa shut himself away in his palace 50 miles outside the capital to watch, over and over again, the film of Queen Elizabeth II's coronation in Westminster. He was very moved by the scenes of pageantry and the spontaneous loyalty and devotion of the Queen's subjects. He decided that his own coronation would be a similarly grand affair, one that would overwhelmingly impress his guests. He wanted to see some of that loyalty and devotion too. So he sent word to the Governor of Bangui Prison to select a dozen prisoners for more humane treatment. He wanted them to be moved to larger cells, allowed exercise, given better food. The prison guards wondered whether a prison amnesty would be part of the coronation celebrations.

The French government, at Valery Giscard D'Estaing's instigation, gave him one million pounds' worth of credit to buy a fleet of Mercedes limousines for his coronation guests. The credit also covered the purchase of 200 motorcycles to act as outriders to accompany the limousines. This was considered by the French President to be an appropriate present to a country with a 10% literacy rate and more than 25 per cent of the children dying of disease and malnutrition before they reached their first birthday.

He had coronation robes specially designed in ivory, black white and gold, with a fur-trimmed, red-lined cape, and naturally an ermine-trimmed gold crown. The throne was a spectacle in itself: a red plush seat embedded in the breast of a colossal golden eagle with wings outstretched. His idea seems to have been to outshine the Emperor Napoleon. He planned to spend £10 million on a two-day binge that would rival that of Napoleon's coronation. Bokassa signalled his intention by taking the title 'emperor' after his crowning.

The country itself was to be renamed Central African Empire.

Many political leaders were repelled by this flagrant waste, and returned their invitation cards. Some made excuses for failing to attend. The British Foreign Office is usually fastidiously polite in dealing with unwanted invitations; there was little covering-up in this case. President Jimmy Carter, the American President at the time, found Bokassa's self-aggrandisement offensive and stopped all aid to the Congo immediately.

Bokassa went ahead with his flummery. He paraded through Bangui in a gilded carriage drawn by eight white horses, along the only two miles of paved road in the city. He went ahead, complete with crown and ermine robes, in the full heat of the African tropics.

The spectacular lavishness of the coronation brought down global ridicule and disapproval upon Bokassa. The errors of judgement and taste were strikingly similar to those of General Amin. As with Amin, the charge of cannibalism has been levelled against Bokassa. The banquet served to the coronation guests on Limoges porcelain was far more unusual and expensive than the privileged guests could possibly have realised. The prisoners at the Bangui Prison who had been given exercise, better cells and better food had been killed, butchered and cooked for the delectation of Bokassa's guests.

The new imperial regime was even more stringent than the old. Dissent was punished severely. France remained a supporter of Bokassa, in spite of Bokassa's high-profile descent into megalomania. The French President Valery Giscard d'Estaing was a friend of Bokassa's and a loyal supporter; he made sure the Bokassa regime had adequate financial and military support. If this support seems strange, Bokassa in return invited Giscard d'Estaing on frequent hunting trips to Africa and supplied France with uranium, which was vital for its nuclear power programme. The French press nevertheless became increasingly critical of President Giscard d'Estaing's excessively friendly relationship with Bokassa, and all the more so after it emerged that Bokassa had given the French President presents of diamonds. The reason for Giscard's support now seemed clear.

The gifts of diamonds were not limited to the French President either. Other foreign visitors were given equally lavish presents – presents the country could ill afford to give.

There were many infringements of human rights in Bokassa's empire, and publicity about these became an increasing embarrassment in France. One high-profile incident received international coverage. Riots in Bangui led to a massacre of civilians. Bokassa was determined to change dusty Bangui into a model of European fashion – ideally French, of course. He ordered the children of Bangui's high school to wear (and therefore buy) expensively tailored school uniforms. Their parents could scarcely afford the textbooks their children needed, let alone expensive uniforms. The clothing factory which manufactured the uniforms was owned by the Emperor himself, which prompted a certain amount of comment. There was understandably a protest about the school uniforms. On 17-19 April some 200 schoolchildren were rounded up by the Imperial Guard and arrested. They were herded into the yard of Bangui Prison where Bokassa swaggered up and down with his gold-topped cane, hectoring and shouting at them.

The children were put in already overcrowded cells. Over the next few weeks, the children were brought out, one by one, for what was described as a 'school uniform inspection'. One by one, the children were beaten to death. Almost incredibly, about a hundred of them were killed. It was alleged that Bokassa himself had taken part in these killings and that he had eaten some of the bodies.

News of the brutal and pointless killings reached the French Embassy in Bangui. At first the French officials did not believe what they heard, but more witnesses appeared, corroborating the story. Then Paris knew what had been going on and it was clear that this was not just a harmlessly eccentric African head of state, a kind of comic opera buffoon, but a dangerous monster. French support for the dictator Bokassa instantly evaporated. David Dacko, the previous president, enlisted French support for a coup. The French were now more than ready to see Bokassa removed and agreed to reinstate Dacko. The opportunity arose when Bokassa was out of the country visiting Libya. On 20 September 1979, French troops staged a coup and deposed him. Emperor Bokassa stepped off the plane at Tripoli to learn that he was no longer emperor. Meanwhile, French Secret Service agents in Paris went to the apartment of David Dacko, shook him awake, gave him a prepared speech to memorize, and pushed him into a waiting car. Ten hours later, Dacko stepped out of a French military jet at Bangui airport. He was the new head of state, though clearly under firm French control. Dacko remained President until he too was overthrown, for a second time, in 1981.

Bokassa had by then been sentenced to death in absentia. After he was deposed, Bokassa went from Libya to the Ivory Coast in West Africa, another French ex-colony, and then to a run-down villa in a Paris suburb.

The French Legionnaires searched the prison grounds, where they found the mass grave of the murdered schoolchildren. Later, they broke into the Emperor's palace, where they claimed to have found the remains of a further 37 children lying on the tiled floor of the swimming pool. Resting beside the swimming pool were Bokassa's four pet crocodiles, which had evidently fed on the children. In the palace kitchens, the Legionnaires were reported to have found a cold store containing the half-eaten remains of another ten children who had been served up at the Emperor's dining table just a week earlier.

Bokassa remained obsessed with uniforms – which were in a sense the cause of his downfall – even in retirement. He started up a new career as a supplier of khaki suits to African tourist shops. President Giscard D'Estaing, now profoundly embarrassed by his association with the cannibal emperor, sent a cheque for £10,000, the value of Bokassa's diamonds, to a charity school for children in Bangui. It does not sound nearly enough, given the circumstances.

Remarkably, and very exceptionally in such cases, Bokassa returned from exile in France to answer his accusers. He arrived back in his empire on 24 October 1986, when he was arrested and put on trial. The charges were treason, murder, cannibalism and embezzlement. The trial was an emotional affair and dragged on for some months. Bokassa was eventually cleared of the charges of cannibalism, but found guilty of the other charges, and sentenced to death on 12 June 1987. Some months later the death sentence was commuted to life imprisonment, then to 20 years. With the return of democracy in 1993, the outgoing President Andre Kolingba announced a general amnesty for all prisoners. Bokassa, who was incredibly lucky not to have been executed back in 1986, now found himself released from prison, a free man, in August 1993.

Bokassa's lucky break was short-lived. He died of a heart attack three years later, on 3 November 1996. Whether he really ate children or not we shall probably never know, but the killings certainly happened – lots of them. Bokassa ruled with the same capricious cruelty that Amin displayed in Uganda, and in a similar way he spread untold misery among his unfortunate subjects. His country was a poor one, and it was entirely inappropriate for him to siphon off such a high proportion of his country's wealth to pay for his own lavish lifestyle. Like many such political leaders, he kept his people poor, instead of enriching them; he took away their rights instead of empowering them.

Idi Amin

Conqueror of the British Empire in Africa in
General and Uganda in Particular

ON WARM TROPICAL nights in Kampala in the 1970s, the lights would dim and go out. Cinemas and cafés blacked out, to the irritation of foreign businessmen and diplomats from overseas, but the local residents would go silently to their homes, knowing the reason for the power failure. The blackouts usually meant one thing – that the hydro-electric power station at the Owen Falls Dam, on the Nile 40 miles away from Kampala, was clogged up with human corpses. The President of Uganda had been on another killing spree, and the massacre had inevitably resulted in a drop in voltage followed by a national blackout. It was somehow emblematic of one of the most grotesque and bloodthirsty regimes imaginable.

General Idi Amin Dada Oumee was born near Koboko in Uganda on 17 May, 1928, as a member of the Kakwa tribe. He was brought up by his mother, who was thought to be a witch doctor, and had very little in the way of an education. In 1946, Amin joined the King's African Rifles as a private in the British colonial army. He saw action in the Mau Mau revolt in Kenya and was promoted to the rank of lieutenant. He was a keen, over-eager soldier with a reputation for cruelty, rising gradually through the ranks to sergeant-major before being made an effendi, which was the highest rank an African could reach in the British army.

The young Amin was a great sportsman. He was a champion swimmer and also Uganda's light heavyweight champion from 1951 to 1960. He was an extraordinary-looking man, a gleaming black hulk, six foot four inches tall and weighing over 20 stone. He was imposing, but unintelligent and violent, and completely oblivious to the subtleties of conventional politics.

After Uganda became independent in 1962, the first Prime Minister of Uganda, Milton Obote, promoted him to Deputy Commander of the army in 1964. The following year, Amin and Obote were involved in a scandalous gold and ivory smuggling deal. An investigation demanded by President Frederick Mutesa II, who was also the Kabaka (King) of Buganda, and known as King Freddie, put Obote on the defensive; he made Amin General and Chief-of-Staff, had five ministers arrested, suspended the constitution and declared himself president. Amin used a 122 mm gun mounted on his own Jeep to go and blow gaping holes in King Freddie's palace. That was the level of Amin's political finesse.

King Freddie had been tipped off that he was going to be the object of this onslaught, and was able to go into hiding. He was forced into exile in 1969; he went to London, where he died the same year under mysterious circumstances. A political assassination was suspected. Once Amin had shown his ability to act in this way, Milton Obote was happy for a time to use his as his strong arm.

Amin started recruiting members of his own tribe into the army and relations with Obote began to deteriorate. Obote tried putting Amin under house-arrest. When Amin heard Obote planned to arrest him for misappropriating army funds, he seized power. The day he chose, 25 January 1971, was when Obote was out of the country, attending a Commonwealth meeting in Singapore. Obote was about to fly home to Kampala when he heard on the radio that Amin had mobilized the army and declared himself the new President of Uganda.

Amin was a dictator from the start. He began to accumulate titles and self-awarded decorations, and called himself 'His Excellency President for Life, Field Marshal Al Hadji Doctor Idi Amin, VC, DSO, MC, Lord of All the Beasts of the Earth and Fishes of the Sea, and Conqueror of the British Empire in Africa in General and Uganda in Particular.'

Amin managed to win some support in Uganda by pacifying his tribal enemies. He made out to the Buganda tribesmen (King Freddie's people) that he had tipped King Freddie off and in effect saved his life. He had the body of the dead king flown from Britain for a state funeral. Amin was deeply impressed by the Buganda tribesmen's lavish expenditure on their dead king, and impressed by the ceremonial too.

Then Amin announced some restructuring in the army, his own power base. He needed to ensure the army's loyalty and remove any potential threat. He ordered 36 senior officers, who were Acholi and Langi tribesmen, to report to Makindye Prison for training in internal security. They were not very pleased, but went as ordered to the prison. Amin had them locked in cells there and then bayonetted to death. The former chief-of-staff, Brigadier Suleiman Hussein, was arrested and taken to another prison. He was beaten to death with rifle butts. Then his severed head was delivered to Amin's new house in Kampala, where the new President kept it in the freezer compartment of his refrigerator. At Mbarara and Jinja, two widely-separated army barracks, the elite of the army officers were lined up on parade grounds, ostensibly to take a salute from an armoured column. As the tanks drove past, they turned and ran them over, crushing most of them to death. Those who survived were shot by riflemen. At a third barracks, officers were assembled in a room to hear a lecture by Idi Amin. As he arrived in his gleaming black Mercedes, grenades were thrown into the lecture room.

In about five months, Amin's 'restructuring' had resulted in the murder of nearly all the trained professional soldiers in the Ugandan army. Somehow, Amin managed to keep this secret from the people of

Uganda, who were told only that a few officers had been court-martialled and executed. Inevitably, the gaps in the army were rapidly filled by Amin's fellow Kakwa tribesmen. Cooks and orderlies became majors and colonels more or less immediately.

Amin was initially welcomed by the international community, and within Uganda. No-one knew then what horrors were in store. He had given King Freddie a state funeral and disbanded the Secret Police. But he also set up killer squads who hunted down Obote supporters. Military leaders who had not supported his coup were executed. By 1974, Amin was murdering hundreds of thousands of his own people, feeding the heads of his enemies to crocodiles, boasting of eating human flesh and keeping human heads in his freezer.

Obote meanwhile had taken refuge in Tanzania, and from there he tried to regain control of Uganda in 1972; it was a failure. In retaliation, Amin did not flinch from bombing Tanzanian towns. After that, Amin became more paranoid and more bloodthirsty than ever. The Nile Mansions Hotel in Kampala became notorious. Far from being a hotel, it was Amin's interrogation and torture centre. The killer squads rampaged across Uganda, abducting, raping, murdering.

Many of the murder victims were dumped in Lake Victoria. There were constant boat patrols, but the power station engineers could not possibly pick out of the lake every corpse before it reached their filter grids. On average, 40 or 50 bodies were dumped in the lake every day.

But word about the massacres trickled out. Two Americans, Nicholas Stroh and Robert Siedle got to hear about the army 'restructuring' massacres. They were granted an interview at Mbarara barracks by the new commander, Major Aiga, a former taxi driver who had gained instant promotion. The questioning from the two Americans became more and more persistent, so Major Aiga phoned the President for advice. He replied briefly but simply, 'Kill them'. The two Americans were shot on the spot. A few days later, Aiga was seen driving round Kampala in Stroh's car. The American embassy demanded an investigation into the disappearance of the two men, but nothing came of it.

Amin even ordered the execution of the Anglican Archbishop of Uganda, Janani Luwum, the Chief Justice, the Chancellor of Makerere University, the Governor of the Bank of Uganda and many others.

A different kind of atrocity followed. On 9 August 1972, Amin gave the 70,000 Asians in Uganda ninety days to leave the country. He claimed he had had a dream in which God told him to expel them. The same year, he severed diplomatic relations with Israel. In 1976, he severed relations with Britain. He turned instead to Libya and the Soviet Union for support. Amin developed links with the PLO, and he offered the PLO the former Israeli Embassy as an HQ. The Air France Airbus hi-jacked from Athens in 1976 was invited to stop at Entebbe. The hi-jackers demanded the release of fifty-three PLO prisoners in return for the

256 hostages. One of the hostages was a frail old woman called Dora Bloch. She choked on some food and was taken to Kampala Hospital. Ironically, it was now Dora Bloch who was in the greatest danger. Amin himself visited the hostages on more than one occasion and was seen on worldwide television hectoring the hostages in a passenger lounge. The Israeli engineers who had been thrown out of Uganda got out their plans of the new buildings at Entebbe airport and worked out exactly where the hostages were. The deadline approached, and the non-Jewish hostages were allowed to go, presumably in preparation for the murder of those who remained.

An extraordinarily daring raid was mounted at very short notice, with the connivance of neighbouring Kenya. Israeli paratroopers landed at Entebbe airport in the early hours of 3 July 1976, and took off again within an hour carrying nearly all of the hostages. The attack badly damaged Uganda's air force, as its fighters were destroyed by the Israelis. When the Israelis took off, they left twenty of Amin's soldiers and all seven of the hijackers dead. Two Israeli paratroopers were killed in the raid.

Idi Amin was furious. Sixteen hours after the Entebbe Raid, the British High Commissioner Peter Chandly was allowed to visit Dora Bloch. He tried to reassure her, though she was justifiably very frightened about what might happen to her. She did not have to wait long to find out. Peter Chandly left the hospital briefly to get some food for her. While he was away, two State Research Bureau officials burst into the ward, hit Mrs Bloch with their pistols, dragged her downstairs and took her away to shoot her. Her bullet-ridden body was found in a field outside Kampala. Peter Chandly was told the next day that Mrs Bloch had left for the airport before the Entebbe Raid, which he knew to be untrue, but there was nothing he could do. The British government had, after all, done nothing about Amin up to this point. Clearly they never would.

Alongside the brutal killings there was economic mismanagement. Within a year of Amin's arrival in office, the country was bankrupt. Amin's unintelligent response to this crisis was to order the Bank of Uganda to print millions of extra banknotes, which had the effect of devaluing the currency. Suddenly a bar of soap cost £6, two weeks wages for an agricultural worker. Colonel Ghadaffi, a new ally, was ready to pour money in as a temporary measure.

Amin's foreign policy was predictably erratic. Alongside the alliance with Libya came repeated verbal attacks on the state of Israel. This was peculiar, in that Israel was giving aid to Uganda in the form of a new passenger terminal, control tower and runway for Entebbe Airport. Amin disregarded this and threw the Israeli engineers out. When they went, they took with them their meticulously detailed plans of the new airport; these plans were to prove invaluable when the Israelis came to mount their raid in 1976. Further madness came when Amin announced his undying admiration for Adolf Hitler; he intended to build a memorial to Hitler in the centre of Kampala. It was now that the world began to realise that Amin was dangerously mad.

One evening in 1972, at a dinner party at his palace, State House, in Entebbe, his guests were horrified when he left the table and returned with the frosted head of Brigadier Hussein. He ranted at the head, threw cutlery at it, then ordered his guests to leave. Two evenings later, Amin announced that God had spoken to him, telling him that all of Uganda's problems were down to the Asian population. There were about 70,000 Asians in Uganda, many of them shopkeepers, trades people, doctors and nurses. They must all go within 90 days. Although many of them had lived in Uganda for several generations, they emigrated, leaving behind their shops, offices, surgeries, plantations. They were not allowed to take anything with them. All these properties were given away to Amin's friends.

Uganda was bankrupt again. His only idea now was to allow the state Research Bureau to kill for profit. A fee of £150 was payable by a family if the body of a family member was found. The Research Bureau had found an easy way of making money; killing people and then extorting a fee from the family by 'finding' the body. The unclaimed bodies – there were many families who could not afford the fee – were thrown to the bloated and overfed crocodiles in Lake Victoria.

Finally, Amin was reduced to trying to scare Ugandans into submission by telling them that they were about to be invaded. Tanzania was about to mount an invasion of Uganda. In order to make this lie more credible, Amin ordered the invasion of Tanzania, sent sorties into the enemy territory and tried to annex the northernmost province of Tanzania, Kagera. This unprovoked invasion of Tanzanian territory was too much for the Tanzanian government under President Julius Nyerere. He ordered his troops to get rid of the Ugandan troops. This they did, and then followed the retreating invaders, pressing deeper into Uganda. Contrary to Amin's expectation, this invasion by Tanzania was welcomed by ordinary Ugandans. By April 1979 President Nyerere had driven the Ugandan and Libyan troops out of his country; he had also succeeded in driving Amin out and taking Kampala, the Ugandan capital. Subsequently, Obote was reinstated.

Idi Amin made a final broadcast, urging his troops to stand by him and make a final stand at Jinja, near the Owen Falls Dam. They did not turn up, but neither did Idi Amin. He instead fled to Libya and gained temporary sanctuary with President Ghadaffi in Libya. At some point, date unknown, he transferred to Saudi Arabia and for the rest of his life he lived in luxury in a hotel suite as the guest of the Saudi royal family. Meanwhile, in Uganda, President Obote took his place, and now the power stayed on.

Amin was in power for eight years. The nature of his

regime was well known, but there was no attempt by American or British governments to intervene to remove him. In recent years there has been intervention in the Middle East, but the absence of oil in Central Africa has meant a lower level of interest in the White House. Amin was nevertheless a criminal on a grand scale. He gratuitously murdered 500,000 of his fellow Ugandans. He ordered the mutilation of one his wives. He killed crusading bishops, excessively intrusive journalists, diplomats, and even children. He killed his political enemies, real or imagined.

There is no doubt that Idi Amin was dangerous and evil, but was he also mad? One expert view is that he was suffering from neurosyphilis. As the years passed, even his harmless child-like eccentricities turned into manias. He began wearing so many medals that his shirts tore under their weight. He thought up ever-grander titles for himself, including President for Life and even King of Scotland. Curiously, in 1975, he was elected President of the Organization of African Unity. Perhaps by flattering Amin the heads of neighbouring states hoped to calm him down. As the Tanzanians found, Amin was not just dangerous to the people of Uganda.

By 1978, he and his killer squads had killed up to 500,000 people. In a final piece of madness, with the help of Libyan troops, Amin ordered the invasion of Tanzania and tried to annex its northernmost province, Kagera. By April 1979 President Nyerere of Tanzania had driven the Ugandan and Libyan troops out of his country; he also succeeded in driving Amin out and taking Kampala, the Ugandan capital. Subsequently, Obote was reinstated.

Amin went into exile, bringing to an end one of the worst regimes since the death of Stalin. First he travelled to Libya. It is not clear how long he stayed there – maybe as little as one year or as much as ten years – before finding asylum in Jeddah in Saudi Arabia. On 20 July 2003, one of his four wives reported that he was in a coma and close to death in hospital in Jeddah. She pleaded with President Museveni of Uganda to let her husband return to die in Uganda. The reply was that if he returned he would have to answer for his sins. He did not return. Amin died in Jeddah on 16 August 2003 and was buried there. David Owen was British Foreign Secretary in 1977—79. While he was in office, he proposed that General Amin should be assassinated in order to bring the bloodshed to an end, but his proposal was turned down. It is certainly remarkable that the same international community that intervened with such alacrity in Kuwait, Afghanistan and Iraq should have stood back from Uganda and watched – while a madman killed half a million innocent people.

Saddam Hussein

Dictator of Iraq

SADDAM HUSSEIN IS one of the most recent examples of a head of state who was also a serial killer – and very recently deposed. He was born in the village of Al-Awja in the Tikrit district of Iraq to a family of shepherds. His father, Hussein Abd al-Majid, either died or disappeared before Saddam was born. When pregnant with Saddam Hussein, his mother, Subha Tulfah al-Mussallat, tried to abort, but failed. She later remarried and by this new marriage Saddam gained three half-brothers. His step-father, Ibrahim al-Hassan, treated him harshly, forcing him to steal. His bond with his home town was strong and his relatives from Tikrit, 'the Tikrit mafia', as they were later called, would be among his most influential advisors and supporters. One of the half-brothers, Barzan Ibrahim Hasan was chief of the Iraqi secret police and ambassador to the UN in Geneva. Another, Sabawi Ibrahim Hasan, became head of Iraqi intelligence. The third half-brother, Watban Ibrahim Hasan, became Iraqi interior minister. Barzan and Watban were both eventually arrested by coalition forces.

When he was 10 years old, Saddam Hussein moved to Baghdad to live with an uncle, Khairallah Tulfah, who was a devout Sunni. From him, Saddam learnt never to back down, no matter how superior the enemy numbers may be. In 1955, he went to secondary school in Baghdad.

The rise of Gamal Nasser in Egypt in 1952 was a highly significant event in the Near East, foreshadowing a series of revolutions that would topple monarchies throughout the region, in Iraq, Egypt and Libya. The collapse of the Iraqi monarchy in 1958 was another landmark for the rising new urban classes; it was not just the monarchies that were going, it was the imperialist collaborator elites that went with them. Nasser's populist pan-Arab nationalism in Egypt made a strong impact on Saddam Hussein. Nasser challenged and faced down the British and the French, nationalized the Suez Canal, and went several steps towards modernizing Egypt.

Saddam became a Ba'ath Party member in 1957, and became known for his brutality. He was 19 years old when he committed his first murder. It was in 1958 that a non-Ba'athist group led by General Abdul Karim Qassim overthrew the king in a massacre. The following year, Saddam Hussein was involved in a plot sponsored by the CIA to assassinate Prime Minister Qassim. Saddam was shot in the leg, managed to get away and remove the bullet from his own leg as he escaped; he fled to Syria and then to Egypt. He was sentenced to death in absentia.

Saddam resumed his education at the University of Cairo. He gained a Law degree from Baghdad University in 1968.

Saddam came to power as a result of the Ba'athist revolution of 1963. He was imprisoned in 1964 following a change in the ruling faction, but he escaped from prison in 1967. In 1968 he played a part in leading the successful – and peaceful – Ba'athist coup. He was then appointed Vice-Chairman of the Revolution Command Council and Vice President of Iraq. In 1973 he was appointed a General in the Iraqi armed forces.

Iraqi society is deeply divided among Arab Sunni, Kurdish Sunni, Assyrian, Turkoman and Arab Shiite camps. A major problem for Saddam Hussein since 1968 has been to consolidate his power in Iraq in the face of such deep divisions. There have also been tribal conflicts, class conflicts, rural-urban conflicts. Saddam's power base was Arab Sunnis of the middle and working classes, which make up perhaps a fifth of the population. The new Ba'athist regime, of which Saddam was a part, was therefore characterized by a very strong – oppressively strong – security regime, in order to prevent coups. The new regime also reduced poverty through the nationalization of oil; oil revenues were used to build schools, hospitals, acquire imported technology. But they were also used to strengthen the security services. In 1972, Saddam led the process of nationalizing the Western-based oil companies who had a monopoly on Iraq's oil. He led a programme of modernization out in the countryside as well as in industry. He worked to raise literacy levels. At the same time he was purging members of the Ba'ath Party who might oppose him. It was a curious mixture of good and evil.

The improvements under Saddam were palpable. There was universal free education up to and including university, support for families of soldiers killed in war, free hospital treatment, subsidies for farmers, land reforms so that peasant farmers could have more land. This was the general pattern up to the point where Saddam began his destructive military adventures. The programme of modernization was looking good, until the invasions of Iran and Kuwait and the twelve years of UN-imposed economic sanctions that were Saddam's – and Iraq's – punishment for lawless behaviour.

Saddam consolidated his power over the Iraqi government and the Ba'ath party in his position as Vice President, while the elderly President, Ahmed Hassan al-Bakr, became increasingly unable to do his job. Saddam began to take a more and more prominent role as the public face of the Iraqi government. It was not long before he was shaping foreign policy, and representing Iraq on visits to foreign countries. By the late 1970s, he was still Vice President, but the country's de facto leader.

In 1979, the President began to make treaties with Syria that would lead to a unification of the two countries. The President of Syria Hafez al-Assad was to become Deputy Leader in this union, and that would have left Saddam nowhere. In order to save his own position, Saddam was forced to act. He compelled Bakr to resign on 16 July 1979 in a bloodless coup, and took over the Presidency. Then the horrors began.

One of Saddam's first acts was to call a meeting of Ba'ath leaders on 22 July and have one of them read out a list of the names of members that Saddam thought might oppose him. These members were labelled 'disloyal'. They were taken out of the room one at a time and immediately shot by firing squad. Then Saddam congratulated those still sitting in front of him. The room erupted in applause and praise of Saddam.

Saddam gave women additional freedoms, opening high-level government and industry posts to them. This was a great surprise and shock to the Islamic fundamentalists in Iraq. He abolished the old Sharia laws except for personal injuries and small claims. He also introduced Western-style banking and legal systems. So, there were some surprisingly enlightened and liberal developments. The strong, oppressive style of government meanwhile had the effect of keeping the lid on tribal, ethnic, class and religious divisions that could easily erupt at any time. But the systematic use of torture for political ends was a very negative development, and it is claimed by human rights groups that there are documented cases of state-sponsored rape.

The end result was the creation of the most

oppressive and suffocating of the Middle East's autocratic regimes. Few sectional interests were satisfied. The traditional Sunni and Shiite aristocracies disliked the populist, modernizing nature of Saddam's policies, even though they had dramatically raised living standards overall. Saddam's later attempts to use some of his giant portraits to show himself off as a devout Muslim were an effort to win round the more religious elements in Iraqi society. However horrible the Saddam Hussein regime was, at least there was no bloody fundamentalist insurgency of the sort seen in Egypt, Algeria and Tunisia.

Saddam espoused the concept of Iraqi patriotism instead, emphasizing the role that Iraq has played through history. In particular he drew attention to the Abbasid period, when Muslim Baghdad was the political, cultural and economic capital of the Arab world. He also referred in his speeches to Iraq's glorious pre-Islamic past when the land between the Tigris and the Euphrates was a cradle of civilization. Saddam's sincerity in this regard seems to have been genuine; he devoted enormous resources to archaeology.

It is hard to say whether Saddam was ever truly popular. In the time-honoured way of dictatorships, there were elections, but with only one presidential candidate and voting was mandatory. In 2002, there was a referendum to find out whether Saddam should continue to lead Iraq. One hundred percent of voters thought he should. The 'show referendum' was one aspect of the Saddam Hussein personality cult. During his time as President, Saddam used propaganda on a big scale, and like other dictators he used his own image to project an identification of leader with state. Gigantic portraits, huge statues and colossal murals appeared all over Iraq. They were all different, some showing him in traditional Arab costume, some in a Western suit. One of the oddest is an image of him in a three-piece 'City' suit, tie and trilby, brandishing a rifle in his right hand. Other dictators, notably Hitler, Stalin and Mao, have used their own portraits to project a personality cult, but nothing on the scale of Saddam. One western commentator said that Saddam's publicity campaign made Stalin look as if he suffered from low self-esteem.

In 1979, the Islamic Revolution in Iran threatened to destabilize Saddam's programme of modernization, not least because the majority of Iraqis were Shiites, and Shiites were on the whole sympathetic to the Ayatollahs who were coming to power in Iran. Saddam found a pretext – a territorial dispute – and declared war on Iran. With hindsight it seems extraordinarily misguided, but Saddam was supported in this war by both the USA and the Soviet Union. Neither of the great powers wanted radical Islamic fundamentalist revolution to spread and destabilize the Middle East; if Saddam was willing to contain it, they would help him. During this bloody and costly war, Saddam ordered the use of chemical weapons on Iranian soldiers. There was no overall victory, just a stalemate with 1.7 million people dead. The economies of both Iran and Iraq were left completely ravaged.

Iraq has been troubled for a long time by the desire of the people in the north of the country, the Kurds, to have their independence. During the Iraq-Iran War, a side-swipe against the separatist Kurds was almost inevitable, and Saddam did not shrink from using chemical weapons against both Kurdish troops and settlements. The worst atrocity took place on 16 March 1988, when Iraqi troops attacked the Kurdish town of Halabjah with poison gas and nerve agents. They killed 5,000 people, most of them women and children. It is also the case that many Kurds have been driven out, in some cases over the mountains into Turkey, and they are no more welcome there. According to one estimate 100,000 Kurds have been driven into exile since 1991.

The Iran-Iraq War left Iraq bankrupt. To rebuild, Iraq needed money. The only country ready to lend money was the USA, but borrowing from the USA would have made Saddam an American 'client-king' rather like the old Shah of Iran. It may be that these consideration drove Saddam into his next military disaster, the attempted conquest of Kuwait.

Saddam Hussein complained to the USA in 1990 about slant drilling in Kuwait. It is possible to drill boreholes vertically or at a slight angle to the vertical. In a deep borehole, this slanting may mean that oil is being siphoned from behind a territorial boundary, and that is what Saddam accused the Western oil companies of doing. Having had no satisfactory response, Saddam drew troops up to the Iraq-Kuwait border. A further problem was that the desert border had been inappropriately defined in relation to some palm trees. Obviously, palm trees come and go, and new ones can be planted in different places. It seems likely that Saddam had additional palms planted further south, in order to make it appear that the correct line of the frontier should be further south. He had exploited a cartographic loophole in order to create an international dispute. Saddam had a meeting with a high-ranking US official, who indicated that the USA would not interfere in border disputes. Saddam interpreted that to mean that the USA would not intervene if he invaded Kuwait. He invaded Kuwait.

The Iraqis had long held the view that Kuwait was really part of Iraq and Saddam lacked the seaport that Kuwait occupied, a grievance that pre-dates and cannot be blamed on Saddam. In 1961, the British narrowly prevented a similar Iraqi invasion. A reluctant UN Security Council declared war on Iraq. By the end of the Gulf War, Iraq had lost at least 20,000 troops and perhaps as many as 100,000, and been ejected from Kuwait.

Following the Gulf War, there were popular risings against Saddam in both the north and the south. They were brutally suppressed. In the south, in addition to a purge, Saddam began a programme of drainage, to destroy the age-old swamps where the Marsh Arabs live.

A UN trade embargo was clamped on Iraq and living conditions in the country deteriorated further.

Relations between Iraq and the US were strained. Bush was criticized for not pursuing the retreating Iraqi troops all the way to Baghdad and 'finishing the job'. An opportunity to seize, depose, possibly kill the now-hated Saddam Hussein had been missed. In 1991, Bush visited Kuwait to meet the restored Emir. Iraqi soldiers tried to assassinate the American president and failed. During the Clinton administration, the Americans complained that Saddam was violating the terms of the Gulf War cease-fire, and accused Saddam of manu-facturing weapons of mass destruction (often abbre-viated to WMD). The Americans tried to intimidate Saddam by making isolated strikes inside Iraqi territory, such as Operation Desert Fox in 1998.

When George Bush Junior, George W. Bush, became US President in 2000, he appeared to have a mission to complete the job his father had begun. Bush alleged that Saddam had WMD, that he was a threat to the West and that the overthrow of Saddam by force was the only solution. In March 2003, American troops together with troops from a few other countries (Britain, Poland and Australia) invaded Iraq. The Iraqi government, and the Saddam Hussein regime with it, fell in about three weeks. The removal of Saddam Hussein from power had been accomplished.

The major problem since that time has been that no amount of searching has produced the weapons of mass destruction that were the United States pretext for invading. The weapons inspectors insisted there were none – and none have been found. It begins to look as if the invasion of Iraq was just as unethical as Iraq's invasions of Iran and Kuwait.

A problem in fighting extreme evil is that sometimes 'clean' methods don't work. The British Prime Minister, Tony Blair, said that Saddam Hussein was an evil man and needed to be got rid of – but that is another argument entirely, and actually transgresses one of the accepted codes of international conduct of the last three centuries. One country may only invade another country if it is itself threatened with invasion; invasion may only be defensive. And how virtuous is it to lie about your reason for going to war? Is there anyone left standing on the moral high ground?

Following the fall of Baghdad on 9 April, 2003, there was a great deal of uncertainty about the whereabouts of Saddam Hussein. Some thought he had retreated to his home area in the north ready for a shoot-out. Some thought he had been killed in the shelling. Some thought he had left the country and was in Syria. Saddam was placed at the top of the US list of most wanted Iraqis. One by one the other leaders were arrested. After a tip-off from an informant, his sons and likely successors, Uday and Qusay, were killed in a shoot-out with American troops in July 2003. It was assumed that Saddam Hussein would choose to go down fighting in a similar way, and the manner of his capture surprised everyone. It was on 14 December, 2003 that Saddam was found cowering in a small concrete-lined underground pit. He was bearded, dirty and dishevelled, and surrendered without a struggle. The problem then was deciding what to do with him. Alive and in captivity, he continues to be a major problem to the 'Coalition'. With his record for waging unprovoked war, indiscriminate use of torture, political murders, war crimes, and attempted genocide of both Kurds and Marsh Arabs, it is difficult to see how, if he was brought to trial in the Middle East, anything but a death sentence could be the outcome. Will the Coalition powers want to make a martyr out of this enigmatic monster?

PART NINE

KILLER
DOCTORS

Dr William Palmer, Surgeon, MRCS

the Rugeley Poisoner

AT 8 O'CLOCK in the morning on Saturday 14 June 1856, at least 30,000 people gathered in Stafford in the English Midlands to watch the execution of William Palmer. He was found guilty of murdering John Cook with poison at a pub called the Talbot Arms in Rugeley and it was suspected that he had killed many others as well. He was a rogue, heavily in debt, a fraud, a forger and gambler – and his wax effigy stood in the Chamber of Horrors at Madame Tussaud's for 127 years. But was he really guilty of murder?

At his trial, Palmer was found guilty of the murder of John Cook by poison, but a coroner's jury found him guilty of murdering his wife Ann and his brother Walter by poison too. These verdicts were based on circumstantial evidence, not on facts or forensic evidence. They had died, and therefore their deaths might as well be laid at his door. Palmer refused to admit to murdering Cook and maintained that Cook did not die of strychnine poisoning at all. A post mortem was carried out on Cook's body, but it was a botched post mortem and no strychnine was found in the body; it was said, even so, that Cook's symptoms could have been caused by strychnine.

Palmer was found guilty as much on the strength of rumour as anything else. At that time, newspapers printed every rumour and accusation that reporters could extract from local gossips, and the gossips said that Palmer was guilty of poisoning Cook and at least a dozen more people besides.

According to the press reports of 1856, Palmer's first victim was thought to have been George Abley a 27-year-old plumber and glazier. Palmer worked for a short time as a 'walking student' at Stafford Infirmary, where a suspicious death occurred in 1846. One published version of events had Palmer inviting George Abley to the Lamb and Flag at Little Haywood in the spring of 1846. He gave him brandy and water to drink, ordering eight pennyworth rather than the usual four penny-worth. Abley soon became drunk and declined to drink any more. Palmer offered him half a sovereign if he could down one more glass of neat brandy. Abley agreed, drank the brandy, was promptly sick and went outside for some air.

A second, slightly different, version had Palmer drinking at the Lamb and Flag with a friend called Timmis, when Abley, a pale and thin man in poor health, came into the pub. Palmer offered to buy him a brandy, but Abley declined, saying he was not much of a brandy drinker. Timmis said Abley was being modest, as he had seen Abley knock back three large brandies one after the other. Then Abley was challenged to drink more than one tumbler full of neat brandy for fifteen shillings. He reluctantly agreed and drank two glasses without any apparent ill effect. There was general laughter because William Palmer had lost his bet. But after a while Abley turned green and went out to the stable for air. Palmer entertained the bar with a funny story and for a while everyone forgot about Abley.

An hour later they realised Abley had not returned, so they went to look for him. They found him stretched out on some sacks in the stable, groaning and holding his stomach. Palmer and Timmis carried him home, but he died later that night.

The inquest on Abley found that he had died from natural causes. He was a thin, weak man in poor health, had drunk two tumblers of brandy on an empty stomach, and then lain in a cold stable for an hour or two. It was not altogether surprising that he had died. The Coroner, William Ward, recorded the cause of death as 'Exhaustion, the result of diseased blood vessels of the lung'. This, rather oddly, leaves out the part played by the brandy, and suggests that the coroner did not believe that the drink was anything to with Abley's death. The wording of the death certificate (issued on 30 November 1846), together with the description of Abley as thin, pale and weak, strongly suggests that Abley was dying of tuberculosis, and that the coroner thought that that was the actual cause of death.

But the foreman of the jury, a man called Edward Jenkinson, strongly disagreed with the verdict passed by the other jurors. During the inquest, rumours had emerged that Palmer had designs on Abley's shapely wife. It was said that Palmer had fallen for her while she had been an outpatient at the Stafford Infirmary. Apparently Palmer had propositioned her and she had made it clear that she intended to remain faithful to her husband. Whether this gossip was true or not, many people saw Jenkinson as a bitter and jealous man, who had had several proposals of marriage rejected, while Palmer was very successful with the ladies. The scandal was even so revived in The Times in 1856, where it was reported, 'At the inquest there was a great deal of talk about Palmer and Abley's wife which was undoubtedly true'.

It is difficult to get anywhere near the truth of the story, because of the absence of any reporting standards in the mid-nineteenth century, but the dates involved are curious. The death certificate for George Abley was dated 30 November 1846, which is some time after Palmer qualified as a doctor and also some time after he left Stafford Infirmary; he could not have been a 'walking student' at the Infirmary at the time of Abley's death.

William Palmer's mother-in-law was another of his alleged victims. Her name was Mary Thornton and she was the housekeeper and mistress of a retired Indian Army officer, Colonel Brookes. Mary had a daughter, Annie, who later became Palmer's wife. Mary Thornton was a drunken brawler, regularly cursing the Colonel for never having married her. Brookes must have bitterly regretted getting mixed up with this harridan in the first place. In 1834 he held a pistol to his head and shot himself. Mary carried on drinking even more heavily than before and as a result of this Annie was made a Ward in Chancery and sent to live with a guardian called Charles Dawson.

After Colonel Brookes' death, Mary lived in a house behind St Mary's Church in Stafford. She had been left fairly well off by Brookes, but she kept no servants and she was in a deteriorating state because of the heavy intake of alcohol. She ate very little; her diet consistently mainly of gin. She kept a swarm of cats, but did not look after them properly. Palmer, now her son-in-law, did what he could for her, organizing repairs to her house for instance, but she made it clear that she hated him. She regularly swore at him and accused him of poisoning her cats.

On 6 January 1849, Mary Thornton was found stretched out straight in a state of delirium brought on by drinking too much alcohol. Palmer took her to his house. She died there twelve days later on 18 January. She was fifty. They buried her at Rugeley on 22 January. None of the circumstances outlined here point to William Palmer as a murderer, and Mary Thornton could simply have died of alcohol poisoning; she could have killed herself with drink.

The nine houses Colonel Brookes had owned in

Stafford, and which Brookes had left to Mary, were not inherited by Annie or William Palmer. One of these properties was the Noah's Ark Inn and Mary Thornton was its drunk and incapable licensee. The Noah's Ark, which was rebuilt in about 1880, is now The Surgery Café Bar, so named after its connection with the infamous Dr Palmer. The Court of Chancery ordered that all this property should be given to Colonel Brookes' next heir, who was a Mr Shallcross, in line with the terms of Colonel Brookes' will.

The press coverage of these events was unfavourable to Palmer. *The Illustrated Times* reported on 19 January 1856 that Palmer's mother-in-law died shortly after Palmer's marriage. Only that. But on 2 February, 1856, the same newspaper carried a far more incriminating and damaging account;

The reader will not be surprised to learn that Mrs Thornton, the mother of Mrs Palmer, was a person of eccentric habits. She still lived at Stafford, not keeping any servants, though possessed of property. Some little time after Palmer's marriage, he called upon her, and requested her to lend him some money. He also invited her to go and live with her daughter. She refused to give him any money, and he left her much incensed. The poor woman afterwards, fearing that Palmer would ill-treat her daughter on his return home if she did not comply with his request, went to the bank, and having procured £20, forwarded it to him. She is reported to have said that if she went to reside under the same roof with him, she would not live a fortnight. These forebodings proved to be true, for she subsequently went to live with her daughter, and four days afterwards she was a corpse. In accordance with Colonel Brooke's will, her property descended to her daughter, whose husband thus became possessed of a respectable income.

This last sentence is certainly not true. The property went to Mr Shallcross. The gossips said that the property was nevertheless the motive for the murder. Palmer did not know the terms of Colonel Brookes' will, and in spite of the outcome he murdered his mother-in-law for her property. The newspaper report was also mischievous in making no mention of Mary Thornton's heavy drinking, which almost certainly caused or contributed to her death. Palmer may have poisoned Mary (and some of her cats), but the newspaper reporting, immediately before he went on trial, made it almost certain that the jurors would think him guilty in advance, whether he was guilty or not.

A Mr Bly was supposed to be a friend of William Palmer's. He lived at a place called Beccles in Norfolk. The two of them often went to the races together. Bly often won his racing bets; Palmer often lost. It was said that Palmer owed Bly the huge sum of £800, when Bly was suddenly taken ill. Palmer offered him treatment. Mrs Bly heard her husband was ill and hurried to see him. Palmer, Mrs Bly later said, tried to prevent her from seeing her husband. While she was sitting at his bedside, Bly suddenly said he thought he was dying. He also said that he regretted his misspent life and that Palmer owed him £800.

After Bly's death, Mrs Bly mentioned the money to Palmer, who said it showed just how bad a state Bly had been in. The truth of the matter, he said, was that Bly owed him £800; he would of course not have mentioned it if she had not raised the matter herself.

But this anecdote was published in the Norfolk Chronicle and then included as part of *The Illustrated Life and Career of William Palmer of Rugeley,* published by Ward Lock in 1856, to cash in on the widespread interest in the Palmer case. It may well have been a complete invention.

The death that led to William Palmer's trial was that of John Parsons Cook. The moment the inquest on Cook was over, officers were sent to arrest Palmer, but when they reached his house they were surprised to find him already under house arrest for debt. He was ill, but as soon as he was well enough to travel he was taken to Stafford Gaol. A large crowd gathered outside Palmer's house, hoping to catch sight of the villain before he was taken off to prison.

The entrance to the Gaol was known as the Lodge. It contained a room for the turnkeys (or warders) and a reception room where prisoners were received, examined and made to change into prison clothes; there was a warm bath and a cold bath and an oven for fumigating prisoners' clothes. Until 1817, condemned prisoners were executed on a gallows erected on the roof of the Lodge. In 1817, at what must rank as one of the most spectacularly botched executions of all time, the scaffold collapsed with everyone on it. From that time on, all executions were carried out on a huge portable gallows that was erected immediately outside the Lodge.

When Dr Palmer arrived at Stafford Gaol, he was still feeling extremely unwell and went straight to bed. He refused to put on the prison clothes and insisted that his own clothes should be returned to him. The turnkeys suspected that he had some poison secretly hidden among his clothes. The prison governor, Captain William Fulford, ordered his clothes to be searched meticulously to see whether any hidden tablets or sachets of powders could be found. Nothing at all was found, and two weeks later the clothes were returned to Palmer.

Palmer stayed in bed and refused to eat. He would only drink small quantities of water. It is not clear whether he had decided to starve himself to death as a way of avoiding the ordeal of the trial and execution. The exercise may alternatively have been a hunger strike, and he may have been hoping that he could bring pressure to bear on the authorities to exhume Cook's body and undertake a proper post mortem – one that would prove beyond any doubt that Cook had not died of strychnine poisoning. It may be that such a post mortem would have provided exactly the scientific evidence needed to acquit him. On the sixth day of the hunger strike, the prison governor visited Palmer and gave him an ultimatum. If he refused to drink his soup voluntarily, in five minutes' time he would be force-fed; the turnkeys would force a rubber tube down his throat and pump the soup directly into his stomach. Palmer was a medic and understood how unpleasant this was going to be, so he agreed to drink the soup voluntarily. From then on he ate his meals normally. The newspapers reported this as 'Palmer's Attempted Suicide' or 'His Voluntary Starvation'.

On 4 May 1856 William Palmer was taken to London. He was accompanied by two men, the deputy governor of Stafford Gaol, Mr Mountford, and one of the turnkeys. They set off on the 6.26 a.m. train. There had been so much speculation and rumour-mongering in the local press that it was quite clear that a Stafford jury would have made up its mind to convict well before the trial began. It was quite clear that Palmer stood no chance of getting a fair trial at Stafford Assizes. An Act of Parliament was rushed through so that Palmer could be tried at the Old Bailey in London. But it was not the local press alone that was publishing prejudicial stories about Palmer: it was the national press too. When Palmer reached the end of his twelve-day trial, Palmer said to the prison governor, 'I am a murdered man'.

According to some observers, the trial of William Palmer was one of the most scandalous miscarriages of justice in British history. The medical evidence against him broke down completely. All that was left was circumstantial evidence – and that was conflicting in any case. From the start, the Lord Chief Justice and the Attorney General were out to secure a guilty verdict from their hand-picked jury.

It was a very high-profile trial, standing out as one of the great landmarks in British legal history. It generated a huge amount of interest nationally and internationally. In spite of this, much of the evidence from expert witnesses was highly technical, consisting of medical men giving evidence regarding (their views on) the symptoms of strychnine poisoning. One reason for the high level of public interest was the social class of the people involved. They were well-educated, middle-class people in apparently respectable positions – people who should have known better. Murders in the slums often had a sordid inevitability about them: they were somehow to be expected. Murders in high society were a little too remote, difficult to empathize with. But middle-class murders had enough about them that was familiar to make the 'soap opera' of the trial exciting as drama.

The fact that the accused man was a doctor, who should have been dedicated to the saving of lives, was the key to the popular sensation that the trial created, something that in modern times has only been paralleled by the Harold Shipman case.

The death of Cook had been suspicious. His stepfather had ordered an inquest and brought in Dr

Taylor to provide expert evidence. This was swiftly followed by the coroner's verdict of murder and Palmer's arrest. William Palmer's past record was examined and the Home Secretary ordered the exhumation of two more bodies. Stories about other suspicious deaths were circulated and then published by the newspapers; there was no restriction on the press to edit their reporting while cases were sub judice. The number of 'Rugeley tragedies' grew and grew, as people gleefully counted his victims – his four children, his mother-in-law, and other acquaintances. Palmer was portrayed as an unrelenting, cold-blooded and mercenary killer. Further stories about Palmer's raffish lifestyle, and his debts in particular, were similarly handed round as gossip, then published. There was another court case at Westminster involving admissions of forgery. And then came the switch to an Old Bailey setting for the show trial.

The trial of Dr William Palmer was one of the most famous in British criminal history and it not surprisingly attracted lots of distinguished spectators, including well-known doctors and judges. Mr Gladstone came, the Lord Mayor of London, the Prince of Saxe-Weimar, the Duke of Cambridge, the Duke of Wellington, the Marquess of Anglesey, Lord Derby and the Earls of Dufferin and Albemarle.

His guilt being a foregone conclusion, William Palmer was condemned to be publicly hanged at 8am on Saturday 14 June, 1856. Palmer's brother, a clergyman, tried to win a reprieve, arguing that Palmer had been convicted on circumstantial evidence alone and it was therefore an unsafe conviction. On the Friday it was solemnly announced in Stafford that Sir George Grey had rejected the appeal for a reprieve; the law must take its course.

When Palmer was visited by his solicitor, Mr Smith, the night before his execution, Palmer said, 'I am innocent of poisoning Cook by strychnine. All I ask is that you have Cook's body exhumed and that you will see to my mother and boy.' Palmer gave Smith a present of a book. Inside he had inscribed, 'The gift of William Palmer, June 13th, 1856.' Later that night, William Palmer had visits from both of his brothers and his sister. They said he seemed to have accepted his fate and was calm, except for a slight twitch in the corner of his mouth.

After his visitors left, Palmer was given brandy and water and slept from 1am. He was awakened at 2.30am by the Prison Chaplain, the Revd Goodacre, who stayed with him for two and a half hours, trying to get him to confess his guilt. But it was no good. William Palmer was still insisting he was innocent. Goodacre went away, then returned at 6.30 and tried for another hour to persuade Palmer to own up to his guilt. Palmer unwaveringly maintained that John Parsons Cook had not died by strychnine poisoning.

At 7.30am, Palmer was given a cup of tea and some brandy. Then he was joined in his cell by the High

Sheriff, Lt Col Dyott, Under Sheriff R. Hand and the prison governor. They led him to the press room to meet George Smith, the hangman, who tied his hands. He received another visit from the Chaplain, who asked him if he was satisfied with the justice of his sentence. Palmer emphatically answered 'No!' Almost unbelievably, the Chaplain tried yet again to make Palmer confess his guilt. Once again Palmer refused.

At 7.53am the prison bell started tolling and the procession to the gallows started. Palmer walked with a jaunty stride and a slight smile on his face as they crossed the prison yard, parading as a solemn warning in front of all the assembled prisoners, out of the Lodge and into the road, where he was met by shouts of 'Murderer' and 'Poisoner'. Palmer seemed unaffected by any of this, taking care to avoid the puddles in the road, which made the crowd laugh. As he reached the gallows there were roars of 'Murderer' and then 'Hats off'.

In spite of heavy rain throughout the hanging, at least 30,000 people had turned up to see William Palmer die. Many of them had walked the ten miles from Rugeley. Many more had come on special trains laid on from Birmingham, Stoke-on-Trent and London. The pubs had stayed open all night. The Greyhound Inn, immediately opposite the prison had done a roaring trade.

The portable gallows, like a colossal Punch and Judy box, had been wheeled out into the roadway at 4am, which was taken by the gathering crowd as a sure sign that there had been no reprieve. At least twenty platforms had been raised around it to give people better views, though they were charged up to a guinea each, a huge sum in those days, for the best places.

The hangman placed Palmer on the centre of the trapdoor, put his head in the noose and pulled a white hood over his head. The crowd were disappointed that Palmer gave them no final speech. There was a general unspoken hope that he would, in the end, own up to his crimes. Smith descended the ladder to pull the bolt, and Palmer fell a short distance. He died quite quickly. Many in the crowd called out 'Cheat' or 'Twister'.

In spite of all that was said about Palmer at the time, and all that has been said since, there is no certainty about his case. He may have poisoned one or more people – he may have poisoned none. His stout denials during his final few hours can be taken as proof of his innocence, in that many prisoners have confessed to their crimes once they realise they have nothing further to gain by lying. On the other hand, many proven murderers, serial killers included, have gone to their graves refusing to own up. William Palmer's stout denial of guilt does not prove his innocence. William Palmer was a thoroughly unpleasant character, a gambler, a womanizer, a fraud, a forger and a poor example to the community in general.

He may, even so, have been innocent of murder.

Joseph Mengele

The Angel of Death

THERE ARE MANY enduring and terrible images of the Second World War preserved on film. Among the most indelible are the short clips of archive film taken by British and American troops arriving to liberate the Auschwitz and Belsen concentration camps in 1945 – static shots of piles of naked corpses, and the emaciated survivors staring blankly through the wire fence. Terrible, unforgettable images. Another, rather subtler, is the film of a trainload of Jews arriving at Auschwitz. In the midst of the milling crowds and gangs of soldiers is a lone figure in immaculate uniform and white gloves. He inspects the inmates and directs some one way, some the other. In one direction lie brutality, starvation and deprivation, but a slender chance of surviving. In the other direction, instant death in the gas chambers awaits. The frighteningly cold and clinical figure making the life and death decisions is one of the camp doctors, Dr Joseph Mengele.

The great Nazi hunter Dr Simon Wiesenthal produced a list of ten names in 1983, at the time when

Klaus Barbie was extradited. These were the Nazis he most wished to bring to justice, in fulfilment of his 'compact with the dead'. Wiesenthal was then 76 years old and must have realised that his chances of bringing all ten to justice were slim. 'If I could get all ten, it would be an achievement. But if I could get only Joseph Mengele, I think my soul would be at peace.'

Who was this hated monster? Who was Joseph Mengele? Joseph Mengele was born in 1911 into a family of upper middle class industrialists in Gunzburg in Bavaria. The family firm manufactured machine tools. At the age of 20, Mengele joined the Stahlheim, a militant right-wing organization founded by discontented former soldiers unhappy about the outcome of the Great War. In 1934, he moved to the SA and became a member of the NSDAP and SS in 1937.

It was while he was at university, in Munich, Bonn, Frankfurt and Vienna that Mengele's Nazi ideology developed. At Munich he was attracted to the racial theories of Alfred Rosenberg, the philosopher of Nazism. At Frankfurt-am-Main he received his medical degree, studying under Otmar von Verschuer, the Director of the Institute for Racial Hygiene at Frankfurt University. He completed a dissertation with a distinctly racist focus on 'The morphology of the lower jaw bone among four racial groups'. He went on to do a similar (and similarly useless) racial study of cleft palates and cleft lips. Mengele was a thorough-going Nazi racist, hating the Jews, but hating the Gypsies even more.

When he was a member of the Institute for Hereditary Biology and Racial Hygiene, Mengele voluntarily joined the Waffen-SS, and began work as a medical officer with several units in the invasion of the Soviet Union. He was awarded four medals but was declared unfit for military service after he was wounded – and that was how he came to get the job at Auschwitz.

In 1943 Mengele went to work at Auschwitz under Eduard Wirths, the chief physician, where he conducted his now-notorious series of medical examinations. One of Mengele's main research interests was on twins, and he was bent on verifying theories of genetic determinism. This involved examining twins both before and after death. Another research interest was dwarfism. One of Mengele's jobs at Auschwitz was to take his turn on the station platform, supervising the selections of incoming transports. Other camp doctors were involved, but of all of them it was Mengele who seemed to enjoy the work, revelling in the overt display of power. He was often on the arrival ramps even when he was not scheduled to be there – the doctors took it in turns to do the selections – using his riding crop to indicate his life-or-death decisions. He often used the riding crop to beat prisoners as well, and it was reported that he used a revolver to kill prisoners who were awkward or unco-operative.

Mengele gloried in his role at Auschwitz, according to the doctors who worked with him there, and was in total accord with the camp's brutal regime. On several occasions Mengele himself murdered inmates, either with his pistol or with fatal injections of phenol. He was technically a doctor, in the sense that he had qualified as a medic, but his behaviour was grotesquely at odds with his training. Instead of saving lives, he took them. Instead of relieving pain, he inflicted it. His ethical standards are vividly shown by his action on arriving at Auschwitz, when he found 600 sick women in the hospital; he immediately ordered all of them off to the gas chambers.

Then there were the experiments.

Mengele's twins, his prized collection, were housed in a special block where he and his staff could examine them. He protected them from harsh labour assignments and made sure they were properly fed, but he still treated them as no more than laboratory animals – and, as with laboratory animals, when it suited him to do so he killed them and dissected them.

Another area that interested Mengele was the connection of eye colour with racial type. He began a series of experiments that involved injecting various chemicals into the eyes of his subjects. The experiments caused pain and infections, and at least one child was killed and another blinded. Mengele also collected 'specimens' for Dr Verschuer. It is known, for example, that seven sets of twins with different coloured eyes were killed with phenol injections, and their eyes sent to Verschuer. Verschuer himself wrote about Mengele's assistance to him in supplying specimens in reports that he wrote at the time, mentioning Himmler's support for the project. Mengele's notes on his experiments did not survive the end of the war, but there is no evidence that any of his experiments had any scientific basis or had any practical application whatever. The suffering was entirely for nothing.

The Auschwitz inmates had good reason to fear Mengele. They nicknamed him 'the Angel of Death'. He went on working at the concentration camp until the experiments stopped, shortly before the end of the war, when he returned to Gunzburg. He never attempted to return to any kind of medicine, and it is not clear what earthly use he would have been as a general practitioner, but instead went back to an earlier phase, working towards rebuilding the family manufacturing firm of Carl Mengele and Son.

Mengele somehow escaped notice until ten years after the Second World was over. It was then, in the mid-1950s, that the author Ernst Schnabel drew attention to Mengele's work at the concentration camp when he was writing about Anne Frank. Reading this, people then naturally started to ask where Mengele was, why he had not been tried already and calling for him to be put on trial as soon as possible for war crimes.

By that time, Mengele had secretly taken his family to South America for safety. He lived as a fugitive in Paraguay from 1973 onwards. The Nazi hunters led by Simon Wiesenthal were on his trail and the net gradually closed in on him. Simon Wiesenthal believed he had traced Mengele to a remote Mennonite community on the border of Paraguay and Bolivia, but as a Paraguayan citizen and a registered refugee Mengele seemed to be immune from extradition.

It would be gratifying to think that Joseph Mengele lived in a state of increasing fear of capture and retribution during those final decades, but that may be no more than wishful thinking. Mengele's Nazi friends in Paraguay circulated a story in 1979 that he was dead. They even published a post mortem photograph of a body on a slab, showing a scar on the right arm where his SS tattoo had been surgically removed. But Wiesenthal was as intelligent as he was committed. He was not to be so easily fooled; he found out that the body was that of SS Captain Roschmann, another war criminal, who sent 80,000 Jews to a concentration camp in Riga.

A skeleton was eventually exhumed that is believed, from forensic examination, to have been Mengele's; and it seems that the old man died of a stroke while swimming in 1985. This is a case where natural justice was not done.

Dr John Bodkin Adams

'At Home' in Eastbourne

IN JULY 1983 an elderly retired doctor died in the quiet East Sussex seaside town of Eastbourne. A lot of retired people, especially from a genteel profession like his, end up in Eastbourne. But this was no ordinary doctor. This 84-year-old general practitioner was firmly believed by the police to be a serial killer, and not only that but a serial killer who had successfully eluded the law.

Because the law of libel is the way it is, it was only after the old man had died that the newspapers were able to open their dossiers about Dr John Bodkin Adams and level the accusations anew. He had been tried at the Old Bailey for the murder of one of his patients, a 72-year-old widow called Edith Morrell. If he had been convicted, he would certainly have been charged with further murders. Two more charges had been prepared and the prosecution service believed they had enough evidence to bring successful prosecutions in three more cases. The police, in other words, were sure that Adams had murdered at least six of his patients. Some officers believed the figure was nine or maybe as high as 25. Detective Chief Superintendent Charles Hewitt of Scotland Yard believed quite early in the investigation that the toll had been that high.

But at the Old Bailey, only the one case was discussed, or fought over. Dr Adams was acquitted after a classic legal duel between two barristers, Sir Reginald Manningham-Buller, the Attorney General, and Adams' defence lawyer, Geoffrey Lawrence. Lawrence was a thorough-going professional. He disliked his client, thoroughly disliked him in fact, but took his side ferociously in the courtroom. Manningham-Buller was sure he could destroy Adams once he had him in the witness box. Lawrence's advice to Adams was to remain silent and avoid cross-examination. The counsel for the prosecution and the police believed that that was what saved Dr Adams from the death sentence. Manningham-Buller had staked everything on cross-questioning Adams, so the basis for the prosecution case collapsed. The jury therefore more or less had to acquit; after a 45 minute deliberation, that was their verdict – and Dr John Bodkin Adams walked free.

The Adams trial was such a disaster that the Director of Public Prosecutions had no confidence that any of the other charges could be made to stick either, so he announced that there would be no further action.

As is customary in all cases, the jury had no knowledge about all the parallel cases that were very similar to Edith Morrell's, and also ended up with the victim's death. Had they known that the police had investigated 400 possibly suspicious deaths with which Dr Adams had been associated, they might have been less willing to give him the benefit of the doubt.

John Bodkin Adams was a very different sort of killer from Harold Shipman. It was purely and simply financial and material gain. He got the old ladies to change their wills in his favour, and then he killed them.

Over a period of 35 years in general practice in Eastbourne, Dr Adams had been named as a beneficiary in 132 of his patients' wills. Most of the bequests were modest, but in all he had amassed £45,000 in cash, which would be worth perhaps ten times as much today, something approaching half a million pounds. He had also been left jewellery, silver, furniture and cars, including two Rolls Royces.

It could be argued that a sympathetic doctor with a good bedside manner and a genuine concern for his elderly patients might well be acknowledged in the wills of old ladies, especially old ladies with no-one else to leave their money to. There need not be anything sinister about the matter. There need not be anything exactly sinister about it if Adams himself had hinted at it or openly asked the old ladies to change their wills in his favour. The key question is – did he kill them?

He was certainly a very popular doctor in Eastbourne, and had made the care of the elderly his speciality ever since he was a young doctor. He arrived in Eastbourne almost straight from medical school in Northern Ireland. He was an unprepossessing little man, only 5 foot 5 inches tall, but weighing 18 stone. His face was pink and fleshy, with small eyes and thin lips. His flabby chin spilled out over the celluloid collars he liked to wear. There was no doubt about it – John Bodkin Adams was ugly. And yet he managed to charm all his old ladies. He stroked their hands as he talked to them and even combed their hair for them.

But the year-long investigation by Sergeant Hewitt and his superior officer, Detective Chief Superintendent Bert Hannam of the Murder Squad, was to show that there was a much darker side to Dr Adams than the tender loving care that he like everyone to see. He prescribed addictive drugs for his elderly patients and made them dependent on the drugs. He in effect turned his genteel old ladies into morphine and heroin addicts. Their dependency on the drugs could so easily, because he was the supplier, be turned into dependency on him. He was then able to use his influence on them to get them to alter their wills in his favour. Once that was done, he was able to ease them gently on their way out of this world by administering an overdose of the drugs they craved.

The Murder Squad's investigation showed that for all the patients for whom Adams signed death certificates 68 per cent were alleged (according to his certificates) to have died of cerebral haemorrhage or cerebral thrombosis. This was a very high percentage – incredibly high.

Well before the outbreak of the Second World War there was gossip going round Eastbourne that Dr Adams did his rounds with a bottle of morphia in one pocket and a blank will form in the other. In 1936, Dr Adams had a windfall from the will of Mrs Alice Whitton, who left him £3,000, a large sum then. Mrs Whitton's niece contested the will, but the court decided in Adams's favour and he kept the money. The gossip in Eastbourne continued through the 1940s and into the 1950s. Dr Adams's racket was an open secret. But it was not until 1956 that the police decided to investigate and the circumstantial evidence started to accumulate. The problem was that most of the evidence was circumstantial.

There was the case of William Mawhood, where Adams made a bad miscalculation. He reckoned without Mrs Mawhood. William Mawhood was a wealthy steel merchant and also a long-standing friend of Adams. He had lent Adams £3,000 to buy his first house. When Mr Mawhood was dying, Adams visited him and asked his wife, Edith, to leave them alone for a moment. She was suspicious and listened outside the door to what was being said. It was just as well she did. She heard Adams telling her husband to leave his estate to him, Adams, and he would look after her.

Edith Mawhood was incensed. She burst back into the room, grabbed her walking stick and struck out at the wicked doctor, chasing him round the bed. He scuttled out of the room and down the stairs. Mrs Mawhood threw her walking stick down the stairs after him. She missed and broke a flower vase instead. She shouted after him to get out of the house. She never wanted to see him there again.

It was scandalous behaviour on Dr Adams's part, and he might perhaps have been charged with unprofessional behaviour, maybe even struck off for it. But it was a far cry from that level of bad behaviour to proving that Dr Adams would have hastened the death of Mr Mawhood – or any of his other patients. Dr Adams was obviously a nasty character. But was he a murderer?

The case of Emily Mortimer was similar to the Mawhood case. In the Mortimer family there was a strict tradition by which they intended to keep the family fortune intact. Whenever a Mortimer died, the bulk of the estate was divided among the surviving members of the family. In that way, each time there was a death, the money was recycled within the family. But Adams persuaded Emily Mortimer to make a break with tradition. The year she died, she changed her will, transferring £3,000 worth of shares from the family (who would have been expecting that sum) to the doctor. Shortly before she died, she changed her will again so that Adams received £5,000 and the Mortimer family was cut out of her will altogether. Emily Mortimer's death certificate gave as the cause of death 'Cerebral thrombosis'.

There was a rather different case of two old ladies who owned the house that they lived in. Adams persuaded them to sell their house and move into a flat – for the good of their health, he argued. He refused to hand over the money he made from the house sale until two years later, and then only when forced to do so by a writ.

The police investigation was very thorough. The Murder Squad had got statements from local solicitors and bank managers, which showed Dr Adams's intense concern with the wills of his patients. There were numerous irregularities. Adams was making visits to banks with his patients to oversee the changes he wanted them to make to their wills. He was making phone calls to solicitors demanding that they come out immediately to change a will or draw up a new one. There was even one patient who was so near to unconsciousness that he could only sign his changed will with a cross. There were also several changes of wills to stipulate cremation instead of burial, which could only be so that there could no exhumation later on to test for levels of morphine or other drugs in the body.

One of the most damning findings of all was the sequence of 32 cheques payable to Dr Adams, totalling £18,000, and all drawn out of one old lady's account during the last few days of her life. The signatures also looked as if they had been forged, presumably by Dr Adams.

But all of this was circumstantial evidence, evidence of Adams's way of thinking, evidence of his determination to get his hands on his patients' money. What evidence did the police managed to find of murder?

They did manage to find evidence that some of the death certificates contained information that Dr Adams must have known was untrue. Clara McNeill-Miller was an elderly single lady who had lived with her sister

Hilda for 13 years. When Hilda died, she left everything to Clara. About a year afterwards, Clara too died, leaving nearly everything to Adams. The sum amounted to £5,000. Three years later the bodies were exhumed and post mortems were carried out. Clara had died, not of coronary thrombosis as Adams had written on the death certificate, but of pneumonia. This was odd in itself, but then the police were able to interview one of the other guests in the rest home. This is what she told the police;

Dr Adams was called to Miss Clara the night before she died. She was suffering from influenza. He remained in her bedroom for nearly 45 minutes before leaving. I later became worried as I heard nothing from the room. I opened the door and was horrified by what I saw.

This was a bitterly cold winter's night. The bed-clothes on her bed had been pulled back and thrown over the bedrail at the base. Her nightdress had been folded back across her body to her neck. All the bedroom windows had been flung open. A cold gush of wind was sweeping through the room. That is how the doctor left her.

It was now very clear to the police from this vital witness evidence that Adams had tried to accelerate the death of Clara Neil-Miller – and probably succeeded. She had indeed died the day after this ordeal. The police also found that in the weeks running up to her death Clara had made out large cheques to Adams; these could not have been for medical treatment or medicines.

Adams also had a financial interest in the residential home where Clara died. He sent many of his patients there. Mrs Sharp, the woman who ran it, was likely to be able to advance the enquiry significantly. Hewitt remembered her later. 'Mrs Sharp was on the point of talking when we left Eastbourne for a week's conferences with the Attorney General in London. She was the witness we needed. She knew much of what went on between Adams and his patients. She knew where the bodies were buried and she was scared and frightened. When we left, she was about to crack.'

Hewitt was sure that with just one more interview, Mrs Sharp would tell them a lot more. He was devastated to find that she had died while he was away in London, and drew the obvious conclusion, that Adams had got to her, killed her, silenced her. Experienced as he was, he was unable to pin any of this on Adams. By the time Hewitt got back to Eastbourne, only a week after leaving, Elizabeth Sharp was dead and cremated – on Dr John Bodkin Adams's orders. Hewitt sensed Adams's role in Elizabeth Sharp's death but was unable to prove a thing. It was just too great a coincidence.

Julia Bradnum was another of Adams's patients. She was a strong and healthy 82-year-old, but woke up one morning with a pain in her stomach. Dr Adams was called and stayed in the room with her for five minutes, presumably administering drugs. Ten minutes later she was dead, presumably of a drugs overdose. Julia Bradnum's body was later exhumed, but it was too badly decomposed to show anything other than that she did not die of cerebral haemorrhage, which is what Dr Adams had written on his certificate. Julia Bradnum was, of course, leaving money in her will to Dr Adams. He had been there only a few weeks earlier with a new will for her to sign.

Harriet Maud Hughes was another of Dr Adams's patients. She was a mere 66 when she died. Adams had only begun to treat her three months before she died. Once again, he declared on the death certificate that death was due to 'cerebral thrombosis'. She spoke of changing her will in his favour. She became seriously ill a few weeks before she died, then recovered just enough to make a trip to the bank with the doctor, who asked the bank manager to make him the executor of her will. Afterwards, she said to her domestic, 'You should have seen the bank manager's face. He was most surprised at my choice of executor.' She made two codicils to her will. One was the instruction that she should be cremated. The other was a bequest of £2000 to Mr and Mrs Thurston, two friends of Adams, but police later discovered that Adams actually took 90 per cent of this sum, giving the Thurstons a 10 per cent 'commission' for the use of their name.

Another Adams case was a well-heeled retired bank

manager, James Downs, who nine times during the last few days of his life tried to put his signature to a will. The tenth time, Mr Downs succeeded in writing a cross, but only with Dr Adams guiding his hand. It almost goes without saying that the will in question left Dr Adams £1000 richer. Mr Downs was being treated for a broken ankle, but under Dr Adams' care he quickly went into a coma and within a month he was dead.

Another case was a widow called Annabelle Kilgour. She had been ill for several weeks, during which time she was being looked after by a State Registered Nurse, Miss Osgood. Adams arrived one night and announced to the nurse that he would give Mrs Kilgour an injection to help her get a good night's rest. Miss Osgood watched helplessly as she watched Adams give Mrs Kilgour what she could see was an excessively large dose. Adams said, 'That will keep her quiet'. Then he left. Mrs Kilgour fell immediately into a coma and died the following morning. He had certainly kept her quiet.

Adams returned to the scene and the nurse told him bluntly that he had been responsible for killing Mrs Kilgour. She later told the police, 'I have never seen a man look so frightened in all my life'. Adams signed the death certificate in his usual way – death, he wrote, was caused by cerebral haemorrhage.

Another case was Margaret Pilling, who was suffering from nothing more than flu when Dr Adams was called out, but within a fortnight she had fallen into a coma. Her family insisted she should stay with them. Her daughter, Irene Richardson, afterwards said that they had imagined their mother was dying of cancer and that the doctor was being kind by not telling them the diagnosis. But they quickly realised that things were not as they should be, and called a family conference. They decided that the treatment was unsatisfactory and in particular they were not happy that their mother was so heavily drugged – and that her condition was worsening fast. Irene Richardson and her family decided to take Mrs Pilling away to a house at Ascot, in effect take her away from Dr Adams, and she began to improve. Irene Richardson later said, 'Had I not taken her away, I am quite sure she would have died.'

Case after case pointed to Dr John Bodkin Adams as a murderer. The police and the Director of Public Prosecution's office were spoilt for choice. For the police, the clinching case was the case of Bobbie Hullett. Bobbie was a lively 49-year-old widow. It seems likely that Adams first killed her husband, Jack, in 1955. Jack Hullett was a retired Lloyds underwriter who had developed a heart condition. Adams gave him a dose of morphia and Jack Hullett died seven hours later, leaving £700 to Adams and the rest to Bobbie. Bobbie was grief-stricken and the friendly doctor was on hand to give her sympathy and drugs to help her sleep. The doses Adams prescribed were excessive and it was noticeable that Bobbie was staggering under the effects of the drug when she got up in the morning.

The comedian Leslie Henson was a close friend of

Bobbie Hullett's and he was distressed to see her disintegrating under the effect of the addictive drugs. Henson and his wife invited her to their house, to try to get her away from the source of the problem, but she had to go back – for more pills. Another of her friends was the Chief Constable, Mr Walker. When Bobbie died, both he and Leslie Henson were very upset, and Walker was in a strong position to make discreet inquiries. He discovered that just a few days before Bobbie Hullett fell into a coma she had given Adams a cheque for £1000; this he had fed into his bank account within hours. By this stage, he had £35,000 in his bank accounts and £125,000 in investments.

Bobbie Hullett's inquest did not go well for Dr Adams. The coroner asked why Adams had not told his medical practice partner about the patient's history of depression? Why had he not put the patient into a nursing home? Why had he not called in a psychiatrist? Why had he stuck to his diagnosis of cerebral haemorrhage after a pathologist had suggested poisoning might be involved? The coroner was unimpressed by Adams's answers and commented, 'There has been an extraordinary degree of careless treatment'. But of course it was much worse than that, and the inquest did not take that critical next step of accusing Adams of killing Bobbie Hullett.

In the end, when the case against Adams was assembled, the prosecution decided to focus not on the death of Bobbie Hullett but on the death of Edith

Morrell, the 72-year-old widow of a Liverpool shipping merchant, instead. The prosecution lawyers chose this case because they thought it was a very clear-cut and obvious case of murder, though the police investigators – Hewitt especially – were alarmed, as they thought other cases were better, especially those where there were bodies to supply forensic evidence. Mrs Morrell's body had gone. It had been cremated. This meant that there was no possibility of bringing in Francis Camps, the leading forensic scientist of the time. It was Manningham-Buller's decision, and he made it against the advice of his junior counsel, Melford Stevenson – and against the advice of Mr Leck at the Director of Public Prosecutions' office. Manningham-Buller knew John Bodkin Adams was by this stage a very frightened man and could easily be worn down in the witness stand. In the event, Adams did not take the stand and therefore escaped being reduced by Manningham-Buller. Manningham-Buller completely miscalculated the situation, bungled the prosecution of one of the worst serial killers of the century, and was responsible for letting him get off scot-free.

The trial of Dr John Bodkin Adams opened on 25 April, 1957. This was six years after Mrs Morrell had died. The prosecution brought witnesses who gave evidence that over a period of six weeks, Adams had prescribed a huge does of drugs – more than 4,000 grains of barbiturate and heroin. The standard recommended maximum daily dosage of morphia was a quarter grain, yet in the final day of Mrs Morrell's life Adams injected 18 grains. The witnesses were giving strong evidence that Adams had administered a huge drug overdose – one that he must have known would be fatal.

This damning evidence was nevertheless overturned by Adams's defence counsel, Geoffrey Lawrence. He had managed to find the nurses' daily record books. these seemed to show that the nurses' memories were at fault; in the six years that had passed they had exaggerated the doses of drugs Dr Adams had administered. Geoffrey Lawrence then played his trump card, which was not to put Adams in the dock. He made it appear that there was no case for him to answer, and denied Manningham-Buller of the chance to break Adams down by cross-questioning him. The case against Adams – at least as far as the death of Mrs Morrell was concerned – just fell apart.

To the huge disappointment of the police investigators, who knew that Adams had killed dozens of elderly people, Adams was acquitted. But irregularities had been uncovered about Adams's professional life that could still be pursued. Three months after he was acquitted, Adams was in the dock at Lewes Assizes on fourteen minor charges, over matters such as forging National Health Service prescriptions and bad record keeping in relation to dangerous drugs. The police were determined, at the very least, to remove Dr Adams from general practice. He pleaded guilty to these charges, perhaps hoping that the investigation would stop there, and he was right.

Adams was fined £2,400. Later in that same year, he was struck off by the General Medical Council. This meant that he was no longer able to practise.

Remarkably, and inexplicably, on 22 November 1961, Adams was allowed back onto the medical register. The police had not forgotten that he was an unconvicted serial killer, and the Home Office had not forgotten either; the Home Office refused to give him a licence to dispense dangerous drugs.

People in general, though, seemed to have short memories. Dr John Bodkin Adams went back into business and his practice in Eastbourne gradually picked up. Almost astonishingly, in 1965 a grateful patient left Adams £2,000 in her will. Now he really was back in business. He even had a brass plate outside his front door announcing the hour when he was 'at home' for sherry and social calls. Somehow, Adams completely escaped retribution. He retired and eventually died in Eastbourne, a constant living reminder to the police and the legal profession that he had got the better of them.

Dr John Bodkin Adam was that very rare being, the serial killer who got away with murder, and got away with it over and over again.

Dr Jeffrey MacDonald

copying Charles Manson

IT WAS ON 17 February 1970 that the Military Police at Fort Bragg answered a distress call from the home of Dr Jeffrey MacDonald. When they arrived in the cold and rain at the MacDonald residence, they found a scene of carnage. The MacDonalds were lying dead all over the darkened house. Dr MacDonald himself was sprawled on the floor of the master bedroom. Colette, his 26-year-old pregnant wife, lay dead, stabbed many times in the chest and beaten severely over the head with a blunt instrument. Both of her arms were broken as she had tried to defend herself from a frenzied attack. Written in blood on the headboard of the bed, was the word 'PIG'. Jeffrey MacDonald's wounds were very minor by comparison with those suffered by his wife. He told the police what he could remember of the attack.

He had been sleeping on the settee in the living room when he had been woken up by Colette's cries. Three men and a woman were standing in the living room chanting, 'Acid is groovy. Kill the pigs'. They were hippies. MacDonald had tried to fight them off, but they had slashed his face with an ice pick. Eventually the hippies had knocked him unconscious with a baseball bat. When he had come round he found his wife and daughters badly injured and unresponsive when he had tried to revive them. That was when he had made the emergency call that brought the Military Police.

The two detectives involved in the case, William Ivory and Franze Grebner, made a thorough search of the crime scene and they did not believe Dr MacDonald's story. It did not ring true. There was very little sign of a fight involving five people in the living room, so that did not tie in with his account a struggle with intruders. Even more suspicious was the fact that one of the magazines on the table had extensive coverage of the Charles Manson murders, which had some very strong parallels with this incident: too many to be coincidental. The ultimate puzzle was why a gang of drug-crazed hippies who had murdered the rest of the family with such ferocity and determination had let Dr McDonald live. All he had to show for the ordeal he described were a few bruises and superficial stab wounds. Why was he let off lightly and everyone else slaughtered out of hand?

The detectives were suspicious of Dr MacDonald's very detailed descriptions of the assailants. He had very poor eyesight without his glasses, so how had he managed to assemble all this detail? And why had he made the emergency phone call in the dark?

There were some other peculiar finds. On the bed where Colette had been attacked was the torn-off finger of a surgical glove, and a knife that McDonald claimed he had pulled out of his wife. Why was that found to be completely clean of fingerprints, including his own? Why would he have put on surgical gloves at any point? Forensic evidence revealed that the knife had in fact not been one used in stabbing Colette. The telephones which McDonald had used to call for help were also free of fingerprints. Why was this? The word 'PIG' had been written with the finger of a right-handed person wearing a glove. Various threads from the pyjama top used by McDonald to make an improvised wrap-round boxing glove for his hand during the fight in the living room were found round the house, though none in the living room where McDonald claimed to have had his fight.

The most damning evidence of all was the blood analysis. Each family member had a different blood group, which was useful, in that it was possible to tell where each of them had been. MacDonald's blood was present in the kitchen, next to a cabinet containing surgical gloves. There was some in the bathroom too, but none in the living room, where he claimed he had been stabbed. There was none of his blood in the hall either, and he was supposed to have lain unconscious there.

In spite of the mounting evidence against MacDonald's version of events and a growing suspicion that Dr MacDonald himself was the murderer, the evidence was mishandled, some of it was even lost and the charges against Dr MacDonald had to be dropped.

One of the FBI's forensic scientists, Paul Stombaugh, was able to show that Colette had been covered by a sheet and moved by someone wearing the blue pyjama top. He also looked at Dr MacDonald's pyjama top and saw that all 48 holes made by the ice pick had smooth edges and a circular shape; this could only have happened if the object had been stationary. Paul Stombaugh then folded the jacket to see how the stab marks matched. They matched perfectly and could have been made by 21 stabs with the pick, exactly matching the number of stab wounds on Colette's body.

The analysis was sufficiently convincing to convict Dr Jeffrey MacDonald on one first-degree and two second-degree murder charges. He was sentenced to three consecutive life sentences. Dr MacDonald disputes the verdict and still claims to be innocent; he portrays himself as the final victim in the case. Even so, his lawyers have been unable to find answers to all the questions raised by his version of events and the clash between that account and the forensic evidence. The police investigators believe that Dr MacDonald had a fight with his wife, knocking either her or his eldest daughter out in the master bedroom. It may be that he was in a blind rage and could not stop once he had started. An alternative is that he had read about the Manson case in the magazine on the living room table and decided that he would copy it – that he planned it and carried it out in cold blood. The wearing of surgical gloves certainly fits this second hypothesis.

Either way, he was found guilty by a jury, who thought that he was a doctor who had it in him to stab to death his entire family and then inflict non-fatal wounds on himself to make it look as if intruders had tried to kill all of them.

Dr Harold Shipman

Britain's worst serial killer

DR HAROLD SHIPMAN has the dubious distinction of being, as far as we know, the most prolific serial killer in the history of Britain. He was born on 14 January, 1946.

After Shipman's trial and conviction, a thorough investigation was set up into the circumstances surrounding the known murders, with the aim of discovering just how many people had been murdered altogether. A report on Shipman's activities published in July 2002 revealed that he had murdered no fewer than 215 of his patients between the years 1975 and 1998, when he was practising as a general practitioner at Todmorden in West Yorkshire (1974–75) and Hyde in Greater Manchester (1977–98). The judge who compiled the report, Dame Janet Smith, said that there were many more suspicious deaths that he may have been responsible for but could not definitely be attributed to him. Altogether, during his career as a general practitioner at Todmorden and Hyde, 459 of Shipman's patients died. A proportion of those will have died naturally, as a result of the conditions he was treating them for, so it is fair to assume that Shipman killed over 200 people, but under 400.

Now a new investigation is being launched, into Shipman's time before Todmorden, when he was an assistant doctor in a practice at Pontefract. If Shipman was killing at Hyde, and killing at his earlier practice at Todmorden, it is not beyond the bounds of possibility that he was killing even before that.

It is hard to imagine the level of human misery Harold Shipman caused. The murder victims themselves had their lives needlessly and undeservedly cut short, but at least they died very quickly and had absolutely no knowledge of what was happening to them; they trusted him completely and felt not even a twinge of fear. It is the families of the victims who have the ongoing torture, living with the knowledge that the doctor they trusted and respected, and in some cases recommended, betrayed them and robbed them of their loved ones. Then there are the families of the possible though not certain victims, who are left with the uncertainty; did their mothers or grandmothers die natural deaths or were they murdered too? The people of Hyde will take a very long time to recover from the trauma of the Shipman murders.

There is still much uncertainty, because Shipman was often the only person in attendance at the time of death, he signed the death certificate, and the death was often followed by cremation, so there was no possibility of a later exhumation and post mortem to establish forensically the true cause of death.

The evil doctor's modus operandi was to visit his victims at home. They were often elderly but in good health, and he persuaded them to let him give them an injection. He injected them with diamorphine in lethal doses, from which they died almost instantly. He never explained why he killed, so we can only speculate. It seems that Shipman enjoyed watching people die and enjoyed having the power of life and death over them. His bedside manner was good, and most of his patients thought he was a wonderful doctor. Just occasionally the mask slipped. He could for instance be inexplicably callous when dealing with bereaved relatives. He nevertheless went unchallenged for a very long time – almost to his retirement, in fact – because of his professional status as a doctor.

Dr Shipman might have got away with this incredibly long series of murders, but for greed. He tried to forge a will for one of his victims. It was a transparently poor forgery, pointing to foul play, and the police had the woman's body exhumed. Traces of diamorphine (heroin) were found. It turned out that Shipman had hoarded diamorphine, which is legally used in Britain in small quantities for pain control. One of the local undertakers became suspicious too; rather a lot of Dr Shipman's patients seemed to be dying. This too was reported. Other suspicious deaths were investigated. There were more exhumations, and Shipman was finally arrested.

The Shipman trial attracted a great amount of press interest, partly because of the potentially large number of victims, but also because of the implicit weaknesses in the NHS system. People began to ask about scrutiny and supervision, about the ethics of single-doctor practices, and so on. The trial culminated in January 2000, when Harold Shipman was convicted of murdering fifteen of his patients with lethal injections of diamorphine. He was sentenced to life imprisonment and given no hope of release; life would mean life. In prison, Shipman continued to behave as though he had professional status and expected to be treated accordingly. The prison staff finally withdrew some of his privileges because of his high-handed behaviour towards them and he became depressed. At 6.20 on the morning of 13 January 2004, Shipman was found dead in his cell at Wakefield Prison in West Yorkshire. He had used bed sheets to hang himself from the bars of his cell. He was pronounced dead at 8.10.

Shipman's motives for murder can only be guessed at. He consistently denied the murders and never explained his actions. We do know that he was, as a youth, profoundly disturbed by seeing his mother die, and it may be that in the series of murders of elderly women he was in some way re-enacting and coming to terms with that traumatic episode. It may also be that the 'will to power' was at work, that it gave Shipman satisfaction to make decisions about whether other people should live or die. Maybe it was a way of asserting his importance as an individual.

These same motives may have been the ones that led

to his unexpected and unpredicted suicide. The prison service prides itself on being able to identify prisoners who are 'at risk' in this way, but in this case they were caught out. He gave no clues to the prison staff that he was planning to kill himself, so he was as deceitful about his suicide as he was about the other killings. It must also be significant that he killed himself on the eve of his birthday; the prison authorities had refused to let him have a visit from his wife on his birthday. Harold Shipman was not getting enough of his own way, so by killing himself he took total control of the situation – for one last time.

PART TEN

MADMEN & MADWOMEN

Elizabeth Bathory

vampire and child-torturer

ELIZABETH BATHORY IS a figure who seems to have stepped straight out of an eighteenth century Gothic novel. It is hard to believe that she – and the appalling things she did – were ever real. Elizabeth Bathory was, nevertheless, a real countess who lived in the Carpathian Mountains in the sixteenth century. It was said that she was a real vampire, a drinker of human blood, and one of the inspirations for Bram Stoker's novel about Dracula. The countess was born in Hungary in 1561. She was a beautiful girl with a good complexion and fair hair. At the age of 15 she was married to an aristocrat and became the mistress of the Castle of Csejthe in the Carpathian Mountains.

Elizabeth's aristocrat husband was a soldier. He was often away on campaigns, and Elizabeth became very bored with life alone in the gloomy castle. She wanted excitement. This, she decided, would take the form of witchcraft, and she gathered around her a gang of alchemists, sorcerers and witches who were ready to teach her all about witchcraft. She armed herself with a special pair of flesh-ripping silver pincers and a manual of torture that her husband had used when fighting the Turks.

In 1604, when she was 43, Elizabeth's husband died. She longed for a lover, but the mirror told her that too many years had passed and her good looks had gone. When one day she slapped the face of a servant girl and drew blood, she noticed, or fancied she noticed, that where the girl's blood had spattered her the skin was much fresher and younger than before. She became convinced that bathing in the blood of young girls, and drinking it, would restore her beauty and preserve it for ever.

At night, Elizabeth and her deadly witch-band rode about the countryside looking for girls. When they found one, they took her back to the castle, drained off her blood for the countess to drink and bathe in. The countess carried on like this for five years before she realised that the blood cure was not working. She assumed it was because the blood was from peasant girls. What she needed was blood from virgins of her own class.

In order to gain access to the girls she wanted, she opened a finishing school and took in 25 girls at a time, ostensibly to teach them the social graces. She treated her aristocratic pupils with the same ruthless cruelty that she had dealt out to the peasant girls before, but now she grew careless. The bloodless bodies of four of the girls were thrown over the castle walls. The villagers took them away for identification, and Elizabeth Bathory's secret was a secret no more.

The countess's secret was out.

Once the authorities knew what had been happening, the Hungarian Emperor, Matthias II, was informed. He ordered that the countess must be made to stand trial for her crimes. As the law then stood, she could not be arrested because she was an aristocrat, so a new law had to be passed to enable this to be accomplished. At her trial in 1610 it was alleged that she had killed as many as 600 girls. Dorotta Szentes, known as Dorka, was the procuress who had supplied first the peasant girls, then the girls of higher class. She was sentenced to be burnt at the stake along with the whole band of witches.

Because of her class, the countess herself could not be sentenced to death, even though she was behind all the mischief. She was, instead, sentenced to be imprisoned in a small room in her own castle and fed only on scraps. She died four miserable years later.

Mary Ann Cotton

'She's dead and she's rotten'

THOMAS RILEY WORKED at the village workhouse in West Auckland, a poor village in County Durham in North-East England. Walking to work one morning along Front Street, he was approached by the widow who lived at No 13 Front Street. She wanted to know if he had room at the workhouse for her seven-year-old stepson, Charles. She said it was hard for her to keep him when he was not her own, and the boy was preventing her from taking in a lodger. Riley joked with her about the 'respectable lodger' she proposed taking in. Was it by any chance the excise officer the village gossips said she hoped to marry? She said it might be, but in any case the boy was in the way.

Only six days later, on Friday 12 July, 1872, as Mr Riley walked to work along Front Street at six o'clock in the morning, he was surprised to see the widow, standing in her doorway, evidently upset. He asked her what was the matter. She said the boy was dead. Mr Riley went to the police and called the doctor. Mary Ann's first action was not to hurry to the doctor, but to hurry to the insurance office to collect on Charles's insurance policy.

Mr Riley was suspicious about the boy's death because the boy had been in perfect health only six days before. The doctor was surprised too. He and his assistant had seen the boy five times that week because he had symptoms of gastro-enteritis, but had not believed it to be a fatal condition. Dr Kilburn decided not to sign a death certificate but ask for a post mortem examination.

Unfortunately, because of the pressure of work, Dr Kilburn was unable to conduct a thorough post mortem in time for the coroner's inquest. He had to admit to the jury assembled in the Rose and Crown inn next to Mary Cotton's house, 'I have found nothing to suggest poisoning. Death could have been from natural causes, possibly gastro-enteritis.' A verdict of natural death was returned and Charles Edward was consigned to a pauper's grave.

But at least Dr Kilburn had taken the precaution of preserving the contents of the boy's stomach in a jar. A few days later he had the time to undertake the proper tests, and he went to the police with the results. There were traces of arsenic. Mrs Cotton was arrested and charged with murder. The boy's body was exhumed and sent to Leeds, where Dr Thomas Scattergood found more arsenic throughout the body.

Meanwhile, Thomas Riley was telling the authorities that this was not the first death in the family. There had been four deaths in the two years that Mary Cotton had lived in West Auckland. Her fourth husband, Frederick Cotton, a coal miner, had died at the age of 39 of what was described as 'gastric fever' in September 1871, just a year after they had been married. Then, in a short period of less than a month in early 1872, three more people had died, a ten-year-old boy who was a son of Frederick Cotton by a previous marriage (another unwanted stepson), Mary's one-year-old son Robert and Joseph Nattrass, Mary's former lover. The baby had apparently died of 'teething convulsions', the others of 'gastric fever'. Before dying, Nattrass had been persuaded by Mary to change his will, leaving everything to her.

Now, seen in context, those deaths looked suspicious. The three bodies were exhume while Mary herself awaited trial in Durham Prison. Dr Scattergood found traces of arsenic in all the bodies.

At this point investigative journalists stepped in, exploring Mary Ann Cotton's past and compiling a horrifying dossier. The oddest aspect of the case was that Mary Ann, the central figure, seemed very kind, well-meaning and good-natured. She was a devout Methodist and to all appearances a good, kind person. And yet she spread death wherever she went.

Mary Ann Cotton was born as Mary Ann Robson in October 1832 in the village of Low Moorsley. She had an unhappy childhood. Her parents were both under twenty when they married. Her father earned perilously little as a miner in East Rainton. Those who knew her in those days spoke of her as a pretty little child and some of that prettiness remained as she grew up. She had no problem in attracting men. The photograph taken when she was forty, in custody and facing trial for her life, naturally does not show her at her best; she looks stunned, dazed, bewildered, plain. But how else would she have looked under those conditions?

Mary Ann's father was fanatically religious, and a fierce disciplinarian. Probably the girl feared her father and his punishments. When she was eight years old, the family moved to Murton, where her father continued mining until he fell to his death down a mine shaft. Her mother remarried. Mary Ann did not like her step-father, and he did not like her. She began to look for a way of escaping.

She left home at the age of sixteen, going into service in a wealthy household in South Hetton. She seems to have worked well there, though she was sexually promiscuous and the South Hetton gossips had plenty to talk about. After working for three years as a domestic servant, Mary Ann trained to be a dressmaker.

In 1852, at the age of 20, she married a labourer called William Mowbray and went to live in Devon. She gave birth to five children, of which four died. Infant mortality rates were high, but even so, the Mowbrays must have been seen by their neighbours as extremely unlucky to lose so many of their children. The Mowbrays' marriage was not a happy one. There were lots of arguments about money, as Mary Ann was obsessed by a fear of poverty. They went back to North-

East England, changing address several times in the Sunderland area. William Mowbray took a job on the steamer Newburn and so was often away from home. They had three more children, and they all died. Then William Mowbray himself died of a sudden intestinal disorder. The doctor went to see Mary Ann shortly after Mowbray's death to offer his condolences to the grieving widow, and was very surprised to find her dancing round the room in a new dress she had bought out of her dead husband's insurance money.

Soon after Mowbray's death, Mary Ann moved her remaining children to Seaham Harbour, where she struck up a new relationship with Joseph Nattrass, who was engaged to another woman. It seems Mary Ann was unable to break the engagement, so she left Seaham Harbour when Nattrass got married. Before leaving, she buried her three-year-old daughter. She returned to Sunderland, where she found a job working at the Sunderland Infirmary. Her one remaining child, Isabella, was sent to live with her grandmother, where she was at least safe for two years. Her work in the Infirmary was much admired; she was diligent and friendly towards the patients. One of the patients, George Ward, took a fancy to Mary Ann, and when he was discharged he married her.

Mary Ann's new husband, who was an engineer, died in October 1866, only a year after they were married. He had chronic stomach problems. The doctor attending George was criticized for treating his patient incorrectly. This was a view Mary Ann encouraged, as it deflected attention away from her own role in George's death. In November, only a month after her husband's death, Mary Ann moved in as housekeeper to a widower called James Robinson. He had three children. She became pregnant and married Robinson. Very quickly after that, James Robinson's children died, one after the other. In May 1867, nine-year-old Isabella, the only surviving child of her marriage to Mowbray, and back from her stay with her grandmother, also died.

Robinson himself survived mainly because he stubbornly refused to take out a life insurance policy. Mary Ann went off to visit her mother, fearing that she 'might be about to die'. Her mother was only 54, so there was no particular reason to suppose that she was going to die, but she certainly did die. Mary Ann moved on, loaded up with her dead mother's clothes and bed linen.

Then Mary Ann met and became friendly with Margaret Cotton and through her met her brother Frederick. Once again, Mary Ann became pregnant and then married her lover. This was a bigamous relationship because, due to some oversight on Mary Ann's part, Robinson was still alive. The wedding was marred by the death, once again totally unexpected, of her new sister-in-law.

It was an extraordinary trail of deaths. Altogether twenty-one people close to Mary Ann Cotton died within the space of under twenty years. She gave birth to eleven children, but only one of them survived, and that was the little girl she gave away. With hindsight it seems extraordinary that someone could leave a trail of so many suspicious deaths. Mary Ann achieved this by moving around rather a lot. She was at different addresses each time; she was breaking the sad news to different friends and different neighbours each time; she was calling in different doctors. There was no overall picture, no central record. She also belonged to a very poor underclass, where poverty, malnutrition and dirt conspired to shorten lives.

The journalists had a field day. The press were unfettered by modern laws of libel or contempt of court, and were able to publish what they liked. One local paper ran a headline, 'The Great Poisoning Case at West Auckland – Horrible Revelations'.

When Mary Ann Cotton, then aged forty, went to trial on 5 March 1873, she was charged with just one murder, the murder of her stepson Charles Edward. The prosecution argued that she had poisoned the boy to get the £8 his life was insured for, and because he was an impediment to her marriage to her lover, a man called Quick-Manning. As usual, she was already pregnant by him.

A former neighbour of Mary Ann's, Mary Dodds, revealed that Mary Ann had bought a mixture of arsenic and soft soap from a village chemist two months before the boy died. She claimed this was to kill bed bugs. A chemist said the mixture contained enough arsenic to kill an adult.

He also thought it significant (and by implication suspicious) that she had not bought the arsenic from the nearest chemist. Thomas Riley was able to give evidence that Mary Ann was eager to get rid of the boy.

Then a problem arose. The prosecution wanted to introduce evidence of the earlier deaths. The defence lawyer, Thomas Campbell Foster, rightly protested that his client was charged with one specific murder, and that discussion of earlier deaths with which she had not been charged would be prejudicial. The judge, Sir Thomas Archibald, overruled Foster, who was of course unprepared to defend his client against twenty murder charges. The result of the trial was from that point predetermined. The defence was not able to produce any witnesses, the lawyer having been appointed only two days before the trial opened, and the inevitable verdict of guilty was returned on the third day of the trial. The jury debated the case for an hour.

The judge passed sentence. 'You seem to have given way to that most awful of all delusions, which sometimes takes possession of persons wanting in proper moral and religious sense, that you could carry out your wicked designs without detection. But while murder by poison is the most detestable of all crimes, and one at which human nature shudders, it is one the nature of which, in the order of God's providence, always leaves behind it complete and incontestable traces of guilt. Poisoning, as it were, in the very act of crime writes an indelible record of guilt.'

Mary Ann Cotton poisoned those about her for their possessions, their insurance money, or because they stood in the way of a new marriage.

There was universal horror at what Mary Ann Cotton had done, but there was also a strong aversion to the idea of hanging her because she was a woman. There were also doubts about the conduct of the case, in particular about the way her defence was organized, and about the propriety of introducing earlier deaths with which she had not been formally charged.

Mary Ann spent her last few days trying to get support for a petition that might bring her a reprieve. She gave birth to a little girl, Margaret, who was Quick-Manning's daughter, and arranged to give her to a couple who were unable to have children. She wrote a letter to her estranged husband, James Robinson, asking him to visit her in prison. She begged Robinson to help her. 'If you have one spark of kindness in you – get my life spared. . . You know yourself there has been most dreadful lies told about me. I must tell you: you are the cause of all my trouble. If you had not abandoned me. I was left to wander the streets with my baby in my arms . . . no place to lay my head.'

Unsurprisingly, given the revelations in the newspapers, James Robinson was reluctant to go anywhere near her or have anything further to do with her. He did not answer the letter. But he did send his brother-in-law to the prison instead. Mary Ann was upset that Robinson had refused to come, but asked the man who had come to set up a petition for her. Petitions were set up and circulated by her former employers and other supporters.

Britain's first ever female serial killer, she was hanged on 24 March 1873, still maintaining that she was innocent. The hangman was elderly and incompetent, misjudging the length of slack rope needed. Instead of dying instantly as intended, she died slowly of strangulation.

Like William Corder, Mary Ann Cotton was demonized. Within only a week of her execution a stage play called *The Life and Death of Mary Ann Cotton* was being performed in theatres. She entered folklore as the bogeywoman who would 'come and get' children if they behaved badly. Children in school playgrounds invented a new skipping rhyme:

'Mary Ann Cotton,
She's dead and she's rotten!
She lies in her bed,
With her eyes wide open.
Sing, sing,
Oh what can I sing?
Mary Ann Cotton
Is tied up with string.
Where, where?
Up in the air,
Selling black puddings,
A penny a pair.'

Herman Mudgett
the Torture Castle

HERMAN WEBSTER MUDGETT is one of those rare serial killers whose activities defy belief even decades after they have happened. The events, the circumstances are so bizarre and extraordinary that they read like a work of cheap sensational fiction – so absurd, as well as so appalling, that they cannot possibly be true.

Herman Mudgett was born in Philadelphia, Pennsylvania, the son of Levi Horton Mudgett and his wife, Theodate Page Price. In 1878 he married Clara Lovering. In 1887 he bigamously married Myrta Belknap in Minneapolis; they had a daughter called Lucy. He married a third time, to Georgiana Yorke, in 1894.

His early career was based mainly on fraud and forgery, including a patent cure for alcoholism and a gadget for making natural gas from water. But Mudgett would also become a sadistic killer who enjoyed dismembering his victims. He researched his methods at the incredibly named Ann Abhor medical school, becoming an expert in acid burns. He found that he could supplement his student allowance by body snatching. He stole corpses, made them unrecognizable by burning them with acid, and claimed on life insurance policies he had taken out under made-up names. He managed to pull off this trick several times before he was stopped. A nightwatchman caught him removing a woman's body from a cemetery, and Mudgett ran off empty-handed.

Then Mudgett went to Chicago, where he ran a pharmacy, ominously adopting an alias, Dr H. H. Holmes. By defrauding the pharmacist, Mudgett acquired not only the pharmacy but the land next to it; in 1890 he was able to build himself a house on the vacant plot. It was to be no ordinary house. The ground floor was shops, the top floor was his personal office, and the floor in between consisted of a maze of over a hundred windowless rooms. Mudgett called it The Castle, and like a medieval castle it contained a remarkable range of special features such as secret passages, trap doors, chutes, shafts and dungeons. He managed to avert any suspicion about what he was up to by commissioning a different builder for each part of the house.

Mudgett's Torture Castle was completed in time for the great Columbian Exposition of 1893. This attracted huge numbers of visitors to the city. He offered rooms to let in his house, and killed several of his guests during the course of the Exposition. He lured young women to his castle where he drugged them, shot them down one of the shafts or chutes into an airtight chamber, which he pumped full of lethal gas. The bodies were sent down chutes into the cellar where he had installed vats of acid and lime – and a dissecting table. Here Mudgett cut his victims up, saved the organs that interested him and put the rest into the vats for disposal. Some victims were cremated, some sold to medical schools.

After his arrest, Mudgett was to admit to killing twenty-eight young women during the period of the Exposition, but he may have killed as many as two hundred. He might have gone on committing more and more murders, but for his greed. Two of his victims were sisters from Texas. Instead of disposing of their bodies in his usual way, he set fire to the house in order to get the insurance money and moved away from Chicago. The insurance company was suspicious and called in the police. Unfortunately, and surprisingly, the initial police investigation revealed no direct or circumstantial evidence of any of the terrible crimes Mudgett had committed in the house.

Mudgett did not know this, and was by now in Texas, where he traced the relatives of the two Texan sisters. He tried to defraud them of 60,000 dollars and they became suspicious. Before any action had been taken, Mudgett took to the road again, stealing a horse to make his getaway. The police stopped him in Missouri, where he was charged with another attempt at fraud. He managed to get a grant of bail, and promptly absconded.

The mass murderer next turned up in Philadelphia, in 1894, where one of his criminal associates had been running an insurance fraud racket for him. Mudgett took the extraordinary risk of murdering him and moving to Toronto with his victim's wife and three children. The children too were to be murdered; their bodies were later found in the cellars of rented houses.

There is so often an ironic twist in these cases that is tempting to think that there is a resistance in the human heart to believing in evil on the grand scale. Right up to this point, no-one had any suspicion that Mudgett had killed anyone at all, let alone that he was a serial killer. The police were on his trail, but for the theft of the horse and for bail-jumping. The police went to Mudgett's mother, who was proud of her successful son and happy to tell them where they could find him. Mudgett was arrested in Boston and charged with horse-stealing, bail-jumping and fraud. Only then did the police return to the burnt-out remains of the Chicago Torture Castle. There, when they inspected the site more closely, they found the remains of many human bodies.

Mudgett confessed to twenty-eight murders and was hanged on 7 May, 1896. He was one of the most spectacular serial killers, indeed serial criminals, in American history.

David Berkowitz

Son of Sam

THE MOORS MURDERER Myra Hindley campaigned for 25 years for her freedom, on the grounds that, according to her version of events, she was not the instigator of the murders and moreover that she was a changed person after her years in prison. David Berkowitz, who has been in prison for about that length of time, also for serial murder, insists that he does not want to be freed. Yet, like Hindley, he claims to be a changed person. In particular he claims to be a born-again Christian.

In 1977, David Berkowitz was sentenced to 365 years in prison for his crimes. Each June he is entitled to a parole hearing, but he does not want it. Berkowitz is, I think, unique among serial killers in having his own website. I have a website (www.rodneycastleden.co.uk), but then I am an author, not a serial killer. The nearest thing to David Berkowitz is Jeremy Bamber, who is serving a life sentence in the UK for the mass murder of his family. Bamber, who protests his innocence, has set up his personal website as part of a campaign to have his case reviewed. Berkowitz posted on his website a letter he wrote to New York Governor George Pataki saying that he was disappointed that there would be a hearing, adding, 'I have no interest in parole. Frankly, I can give you no good reason why I should even be considered for parole. I can, however, give you many reasons why I should not be. The loss of six lives and the wounding of even more are reasons enough.'

David Berkowitz remains an enigmatic figure. I have often wished that Jack the Ripper had been caught, not just to stop the killing, but so that we could have heard from the man himself why he was doing it. I sense that if I could meet and know the man, all would become clear. But Berkowitz is articulate, freely expressing himself on his website and even ready to give television interviews – yet still the fundamental mystery remains.

Somewhere along the way, as with the notorious Jack, the victims have been almost forgotten while the murderer remains the celebrity. But the relatives of Berkowitz's victims have certainly not forgotten them. Mike Lauria, whose teenage daughter Donna was the first of Berkowitz's victims, has said in recent years, 'He claims he's a born-again Christian, but I don't believe God has forgiven him. I haven't forgiven him'. This is typical of the deep and tormenting injury felt by the relatives and friends of the victims of serial killers; they are tortured for the rest of their lives by the knowledge that their loved ones have been contemptuously torn up and thrown away as part of some entirely impersonal hate campaign.

Donna Lauria was killed on 29 July, 1976. Her murder did not trigger a great deal of media interest in New York. Her murder was, after all, one of around 20,000 murders that take place in the USA every year. Donna was killed in area of the Bronx where the Mafia ran things. The New York journalists took little notice of Donna's murder, perhaps because they thought she saw or heard something she shouldn't have seen or heard, or said something the Mafia did not like. An isolated murder can happen for any number of reasons.

It was only when two further murders happened and several other people were injured that police and journalists began to think there was something unusual going on. There was a press conference at the New York Police Department's headquarters at One Police Plaza on 10 March 1977. The crime reporters gathered to hear that the same .44 calibre revolver had been used to shoot Donna Lauria and Virginia Voskerichian, a 19-year-old American, two days earlier. The Police Commissioner, Mike Codd, said the gun was a Charter Arms Bulldog and the same weapon had been used in the murder of Christine Freund and in two other shootings in the Bronx and Queens.

The press took up the story with alacrity and soon everyone in New York knew about the serial killer the journalists were nicknaming The .44 Killer. This was not good enough for Berkowitz. In common with many other serial killers, he wanted to be a celebrity, a big-shot in every sense. He was not content with this '.44 Killer' label, which was not nearly glamorous enough for him. He was an attention-seeker, and in a sense he still is.

In the small hours of 17 April 1977 he shot and killed two young lovers, Valentina Suriani and Alexander Esau. He also left a handwritten note in the middle of the street nearby. It was addressed to Captain Joe Borelli, the Deputy Chief of the Omega Task Force, which had been set up a month earlier to find The .44 Killer.

The writer of this peculiar letter claimed he had been ordered to kill by his father, whose name was Sam. Sam was a vampire. The letter was scrutinized by the police investigators, but not released to the public. Some journalists were told some of the contents of the letter and one of the New York Daily News journalists, Jimmy Breslin, dropped several hints about it in articles. On 30 May 1977 Berkowitz wrote another letter, this time directly to Breslin; this time the Daily News published it and gave Berkowitz a new nickname. They now called him 'Son of Sam'.

The summer of 1977 was a hot one in New York. Hot summers in New York are notoriously times of tension and trouble. In the small hours of 26 June 1977 a young Italian-American woman called Sal Lupo left a disco in Queens with 17-year-old Judy Placido. They sat together in Sal Lupo's car. The lateness of the hour and their vulnerability made them start talking about the dangerous predator stalking the streets. Judy said, 'This Son of Sam is really scary – the way that guy comes out of nowhere. You never know where he'll hit next.' Suddenly the car window shattered and they were hit by three bullets from a .44 revolver. Remarkably, neither of the girls was badly hurt. Sal staggered from the car and ran back into the disco to get help, and the killer vanished. Both girls recovered from their minor injuries, but they had nevertheless had a very frightening and painful experience.

Four weeks passed and there was no sign of Son of Sam. It was obviously a cooling off period. During that time, the police made no progress towards finding the attacker.

On the night of 31 July 1977, Bobby Violante and Stacy Moskowitz went out together on a first date. Up to now the hunting ground of Son of Sam had been Bronx and Queens, so the couple thought they were safe in Brooklyn. They had been to see the film New York, New York. Afterwards, they took their car and parked under a street-light in a well-known lovers lane in south Brooklyn. It was 2am.

Stacy and Bobby were sitting in the front seats of the car, kissing, when the windows shattered and Stacy jerked forward. The blast from the gunfire burst Bobby's eardrums, he lost his left eye and much of the vision in the right eye. He may have been disabled by the attack, but at least he survived it. But poor Stacy was in a very bad way. She was taken to hospital and surgeons worked on her for two days to save her, but she was too badly injured to survive. Stacy became David Berkowitz's sixth victim.

Then Berkowitz made a mistake. He committed a minor offence which got him noticed by the authorities. He parked his white Ford Galaxie beside a fire hydrant, which is an offence in most American cities, because of the dangerous obstruction it causes. Berkowitz was given a parking ticket. He returned to his car at 2.20 a.m. He was seen by a woman who lived nearby, Cacilia Davis; she noticed him ripping the ticket from his windscreen and throwing it into the gutter.

Mrs Davis was a widow of 49, and she was frightened. She knew about the attack nearby and realised that the man she saw angrily tearing the parking ticket from his car windscreen was probably Son of Sam. She feared that she might be attacked herself. For three days she did nothing, said nothing. Then she decided to go to the police. But the police ignored her, because they had been told by other witnesses that the killer was a fair-haired man driving a yellow Volkswagen. They also told her no parking tickets had been give out that night.

Although she had at first been undecided about coming forward, she now became determined to make the police listen to her. They were obviously wrong. A parking ticket had been issued. She had seen it. Finally, ten days after the shooting, the police found a ticket that had been issued to a Ford Galaxie, registration number 561 XLB. The registered owner was a man called David Berkowitz, and he lived at 35 Pine Street in the north of New York.

When the police arrived to arrest him, Berkowitz was about to get into his car. They asked him who he was and he gave them a crazed smile; 'I'm Sam!' he said. It was as if he was delighted to have been recognized – the limelight at last.

Berkowitz was taken into custody and he quickly confessed to all six murders as well as several other shootings, all within half an hour of questioning. The detectives asked him about the references to Sam. Berkowitz explained that he had a neighbour called Sam Carr and claimed that it was Sam Carr who had ordered the murders. The account got madder by the second, as Berkowitz went on to explain that the orders had not been given him directly by Sam Carr but by Sam Carr's demon dog, a black Labrador by the name of Harvey.

It began to look like the classic 'I'm guilty but I'm mad' self-account that is all too familiar to police interviewers. Some parts of what Berkowitz said were true. There was a Carr family, they knew of Berkowitz, knew he was unstable, and suspected him of shooting their dog Harvey, who had survived the attack. They also suspected Berkowitz of throwing a petrol bomb through a window into their home. The court appointed several psychiatrists to report on Berkowitz. They could not agree on a diagnosis. Some thought he was suffering from paranoid schizophrenia.

The letters clearly show signs of an abnormal personality. For a start they are written in capital letters

– the trademark of the madman. One contained the remark, 'BECAUSE CRAIG IS CRAIG SO MUST THE STREETS BE FILLED WITH CRAIG (DEATH)', followed by cabbalistic signs. This was clearly deranged. Another included what passes for poetry, but still in capitals

'AND HUGE DROPS OF LEAD
POURED DOWN UPON HER HEAD
UNTIL SHE WAS DEAD
YET, THE CATS STILL COME OUT
AT NIGHT TO MATE
AND THE SPARROWS STILL
SING IN THE MORNING.'

As it turned out the question of Berkowitz's sanity was not central in his trial, and he pleaded guilty to all the murders. He was sentenced to 365 years.

Prisons are dangerous places, full of dangerous people. In July 1979, David Berkowitz was attacked by another prisoner in Attica Prison. He had his throat slashed with a razor. He had to have 56 stitches in his throat and the wound has left him with a scar eight inches long.

After he was convicted, Berkowitz admitted that the demon dog and the voices were an invention. He attributed his murder spree to a deep-seated loathing of women, rooted in his sexual frustration. But there are some people, including relatives of some of the victims, who believe that there was some other motive. They think Berkowitz was a member of a coven and that the killings were not carried out by Berkowitz alone. The investigative journalist Maury Terry believes that the coven was called the Twenty-Two Disciples of Hell and alleges that Sam Carr's sons John and Michael were also members. Sam Carr's sons are said to have hated their father. Terry studied the contents of the letters Berkowitz wrote. In the text of the letter Berkowitz wrote to Captain Borelli, Berkowitz referred to both the Twenty-Two Disciples of Hell and John 'Wheaties', who was described as a rapist and suffocator of young girls. John Carr's nickname was 'Wheaties' and he closely resembled a composite picture of the gunman involved in one of the shootings. It began to look as if there was at least one more person involved in Berkowitz's attacks. But John Carr was found shot dead in February 1978, before Maury Terry had a chance to interview him about the case.

Scrawled on the skirting board next to the body were the letters 'SSNYC', which conceivably stood for 'Son of Sam, New York City'. Whether the letters were scrawled by John Carr before he died or by his murderer is not known. His brother Michael Carr also died under mysterious circumstances. In October 1979, he was driving his car towards Manhattan and he drove off the road straight into a lamp-post. Michael's sister, Wheat Carr, is certain that it was not an accident; she is sure he was either driven off the road or had a tyre shot out.

The District Attorney of Queens, John Santucci, was very interested in the results of Maury Terry's investigation, and agreed to reopen the Son of Sam case with a view to finding out if more people were involved than just David Berkowitz. So far, no-one else has been charged in connection with the shootings. Berkowitz himself is helpful but unhelpful. He admits that he was not entirely alone. 'There were others who knew about them [the killings] and urged me on. But I carried out the killings. I take full responsibility for my actions.' Berkowitz consistently maintains his own guilt and has never tried to implicate anyone else. In his letter to the state governor, he wrote, 'In all honesty, I believe that I deserve to be in prison for the rest of my life. I have, with God's help, long ago come to terms with my situation and I have accepted my punishment.'

What exactly the Carr brothers had to do with the Son of Sam attacks, we will probably never know.

Revd Jim Jones

The People's Temple

THE STORY OF the Revd Jim Jones is an unusual one. He seems to have set out initially with genuinely good intentions, to champion the cause of the oppressed and the poor of the world. Excessive zeal can sometimes lead people into fanaticism, and that can lead on to all kinds of mayhem. Jim Jones ended up killing a huge number of people, but at the outset thousands of people flocked to him, inspired by his Christian message of brotherhood and justice.

Jim Jones's peculiar story began on 13 May 1931, when he was born in the farming town of Lynn, Indiana. He grew up a lonely child. His father was a First World War veteran who suffered from a debilitating lung disease and was unable to work; all he could do was to draw a small pension to support his family. He, the father, was a very bitter man and he used such strength as remained destructively, to support the racist rallies of the Ku Klux Klan.

Mrs Jones, Jim's mother, had to work in a factory to bring in some extra money. Jones later claimed that she was a full-blooded Cherokee Indian. It was certainly true that Jones himself had the dark complexion and handsome features that could have come from a Cherokee ancestry. Jones knew from early on that he had to devote himself to a different message from the one his father was propagating – how, after all, could he marry a Cherokee and be a racist?

At school, Jim Jones was only an average student but he showed unusual zeal for Bible study. His schoolmates expended their energies on the playing fields. Jim Jones stood on the porch of his parents' run-down house and preached sermons at passers-by.

In 1949, when he was 18, Jones became a porter at a hospital in Richmond. This was to earn enough money to pay for him to do a religious studies course at Indiana University. He also got married, to a hospital nurse called Marceline Baldwin. The following year he became a pastor at a church in Indianapolis, helping to run its racially integrated youth centre. This was the predictable rebellion against his father's extreme racism. It inevitably brought him into conflict with the racist bigots of the city, and he suffered a good deal of abuse from them. Even the conservative members of his own church protested at his plan to welcome black worshippers into the congregation. It was a sharply segregated society, and Jim Jones was one of the few pioneers who was prepared to take significant risks to bring the racism to an end. The opposition to Jim Jones made some members of his congregation who had at first only been tepid in their support for him into vehement supporters.

Jim Jones rapidly became a cult figure, with a fiercely loyal band of supporters. Using money given by his supporters. Jones was eventually able to buy his own church, which was called The People's Temple, an alarmingly grandiose title. The church was located in a run-down white area, and the creation of the racially integrated church quickly turned the area into a black ghetto.

Jones and his wife adopted seven children, white, black and Asian. He was able to boast about his mother being a Cherokee and therefore claim to be 'bi-racial'.

Jim Jones now found himself with a predominantly black congregation, so he studied the style and technique of the black preachers they were used to, and who commanded extreme devotion. He watched one black preacher in Philadelphia who held his congregation in the palm of his hand. It was Father Divine, a fire and brimstone orator and faith healer, who also led a life of luxury on the gifts of his followers. Jones was captivated by what he saw, and what he believed he might be able to achieve for himself.

Jones decided to test the allegiance of his followers. The campaign of racial abuse against him suddenly accelerated. He said he was beaten over the head on his doorstep with a bottle wielded by a Ku Klux Klan member. Dynamite was thrown into his garden, where it exploded without causing any damage or injuries.

The incidents were reported in the press, and the source of the information was Jones himself, who told how he and his family were bravely resisting the threats.

The Mayor of Indianapolis gave Jones a paid position on the city's Human Rights Commission, and his congregation gave him their undivided devotion.

Then Jones decided to weld his following with and even greater external threat. It was now 1960, and there was a nuclear war fever. Millions of Americans were building themselves fall-out shelters. One magazine ran a satirical piece, claiming to have identified the ten safest places to live in the event of a nuclear war.

These are not always where you might expect them to be. I remember once, during the Cold War, seeing a secret Russian map that showed the locations of first, second and third priority targets for a Russian missile attack on Britain. I assumed that Westminster would be a first priority target and that the place where I lived, Newhaven, was relatively safe, except for radioactive fall-out. Not a bit of it. The Russians would have landed a nuclear missile on nearby Seaford Head. I went up there out of curiosity to see what they might be hoping to knock out. At first sight there was nothing, just downland grass and scrub. Had the Russians made a mistake? Then I noticed hidden among the scrub a small unmarked installation – I found out eventually that it was a flight navigation device to guide aircraft approaching Gatwick. Suddenly living at Newhaven seemed not such a good idea. But where is safe in a nuclear war? The choice seemed, even in the Cold War, to be between dying quickly and dying slowly.

Jim Jones found, from the completely non-scientific satirical piece in the magazine, that one of the safest places from nuclear attack was Belo Horizonte in Brazil. He announced to his congregation that he had had a personal vision of the nuclear holocaust and that they should prepare to follow him to a remote place where they would be safe. Jones and his family took a trip to Brazil, at the church's expense, to see whether it really was the promised land. It was not. But on his return journey he stopped over in Guyana for a few days, and was far more impressed with that. Guyana had been a British colony, and was now a newly independent socialist democracy. It seemed to satisfy his dream of a utopian state where there was social equality.

When he returned home, Jones announced that the prospect of a nuclear emergency had receded, but that the option of fleeing to South America should be held in reserve. Meanwhile, he launched into the very lucrative faith-healing industry. In a frenzy of religious zeal Jones laid hands on a succession of disabled and sick newcomers to his church. Selected patients, possibly planted, would leap up to say that they were cured.

But Jones's claims were too wild. His inner circle started to claim, presumably at his prompting, that he had raised forty of his followers from the dead. Then the press and the State Board of Psychology started to show an unwelcome interest. He and his followers needed to leave. He decided that the ideal bolt-hole would be the Redwood Valley near Ukiah in California. This was one of the top ten nuclear 'safe houses' Jones had seen listed. California in the mid-Sixties was full of hippy groups dropping out for all sorts of reasons, so Jim Jones's People's Temple attracted no particular attention.

To ensure that his church would not be subjected to destructive attention by the press and local authorities, Jones set up a campaign to win hearts and minds. Temple members became unpaid charity workers, foster parents. Jones himself courted local politicians until he was elected foreman of the County Grand Jury. He made it very clear that he wanted political power, in order to bring about greater social justice, and the only way for people to help him to achieve that was for them to hand over their earnings to him. The People's Temple became a state-registered, tax-exempt religious organization.

With the Temple treasure mounting up, Jones was able to set up a new Temple in San Francisco. The membership of his church now reached 7,500. The city officials were impressed to see Jones dispensing thousands of free hot meals every day to the needy. What they did not realise was that many of the needy were church members who were handing over their wages, savings and social security payments.

In 1976, a meeting was planned to greet Rosalynn Carter, the wife of the presidential candidate, Jimmy Carter. A nervous political worker responsible for organizing this meeting turned to Jones to see if he could swell the numbers for him. Jones obligingly filled the hall with his own supporters. He was duly photographed with Rosalynn Carter. Jones was not the only odd ally the Carters made on their way to – and through – the White House. Rosalynn Carter was also to be photographed with another serial killer, John Wayne Gacy.

But, for the time being, Jim Jones gave every appearance of being a pillar of society. He began talking about funnelling huge sums of Temple funds into South America to aid starving children in Guyana. Civic leaders and politicians paid tribute to Jones's work as a tireless worker making huge personal sacrifices in order to improve the social and living conditions for millions of poor people in America.

As time passed, some of his supporters began to question what he was doing, and what he was saying. The defectors spoke out against Jim Jones. Jones was launching into long tirades about sex in his sermons. He was demanding that couples, even if they were happily married, must be divorced and remarry partners that he chose for them among his inner circle of church elders. He insisted that as the Temple's spiritual leader he had the right to have sex with any woman – or girl – in the congregation; he even forced his sexual demands on them. He browbeat Temple members into confessing to completely imaginary homosexual acts. He was, in other words, abusing his power to give rein to his own psychosexual hang-ups.

There was physical abuse too. Young girls were made to participate in boxing matches against teams of bigger opponents who would knock them senseless. Other children were taken into a private room where they were tortured with cattle prods.

Meanwhile, Jones was buying press support by offering large cash bonuses in the form of Temple Awards for 'outstanding journalistic contributions to peace and public enlightenment'. The police department were similarly bought off by Jones's generous donations to the widows and orphans of police officers killed in the line of duty. But word was beginning to filter through, right up to the White House, that Jim Jones might turn out to be no more than a vicious maniac. Jones needed to activate his escape plan now. He had for some time been sending money to Guyana. It had been sued to buy a lease on a tract of forest and swamp not far from Port Kaituma. A pavilion had been built as the headquarters of what would now be called 'Jonestown'. Dormitories were built, where a thousand followers could join Jones in setting up a new socialist society, presumably complete with bullying, child abuse and cattle prods.

Jones succeeded in persuading a thousand volunteers to travel with him to Jonestown in November 1977. There was general relief in San Francisco that the Jim Jones problem had gone away. But one local politician, Leo Ryan, was concerned about the fate of the thousand followers. Anxious constituents told Ryan that they were hearing that their friends and relatives were being held in Guyana against their will. Ryan pressed the Guyanese government to allow him to fly to Jonestown.

Ryan found that the cult members appeared to be fanatically devoted to Jones, but were gaunt, hungry and deprived of their passports. They couldn't leave if they wanted to. Ryan addressed them. 'I am sure that there are some of you who think this is the best thing that has ever happened to you'. There were shouts and cheers. 'But I promise if any of you want to leave you can come with me under my personal guarantee of protection'. There was silence. One volunteer stepped forward.

That night, Ryan was allowed to stay to talk to the settlers. The party of journalists who had gone with him was sent back to Port Kaitumu, six miles away. When they got there, one of them reached into his pocket to read a note that had been pushed into his hand in Jonestown. 'Please, please get us out of here before Jones kills us.' It was signed by four people.

The next day, when the journalists went back, Ryan was waiting with the twenty frightened Temple members who wanted to leave. There were too many for the small plane, so Ryan stayed with those who were left, to wait for the plane to make a second trip. As they were about to leave, one of the elders tried to stab Ryan but succeeded only in stabbing himself. The journalists pulled Ryan onto the truck and made for the airfield.

They were on the runway, when a tractor drove out of the undergrowth onto the runway. The men on the tractor fired a volley of shots at them. Leo Ryan and a TV reporter were killed outright. A cameraman and a stills photographer were both killed as they recorded the scene.It turned out that some of the 'defectors' were actually fifth columnists. One of them pulled out a gun and shot the pilot.

Back at the Jonestown settlement, Jim Jones started to say an emotional goodbye to his followers. 'We were too good for this world. Now come with me a to a better place.' What he had created in the tropical forest was not a paradise but a living Hell. He could not of course keep the outside world at bay for ever. And the disastrous religious community had created started to crumble and implode. So he organized its total destruction. He ordered his followers to commit suicide. The followers prayed or cried as the elders brought out of the pavilion vats of soft drink laced with fast-acting poison. There was some gospel singing as the followers queued up to take their cups of poison. The babies died first, poison squirted into their mouths with syringes. The children were killed next. Then their parents. Along the way, as Jones became more fanatical and more egotistical, he became more dictatorial, eventually tuning into a tyrant and torturer.

There were some followers, of course, who were unpersuaded, or whose nerve failed them. For them the elders of the Revd Jim Jones evil church were on hand to cut their throats or shoot them through the head. One way or another, almost his entire congregation died.

When Guyanese soldiers arrived the next day, they found a scene of terrible carnage. The bodies of entire families lay on the ground, their arms locked together in a final embrace. The Revd Jim Jones, the mastermind behind this massacre, lay sprawled on the ground, killed with a single bullet through the brain. There were just one or two survivors, terrified escapees who had managed to hide in the crawl spaces under buildings.

Leo Ryan, who had tried as hard as anyone could to stop the tragedy from unfolding, was dead too, but he left a tape. Just before he died on the airstrip, he was interviewed by the television crew, many of whom were also about to die. The tape recorder on which Leo Ryan's last words were recorded was found under the pile of bodies on the runway. 'Jim Jones talks a lot about love, brotherhood and humanity and his faith and the power of religion. But never once did I hear him mention God.'

Andrei Chikatilo

the Forest Strip Killer

IN THE OLD days in the Soviet Union the official line was that serial killers were a product of the decadent West: the Soviets did not have serial killers. It is certainly true that there have been far more serial killers in the USA than in the Soviet Union or the Russian Federation, because of all kinds of social and political differences, not least the difference in freedom of action. But Andrei Chikatilo was a serial killer – in a very big way – and he was a Soviet citizen. The Soviet Union did have serial killers, after all.

Chikatilo is known to have killed 53 people, but he may have killed many more, in and near the city of Rostov, near the Black Sea. His job was as a travelling buyer of raw materials for a Rostov factory. A job involving travelling is always helpful to a serial killer. If the killings are in widely separated locations, there is less chance that the police will make the significant connections that will lead back to the killer. Chikatilo's travelling meant that he claimed some victims as far afield as Leningrad and Tashkent.

Chikatilo's favourite method was to engage a young woman (or sometimes a young man) in conversation at a railway or bus station, then lure them to a strip of woodland where he would murder them. This specific choice of location for killing earned him the nickname 'Forest Strip Killer' or Lesopolosa.

As the body count mounted, a huge manhunt was set up by the powerful Soviet establishment, which was, as it happened, itself about to implode under Gorbachev's glasnost and perestroika policies. By the time Chikatilo was brought to justice in 1994, the huge administrative machine that had organized his manhunt had vanished completely.

As with so many serial killers in the West, it is clear that Chikatilo's dysfunctional behaviour had its roots in the dynamics of his childhood, and in his serious sexual problems. Andrei Romanovich Chikatilo was born in October 1936 in Yablochnoye, a village in the Ukraine. The 1930s were a period of intense upheaval under Stalin's regime, especially in the Ukraine. Ukraine was the bread basket of the Soviet Union but Stalin's collectivization programme was brought in with such catastrophic effects that millions of Ukrainians died of starvation.

In 1931, Andrei's older brother Stefan vanished. His parents believed he was abducted, killed and eaten by starving neighbours. The thought of what had happened – or might have happened – to Stefan preyed on the young Andrei's mind.

When he was only five, Andrei witnessed Nazi atrocities when the German army overran his village. Even worse was to follow. His father, Roman, was captured by the Germans and was only released from a prisoner of war camp when the war ended in 1945. Roman Chikatilo returned to Yablochnoye a broken man. Instead of being rehabilitated by the Soviet authorities, they callously accused him – and many others like him – of treachery, in allowing themselves to be caught. Andrei, already a committed Communist, joined in the general denunciation of his father's betrayal of the motherland, but he was still taunted at school for what his father was.

Andrei was quiet and slightly effeminate, and this meant that he tended to be picked on at school. He became extremely shy. He was seriously short-sighted, but refused to wear his glasses for fear of being ridiculed. He was also a bed-wetter, and like many others so afflicted went to great lengths to cover up the problem. Overall, Andrei Chikatilo had a more painful adolescence that most boys. His shyness, insecurity and lack of social skills made it very difficult for him to interact with girls. When he did finally persuade a girl to go to bed with him, because of his anxiety he was unable to get an erection and was almost inevitably exposed to further ridicule.

He came by stages to realise that violence was more exciting to him than sex.

He left school, having failed to qualify for university,

did his national service and then got a job as a telephone engineer in the town of Rodionovo-Nesvatayevsky, not far from Rostov. In 1963 his sister, who had moved in with him, introduced him to a local girl called Fayina. They were married. Andrei was very shy where sex was concerned and Fayina realised that he had little interest in sex. Even so, she managed to coax him into performing, and they somehow produced two children, Lyudmilla and Yuri.

In 1971, Chikatilo completed a correspondence course and obtained a degree. His new qualification enabled him to get a post as a teacher, but his shyness and weakness made normal classroom discipline difficult for him. His pupils did not respect him and his colleagues thought him odd. Unfortunately, Chikatilo enjoyed being surrounded by children, and found them sexually arousing. He started committing indecent acts on both girls and boys. Complaints were made and he was forced to resign, though criminal charges were never brought. He got a job at another school. On one occasion he tried to perform oral sex on a sleeping boy; he was caught by some of the older boys and severely beaten for it. After that salutory incident, Chikatilo always carried a knife.

Despite the oral sex incident, Chikatilo was still not formally charged. The principals of Soviet schools did not want anything to reflect badly on their schools' reputations, so problems like these were often swept under the carpet.

In 1978, Chikatilo moved to the town of Shakhty, not far away from Rostov, and got a post at a mining school.

It was on 22 December 1978 that he killed his first child. He befriended a nine-year-old girl called Lena Zakotnova, who was waiting for a tram. He promised her some American chewing gum if she would go with him, and he took her to a shack he owned next to the Grushevka River. Once inside the shack, he pushed the terrified little girl to the floor, blindfolded her and tried to rape her. He found he was only able to become sexually aroused when the girl became distressed and started gasping for breath. He knew that if he let Lena go now she would report him and he would go to prison for what he had done. He had to kill her to silence her. He stabbed her three times in the stomach, then dragged her outside and threw her into the river. She was still alive at that point but quickly died as a result of bleeding, hypothermia and drowning.

One of Lena's friends told the police she had seen Lena with a tall, thin, middle-aged man wearing glasses and a dark coat. The artist's impression based on her description was shown to the principal of the mining school, who noticed the similarity between the sketch and Chikatilo. The police noticed splashes of blood on the steps of Chikatilo's shack and took him in for questioning. That should really have been the end of the matter, but for some reason Fayina gave Andrei an alibi, and the police turned their attention to another suspect. A poor young man called Kravchenko, who had a conviction for rape, was questioned mercilessly by the police until he confessed, and he was executed for Lena's murder in 1984.

It was only much later that it became clear that Lena's killer was still at large, but the tightly controlled Soviet media were hardly likely to comment on this appalling miscarriage of justice.

Meanwhile, Chikatilo managed to restrain his homicidal urges for three years. In 1981 he lost his teaching job, and was unable to get another because of his terrible reputation for lecherous behaviour. He worked next as a clerk at a factory.

Six months after this, Chikatilo carried out his second murder. This time it was a 17-year-old girl, Larisa Tkachenko, who was well known for her generosity in offering sexual favours in exchange for food and drink. He took her to a strip of woodland, undressed her, then punched and strangled her, forcing handfuls of earth into her mouth to stifle her screams. This killing left Chikatilo feeling elated. He 'danced with joy' round his young victim's body. This was something he would want to do again.

In June 1982 He killed a thirteen-year-old girl, Lyuba Biryuk, while he was away on a trip, and during the following year he killed six more people, and two of them were young men. The police understandably assumed the person killing the young men was a different killer – but they were all Chikatilo's. After killing a 15-year-old girl in December 1982, Chikatilo did no more killing for six months, then killed three people in the summer of 1983, including the savage killing of a seven-year-old boy, Igor Gudkov.

The Central Moscow militia sent an experienced detective, Major Mikhail Fetisov, to Rostov to take charge of the murder investigation in September 1983. Fetisov was very critical of the local police, who he thought were totally inept. He succeeded in convincing his senior officers that all 14 murders (so far) were the work of a single maniac, but he stopped short of using the dreaded phrase 'serial killer' because it was ideologically unacceptable to countenance serial killing in the Soviet Union. Fetisov had his team trawl through the criminal records and mental health records in the hope of finding someone who might match the killer's profile. Here, of course, it would have been helpful if criminal charges had been brought against Chikatilo for his early sexual assaults while school-teaching; he would then have appeared in this trawl.

Chikatilo was actually arrested, but his blood sample did not match the AB blood group the police had attributed to the killer. It was only afterwards that the investigators realised their mistake. The AB sample came from semen. Chikatilo was type AB, but the B antigens did not show up in his blood sample. The investigators did find someone who fitted the killer profile. His name was Alexei Shaburov, a car thief of low intelligence who confessed to killing four children along with four other men. None of the men allegedly involved could give any details. In spite of several days of brutal interrogation, it was evident that the 'gang' was just a group of time-wasters.

The police in Rostov became more vigilant. They realised that the killer was picking up most of his victims at railway and bus stations, and patrolled them conscientiously. Inspector Zanosovsky watched a middle-aged man wearing glasses showing an undue interest in young girls. Zanosovsky approached him and asked to see his identification papers. It was Andrei Chikatilo, a freelance employee of the Department of Internal Affairs, a branch of the KGB. Zanosovsky let him go, probably because of the KGB link. A few weeks later, though, Zanosovsky saw Chikatilo again and followed him for hours as he took bus after bus round the area. He could see that Chikatilo was not actually going anywhere, but he was repeatedly approaching young women. Most of them brushed him off, but eventually he found one who was drunk, and she rested her head on his lap and let him fondle her.

Zanosovsky approached Chikatilo, who started sweating profusely. The policeman insisted that he open his briefcase. Inside was Chikatilo's serial killer kit: a jar of lubricant, a length of rope and a knife with a long blade. He was taken to the police station where it emerged that he was being investigated for stealing a car battery from his work place. It was enough to justify keeping him in custody while the police ran some checks. Unfortunately the blood type did not match –

as before – and to make things worse a policeman sent the damning contents of the briefcase back to Chikatilo's home, where they were disposed of. Suddenly there was no case to answer except the theft of the car battery, for which he received a three month prison sentence.

Chikatilo lost his job as a result of the conviction, but got another in January 1985, as a travelling buyer for a locomotive factory at Novocherkassk. He did no killings for six months, but then killed an 18-year-old girl in Rostov. There was another lull of almost a year and a half before the next killing, a 13-year-old boy in Revda in the Urals.

Andrei Chikatilo was now running out of control. It was the final phase. He killed eight young people in 1988. In 1990 he killed nine, and many of these were boys. A new man was in charge of the investigation, Issa Kostoyev, who was Director of the Central Department for Violent Crime. When on 3 November 1990 the body of a 16-year-old boy, Vadim Tishchenko, was found near the railway station in Rostov, Kostoyev decided he had to saturate the area with plain clothes men, equipped with night vision goggles. In spite of this strenuous response, Chikatilo was still able to kill once more. He succeeded in luring Svetlana Korostik away from a railway station and murdered her in some nearby woodland. He cut off parts of her body and ate them, then covered her remains with branches and walked back to the station.

One of the plain clothes officers saw Chikatilo sweating heavily and noticed spots of blood on his face. He checked Chikatilo's papers but let him go. At that point he knew nothing of Svetlana's death and had no particular reason to detain him. But later, when her body was discovered, Kostoyev read the plain clothes officer's report of the meeting with Chikatilo and realised what it meant. He checked Chikatilo's works records and saw that his business trips put him in the right place at the right time for many of the murders. Chikatilo was the man they had been looking for. Kostoyev detailed a team of undercover officers to follow Chikatilo.

On 20 November 1990, he left work to visit the doctor. He needed treatment for a broken finger – it had been bitten by one of his victims – and then went off to look for young boys. He was chatting to one young boy when his mother called him away. He carried on down the street to try to find another, when he was stopped by three police officers. He was under arrest. The briefcase he was carrying contained, exactly as before, his serial murder kit.

Eventually Chikatilo confessed to all the murders. His trial took place in April 1992. For the trial he was locked in a cage like a wild animal; it was designed to defend him from attack by his victims' relatives. Chikatilo ranted and raved and generally behaved outlandishly. It is possible that his mental condition had deteriorated under the severe questioning he would undoubtedly have been subjected to. But it is also possible that he was trying to persuade the judge that he was insane and so escape the death penalty. At one point he took all his clothes off and waved his penis at the public gallery, shouting, 'Look at this useless thing! What do you think I could do with that?'

Chikatilo's defence lawyer had a difficult task. He tried to argue that there was no solid evidence against his client. The only evidence was the confessions. The judge was nevertheless convinced of Chikatilo's guilt, giving him 52 death sentences. The evidence against Chikatilo in the fifty-third case was not overwhelming. It scarcely mattered. Chikatilo was led away shouting, 'I'm not going to listen to your lies!'

A year and a half later Andrei Chikatilo, the Forest Strip Killer or the Rostov Ripper, was executed with single bullet in the back of the head.

Aileen Wuornos

killing the clients

AILEEN WUORNOS HAS been described as the first woman serial killer in America. It is true that female serial killers are very rare, but she was not the first: she did have her predecessors. Wuornos was different from most other female murderers in that she attacked total strangers, which makes her more like the classic predatory type of male serial killer. Women nearly always kill someone with whom they already have some sort of relationship; with women, killing is usually an intensely personal thing. Aileen's use of a gun is also unusual. Women have, historically, tended to prefer indirect methods of killing such as poison.

Her criminal activities first came to the attention of the police in December 1989, when a car was found abandoned in Florida, near Daytona Beach. Ominously, there was blood on the seats. It emerged that the car had belonged to a man called Richard Mallory, who was known to pick up prostitutes. Two weeks later, the body of Richard Mallory was found in woodland. He had been shot four times. On the day of the murder,

Aileen Wuornos had returned to the motel room where she was staying with her lover, Tyria Moore, and blurted out that she had just killed a man. Tyria told the court this at Wuornos's trial.

This seems to have been the first murder Aileen Wuornos committed, but the desire to kill men must have been developing within her for a long time beforehand. Her schizophrenic father was imprisoned for raping a seven-year-old girl; then he hanged himself. A friend of her grandfather's had made her pregnant at the age of 14. She was made to have the baby then give it up to be adopted. After that she was thrown out and had to make her living by prostitution. She had been raped and beaten several times during the course of her life as a prostitute.

The terrible experiences of her early life – at the hands of several different men – predisposed her to take revenge on men in general. Any men would do.

She met Tyria Moore in Florida. Then she got herself a gun, perhaps initially so that she could defend herself if she was threatened with a beating. What Richard Mallory did to provoke Wuornos to shoot him is not known, but he had a history of sexual offences and may well have tried something violent that made her reach for the gun.

Several months after the initial murder she killed again. A truck was found beside a main road in Florida. Its registered owner was David Spears, and his body was found 60 miles away. Like Mallory, he had been shot in the chest with a .22. The police found no fingerprints in the vehicle, but they did find a blonde hair. At this stage, the police made no connection between the two murders.

The police were given an important lead when a peculiar incident was noticed and reported. Two women were seen driving a car off a road, changing its number plates, then running off into a wood. The car, it turned out, belonged to a missionary who had gone missing. After the bodies of three more men were found, all of them killed in the same way, sketches of the two women were circulated. Progress in solving the crimes was slow because the crimes were committed in five different counties. In the end a special task force was formed.

Several people identified the two women in the sketches as a lesbian couple, Tyria Moore and 'Lee', who was Aileen Wuornos. This was a major breakthrough. The police were able to take Wuornos in for questioning without formally arresting her as she was guilty of a parole violation. Tyria Moore was interviewed too and pressed to tell everything she knew. Then the decisive moment came as the police discovered items belonging to the dead men, locked in storage by Wuornos.

Tyria Moore was the weak link. She told the police interviewers what she knew and agreed to try to get Wuornos to confess. Finally, in January 1991, Aileen Wuornos went to the police and confessed to the murder of seven men. Even when she was told that one of the men had been a missionary, she still insisted that all the murders had been in self-defence. She had been hitch-hiking, they had picked her up, propositioned her and then got violent. And then she had shot them.

The self-defence plea was unconvincing, because it did not tally with what Tyria Moore had said in evidence; she had said nothing at all about self-defence.

As Wuornos's trial drew to a close in January 1992, the jury recommended the death penalty and she was sentenced to the death penalty six times over. It was emerging that she had killed at least eleven men. In 2001, she went to court to dismiss her lawyers, and the judge told her she was heading for the electric chair. He was right. Aileen Wuornos was executed in 2002.

The Monster of Florence

more than one madman?

IL MOSTRO, THE Monster of Florence, carried out a string of grisly murders over a long period in the country lanes and camping sites of Tuscany. All were carried out in quiet rural locations in the hills around Florence. It was an extraordinary campaign, partly because it went on for such a long period – 17 years – and partly because of the many unlikely conspiracy theories surrounding the case, most of them generated by the authorities.

The killings began one hot summer night in 1968. At first it looked as if the death of Barbara Locci and her lover, Antonio Lo Bianco, was a straightforward and isolated domestic tragedy. Barbara lived in the town of Lastra a Signa, a few miles down the River Arno from Florence. She was a 32-year-old housewife and notoriously promiscuous. She had had several lovers and was known locally as The Queen Bee. On this particular summer evening, 21 August 1968, she had gone to the cinema with Antonio Lo Bianco and her young son Natalino. Afterwards, the boy had fallen asleep in the back of the car, and Barbara and Antonio had driven to a quiet spot to make love.

An unidentified gunman had then crept up to the car and fired eight shots at them, killing them outright. The gunman had then picked up the boy and carried him to a nearby farmhouse before running off into the night. The act of taking the boy away from scene of mayhem and leaving him within reach of help was a significant act of humanity, suggesting that this was not the action of a typical serial killer. Little Natalino knocked on the farmhouse door and told the farmer, 'My mother and my uncle are dead.'

Not surprisingly the local police immediately suspected Barbara Locci's husband, Stefano Mele, and their initial suspicion was confirmed when they found him with a suitcase already packed as if he was about to leave. When the police interviewed Mele, more detail emerged. He first accused one of his wife's several lovers, then admitted his own involvement, claiming that a friend, Salvatore Vinci, had lent him a gun. Later, Mele withdrew his confession and blamed Vinci's brother Francesco, who was also one of his wife's lovers. His frequent changes of mind irritated the police and the judges. In 1970 he was found guilty of the murders and given a 14-year sentence. The sentence was lenient partly because of his wife's provocation, partly because he was thought to be insane.

By 1974, the Barbara Locci killing had been forgotten, but then a similar attack took place at Borgo San Lorenzo, a few miles north of Florence. One dark night in September 1974 two teenage lovers, Pasquale Gentilcore and Stefania Pettini, were making love in their Fiat when someone came up to the car and fired ten shots at them. Instead of leaving the scene straight away, the attacker stabbed Pasquale twice. He also lifted Stefania out of the car and slashed her with his knife, wounding her 96 times.

This time there were no obvious suspects. A man walked into a police station and confessed, but he turned out to be an attention-seeker. He was unable to give any significant detail about the manner of the killings. The police did not notice any link with any previous attack, and did not make the obvious connection with the 1968 attack at Signa. The police could find no suspect at all and had to file the case away as unsolved.

Again there was a long time gap before another slaying. It was seven years later, on a warm summer night, that the next double killing took place. On 6 June 1981, the mad gunman fired eight shots into a Fiat with a young man and woman inside, Giovanni Foggi and his lover Carmela De Nuccio. Once again, after the shootings, the killer indulged himself with his knife. He lifted the body of Carmela from the car, put her body in a ditch, stabbed her in the abdomen and cut out and removed the genital area completely. As in the 1974 murders, her purse was emptied onto the ground near the car; this act evidently had some symbolic meaning to the killer.

This time the police did notice the connections and similarities with the earlier killings. They set about comparing the Winchester bullets found in all four bodies from the 1981 and 1974 killings. They had all been fired from the same Beretta pistol. They all came from the same batch of ammunition. These were not isolated killings but the work of a serial killer. As yet, no-one had made any connection with the killings of 1968. The police found a suspect. Enzo Spalletti was a Peeping Tom who had told his wife about the murders of Giovanni and Carmela before they were public knowledge. He said he had read about them in the newspaper, whereas they were not reported until the following day. He was arrested and taken into custody.

Four months later, while Enzo Spalletti was still in prison, there was another double killing. Spalletti was immediately released, as he could not possibly have carried out this new attack. Stefano Baldi and Susanna Cambi were shot dead at a beauty spot to the north-west of Florence. Susanna's body was subjected to the same mutilations as Carmela's.

The following summer, yet another couple was attacked as they were dressing after having sex in a car parked at Montespertoli, south-west of Florence. The girl, Antonella Migliorini, died instantly when the gunman opened fire. The boy, Paolo Mainardi, survived the initial gunshots, was able to turn the car's ignition key and put the car into reverse. Weakened by his wounds, he ran the car into a ditch. The gunman walked over, shot out the car headlamps, pulled the car keys from Paolo's hand and threw them into under-growth. The gunman disappeared, leaving Paolo slowly bleeding to death. The young man survived until the next morning, but died in hospital without giving the police any description of the attacker.

Shortly after this double murder, Sergeant Francesco Fiore remembered the 1968 murders. He had at that time been assigned to Signa. Sergeant Fiore insisted that a comparison must be made of the bullets from the 1968 killings with those of the later double murders. The test results showed what he suspected – that all the bullets came from the same box of 50 Winchester bullets and all had been fired from the same Beretta pistol. The police did not immediately order the release of Stefano Mele, because they assumed he was working with an accomplice, who had continued killing while Mele was in prison. In August 1982 they arrested Francesco Vinci, who had been accused by Mele 14 years before, but he was to be cleared of suspicion by the way events developed subsequently.

The killer struck again in September 1983. This time he killed two young men in a camper van, though it is likely that the killer mistook one of them for a woman because he had long hair. The men were German holiday-makers, Wilhelm Meyer and Uwe Sens. The gunmen shot them through the van window, killing them instantly. Vinci was in custody, just as Mele was, at the time of this double killing, yet Vinci's lawyer was unable to get him released. The State Prosecutor Mario Rotella was working on the assumption that the killings were being carried out by a Sardinian peasant gang; Mele, he assumed, was a member of that gang. On that basis, Mele's brother Giovanni and Stefano's friend Piero Mucciarini were also arrested. They too were to remain in custody until months after the next murder – all of these men were put, and kept, in prison on the strength of a hypothesis based on no evidence whatever.

The next double murder took place in July 1984. The unlucky couple were Claudio Stefanacci and Pia Rontini.

The killing spree of the Monster of Florence came to an end on 8 September 1985. With his knife, he ripped open a tent on a camp site at San Casciano. He fired several shots into two French tourists, Jean Michel Kraveichvilj and Nadine Mauriot. Jean managed to get to his feet, scramble out of the tent and run a few yards. But the merciless killer chased him and stabbed him to death. Then he went back to the tent, pulled Nadine's body out and started to mutilate her. The next day, the public prosecutor's office received a packet. Inside was a sheet of paper folded round a plastic bag containing a piece of flesh from Nadine's body.

By 1986, the Italian authorities had to admit that their Sardinian gang theory was wrong. The enquiry had to start from scratch. Ten thousand people were questioned.

By 1991, several leads were pointing in the direction of Pietro Pacciani, a farm labourer who had convictions for wife-beating, sexual assault – and murder. There was some hearsay evidence that Pacciani and Mario Vanni were conducting occult ceremonies in San Casciano, rituals that involved female body parts. The ceremonies were supposed to be presided over by a doctor.

The 69-year-old Pietro Pacciani was put on trial late in 1994. The trial was televised and became a great media event. Pacciani protested his innocence, but he was convicted of fourteen murders and sentenced to life imprisonment. He was taken from court shouting, 'I am as innocent as Christ on the cross'. And he may have been. There was no real forensic evidence against him. The only evidence was circumstantial and anecdotal.

In February 1996, an appeal court quashed the earlier guilty verdict, but later in the same year Pacciani was ordered to face a new trial. In the meantime, his friend, the 70-year-old Mario Vanni, and a third man, the 54-year-old Giancarlo Lotti, were arrested. They too were convicted of involvement in five of the double murders. Vanni was sentenced to life, Lotti to 26 years.

Then the story took a very peculiar turn. On 23 February 1998, Pacciani was found dead while awaiting a further trial. He was found at his home, lying face down on the floor , his trousers round his ankles and his shirt up round his neck. His face was contorted and blue and, at first, the police believed the 71-year-old might have died of a heart attack. The post mortem showed that he had died of a combination of drugs. The investigating magistrate, Paolo Canessa, believed that the man had been murdered before he could reveal significant new details about the killer cult of which he was a member.

The story of these serial killings may be over, or it may not. The killings round Florence seem to have ceased, but there are still a lot of loose ends. Were the killings the work of one pathetic psychopath, a peeping tom stalking young lovers and killing them out of sexual frustration and envy? Were they the work of a single missionary serial killer on some warped moral crusade? Or were they, as the Italian authorities seem to have believed, the work of a cult group? It is hard to see, unless they have some additional evidence, why they should believe this. The killings have all the hallmarks of the lone psychopathic killer with a particular hatred of women.

Whoever Il Mostro, the Monster of Florence, is, he is still at large. Serial killers disturb us for a variety of reasons. We – none of us – like the idea that we are being stalked by predators. We feel uncomfortable with the thought that someone close to us, whether a relative, a friend, a colleague at work, or even a stranger who passes us in the street, is insane enough not only to want to kill us, but to kill lots of us. But it is also clear from the cases described in this book that we are psychologically ill-equipped to identify these people, let alone defend ourselves against them – probably because what they are doing goes right against the grain of normal human relationships. We need to pick up the signals of abnormal behaviour early. There are often warning signs, as there were with Cary Stayner, and we have to act upon them in order to save ourselves.

Some serial killers are stopped relatively quickly, thanks sometimes to good luck, sometimes to an observant witness and sometimes to good policing, and relatively few people are killed. But other serial killers are lucky enough or clever enough to go on and on killing, sometimes, as with Tommy Sells, murdering scores of people, sometimes, as with Harold Shipman, murdering hundreds of people before being detected. One criminologist who has catalogued almost two thousand cases of serial killing has commented that 20% of them have remained unresolved. In other words, 20% of serial killers literally get away with murder.

In a different league again are those who use, or abuse, political power to cause the deaths of others. We see it overtly in the careers of dictators like Adolf Hitler and Joseph Stalin, who were serial killers by proxy, ordering other people to do their killing for them – and on a grand scale. We see it covertly in the reigns of monarchs who have used their position to persecute certain religious or racial groups (and not just minorities) within their own kingdoms, like Mary Tudor. We see it in the careers of modern terrorists or politicians who as 'a matter of principle' declare war on regimes in other countries far away from their own natural sphere of influence; Osama bin Laden springs to mind as an example, but there are others less obvious.

There are many routes to serial killing. The serial killer wears many masks. Some brood, scowl or leer and are obviously evil-looking, like Henri Landru, Charles Manson or Ian Brady. Others are open-faced and innocent-looking, like Harold Shipman. The reason, the motive, the justification for the killing spree varies endlessly, from sexual gratification to the alleged best interests of the state. But if the end result is the deaths of many innocent people the background reason for the killing does not matter at all. Serial killing can never be justified.